IDENTIFICATION GUIDE TO NORTH AMERICAN PASSERINES

The gropings and conjecturings of Science-in-the-making afford amusing reading after the clew is found. We are not out of the woods yet, but the timber is thinning . . . The Gray Flycatcher is beginning to take on the semblance of reality.

William Leon Dawson
The Birds of California, 1923.

Identification Guide to North American Passerines

by
Peter Pyle
Steve N. G. Howell
Robert P. Yunick
David F. DeSante

A compendium of information on identifying,
ageing, and sexing passerines in the hand.

Illustrations by Steve N. G. Howell

Slate Creek Press
Bolinas, California

Identification Guide to North American Passerines
Copyright © 1987 by Peter Pyle. All rights reserved.

ISBN: 0-9618940-0-8.
Library of Congress Catalog Card Number: 87-90700.

Cover designed and illustrated by Steve N. G. Howell and
Moody Graphics, San Francisco, California.

Printed in the United States of America by Braun-Brumfield Inc., Ann Arbor, Michigan.

Special thanks to Paul de Fremery, Terry Cobb and Barbara Wasneski of
Braun-Brumfield, and Carole Moody of Moody Graphics.

Designed and produced by Peter Pyle and David DeSante for Slate Creek Press,
P.O. Box 219, Bolinas, California 94924.

A product of the:

4990 Shoreline Highway
Stinson Beach, CA 94970

We dedicate this work to the birds.

Especially those that have been captured, handled, blown upon, wetted, collected . . . that have generally had their lives disrupted such that we may present the information herein. May it help them and their kind as much as they have helped us.

Table of Contents

Preface and Acknowledgements

Crucial to the conception of this guide was a late November, 1981, drive through the Swedish countryside. I had just finished a term as Ringing Assistant at the Falsterbo Bird Observatory and had journeyed to Stockholm for a few weeks of holiday season employment. Lars Svensson, author of *Identification Guide to European Passerines*, kindly took a day from his busy schedule to escort me in search of White-tailed Eagles at a few of their local nesting areas.

I had met Lars at Falsterbo earlier that fall, and while there, had certainly become familiar with the second edition of his guide, a compendium of identification, ageing and sexing information on European passerines and the "bible" for European ringers. Much of our discussion that day focused on the need for both a North American counterpart to his guide and for a better communication between North American banders and European ringers concerning identification, ageing, and sexing techniques. Although we "dipped" on the White-tailed Eagle, a more important "tick" for me that trip was the initial inspiration to someday create *Identification Guide to North American Passerines*.

In early 1984, Lars sent me a copy of the recently published, third edition of his guide for promotion in North America, referring me to the top of page six where his appeal was repeated: "when do we get an American guide?" Since 1981 I had worked periodically at several banding stations, particularly those of the Point Reyes Bird Observatory (PRBO), and the need for such a thorough compilation had become increasingly apparent. In November, 1984, I approached PRBO for sponsorship of the project, and during the following winter undertook the initial jobs of researching the literature and establishing a standard format. It did not take long, however, for that sinking feeling to consume me — the impending mountain seemed just too high to climb alone.

I had already recruited Steve Howell, a birding *compadre* and capable technical artist to do the illustrations for the guide. As the months wore on, however, I found myself increasingly reliant on Steve for more than just the illustrations, especially for help in the museum skin collections, as a valuable sounding-board off of which to bounce new ageing and sexing ideas, and as a companion during the long hours of work during the summers of 1985 and 1986 and during the one frantic night in which we labled all the illustrations (explaining the several crooked lables, which sure looked straight at six that morning). To complete the team, I enlisted the help of Bob Yunick and Dave DeSante to serve as primary East and West Coast reviewers, respectively. With the extensive banding experience and knowledge possessed by these two reviewers, and Steve's critical technical artwork, I am confident that we have produced an adequate North American counterpart to Lars Svensson's guide.

Of course, such an undertaking could not have been completed without the assistance and cooperation of many others, as well. To begin with, we would like to acknowledge the work of those ornithologists, both amateur and professional, that have made substantial contributions to recent developments in North American, in-hand, identification, ageing, and sexing techniques. Charles H. Blake, Charles T. Collins, Erma J. Fisk, Ned K. Johnson, M. Kathleen Klimkiewicz, Robert C. Leberman, L. Richard Mewaldt, Allan R. Phillips, Kenneth C. Parkes, Amadeo M. Rea, Chandler S. Robbins, Jay M. Sheppard, Robert M. Stewart, and Merril S. Wood were names that kept resurfacing. This guide is essentially a product of us all.

We extend our appreciation to the PRBO family for supporting this project and assisting in many ways: to Don McCrimmon and the PRBO board of directors for initial support; to Farallon and Palomarin biologists Harry Carter, Geoff Geupel, Phil Henderson, Jay and Teya Penniman, Bill Sydeman, and Dan Taylor for comments and assistance throughout the duration of this project; to previous staff and, especially, to all of the many volunteers at the Palomarin and

Farallon Island Research Stations for the many years of quality data; and to the two stations themselves for being such inspirational places to work. This is contribution # 369 of the Point Reyes Bird Observatory.

We are especially indebted to Steven F. Bailey and Luis K. Baptista at the California Academy of Sciences, San Francisco, and to Barbara Stein and Ned K. Johnson at the Museum of Vertebrate Zoology, Berkeley, for allowing us the free and extensive use of each institution's bird skin collections.

Philip Ashman, Richard K. Bowers Jr., Dawn Breese, Carolee Caffrey, L. Richard Mewaldt, Peter Paton, C. J. Ralph, Ginny Rosenberg, Rich Stallcup, Lars Svensson, Christopher F. Thompson, and George Wallace (Long Point Bird Observatory) provided us with valuable encouragement, inspiration, comments, reviews and/or unpublished information; and Farallon Island visitants Western Meadowlark band # 1023-43241, Gambel's White-crowned Sparrow # 1292-03793, and Bullock's Oriole # 751-36689 patiently posed for illustrations. The support and help is appreciated. I would also like to acknowledge my parents, Robert and Leilani Pyle for indoctrinating me into the world of bird-banding at the impressionable age of four. I guess the impression has lasted.

Finally, we offer an appeal of our own, to banders, birders, and museum workers interested in the subject matter of this book, to give us a hand with future editions. With the profusion of little details we present—timing and extent of molts, wing length ranges, timing of skull pneumatization, etc.—users are bound to find a few discrepancies, or gaps in our knowledge to fill. Just two days ago, for instance, I banded a Western Wood-Pewee with "windows" in the skull but flight feathers in perfect condition.They must have a complete first-winter molt! A tidbit, at this point, for the second edition. Will you help us find others? We would like to add your name to the above list of acknowledgements.

Peter Pyle
Southeast Farallon Island
13 May 1987

Introduction

During the past decade we have witnessed a surge of interest in the identification, ageing, and sexing of North American birds in the field, resulting in many excellent articles and several detailed field-identification guides. Unfortunately, a similar development of information has not occurred for birds in the hand. Of course, some of what we have learned in the field is applicable and even more easily used with birds in the hand. In-hand examination and measurements, furthermore, substantially increase the potential for accurate ageing, sexing, and specific or subspecific identifications. But other field criteria, notably environmental, behavioral, posture related, and vocal characteristics, are not as readily used with captive birds and, with museum specimens, cannot be used at all.

Individual banders and ornithologists have made numerous contributions toward the development of in-hand identification, ageing, and sexing criteria for certain North American passerine species. A primary reason for the slow general progress, however, has been the previous lack of an overall compilation of, and an effective central repository for, in-hand information and techniques. In Europe, this information has been compiled, circulated, and refined for over 16 years (see Svensson 1970, 1975, 1984), resulting in a comparatively advanced knowledge of in-hand criteria and, in particular, more familiarity with such topics as passerine wing formulas, molt strategies and molt-related ageing characteristics. This guide attempts to summarize and bring up-to-date such information for North American passerines.

The purpose of this guide is essentially threefold. First, the information within is illustrated and presented in a format that can be readily used by banders, museum workers, and birders interested in quick and accurate in-hand determinations of the identification, age, and sex of North American passerines. For banders, this should serve as a convenient replacement for the bulky binders crammed with worksheets, reprints, and other scattered information commonly found in banding labs. Second, in addition to summarizing the published literature, some new information is presented that was discovered by the authors during the preparation of this guide. Much of this applies to species about which little previous information has been published, and was discovered primarily through the examination of museum specimens and captured birds for the application of ageing criteria which are useful for related species. Finally, the summarization of current information on in-hand identification, ageing, and sexing criteria and techniques will provide a basis for the further development of our knowledge in this field. In this regard, the senior author strongly encourages users to publish contradicting, additional, or supporting information (or to contact him at Identification Guide, PRBO, 4990 Shoreline Hwy, Stinson Beach, CA. 94970), so that it may be incorporated into future editions.

SCOPE

276 species of passerines and an additional 20 well defined subspecies or hybrids are treated in this guide. Included are all passerine species which regularly breed in North America (north of Mexico) except for a few primarily Palearctic species which breed only in Alaska and/or arctic Canada and Greenland. Svensson (1984) should be consulted for accounts of these species. Also not included are a few introduced species, such as Eurasian Skylark (*Alauda arvensis*) and Spot-breasted Oriole (*Icterus pectoralis*), which are seldom captured for banding and have small and locally distributed populations. Although strictly tropical species are not included, the information presented in the accounts of many migrants is applicable on both their breeding and tropical wintering grounds. The only subspecies treated are those which the Bird Banding Manual (Canadian Wildlife Service 1984) recognizes by assigning to them separate "species numbers". Most of these were considered as separate species by the American Ornithologist's Union (1957). Otherwise, taxonomy and order follow those of the A.O.U. (1983).

1

BIRD TOPOGRAPHY

The names of soft parts and feather tracts found in this guide follow those most widely used in the current ornithological literature (see figs. 1 & 2). Primaries are numbered ascendantly (innermost to outermost) and secondaries descendantly (outermost to innermost) following the scheme used in the American banding and molt related literature. Thus, it is primary # 10, the outermost, that is absent on some and present on other North American passerines. The naming of the wing coverts follows Svensson (1984).

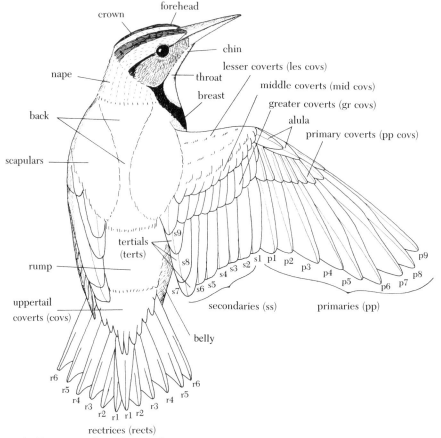

Figure 1. Terms used in this guide (including many abbreviations) for feather tracts and anatomical areas.

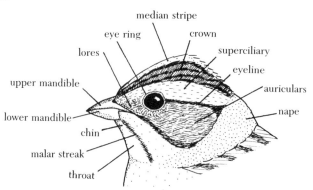

Figure 2. Terms used in this guide for areas of the head.

IDENTIFICATION, AGEING, AND SEXING TECHNIQUES

The accurate identification, ageing and sexing of North American passerines is generally complicated by the highly variable nature of size, plumage, and molt patterns found within each species and age-sex class. In this guide, a format which summarizes the distinguishing features of each species or age-sex class was chosen over the popular but oversimplified dichotomous key approach because it better represents this variability and the complexity of the subject. It also emphasizes two important aspects of accurate identification, ageing and sexing that should always be kept in mind by users of the accounts:

1. **Determinations should be based on a synthesis or combination of all available characteristics (whether or not they are definitive), all of which may or may not coincide with those of one particular species or age-sex class.**

2. **Intermediate individuals and exceptions will always occur which are not reliably placed in a particular species or age-sex class by in-hand criteria alone.**

By combining all criteria with in-hand experience of the different species, classes, and determination methods, and by realizing that a certain percentage (up to 50% in some cases) of individuals cannot be reliably aged, sexed, and/or identified with any one or all of the criteria given, users of this guide should be able to make determinations with confidence intervals of well above 95%. References to the combination of criteria and to the potential for intermediates in specific cases will be found throughout the species accounts.

In this section, general information and methods for identifying, ageing, and sexing birds in the hand are detailed. Accurate determinations are best achieved by combining the information gained from all applicable techniques with that presented in the species accounts.

MEASUREMENTS

Size is often a useful characteristic for identifying, ageing, and especially, for sexing passerines in the hand. In both live birds and museum skins, size is best indicated by specific measurements. In this guide, ranges of wing chords are given for every species as an indicator of sex, but other measurements may be of equal use, and a formula consisting of several measurements (see Reese & Kadlec 1982, for example) may be the best indicator of all. Users are encouraged to always consider size when sexing and ageing the birds they handle, and to publish measurement data (see Bowers & Dunning 1986).

In almost every passerine species, the males of a given population will average larger than the females. The extent to which the sexes overlap in size depends both on the species and the particular measurement being considered. With wing chord, for example, overlap can range from almost complete (e.g. in the Wrentit and some vireos) to little or none (Dickcissel and many icterids). With most North American passerines there is 60-80% overlap. Wing chord, therefore, varies from being practically useless to entirely reliable for sexing, and most often will reliably separate 20-40% of the individuals. Other measurements, such as the tail and culmen lengths are probably of similar usefulness.

Certain measurements vary with age, but to a lesser extent than with sex. In passerines, juvenal primaries tend to be slightly (2-5%) shorter than adult primaries. Thus, the wing chords of juveniles, and of birds that retain their longest primaries during the first prebasic (postjuvenal) molt (see pp. 12–13) will be slightly shorter than birds with adult primaries. Because of the individual and sex related variation found in bird size, measurements are not recommended for ageing, except in a few blackbirds where there is a considerable difference between adult and first-year birds (see species accounts). However, the tendency for juvenal primaries to be slightly shorter than those of adults can be used to help sex known aged birds. Individuals with juvenal primaries usually have wing chords falling in the bottom portions of the ranges for each sex, while those of adults will be longer, falling in the upper portions of the ranges. By considering age, the percentages of birds that can be sexed by wing length (and other measurements) can be increased (see, for instance, Blake 1965c and Mewaldt & King 1986).

When using measurements for identifying, ageing, or sexing passerines it is important that the measuring techniques of the user be strictly standardized with those used in obtaining published samples. In the following sections the methods of obtaining the measurements used in this guide are outlined. All linear measurements given are in millimeters (mm).

Wing

At least three methods of measuring the wing length have been described in the literature. The wing chord, or "unflattened" wing length is the measurement most frequently used and published in North America, the "flattened" wing length is widely used with museum specimens and was previously popular in Europe, and the "maximum flattened" wing length is the measurement presently gaining popularity in Europe. Depending on the species and handling conditions, the flattened wing length is 0.5-2% longer than the wing chord, and the maximum length, in turn, is 0.5-3% longer than the flattened length (see Nisbet *et al.* 1970 and Svensson 1984 for thorough discussions of the differences between these methods).

In this guide, measurements of the wing primarily refer to the wing chord (wg), as this is the length most frequently used by North American banders and most widely published for North American passerines. In a few accounts (e.g. the *Oporornis* warblers) the flattened wing length (wg flat) is indicated because previous major studies of these species have been with museum skins and have used this wing measurement method. A primary concern with the wing chord method is the potential for non-conformity between different species, handlers and handling conditions. When performed properly and in a standardized way, however, the wing chord method should result in consistent and reproducible measurements.

To measure the wing chord it is best to have a thin ruler with a perpendicular stop at zero. Alternatively, one's thumb or forefinger can, with care, serve as a stop. The ruler should be inserted under the wing, and the bend of the wing (carpal joint or "shoulder") should be pressed snugly against the stop. A source of potential variation with wing measurements is the amount of carpal compression applied by the pressure on the stop by the bend of the wing (see Yunick 1986). It is recommended that the bend of the wing be pushed against the stop with no more pressure than the wing itself applies when the ruler is moved in a posterior direction. Once the wing is in place, make sure that the line between the carpal joint and the tip of the longest primary is parallel with the edge of the ruler, gently lower its tip to the ruler so that it touches it, and read the wing chord length (figs. 3 & 4). To achieve a flattened wing length, gently press the wing flat against the ruler with the thumb on the wing coverts (fig. 4) and read the resulting, slightly longer measurement.

When measuring the wing it is important to make sure that the longest primary is not broken or molting, and to realize that older and more worn primaries will result in a slightly shorter measurement than freshly grown ones. Also, a source of minor error with the wing chord method on live birds is that damp wings will be slightly flatter, hence longer, than dry wings. This should be taken into consideration when measuring the wing chord of damp or wet birds. Finally, museum skins will show a slightly shorter wing length (up to 3%) due to slight shrinking as the skin dries. On the other hand, the arc of the wing often becomes shallower (and even flat) during drying, resulting in a slightly longer length than the chord of the wing in its natural (living) position. These factors probably cancel each other somewhat, resulting in fairly similar measurements between wing chords on living birds and museum specimens.

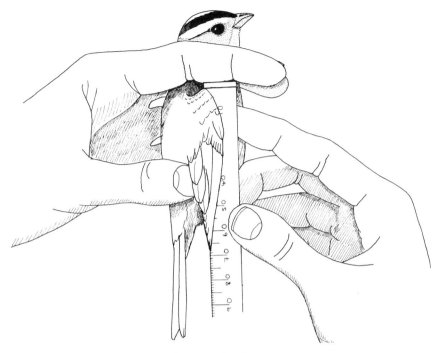

Figure 3. A good hold for measuring the wing chord.

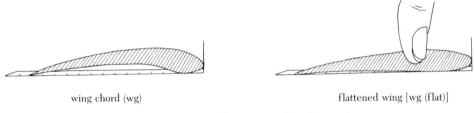

wing chord (wg)

flattened wing [wg (flat)]

Figure 4. Profiles of wing measurement techniques used in this guide.

Tail

Although it has received less attention than the wing length, the length of the tail is probably of equal use in identifying, sexing, and ageing passerines. The tail length is defined as the distance between the tip of the longest rectrix and the point of insertion of the two central rectrices. Ideally, this distance should be measured with calipers, especially on museum specimens. But calipers can be difficult to use with live birds in the hand, and a more standardized and nearly, if not completely, as accurate measurement can be achieved with a ruler.

Two methods of measuring the tail with a ruler are currently practiced. In both cases it is imperative to use as thin a ruler as possible, with the end of the ruler coinciding with zero. One method is to hold the ruler parallel to the tail and insert it between the tail and the undertail coverts (see Svensson 1984). The other method is to hold the ruler perpendicular to the tail and insert it between the two central rectrices (fig. 5). In both cases, the zero end of the ruler should be pushed firmly against the root or point of insertion of the feathers. At PRBO, both of these methods were tried on a series of live birds. The differences found between the two methods was negligible. The latter method (inserting the ruler between the two central rectrices) is, perhaps, easier and more consistent than the former method, but with practice, either technique should yield reproducible results.

As with the wing, it is important to make sure that the longest rectrices are not broken or molted and to realize that older and more worn feathers will result in a shorter measurement (by up to 10% on very worn tails) than when they are fresh.

Another measurement of the tail that is useful for separating certain species is the difference in length between the outer and central rectrices. A clear plastic ruler placed flush with the closed tail is the best way of achieving this measurement. Be sure to measure along the axis of the tail rather than at a slight angle.

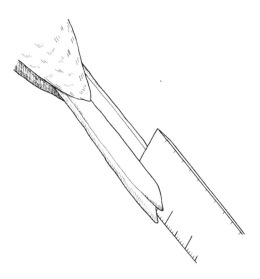

Bill Length

Figure 5. Measuring the tail between the central rectrices.

As with the wing, at least three methods of measuring the bill length are currently employed, depending on the point at the base of the bill from which the measurement is taken. In this guide, the "culmen" is most often used and refers to the distance between the anterior end of the nostril and the tip of the bill. This is probably the most consistent and easiest of the methods, although the length of the nostril itself may vary somewhat, affecting the culmen length to a slight degree. The "exposed culmen" (exp. culmen) is referred to in a few instances and indicates the length between the tip and the edge of the feathering at the base of the bill. A third method, the length between the bill tip and where the upper mandible enters the base of the skull is not used in this guide.

Since the length of the culmen or exposed culmen is actually a chord measurement (notably

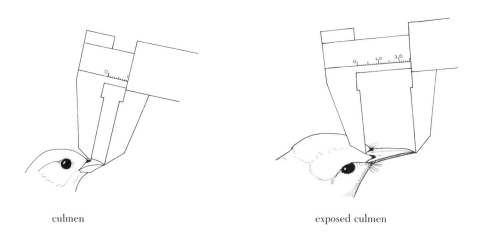

culmen   exposed culmen

Figure 6. Measuring the culmen and exposed culmen.

on species with curved upper mandibles) it is best to use calipers for an accurate measurement (fig. 6). A general measurement can be achieved with a ruler. Begin by making sure that the bill tip is not broken or deformed. Place the tip of the bill against the inner jaw (it is easier with calipers constructed of thick material) and gently slide the tip of the outer jaw to the anterior edge of the nostril (culmen) or to the base of the forehead feathering (exp. culmen). With the exposed culmen the measurement is taken from the base of the feathers along the ridge (culmen) of the bill, not the nostril feathers or those on the sides of the forehead (fig. 6).

When using bill lengths, it should be kept in mind that slight seasonal varation may occur, with lengths generally being slightly longer in the summer than in the winter (Davis 1954).

Bill Depth and Width

All references to bill depth and width in this guide indicate measurements taken at the anterior end of the nostril. Again, calipers should be used. For the bill depth, place the outer jaw on the point of the culmen even with the anterior ends of the nostrils and bring the inner jaw up to the lower mandible such that the calipers are oriented at a 90° angle to the axis of the bill. To get the bill width, open the calipers to the point where they stop at the anterior end of the nostrils when they are gently moved toward the base of the bill. Again, the calipers should be oriented at a 90° angle to the axis of the bill.

Crown Patch

The crown patch length is useful for sexing and ageing a few of the warblers and is interpreted as the length, along the median axis of the crown, between the anterior and posterior points of the patch (these not necessarily being on the median axis; fig. 7). In this guide, this measurement refers to the patch when the feathers are lying in their natural position (the length will increase if the feathers are lifted).

Figure 7. An example of a crown patch measurement.

Tarsus

The length of the tarsus is referred to in only a few instances in this guide because it is a relatively difficult measurement to perform on live birds and because variations in tarsus length between similar species and sexes is comparatively slight. Again, the measurement is best obtained with calipers. It is the length between the intertarsal joint and the distal end of the last leg scale before the toes emerge (fig. 8).

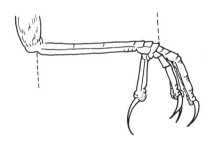

Figure 8. The tarsus.

Weight

Since bird weight varies substantially with geographic population, condition of the individual, and season or period within the life cycle of each particular species, this measurement is not as useful for ageing, sexing or identifying birds as are the above linear measurements. In a couple of instances, however, weights are given in this guide as a useful character for sexing. The most important considerations to make when weighing birds are how much fat is present (see Leberman 1967), and whether or not females have eggs in the oviducts, both of which can substantially increase the weight (Reese & Kadlec 1982). Dunning (1984) provides sample weights in grams for most North American birds, including 283 species of passerines, and should be referred to when considering bird weights.

WING FORMULA

"Wing formula" refers essentially to three aspects of the primaries of birds: the relative lengths, hence position of the tips of each primary; the occurrence and length of notches on the inner webs of each primary; and the occurrence of emargination to the outer webs of these feathers (fig. 9). Because of such factors as distance of migration, wing formulas usually differ slightly between species and, thus, can be very useful in the separation of similar appearing species in the hand. The finer details of wing formulas, furthermore, have been found useful for sexing certain flycatchers (Phillips *et al.* 1966; see also Hedenström & Petterson 1986) and are probably useful for sexing other passerine species as well.

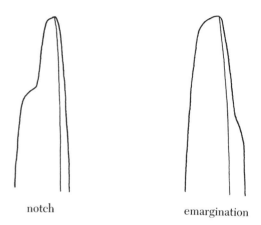

notch   emargination

Figure 9. Examples of notched and emarginated primaries.

In this guide, the use of wing formulas is limited primarily to the positions of the tips of the outer one or two primaries (p9 and p10) relative to the positions of the tips of the other primaries, the tip of the longest secondary, or the tips of the primary coverts. It should be noted that the illustrations of these wing formula features are drawn with the wing open such that the relative positions of the primary tips are clearly shown. When performing wing formula measurements, however, it is important that the wing be closed and in its natural position.

When determining the distance between primary tips, it is best to measure the distance between the tip of the longest primary and that of each of the primaries being considered, and taking the difference between these lengths. The measurements are best achieved by placing calipers or a transparent ruler next to the wing in its naturally closed position and putting the tip of the longest primary against the outer jaw of the calipers or at the zero of the transparent ruler (fig. 10). Always make sure that none of the primaries are broken, missing, or molting. If a molting feather is still in its sheath it may not be fully grown and should not be used in the wing formula. In this guide, the measurement between the tips of two primaries, the 9th and the 5th, for example, is abbreviated as "p9-p5". A more complete knowledge of wing formulas has developed in Europe (see Svensson 1984) than in North America, in part because of

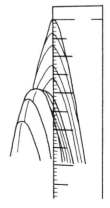

Figure 10. A good way to measure the distance between primary tips.

the relative prevalence of difficult-to-identify species found there. Further study in the use of wing formulas in North American passerines is encouraged, especially in regards to sexing and possibly to ageing by the length of the tenth primary or by the length of the notch in the outer primaries.

SKULLING

The art of skulling, and the usefulness of skull pneumatization for ageing passerines in the hand have steadily improved since Miller (1946), Norris (1961), and Baird (1964) first described and modified the process (see also Wiseman 1968a). Skulling is now recognized as being the most reliable technique for ageing passerines during the fall months and, for many species, is proving useful through the early winter and even into spring. The authors strongly encourage banders to become proficient at skulling and to skull most passerine species throughout the year, so that a better understanding of the exact timing, variation, and reliability of the pneumatization process for ageing each passerine species can be achieved.

Skull Pneumatization

When a fledgling passerine leaves the nest, the section of the skull overlaying the brain (frontals and parietal) consists of a single layer of bone. From this time until the bird is four to twelve months old (depending mostly on the species), a second layer develops underneath the first, the two layers being slightly separated by spaces or air pockets, and joined by small columns of bone. The process by which this second layer, the air pockets, and the columns develop is called skull pneumatization.

The pattern and rate of skull pneumatization varies both within and among the different passerine species. The pattern generally follows one of the two progressions illustrated in fig. 11, but may show other variations (see Yunick 1979a, 1981a). Smaller species tend to show the peripheral pneumatization pattern and larger species the median line pattern (Yunick 1981a). Individuals of certain species may show either pattern, however, and the exact shapes of the unpneumatized areas or "windows" will also show substantial individual variation.

Generally, the skulls of smaller species become pneumatized more quickly than those of larger ones, but this may vary somewhat depending on the family. Warblers, for instance, show a faster rate than flycatchers of the same size. The rate of

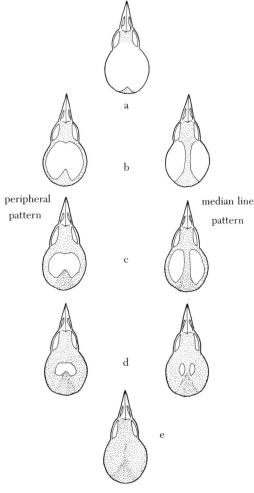

Figure 11. The two common sequence patterns of skull pneumatization.

pneumatization also depends more on the age of the bird than on the season, yet both factors are involved. Pneumatization appears to slow, for example, in stressful times such as during fall migration and winter, and is probably more rapid in southern populations than northern ones. Thus, the time of the year when the skull becomes fully pneumatized depends on the species, the age of the bird, and the amount of stress the individual endures during the fall and early winter months.

Any passerine found with a partially pneumatized skull (fig. 11a-d) can be reliably aged as a first-year bird, with the exception, perhaps, of occasional summer or early fall birds with small windows (fig. 11d; see next paragraph). In most North American passerine species, the skulls of the earliest first-year birds become completely pneumatized in October and November, and the latest birds between November and January. The exact date when the earliest birds complete pneumatization is important for ageing as this is when adults can no longer be aged reliably by skulling alone. However, completely pneumatized skulls should still support other ageing criteria indicating adult, for at least a month following the initial date given in the species accounts (see p. 25).

In some (perhaps many) species, small unpneumatized windows may normally be retained until spring and even early summer. This is most commonly seen in the longer distant migrants such as certain flycatchers, swallows, thrushes, and vireos. Birds with windows greater than one millimeter in diameter (fig. 11d) are probably reliably aged as first-year through June. Birds with these windows in July through August, and birds with smaller windows or "pinholes" should not necessarily be aged as first-year because a small number (less than 5%) of individuals will never show complete pneumatization. [The occurrence and size of windows in spring and their relationship to age deserves further study.] Thus, extent of skull pneumatization is useful for ageing first-year birds through October to June, and adults through September to November, depending on the species and individual.

Skulling

Unpnuematized areas of the passerine skull usually appear pinkish while pneumatized areas appear grayish, whitish, or pinkish-white, with small white dots indicating the columns of bone. The color and/or contrast (when present) between these two color patterns can usually be seen through the skin of the head, especially after the head has been wetted to allow parting of the feathers.

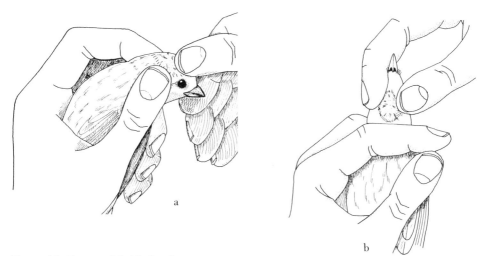

Figure 12. Two good holds for skulling.

To skull a passerine, start by holding the bird in one of the two positions shown in fig. 12. The hold illustrated in 12a may be easier to use because the skin can more readily be moved around the skull, allowing a larger area of the skull to be viewed through a smaller area of skin. With experience, however, both holds can be used with equal effectiveness. In order to see the skull the feathers need to be parted such that a small opening of bare skin is created. This can be accomplished without wetting the feathers but is more easily done if a small amount of water or saliva is applied. The use of detergent or alcohol solutions do not enhance the viewing conditions significantly and should be avoided due to the potential of harming the bird. Those with extensive experience in skulling will be able to part the feathers and see the skull simply by blowing or by licking their thumb or finger. Beginners, until they are familiar with the appearance of the skull in its various stages of pneumatization, should wet the feathers a greater amount in order to create larger viewing areas. In cold weather, however, substantial wetting should be avoided so as not to chill the bird.

It is usually easiest to part the feathers by running the thumb or finger forward over the crown, against the direction in which the feathers lay. In the early fall, when most young birds are just beginning the pneumatization process, it is good to start at the rear of the skull and work up towards the crown. Later in the fall the parting should be made higher up on the crown (in the areas just above and behind the eyes), where the last unpneumatized windows usually occur. With thicker skinned birds, a parting made on the side of the head or neck (where the skin is more transparent) and moved up to the crown will often improve viewing conditions. When the skulling process is finished, the feathers can be smoothed back into place.

Once an opening between the feathers has been created, gently move the skin around so that a larger area of the skull can be examined. If the skin is still dry, wetting it will make it more transparent. Hold the bird under a fairly strong light bulb or in shaded or indirect sunlight to achieve the best lighting conditions for viewing the skull. Direct sunlight may reflect off the skin too much, hindering the viewing process. It is often helpful to move the head around as different angles of light can make it easier to see through the skin. Finally, some banders may find it easier to look through a mounted loupe or other magnifying device, although the unaided eyes are usually quite sufficient.

Look for entirely pinkish skulls in very young birds (fig. 11a; June-July), for contrasts between the pneumatized and unpneumatized areas (fig. 11b-d; most frequently in August to December), or for the entirely grayish or pinkish-gray skulls, with white dots, indicating complete pneumatization (fig. 11e; all months). Small windows (fig. 11d) should be carefully looked for in winter and spring. With experience, these pneumatization conditions will be readily distinguished.

Any of several factors, however, may make it difficult or impossible to see the pneumatization of the skull. In larger passerines or those with large bills (notably the corvids, grosbeaks, and icterids) the skin of the head is often too thick to adequately discern the pneumatization pattern, particularly when no contrasts can be seen. Birds of northern populations will increase the amount of fat in the skin during the winter, which can further hinder visibility and thick, dark, or otherwise opaque skin is occasionally found on individuals of all species. In addition, the skin of molting birds becomes flaked and less transparent, and injury-related blood hemorraging is sometimes encountered which can partially or totally obscure the pneumatization pattern or cause the skull to appear unpneumatized. Finally, in some birds the demarcation line between pneumatized areas and windows is very subtle and only discernable after close scrutiny.

Despite these pitfalls, the pattern of skull pneumatization of most passerine individuals is readily seen and provides a reliable means of ageing during at least the fall. Finally, when the skull is visible, the pattern should always be combined with all other ageing criteria, so that the reliability of both skull pneumatization and the other criteria can be more fully understood.

MOLT

A complete understanding of the general timing, sequence, and extent of passerine molts is an essential aspect of accurate ageing and sexing of passerines in the hand. Several good summaries are available on the subject of bird molt (see Humphrey & Parkes 1959, 1963; Palmer 1972; and Payne 1972). Readers should consult these articles for an overall understanding of the mechanisms and finer details of bird molt. Herein is a brief summary and a discussion of the aspects of molt that pertain directly to ageing and sexing passerines.

With a few known exceptions, molting is confined to two periods within the annual life cycle of North American passerines, just before and just after the breeding season. Thus, most passerines display two plumages, the basic (winter) plumage and the alternate (summer or breeding) plumage. The molt that occurs just before the breeding season is called the prealternate molt; that just after the breeding season, the prebasic molt (see p. 24 and p. 278). All North American passerines have a prebasic molt while just over half (predominantly migratory species) have a prealternate molt. Those that lack a prealternate molt acquire their alternate plumage by the natural wearing of the tips of the contour (body) feathers.

Prebasic Molt

The prebasic molt usually takes place from July to September (occasionally as early as May and as late as December) and occurs in both recently fledged birds and adults that have completed nesting activities for the year. It usually occurs on the summer grounds, often in the breeding territory, but sometimes takes place during fall migration or on the winter grounds. It can also start on the summer grounds, be delayed or suspended during fall migration, and be completed on the winter grounds. In most passerines, the prebasic molt differs in extent, timing, and/or locality between first-year and adult birds. These differences result in many useful ageing characteristics.

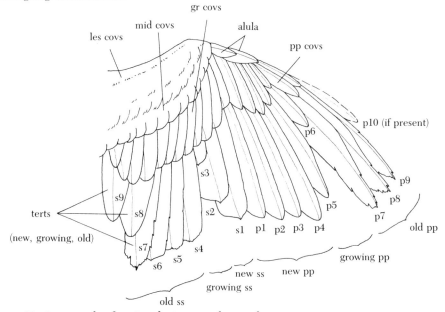

Figure 13. An example of a wing during complete molt.

With one or two exceptions, the prebasic molt in adult passerines is "complete" (includes all body and flight feathers), whereas in first-year birds it is most often less than complete. In the complete molt (fig. 13), replacement of flight feathers usually begins with the innermost primary (p1) and proceeds, one at a time, to the outermost primary (p9 or p10). Replacement of all wing feathers normally occurs symmetrically, that is, the same feathers molt on both wings at the same time. After a few primaries have been replaced, molting of the secondaries usually begins, starting with the outermost and proceeding toward the innermost. The three innermost secondaries, or tertials, however, are usually replaced as a unit before the rest of the secondaries have been molted, and the rectrices are usually replaced from the innermost (r1) to the outermost (r6), often but not always symmetrically, during the molt of the primaries and secondaries. The last flight feathers to be molted are the outermost primary, the sixth (from the outside) secondary, and the outermost rectrix. A bird in the process of a complete molt can usually be identified by the contrasting new and old flight feathers, especially apparent among the rectrices and outer primaries.

In contrast to the adults, first-year birds of most passerine species normally replace only the body feathers, lesser and middle coverts, and none, some, or all of the greater coverts during the first prebasic molt. The number of greater coverts that are molted varies considerably among and within these species. Earlier broods and southern populations of a species often molt more greater coverts than later broods and northern populations, and this can vary overall from season to season. When the molt involves some but not all greater coverts, it is usually consecutive inner coverts that are replaced. In these species, however, no primary coverts, alula, or flight feathers are usually molted. In this guide, this is referred to as a "partial" molt (see p. 25).

In other first-year passerines, all of the above feathers are replaced during the first prebasic molt, as well as some, but not all of the flight feathers. The number of flight feathers replaced during these "incomplete" molts varies both among and within species as it does with the greater coverts during a partial molt. In some species, this variation ranges from none to all of the flight feathers, depending on the individual or population. Flight feathers commonly replaced during incomplete molts are the tertials, some (often the central) or all rectrices, and a variable number and distribution of primaries and/or secondaries. Unlike the complete molt, these wing feathers can be replaced in various sequences. They should always be replaced symmetrically, however. Accidental or adventitious loss can often result in the replacement of a rectrix, primary or secondary on one side but not the other. Individually and assymetrically replaced feathers should not be considered as part of the normal molting process.

A few first-year passerines normally have a complete prebasic molt. These, however, often occur during different months or localities than the adult prebasic molts (also complete) of the same species. Complete first prebasic molts generally occur later in the fall than adult molts and often take place partially or entirely on the winter grounds. This can vary substantially, however, depending on conditions during the breeding season (see Phillips 1951 for example). In a couple of species (e.g. the Cliff Swallow) the first molt occurs in the late winter and spring, such that it is, perhaps, more aptly considered a first prealternate molt. In only a few North American passerines (e.g. Wrentit and Bushtit) do complete prebasic molts of adult and first-year birds occur during the same months and in the same location.

Finally, recent studies (Rowher 1986, Willoughby 1986) have found that certain passerine species will replace the body feathers twice during the first prebasic molt. The first replacement in these migratory species occurs on the summer grounds and the second replacement, or "supplemental" molt occurs in October through December, after the birds have reached their winter grounds. It is quite possible that other migratory species may also have these partial, supplemental molts.

The differences in extent, timing, and/or locality between the first and adult prebasic molts results in several useful ageing criteria. In species where the first prebasic molt is "partial", for instance, any bird showing symmetrical and sequential flight (especially wing) feather molt during June to September, or showing evidence of a complete molt, can be reliably aged as an adult. With consideration of the flight feathers being molted, this is often reliable in species with incomplete first prebasic molts, as well. Late in the molting period, a complete molt can still be detected by the condition of the sixth secondary, the last flight feather normally replaced. Check for the presence of a sheath or see if this feather is still growing (it should not be shorter than both the fifth and seventh secondaries when fully grown). A contrast between new and old greater coverts, although often subtle, is another indicator of birds having undergone a partial first prebasic molt. The lack of a contrast in the greater coverts does not necessarily indicate an adult, however.

Differences in the timing and locality between the adult and first prebasic molts can also lead to separation between adult and first-year birds. This may be especially useful in species where the first prebasic molt is complete. In certain species of swallows, for example, first-year birds do not start molting flight feathers until October to December, when they have reached the winter grounds. Adults of the same species may begin flight feather molt in July to September, before or during the fall migration. Differences in locality of the molt may also cause differences between first-year and adult birds in the timing of the fall migration (see Hussel 1980, 1982a).

Most importantly, however, almost all ageing criteria related to variation in flight feather color, shape, and wear are based on differences between the first and adult prebasic molts. When ageing birds in basic plumage (early fall through early spring), users of this guide are encouraged to always check the molt accounts for differences in the extent, timing, and locality of the prebasic molts, and accordingly, to look for feather wear and shape related ageing clues (see p. 17).

Prealternate Molt

The prealternate molt, as mentioned above, does not take place in all passerine species. When it does occur, however, the extent can vary from a few throat and/or head feathers to complete replacement of both body and flight feathers. In most North American passerines the prealternate molt occurs from late January or February through April, occasionally as early as December and as late as early June. In migratory species it takes place mostly on the winter grounds although individuals of certain species may still be molting during spring migration, and even after they reach their breeding grounds. For some (possibly many) species, the prealternate molt may be an extended, winter-long process.

Unlike the prebasic molt, differences between first-year and adult prealternate molts have been documented for relatively few passerine species. Recent studies (e.g. Greenwood *et al.* 1983 and Cannell *et al.* 1983), however, have found that this molt in first-year males tends to be more extensive than in the other age/sex classes. It is possible that this trend occurs in most species that have a prealternate molt, especially those in which males in first basic plumage resemble females, but adult males do not. Users of this guide (especially those in tropical America) are urged to consider this when handling molting birds in the spring.

Although a few species replace flight feathers during the prealternate molt the majority do not. Thus, the most important aspect of this molt for ageing and sexing is the resulting change in plumage that occurs. The timing of plumage-related ageing and sexing criteria of many passerine species depends on the timing of the prealternate molt (see p. 15).

Words of Caution and Encouragement

Much of the molt information presented in this guide is derived from Bent (1942-1968) who in turn based much of his information for eastern passerines on Dwight (1900). The importance of these references to the development of our understanding of molt sequences cannot be overstated. However, many recent investigations into the molt sequences of specific passerines (eg. Norris 1952; Johnson 1963b, 1974; Thompson 1973; Rowher 1986; Willoughby 1986; *et al.*) have found significant new information that was presented inaccurately or not at all by the former authors. Likewise, the molt information found in the species accounts (especially concerning molts that take place in tropical America) may need subsequent revision when new information comes to light. Users of this guide are strongly encouraged to pay close attention to all aspects of passerine molt and to publish any new or conflicting information found.

PLUMAGE

The most obvious method for determining both the age and the sex of many birds is by examining the plumage characteristics. Among North American passerines, plumage patterns vary widely according to age and sex. In some species the sexes differ markedly but the different age classes do not; in others the plumage is similar in the sexes but varies with age. Many species show three or four different plumages, one for each age/sex class, while others have the same plumage regardless of age or sex. And plumage patterns may change during either or both molts. One only has to look at the different plumages displayed by one passerine subfamily, the North American warblers, to realize how complex and varying these patterns and sequences can be.

In this guide, the bulk of the age and/or sex portions of the species accounts are comprised of plumage related characteristics. Criteria are given only when clearly defined and consistent age/sex-related plumage patterns occur. However, it is important that users understand the variable nature of plumage. Variation occurs both within each defined age/sex plumage association, and between the different age and sex classes, even in species with no clearly defined plumage patterns. These variations can respectively hinder or assist with the ageing and sexing process.

In species otherwise showing little plumage variation, males and adults will often exhibit slightly brighter or more contrasting plumages than females and first-year birds. The extent to which this plumage variation is found, itself varies substantially among the species, from practically none to the point where plumage can almost be used reliably on its own. In many cases, when either the age or the sex is known from other criteria, the relative brightness of the plumage can assist in determining the other class. Bright or well-marked immatures are likely to be males, for instance, and bright females could well be adults. The same might work in reverse, for particularly dull or indistinctly marked birds. In many cases, a small to moderate percentage of extremes may be accurately aged or sexed, especially if one is familiar with the species. [See Heydweiller (1936) for an example of this with the American Tree Sparrow (p. 203), a species which shows no definitive age/sex plumage associations.]

On the other hand, plumage variation within each age/sex class is often such that intermediates between the classes occur. In these cases it is again best to incorporate other ageing and sexing information. When plumage overlap exists, it is most often between young males and adult females, and in certain species this is the normal pattern (see Rohwer *et al.* 1980). In these cases, knowing the age can result in accurate sexing, and vice versa. Plumage exceptions can also occur, even in species that normally show no overlap between age/sex classes. In many cases these are older females which suddenly may acquire male-like plumage (see Goodpasture 1972, Baumgartner 1986). Males with plumage typical of females may also show up. When ageing and/or sexing, users are encouraged to always confirm plumage-based determinations with all other available criteria.

Finally, it should be noted that plumages, hence plumage-related ageing and sexing criteria, change during periods of molt. These periods can be quite extended, and may vary substantially with different individuals of the same species. Users should always consider how the molt might affect the reliability of the plumage criteria when ageing and sexing birds during molting periods.

JUVENILES AND SOFT PARTS

The first plumage (subsequent to the natal down) acquired by the nestling and retained by the juvenile is called the juvenal plumage (note the difference in spellings). The body feathers of this plumage are replaced during the first prebasic molt, which almost always occurs within three monthes of fledging, and usually takes place on the breeding grounds. Because juveniles are readily aged by many criteria and are generally sexually indistinguishable by plumage, their treatment in the species accounts is usually restricted to a brief description of the differences between juvenal and subsequent plumages and the months of the year in which they are usually found (see p. 26). Herein, therefore, is a brief summary of useful characters for ageing and (when possible) sexing juveniles.

Ageing Juveniles

In many North American passerines, the juvenal plumage differs quite substantially from subsequent plumages, allowing easy separation of juveniles from adults at the same time of year. In these cases, the juvenal plumage is usually more streaked or spotted than that of the adult, will often have wing bars where the adult has none, and is displayed on more loosely textured contour feathers (fig. 14). In certain species where the juvenal plumage otherwise resembles that of the adult (eg. corvids, parids, gnatcatchers, most mimids) these feather structure differences can often (but not always) be used for ageing. They are most evident in the feathers of the nape, back, and undertail coverts.

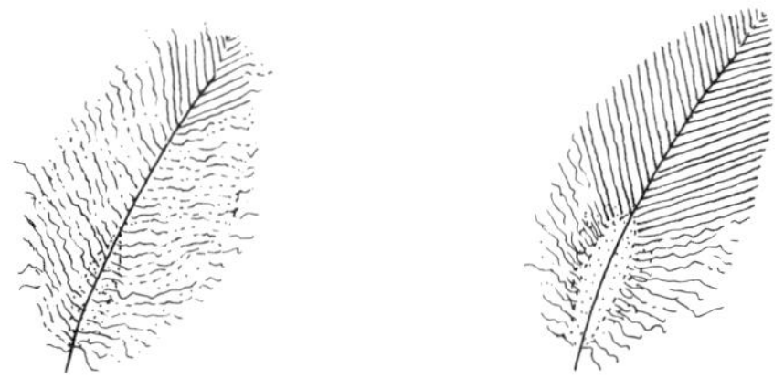

juvenal   non-juvenal

Figure 14. Juvenal and non-juvenal body feathers. The differences are most apparent with undertail coverts and feathers of the nape and back.

In addition, many nestling characteristics are evident in juveniles which can be helpful in separating them from adults. Most of these are more apparent through the early stages of the juvenal period, becoming less so as the juvenile ages. Some remain useful for separating first-year birds from adults well after the first prebasic molt.

The feathers of the tibiotarsus (leg) and axillaries develop much later in juveniles than other feathers, hence, these areas are often devoid of feathers for a short time after the bird has fledged. The gape of nestlings and early juveniles is swollen and more brightly colored, and the inside of the mouth is also brighter in tone and/or paler in hue in juveniles than in adults. This latter feature is often useful well after the first prebasic molt (e.g. in the corvids, but look for similar situations in other species). The legs of nestlings and early juveniles are also more swollen and fleshier than those of adults, and the bill, and sometimes the wing, can take up to a month after fledging to reach full size.

In return, several characters useful for separating first-year birds from adults can be applied to juveniles. Molt related criteria such as the occurrence of molting flight feathers (p. 14) and the differences in shape and wear of juvenal feathers (p. 17) are applicable. In particular, summer adults in alternate plumage should show very worn flight feathers while those of juveniles should be relatively much fresher. And, of course, the pneumatization process is just beginning in juveniles whereas it should be complete (or nearly so) in adults. Finally, the eye color differences as indicated in the species accounts for the separation of first-year birds from adults of certain species should be even easier to use with juveniles. Eye color is probably useful for separating juveniles of many other species, as well (see Wood & Wood 1972).

In summary, bird handlers should have no trouble with the separation of juveniles from adults during the summer months, when all criteria are used.

Sexing Juveniles

In most passerine species, birds in juvenal plumage cannot be reliably sexed by in-hand criteria alone. Only in a few species, where differences occur in the color pattern of the flight feathers, can juveniles be sexed by plumage. These differences are noted in the species accounts. The only other potential method is by the wing length, which can probably be used to sex larger males only. Juveniles with wing lengths indicative of females may actually be males that have not completed growth of the primaries. When attempting to sex juveniles by wing length, note that the length will average 1-3 mm shorter than on birds of the same sex with adult primaries. Thus, the wing length of most juveniles should fall in the bottom half of the ranges for each sex, once the primaries are fully grown.

FEATHER SHAPE AND WEAR

In passerine species where the first prebasic molt is partial or incomplete, the shape and the amount of wear and fadedness of certain flight feathers or primary coverts can serve as very useful clues for ageing. Juvenal feathers are typically thinner and more tapered than adult feathers and may often be of a less durable quality, resulting in their becoming abraded and worn at a quicker pace. These differences are particularly noticeable in first-year birds that have an incomplete first prebasic molt, resulting in the juxtaposition of retained and replaced flight feathers. In using feather shape and wear for ageing, it is important to take into account both the molt sequences and the time of year.

Feather Shape

During the preparation of this guide, the senior and second authors checked all North American passerine species with partial or incomplete first prebasic molts for the usefulness of rectrix shape for ageing. With experience, we believe that up to 100% of certain species can be reliably aged by this criterion, at least during certain times of the year.

The outer two or three rectrices usually show the greatest difference, being slenderer and having more tapered inner webs in juvenal feathers and being typically more truncate in adults (see fig. 15). Note that the presence (adult) or absence (juvenal) of a corner in the outer web and the angle at which the outer web descends from the tip are often the most apparent differences. North American passerine groups where rectrix shape is particularly useful for ageing are the corvids, chickadees, thrushes, most warblers, orioles, and fringillids. It is useful to varying degrees with many other species, as well.

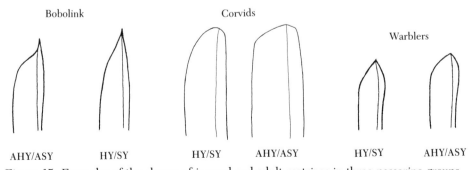

Figure 15. Examples of the shapes of juvenal and adult rectrices in three passerine groups.

Thrushes   Warblers

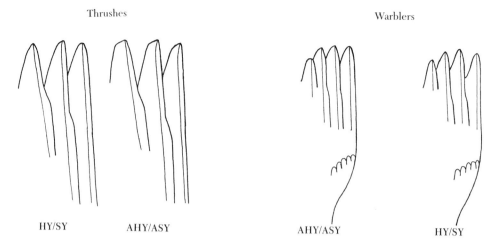

HY/SY   AHY/ASY   AHY/ASY   HY/SY

Figure 16. Examples of the shapes of juvenal and adult primaries in two passerine groups. Look for similar differences in others.

In most of these species, however, a significant percentage of individuals will show intermediate rectrix shapes, and should not be reliably aged, especially without experience with the variation of this feature in the species at hand. Caution is advised with late spring and summer birds, as the increasing degree of wear found in both juvenal and adult feathers can obscure the differences between the two age groups. Reliable ageing also becomes more difficult with birds that have wet or otherwise displaced rectrices, as can often happen during the capture and confinement of passerines for banding. In most species, only obvious examples should be reliably aged by rectrix shape alone. Information on rectrix shape is included in all species accounts, and users of this guide are encouraged to become familiar with its usefulness for ageing the different passerine species (see Scott 1967 and Meigs *et al.* 1983 for specific examples of rectrix shape use).

The shape of the outer primaries (fig. 16) and primary coverts (fig. 17) are also useful for ageing certain species with partial or incomplete prebasic molts. Like the rectrices, the juvenal primaries and primary coverts tend to be more tapered than those of adults. With the primaries, these differences are most easily seen in the longest feathers (p6-p9). The usefulness of these criteria, however, is not as well known as for the rectrices. Users of this guide are encouraged to check the shapes of these feathers on all passerines with less than complete first prebasic molts.

Dippers

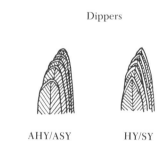

AHY/ASY   HY/SY

Figure 17. Examples of the shapes of the primary coverts in dippers. Look for similar differences in other passerine groups.

Feather Wear

As with feather shape, differences in the amount of wear between juvenal and adult rectrices, primaries, and primary coverts can provide useful clues for ageing. These differences are related primarily to the age of the feathers and to the fact that juvenal feathers often wear more quickly than those of adults. However, feather wear also varies with the habits of the species and of individuals, the amount of exposure the feather receives, and the extent and timing of the molts. All of these factors need to be considered when correlating feather wear with age.

In the early fall, after the prebasic molt, retained juvenal feathers are usually 2-3 months older than the corresponding adult feathers, and are usually showing signs of wear. Look for small nicks in the outer webs and less glossiness, especially in the rectrices and outer primaries. Adult feathers at this time should be quite glossy and contain no nicks. On first-year birds that have replaced some but not all flight feathers, contrasts in wear between the old and the new should be visible. Fig. 114 (p. 135) illustrates typical differences in wear between juvenal and adult feathers in fall and spring.

By spring the juvenal feathers are considerably worn and abraded while those of the adults are usually only moderately so, and should still show some glossiness. Check especially for differences in wear of the central rectrices, as they are the flight feathers that generally receive the most exposure (but note that these are often replaced during incomplete first prebasic molts). By mid summer, however, when the birds are well into the breeding season, the feathers of both first-year and adult birds become very abraded, such that it becomes increasingly difficult to distinguish them. They will, however, be easy to tell from the fresh feathers of newly fledged juveniles.

With the primary coverts, it is often useful to compare them with the adjacent, greater (secondary) coverts. First-year birds with partial or incomplete molts will almost always retain the primary coverts, and replace some or all of the greater coverts. Next to the new and glossier greater coverts, therefore, the primary coverts will appear contrastingly faded and worn, and will usually lack pale edges. On adults they will all appear uniform in coloration and glossiness, and will often display fresher and paler edges. The condition of the primary coverts has been found useful for ageing corvids, bluebirds, many warblers, and various other species well into the spring. After March, however, care and consideration of the prealternate molt should be taken when using covert contrasts for ageing. Both adults and first-year birds in species with a partial prealternate molt may replace the greater coverts again, creating contrasts in both age groups.

The combination of feather shape and wear has proven quite useful for ageing North American passerine species that have a less than complete first prebasic molt, especially in the spring when skulling and other plumage related criteria usually become less valuable. Unless one is quite experienced with these characteristics in a particular species or group, however, these criteria should not be relied upon alone. They are best used in combination with all other ageing criteria.

GROWTH BARS

The examination of the growth bars is an ageing technique which has been found useful in some European passerines (Svensson 1984). Growth bars (fig. 18) are caused by small structural differences in the flight feathers, that result from inconsistencies in the bird's diet when the feathers were growing. Major diet deficiencies, for example, cause actual breaks in the feather

juvenal rects   adult rects

Figure 18. Examples of growth bars in juvenal and adult rectrices.

vein which are known as fault bars. Growth bars are easiest to see on the rectrices and to a lesser extent the secondaries, and are best viewed when the feathers are held at an angle and with a strong source of backlighting. Both juvenal and adult feathers can develop growth bars although they are probably more common in juveniles.

Growth bars can only be used in species with less than complete first prebasic molts, and the pattern of the growth bars is the best clue to the age of the bird. A pattern as shown in fig. 18a indicates that the rectrices have grown simultaneously, which is always the case with nestlings. The pattern of fig. 18b is typical of rectrices which were not grown simultaneously, usually the case during the adult prebasic molt. Distinguishing these two pattern types can assist with the ageing of these passerines.

Several problems occur with this ageing technique, however. The growth bars can often be difficult or impossible to see, especially as the feathers become older and more worn. Adults will sometimes replace rectrices simultaneously during the prebasic molt, resulting in a growth bar pattern typical of juveniles. Birds that have accidentally lost their tails will also replace rectrices simultaneously, and many species may molt some of their rectrices during the first prebasic molt, producing an adult-like pattern in first-year birds (although with these, the new and old feathers are usually separable). In summary, therefore, growth bars should be used only to support other ageing criteria. For more information on growth bars see Svensson (1984).

BREEDING CHARACTERISTICS

The best method for sexing simarly plumaged passerines during the breeding season is by the presence or absence of the breeding characteristics: the cloacal protuberance and the brood patch. All North American passerines develop these characteristics at least partially, and most are reliably sexed by them during the late spring and summer months. As the user gains experience, cloacal protuberances and brood patches can be detected earlier and later in the season.

Cloacal Protuberance

In order to store sperm and to assist with copulation, external cloacal protuberances, or bulbs, are developed by male passerines during the breeding season. They usually begin to develop early in the spring, reaching their peak size 3-5 weeks later, around the time the eggs are laid. Depending on the species and the number of clutches attempted during the breeding season, cloacal protuberances will recede from mid to late summer (more study is needed on this timing for each species). Although the cloacal regions in females will sometimes swell slightly or show a small protuberance, it rarely approaches the size of the males. During the breeding season, the presence of a strong protuberance can be used to reliably sex males of all North American passerines except one, the Wrentit (p. 101).

To view the cloacal protuberance, simply blow the feathers apart in the region of the vent. Figure 19 shows a cloacal protuberance at the height of its development, as viewed from above. Figure 20 illustrates the sequence with which it develops and recedes, and a typical profile displayed by female passerines during the breeding season. The shape of the protuberance, however, can be somewhat variable (see Wolfson 1952), and non-breeding males may not always develop one. When the female is most swollen in this area, she will usually have a brood patch as well (see below). After a little experience with the shape of the cloacal region during the nesting season, bird handlers should have no problem separating breeding males from females.

In the species accounts, the cloacal protuberance and brood patch are often listed together, followed by the months in which they are most easily used for sexing (see p. 26). Males should probably be sexed by cloacal protuberance only during these months, although it is possible that certain individuals can be sexed by the shape of the cloacal region at all times of the year (see

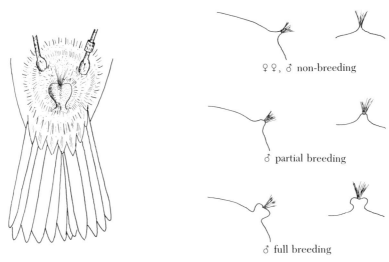

Figure 19. A cloacal protuberance (at its peak) in male passerines.

Figure 20. Profiles of passerine cloacal protuberances in different breeding conditions.

Svensson 1984). The lack of a cloacal protuberance, of course, should not necessarily be used to indicate females. Banders are encouraged to routinely examine the cloacal region of both males and females, so that the timing and usefulness of sexual differences in cloacal shape in North American species can be better understood.

Brood Patch

Incubation or brood patches are developed by incubating birds as a means of transferring as much body heat as possible to eggs in the nest. In almost all passerines, females perform all or most of the incubating, and develop more complete brood patches. The presence of a distinct brood patch thus can be used to reliably sex breeding females of almost all passerine species.

The development of the brood patch begins with the loss of the feathers of the abdomen, about 3-5 days before the first eggs are laid. Shortly thereafter, the blood vessels of the region begin to increase in size and the skin becomes thicker and more fluid-filled. Figure 21 illustrates a full brood patch as viewed by blowing the feathers of the breast aside. A few days after the fledglings leave the nest, the swelling and blood vascularization will begin to subside. If a second clutch of eggs is laid, the process (except for defeathering) will be repeated. A new set of feathers on the abdomen are usually not grown until the prebasic molt, after completion of breeding. Between the end of nesting and the onset of molt, the skin of the abdomen will often appear grayish and wrinkled. With experience, the abdomens of adults are distinguished from those of juveniles, which can lack feathers but are otherwise much smoother and pinker than those of the adult females. See Bailey (1952) and Lloyd (1965) for more information about brood patches.

In most North American passerines, the male does not develop a brood patch in the breeding season. Slightly fewer feathers may be present on the abdomen than are found in the winter, but the breast basically retains a feathered appearance (fig. 21). In a few groups, notably the mimids, vireos, *Myiarchis* flycatchers, and a few other species (see accounts), the male will assist with incubation and develop an incomplete brood patch. These will include partial or complete feather loss and slight to moderate vascularization and swelling, which rarely or never approach the extent of development typically found in females of the same species. With experience, bird handlers should be able to readily distinguish male brood patches in

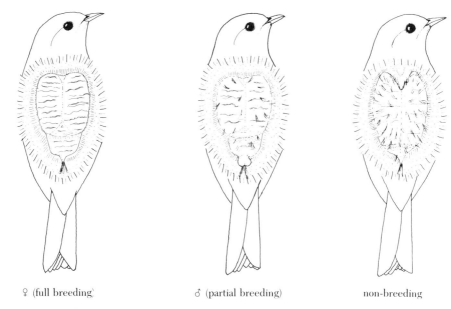

♀ (full breeding)   ♂ (partial breeding)   non-breeding

Figure 21. Brood patches in different stages of development.

these species (it may be harder to distinguish developing female brood patches, however). In only one North American passerine (again, the Wrentit) do males develop full brood patches that are not reliably separated from those of the female, and in two others (the cowbirds), the female does not develop a brood patch at all.

In most North American species, brood patches should be expected only from April through September, but exceptions are found, especially in southern and California populations (see species accounts) and in erratic breeders such as the Red Crossbill (p. 249). Finally, non-breeding females may not develop a brood patch or may only develop a partial one. Hence, males should never be reliably sexed solely by the lack of a brood patch during the breeding season.

A SUGGESTED APPROACH TO AGEING AND SEXING

The emphases and format of this guide (see p. 3) coupled with the variability and complexity inherent in the ageing and sexing criteria, will likely present an overwhelming scenario at first, especially to those used to dichotomous keys. Do not despair. With time and practice, users will learn this system and find it quite useful for ageing and sexing. For beginners, here are some suggested steps to accurate ageing and sexing:

1. Look for obvious and reliable age or sex indicators. From early fall through winter check the skull. Look for molting flight feathers in late summer. Are there any definitive age or sex related plumage characteristics? Check for breeding characteristics during the nesting season.
2. Add ageing information derived from more subtle characteristics. What is the extent and timing of the molts, particularly that of the first prebasic? Examine the shape of and amount of wear on the flight feathers. Are these useful with this species? Check the skull in winter-spring. Any windows? Check the plumage for non-definitive, age related variations.
3. Add similar sexing information. What does the wing chord indicate? Check for subtle plumage indicators.

4. Combine ageing and sexing criteria. Have you reliably determined either the age or the sex? Knowing the age or the sex, can the wing length or the plumage assist with the determination of the other class? Determine which of the age/sex classes fits best when all ageing and sexing information are combined.
5. Based on your experience with the species, what do you think? Can the combination of all criteria lead to reliable determinations? Are you sure of the choices you made? If not, perhaps you should write down what you think on the back of the data sheet, and leave it "unknown" in the data.
6. Is the information presented in these species accounts complete? Is it accurate? Maybe you should publish your data, or notify the author. And, most importantly, is the bird getting tired? Perhaps it should be released.

DIRECTIONS FOR USE

In this section, the abbreviations, definitions, and format used in the species accounts are provided.

COLORS

Strictly defined and standardized color names are not used in this guide. Rather, the names used for colors are considered in a relative context when comparing those of different species or age/sex classes. The geographically and seasonally dependent variation in coloration among individuals of the same species or age/sex class, and the different appearances that colors can assume under different lighting circumstances considerably lessen the usefulness of strictly defined color names.

The color names used follow those of the current ornithological literature, especially of recent field guides and other identification, ageing and sexing articles. Compound color names should be interpreted as the second color tinged with the first (ie. grayish-green is basically green with a gray tinge). For the definitions of other color names used and for other information and examples of colors commonly found on birds, readers are referred to Smithe (1975, 1981) or Wood and Wood (1972).

MONTHS

All months are abbreviated to the first three letters. Parentheses surrounding the months indicate that the plumage or condition described may be encountered between and/or within the range of months listed, but is usually not found or can not be reliably used outside of them. Note also that not all birds will show the plumage or condition for the entire period (especially during the two extreme months), and that exceptions, occurring outside of the given month ranges, are always possible.

FORMAT

The species accounts are divided into the following sections:

Heading

For each species, the heading includes the English and scientific names, a four-letter code derived from the English name, the A.O.U. or "species" number, and the recommended band size. The English and scientific names follow those found in the A.O.U. Checklist (1983) and the species numbers (for both species and subspecies) and band sizes are those recommended by the Bird Banding Manual (Canadian Wildlife Service 1984; basically the same as those in the A.O.U. 1983). A few of the listed band sizes (Black-capped Vireo, for example) differ from what the Bird Banding Manual suggests, the result of recommendations by banders familiar with these species. When two band sizes are given, the first usually indicates the size which best fits a majority of the individuals of the species.

The four-letter codes are suggested abbreviations for computer data entry. For the most part, they are based on the rules and codes outlined by Klimkiewicz and Robbins (1978) and Hamel and Klimkiewicz (1981). In this guide, a few of their codes have been changed to avoid duplication and because of a stronger adherence here to the principle that the second two letters of the code should correspond to the first two letters of the last name of the species. With only one exception (the two waxwings), this latter principle is followed.

Species

In this guide, accounts for identifying the species are given only when there exists a potentially occurring species which may be difficult to distinguish in the hand. A certain basic knowledge by the user is assumed (the ability to separate a flycatcher from a vireo, for example). The determination of when and when not to use species identifying accounts has been made by the senior author and is based on experience with the identification of most North American passerines in the hand. To assist with identifications, banders and other users of this guide should refer to one of the many recent field guides in conjunction with the use of these accounts.

Within the species identification accounts, the potentially confusing species are listed along with the age and sex class (if applicable) and a list of characters which are useful for separating the species at hand. When only one or two characters are given it should be assumed that these will separate all or a vast majority of the potentially confusing species. When many characters are given, the user should combine all of them for accurate determinations. It should also be kept in mind that the potential usually exists for one or more characters not to coincide with the other characters or with what is normal for the species. Occasional oddities, hybrids or intermediates can occur that may not be identifiable to species in the hand, using the characters given.

Subspecies

As mentioned before, subspecies are only separated in the species accounts for a few, well marked forms, most of which were earlier considered species by the A.O.U. (1957). The same information is given for the separation of these subspecies as is given for the separation of species. With subspecies, however, the user should exercize even more caution as the likelihood of intergrades between subspecies is generally higher than that of hybrids between species.

Molt

The sequence, extent, timing, and location of each molt is given for each species. Molt terminology follows that suggested by Humphrey & Parkes (1959) and is abbreviated as follows:

PB—Prebasic (postjuvenal or postnuptial) molt.
1st PB—First prebasic (postjuvenal) molt.

Adult PB—Adult prebasic (postnuptial) molt.
PA—Prealternate (prenuptial) molt.
1st PA—Prealternate molt in first-year birds.
Adult PA—Prealternate molt in adults (at least 1 1/2 years old).

For most species, the extent of only three molts is given, that of the prebasic in first-year birds (postjuvenal molt), the prebasic in adults (postnuptial molt), and the prealternate (prenuptial) molt for the species. In a few cases, the prealternate molt is known to differ in extent between first-year birds and adults; for these, four molts are given. Five categories define the extent of each molt, as follows:

Absent—No molt or feather replacement occurs (many PAs).
Limited—Some, but not all, body feathers and no flight feathers are replaced (some PAs).
Partial—Most or all body feathers but no flight feathers are replaced (many 1st PBs, some PAs).
Incomplete—Usually all body feathers and some, but not all, flight feathers are replaced (some 1st PBs, a few PAs).
Complete—All body and flight feathers are replaced (all adult PBs, some 1st PBs, a few PAs).

For convenience, all abbreviations and these definitions are repeated on p. 278.

It must be emphasized that the extent of molt is always subject to individual, geographic, and yearly variation. When a single extent is given it is intended to include what is normal for at least 95% of the population. When two molt extents are given it indicates that there is substantial variation in the extent of that particular molt, usually ranging between the two given extremes.

The timing of the molt, as indicated by the range in months, is given after the extent. As with the extent, the timing is subject to much geographic, yearly, and individual variation. Here, the month ranges are intended to encompass at least 95% of the body molt and 100% of the flight feather molt over the range of the species. Note also that the months include the normal molting period of the entire species. Individual birds will take less time to molt and, thus, some percentage of individuals will show no molt during most or all times within the given range.

Finally, after the molt sequence, extent, and timing are indicated, notes pertaining to the locality of the prebasic molts in migrant species, and the extent to which the flight feathers are normally replaced during incomplete molts, are provided. Localities are expressed by the terms "summer grounds" and "winter grounds". Note that these pertain to the general breeding and wintering areas of the species, not necessarily to the actual territory of the molting individual. Some individuals disburse from their breeding or winter territories during part or all of their molts. Unless otherwise stated, prealternate molts in migrant species occur on the winter grounds.

Skull

For each species, the seasonal timing of skull pneumatization is furnished, followed by specific notes (if applicable) on the occurrence of "windows" and/or conditions increasing the difficulty of skulling (such as thickness of skin) for that species. The specific date when the earliest first-year birds usually complete pneumatization is followed by the month when the last individuals complete or nearly complete the process. The first date is more important to banders because it indicates the onset of the period when completely pneumatized birds can no longer be assumed to be adults. This date is derived from the timing of both the pneumatization process and the breeding season of each species, and is generally a conservative estimate. Most first-year birds will show areas without pneumatization well after the initial dates given in this guide.

Since skulling is possible only on live or freshly dead birds and is potentially useful for ageing every passerine species, it is afforded its own section. However, banders should always combine skulling information with the characteristics furnished under Age and/or Sex.

Age/Sex

In this section, specific plumage and soft part criteria are given for ageing and sexing each species. Depending on the species and its plumage patterns, age and sex criteria may be given together or separately. A primary emphasis of this guide, however, is that ageing and sexing information should always be combined before either age or sex determinations are made. Even when these criteria are separated, therefore, users are encouraged to consider them at the same time. As with the accounts dealing with species identification, a field guide can provide additional helpful illustrations of the different age/sex classes. Note, however, that some of the age/sex representations found in field guides may not be entirely reliable.

Before these age/sex-specific characters are given, some general characteristics about the species are provided. These include a brief description and the timing of the juvenal plumage, the occurrence and timing of the breeding characteristics [cloacal protuberance (CP) and brood patch (BP)], and a range of wing chord lengths (wg) for males and females. Unless they are present through the fall migration, juvenal plumages are not otherwise included in the age/sex breakdowns, as in most passerines they are easy to distinguish from other age classes and are not usually sexually dimorphic (see p. 16).

As with the timing of the molt, month ranges are indicated for both the juvenal plumage and the breeding characteristics. When the cloacal protuberance and the brood patch are listed together (as CP/BP, in most cases), the month range should be interpreted as the month when the first CP is in evidence to the month when the last BP becomes obscured. Note that the CP usually develops about two weeks before, and recedes from one to two months earlier than the BP. Thus, BPs might not be expected in the first month, and CPs may not be found during the latter month or two, of the given ranges.

Wing length ranges are derived from the literature, from data collected at the Palomarin and Farallon Island Research Stations of the Point Reyes Bird Observatory, from data collected in New York and New Jersey by Robert P. Yunick, and from extensive measurements by the senior author of museum skins at the California Academy of Sciences, San Francisco and the Museum of Vertebrate Zoology, Berkeley. If available, a sample of thirty wing chords for each sex of each species is listed. An attempt was made to include samples from all parts of the species' North American range, and to establish the upper and lower extremes within the sample of each sex. When the species shows considerable geographic variation, the ranges are followed by a general, abbreviated indication of which populations are larger (e.g. "N > S" indicates that northern populations of the species are substantially larger than southern populations). When the sample size is listed as 30, it indicates that *at least* 30 measurements are included, and that birds with extreme wing lengths (outside of the overlap in the given ranges) are *probably* reliably sexed. A little more information on the geographic variation in size is probably needed for these species. Sample sizes of 100 indicate that sexing by the ranges *per se* will lead to less than 5% error (i.e. the species is reliably sexed by wing length).

Age coding used in this guide follows, for the most part, the system used by the Bird Banding Laboratory as listed in the Bird Banding Manual (Canadian Wildlife Service 1984), and is based primarily on the calender year. The following age codes are used:

Juv—Juvenile. A bird in juvenal plumage, before the first prebasic molt.
HY—A bird in first basic plumage in its first calender year (i.e. from the first prebasic molt

until December 31st of the year it fledged). [Banders may wish to combine this category with juvenile, as is the case in the Bird Banding Manual. Note, however, that the month ranges given in the species accounts assume this distinction.]

SY—A bird in its second calender year (i.e. January 1st of the year following fledging through December 31st of the same year). With one exception, this code is only used for birds in their first basic and first alternate plumages.

AHY—A bird in *at least* its second calender year. This code is more significant after the breeding season, when it implies an adult. Before the breeding season, it essentially means "unknown" (either SY or ASY).

TY—A bird in its third calender year. This code is more applicable in birds such as gulls that take several years to reach the adult plumage, than it is in passerines. In this guide it is only found in one species account.

ASY—An adult in at least its third calender year (i.e. a bird in at least the year following its first breeding season and 2nd prebasic molt).

The terms "first-year", interpreted as a bird in its first 12-16 months (or until its 2nd prebasic molt), and adult, as interpreted as a bird in at least its second 12-16 month period (or as one having completed its 2nd prebasic molt), are not used in the species accounts. These concepts are replaced by "HY/SY" and "AHY/ASY", respectively, where the "/" indicates the separation of one calender year from the next.

The age (or age/sex) code is followed by the range, in months, when the code can be reliably assigned to *at least a portion* of the individuals in the class. Note that not all birds of a specific age (or age/sex) class may be determined during the entire range of months. In most cases, the extreme months roughly indicate the central period of molts. During these months, users should always consider the molt and how it might affect the reliability of the plumage criteria. If the individual has completed the molt, for instance, the criteria may no longer apply. Alternatively, it may be reliable on molting birds a month or so before or after the period given. Both incoming and outgoing plumages should be carefully considered when ageing molting birds. Finally, when a range of months does not span an entire year (most often used with the code, "AHY"), birds found in that category during months outside of the range should be considered unageable ("unknown").

The age/sex characteristics given are those that have been found helpful for ageing and sexing each species. They should always be used not only in combination with each other, but also in combination with molt and skull information, measurements, time of year, breeding characteristics, and previous experience by the user with the species at hand. Two types of characteristics are often referred to in these sections, and should be interpreted as follows: **Reliable** characteristics are those that should, on their own, accurately separate greater than 95% of individuals. **Useful** characteristics are those that accurately separate between 50% and 95% of individuals (i.e. there is 5-50% overlap), and should either be used only in combination with other ageing or sexing criteria, or used only to separate extremes.

References

Both general and specific references used for each species account are listed in this section. Since this guide deals with North American passerines, references used are derived almost entirely from the American literature. For general and specific references in the European literature (some of which pertain to Holarctic species), Svensson (1984) should be consulted.

In the species accounts, encoded, general references are given first, followed by specific, published references and then unpublished references or data sets. Within each group, the references are listed chronologically. General reference codes are as follows:

B—Bent (1942—1958) and Bent *et al.*, comps. (1968).

BBM— Bird Banding Manual (Canadian Wildlife Service and U.S. Fish and Wildlife Service 1977).

C—Banding worksheets for western birds, supplements to *Western Bird Bander* or *N. Am. Bird Bander*, 1973-1984. (Worksheets prepared by Charles T. Collins unless otherwise specified.)

DVR—Dickey and Van Rossem (1938).

O—Oberholser (1974).

R—Roberts (1955).

SK—Sheppard and Klimkiewicz (1976).

Sv—Svensson (1984).

W—Wood (1969, 1970).

The senior author would appreciate receiving reprints of any applicable references that are not included in the species accounts.

A NOTE TO BANDERS

For many species, this guide indicates the potential for assigning age/sex classes that the Bird Banding Laboratory (BBL) does not currently accept on schedules from banders. This is not because the senior author is promoting the use of age/sex criteria which are less than 95% reliable (the standards accepted by the BBL). It results, rather, from a difference in emphasis of technique, as outlined by the two tenets on p. 3, and in a few instances, from the incorporation of previously unpublished information discovered by the senior author and/or other ornithologists. Until the BBL makes a statement on the information supplied in this guide, however, banders should adhere to the BBL's standards when submitting their schedules. The senior author recommends that they record in their own data, age/sex classes according to the criteria presented in this guide.

Species Accounts

TYRANT FLYCATCHERS   *TYRANNIDAE*

Thirty-four species. Family characteristics include wide and flat bills, whiskers, and pointed wings. They have 10 primaries (10th full-lengthed), 9 secondaries, and 12 rectrices. The first prebasic molt is often (but not always) complete, and usually occurs on the winter grounds. Windows in the pneumatization of the skull are often present thru spring, and should be looked for at all times of the year. Generally, plumages are similar between young and old and male and female.

NORTHERN BEARDLESS-TYRANNULET
Camptostoma imberbe

NBTY
Species # 472.0
Band size: 0

Species—From other flycatchers by narrow, vireo-like bill, lack of whiskers, and small size: wg 46-59. From Hutton's Vireo and Ruby-crowned Kinglet by less distinct and buffier wing bars, and by the presence of a small but distinct crest.

Molt—PB: HY complete (Aug-Oct), AHY complete (Aug-Sep); PA: partial (Feb-Mar). PBs probably occur on the winter grounds.

Skull—Completes in HY from 15 Sep thru Dec.

Age—Juv (May-Sep) has relatively brownish upperparts and cinnamon-buff edging to ss, terts, and wing covs. Otherwise, no criteria known after the 1st PB.

Sex—♂ = ♀ by plumage. CP/BP (Apr-Aug). Wg: ♂(n30) 50-59, ♀(n30) 46-55

References—B,O.

OLIVE-SIDED FLYCATCHER
Contopus borealis

OSFL
Species # 459.0
Band size: 1B

Species—Sides of underparts heavily streaked or mottled; sides of rump with white patches; lower mandible horn colored to blackish; wg 96-117; tail 63-74. From wood-pewees by longer wg; from Greater Pewee by plumage, tail length, and color of lower mandible.

Molt—PB: HY complete (Sep-Nov), AHY complete (Aug-Oct); PA absent-limited (Mar-Apr). PBs occur on the winter grounds. PA may occur on SY only; this needs further study.

Skull—Completes in HY/SY from 15 Oct thru Jan. Some SYs may retain windows thru spring.

Age—The following is reliable on all autumn birds N of winter grounds. Otherwise, rect shape is not useful and no plumage criteria are known for ageing after completion of the PBs:

Juv-HY (Jun-Nov): Upperparts dark brown; wing bars distinct, brownish-buffy or brownish-white; flight feathers relatively fresh.

AHY (Jan-Oct): Upperparts grayish-olive; wing bars indistinct, pale grayish-olive; flight feathers relatively worn.

Sex—♂ = ♀ by plumage. CP/BP (Apr-Aug). Wg: ♂(n100) 103-117, ♀(n100) 96-109; W > E.

References—B,R,W,O; PRBO data.

GREATER PEWEE
Contopus pertinax

GRPE
Species # 460.0
Band size: 1B

Species—Sides of underparts without streaks; sides of rump without white patches; lower mandible bright orange-yellow; wg 97-113; tail 73-84. From wood-pewees by longer wing. See Olive-sided Flycatcher.

Molt—PB: HY complete (Sep-Nov), AHY complete (Aug-Oct); PA: absent-limited (Mar-Apr). 1st PB probably occurs on the winter grounds; adult PBs may be suspended over fall migration.

Skull—Completes in HY/SY from 15 Oct thru Jan. Some SYs may retain windows thru spring.

Age—The following is reliable on all autumn birds N of winter grounds. Otherwise, rect shape is not useful and no reliable plumage criteria are known after completion of the PBs:

Juv-HY (May-Nov): Wing covs and uppertail covs distinctly tipped cinnamon; flight feathers relatively fresh.

AHY (Jan-Oct): Wing covs and uppertail covs uniform in color or indistinctly tipped with pale grayish-olive; flight feathers relatively worn.

Sex—♂ = ♀ by plumage. CP/BP (Apr-Aug). Wg ♂(n28) 101-113, ♀(n18) 97-108.

References—B.

WESTERN WOOD-PEWEE
Contopus sordidulus

WWPE
Species # 462.0
Band size: 0

Species—No eye ring; wing bars relatively indistinct; wg 78-93, p10 > p6; tail 55-74. Separated from all *Empidonax* flycatchers by longer and more pointed wing (fig. 22); from Olive-sided Flycatcher and Greater Pewee by shorter wg. From Eastern Wood-Pewee (which see) with extreme caution; some individuals (especially Juv-HYs) may be impossible to identify reliably: AHYs with upperparts (including rump and uppertail covs) uniformly brown, lacking greenish tones; chest band broad, usually uninterupted; underwing covs and bend of wing dusky-brownish; longest undertail covs with distinct dusky centers (fig. 23); black tip on lower mandible usually > 3.5 (but variable); length between unruffled undertail covs and tip of tail usually < 32.5. Juv-HYs more difficult to separate; most of the above criteria can be applied; upper wing bar tends to be narrower and darker than lower. See also wing and tail lengths by sex.

Molt—PB: HY partial-complete? (Aug-Nov), AHY complete (Aug-Oct); PA absent.PBs suspended, primarily accomplished on winter grounds. 1st PB may be complete and extended over winter; more investigation is needed.

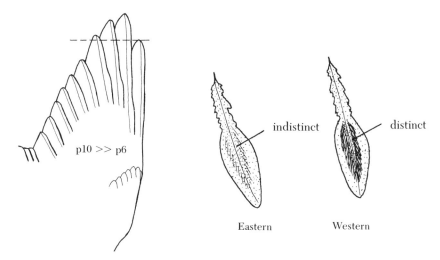

Figure 22. Wing formula in wood-pewees, to separate them from *Empidonax* flycatchers.

Figure 23. The longest undertail coverts of Eastern vs. Western wood-pewees.

Skull—Completes in HY/SY from 1 Oct thru Jan. Some SYs may retain windows thru spring.

Age—Rect shape seems unhelpful for ageing in spring, indicating that the tail may be replaced on HY/SYs during the winter. The following is reliable on all autumn birds N of winter grounds; no reliable plumage criteria known after completion of the 1st PB:

Juv-HY (Jun-Nov): Upperpart feathering with cinnamon edging; wing bars (especially lower) wide, relatively distinct, cinnamon or buffy; flight feathers relatively fresh.

AHY (Jan-Oct): Upperpart feathering uniform in coloration (possibly with narrow, pale grayish edging when fresh); wing bars narrow, indistinct, pale grayish; flight feathers relatively worn in fall.

Sex—♂ = ♀ by plumage. CP/BP (Apr-Aug). Wg ♂(n66) 82-93, ♀(n64) 78-88; tail ♂(n66) 60-74, ♀(n64) 55-69.

References—B,O; Phillips *et al.* (1964), Phillips *et al.* (1966); Rising & Schueler (1980); PRBO data.

EASTERN WOOD-PEWEE
Contopus virens

EWPE
Species # 461.0
Band size: 0

Species—No eye ring; wing bars relatively indistinct; wg 75-90, p10 > p6; tail 55-71; lower mandible with yellow base. Separated from all *Empidonax* flycatchers by longer and more pointed wing (fig. 22); from Olive-sided Flycatcher and Greater Pewee by shorter wg; from Eastern Pheobe by lower mandible color and shorter tail. From Western Wood-Pewee (which see) with extreme caution; some individuals (especially Juv-HYs) may be impossible to reliably identify: AHYs with upperparts dark olive to grayish, rump and uppertail covs often contrastingly grayer; chest band narrow, usually interrupted by narrow pale break down the center; underwing covs and bend of wing pale olive; longest undertail cov usually without cov centers (fig. 23); lower mandible completely or mostly yellow, with dusky tip usually measuring < 3.5; length between unruffled undertail covs and tip of tail usually ≥ 31.0. Juv-HYs more difficult to separate; most of the above criteria can be applied; upper wing bar tends to be bold and similar in coloration or only slightly darker than lower. See also wing and tail lengths by sex.

Molt—PB: HY partial-complete? (Aug-Oct), AHY complete (Aug-Oct); PA absent. PBs suspended in some birds, partially occurring on winter grounds. 1st PB possibly is complete and extended over winter; further investigation is needed.

Skull—Completes in HY/SY from 15 Oct thru Feb. Some SYs may retain windows thru spring.

Age—Rect shape seems unhelpful for ageing in spring, indicating replacement of the tail during the winter. The following is reliable on all birds N of winter grounds; no reliable plumage criteria known after completion of the 1st PB:

Juv-HY (Jun-Oct): Upperpart feathering with pale or buffy edging; wing bars wide, relatively distinct, buffy; flight feathers relatively fresh; rects tapered (see fig. 26).

AHY (Jan-Oct) upperpart feathering uniform in coloration (possibly with narrow, pale grayish-olive edging when fresh); wing bars narrow, indistinct, pale grayish-olive; flight feathers relatively worn in fall; rects truncate (fig. 26).

Sex—♂ = ♀ by plumage. CP/BP (May-Sep). Wg ♂(n73) 78-90, ♀(n71) 75-86; tail ♂(n53) 61-71, ♀(n50) 55-69.

References—B,R,W,O; Phillips *et al.* (1964), Phillips *et al.* (1966); Rising & Schueler (1980).

Identifying *Empidonax* Flycatchers

We have come a long way since the 1960s, when many, if not all *Empidonax* flycatchers were considered impossible to identify in the hand without a series of skins with which to compare. And, yet, how many banders or birders in either the east or the west would today recognize a vagrant of this genus from the other coast? The following accounts should enable users to readily distinguish virtually all *Empidonax* flycatchers (with the exception of many Willows and Alders), and will especially emphasize the separation of similar eastern and western species.

A couple of general points should be mentioned, however. First, when using the finer details of wing formula, note that males average slightly more pointed wings then females, generally resulting in primaries 7-10 being slightly longer in comparison with primaries 4-6. Knowing or surmising the sex of the bird (by BP/CP or wg), therefore, may help in identifying it. Second, as with ageing and sexing, all criteria should be considered before confirming the

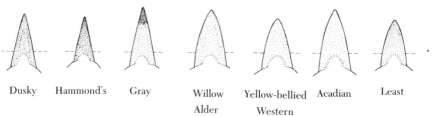

Figure 24. Relative sizes and shapes of the bills, and color patterns of the lower mandibles of *Empidonax* flycatchers.

identification. Many features are given, and reliable identifications are made when all or almost all features coincide to one species. This should usually be the case, but note that occasional individuals will not be identifiable by in-hand criteria alone. Table 1 summarizes the more important identifying features, and fig. 24 illustrates the size, shape, and typical color pattern of the lower mandible for each species. These should be consulted for a preliminary identification, which should then be confirmed with the species accounts.

TABLE 1.
Some key characteristics for the separation of *Empidonax* flycatchers.
(Measurements in mm; see accounts for more information.)

	Yellow-bellied	Acadian	Trail's	Least	Hammond's	Dusky	Gray	Western
Upperparts	green	olive	brownish-olive	grayish-olive	olive to grayish	olive to brownish	pale gray or tinged olive	olive
Wing chord	60–71	67–80	64–77	57–67	63–75	61–73	64–76	56–72
Tail length	46–55	52–62	52–66	51–58	52–62	57–68	56–66	50–63
Wing-tail	12–20	13–21	7–17	4–12	7–16	0–8	6–13	3–14
Culmen	7.0–9.4	9.2–10.1	7.6–10.0	6.3–8.4	6.0–7.9	6.5–8.9	7.6–10.4	7.7–9.0
Wing Formula	p10<p6 p8–p6<5.0 p10>p5	p10>p6 p8–p6>5.5	p9–p5, 8–	wing tip <13.5 p9–p6<5.0	wing tip >13.0 p9–p5<5.0	p10 often <p4. p9–p5<5.0	p10>p4 p9–p5 4–10.	p10<p5
p6 emarg?	variable	no	no	yes	yes	yes	yes	yes

YELLOW-BELLIED FLYCATCHER
Empidonax flaviventris

YBFL
Species # 463.0
Band size: 0

Species—Separated from other species of *Empidonax* with caution. Upperparts green; underparts (including throat) strongly washed yellow; eye ring narrow, yellow, rounded; bend of wing and underwing covs lemon yellow; pp and ss blackish, contrasting distinctly with lemon ss edging and wing bars; lower mandible yellow (fig. 24); culmen 7.0-9.4; inside lining of mouth orangish; wg 60-71; p6 often, but not always emarginated; p10 usually ≤ p6 and ≥ p5; longest p—p6 ≤ 5.0; tail 46-55; wg—tail 12-20; legs gray. Plumage and leg coloration eliminates all other species of *Empidonax* except Acadian and Western flycatchers. From Acadian Flycatcher by yellower underpart coloration (especially throat and chin); shorter bill, wing, and tail; mouth coloration; and wing formula features. From Western Flycatcher by brighter upperpart coloration, rounded eye ring, color of underwing and pp and ss, wing formula features, and wg—tail. See also differences in molt strategy for further identification clues.

Molt—PB: HY partial (Jul-Sep), AHY incomplete (Sep-Dec); PA incomplete-

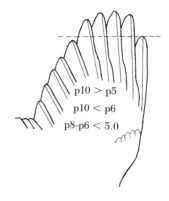

Figure 25. Wing formula of the Yellow-bellied Flycatcher.

p10 > p5
p10 < p6
p8-p6 < 5.0

complete (Feb-May). 1st PB occurs primarily on the summer grounds but may be suspended; adult PB occurs on the winter grounds and may be continuous with the adult PA. The difference in locality is useful for ageing. All flight feathers are usually molted during the winter; a few juvenal feathers may occasionally be retained during the 1st PA.

Skull— Completes in HY from 15 Oct thru Dec. Some SYs may retain windows thru spring.

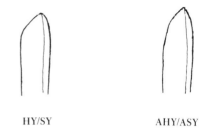

HY/SY   AHY/ASY

Figure 26. Rectrix shape by age in *Empidonax* flycatchers. See accounts for the relative timing and usefulness for each species.

Age—The following is reliable for all autumn birds N of the wintering grounds, but becomes increasingly difficult to use due to wear. Some intermediates may be difficult to determine and are not reliably aged by plumage alone. No reliable plumage criteria are known in alternate plumage, except by contrasting adult and juvenal flight feathers on occasional SYs (see Molt):

Juv-HY/SY (Jun-Feb): Wing bars buffy yellow; flight feathers relatively fresh (fall migrants); some or all rects tapered (fig. 26).

AHY (Jan-Dec): Wing-bars whitish to lemon yellow; all or some flight feathers relatively worn (Jun-Dec); all rects truncate (fig. 26). [This plumage is possibly reliable for ASY through Mar.]

Sex—♂ = ♀ by plumage. CP/BP (May-Aug). Wg: ♂(n80) 62-71, ♀(n41) 60-69. Also, Phillips *et al.* (1966) correctly sexed 97% of their sample using the following formula: ♂ Wg (flat) > 63.4 + .42 × (p10-p6); ♀ Wg (flat) < 63.4 + .42 × (p10-p6).

References—DVR,B,R,W,SK,O,BBM; Mengel (1952), Robbins (1959), Johnson (1963a), Phillips *et al.* (1966), Phillips & Lanyon (1970), Hussel (1982a, 1982b), DeSante *et al.* (1985); PRBO data.

ACADIAN FLYCATCHER
Empidonax virescens

ACFL
Species # 465.0
Band size: 0

Species—From other species of *Empidonax* with caution. Upperparts greenish-olive; underparts washed variably with yellow; chin usually white; throat white (AHY) to yellowish (Juv); pp and ss brown; lower mandible yellow (fig. 24); culmen 9.2-10.1; inside lining of mouth flesh to pale yellowish; wg 67-80; p6 not emarginated; p10 usually ≥ p6; longest p— p6 ≥ 5.5; tail 52-62; wg—tail 13-21; legs gray. From most *Empidonax* by green and yellow plumage and gray legs. From Yellow-bellied and Western flycatchers by a combination of plumage, mouth coloration, larger size, and wing formula features. See also differences in molt strategy for further identification clues.

Molt—PB: HY partial (Jul-Aug), AHY complete (Aug-Sep); PA partial (Dec-Apr). PBs occur on the summer grounds.

Skull—Completes in HY/SY from 15 Nov (as early as 15 Oct in SE populations) thru Jan. Some SYs may retain windows thru spring.

Age—Juv (May-Aug) has upperpart feathers edged buff, wide wing bars, and underparts dull white or faintly suffused with brownish.

> HY/SY (Aug-Jul): Underparts, often including throat, strongly washed yellow (thru Jan); wing bars wide, buffy (thru Feb); rects tapered (fig. 26), tipped buffy when fresh.

> AHY/ASY (Aug-Jul): Underparts with moderate yellow wash on breast and belly, throat whitish; wing bars narrow, white or tinged yellow; rects truncate (fig. 26), without buff tips.

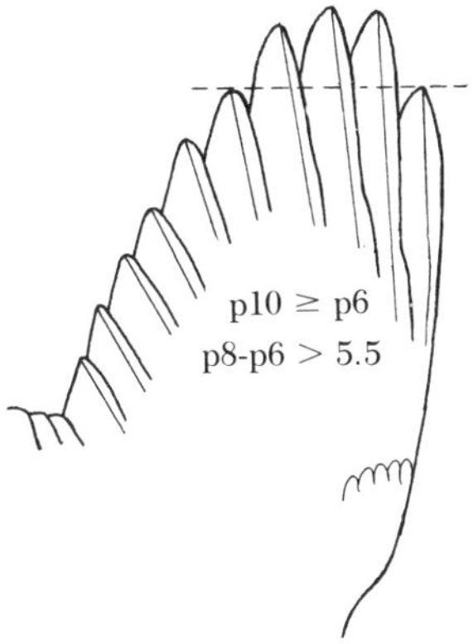

Sex—♂ = ♀ by plumage. CP/BP (Apr-Aug). Wg: ♂(n65) 70-80, ♀(n33) 67-75.

References—B,R,W,SK,O,BBM; Mengel (1952), Robbins (1959), Phillips *et al.* (1966), Traylor (1968).

[Figure at top right of page]

p10 ≥ p6
p8-p6 > 5.5

Figure 27. Wing formula of the Acadian Flycatcher.

TRAILL'S FLYCATCHER

TRFL
Species # 466.9
Band size: 0

ALDER FLYCATCHER
Empidonax alnorum

ALFL
Species # 466.1

WILLOW FLYCATCHER
Empidonax traillii

WIFL
Species # 466.0

Species—Upperparts brownish to olive; eye ring absent or indistinct (sometimes with distinctly paler lores); culmen 7.6-10.0; bill width > 5/8 culmen; lower mandible entirely or mostly yellowish (fig. 24); wg 64-77, p6 not (occasionally slightly emarginated; p10 ≤ p6; p9-p5 usually 8-13; wg—tail 7-17; legs blackish. From wood-pewees by shorter and less pointed wing. From other species of *Empidonax* by plumage and leg coloration, lack of distinct eye ring, large bill, and lack of emargination to p6.

Willow and Alder flycatchers should be separated with great caution, and only with extreme individuals, if at all (see Note, p 36). Alder Flycatchers generally

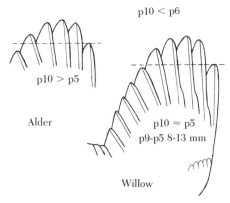

p10 < p6

p10 > p5

Alder

p10 ≈ p5
p9-p5 8-13 mm

Willow

Figure 28. Wing formulas of Willow and Alder flycatchers.

have slightly longer and more pointed wings and slightly smaller bills, such that a scatter diagram involving these characteristics provides the best clue to their identities (see below). As with all species of *Empidonax*, ♂♂ have longer and more pointed wings than ♀♀, hence knowing the sex can be of use. Also, eastern forms of Willow Flycatcher tend to have slightly shorter and less pointed wings than western forms, and may be easier to separate from Alder Flycatcher. The following measurements and scatter diagram are derived from Stein (1963):

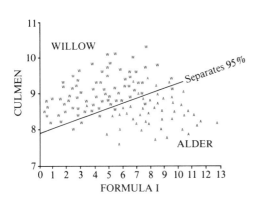

TABLE 2.

Some measurement ranges and means (in mm) of Alder and Willow Flycatchers (mostly from Stein 1963). See Sex for breakdown of ♂ and ♀

	Alder	Willow
Sample	56–57	66–68
Wing chord (mean)	65.8–76.5 (70.35)	63.2–74.5 (68.78)
p10–p5 (mean)	0.0–5.8 (2.27)	−2.6–2.9 (0.27)
Longest p–p6 (mean)	3.4–7.2 (5.14)	2.3–6.4 (3.97)
Culmen (mean)	7.6–9.3 (8.50)	8.0–10.3 (8.99)

Figure 29. A scatter diagram of culmen length vs. a wing formula equation in Willow and Alder flycatchers. Formula I is the difference between the longest p–p6 and p10–p5 (positive or negative). This comparison was used to separate 90–95% of these two species in both sympatric and allopatric populations (see Stein 1963).

[Note: A recent examination of these features indicates that much more study is needed before this identification problem is resolved. The above should be applied to captured birds in the interest of learning more, however, birds should probably not yet be reliably separated by in-hand criteria alone.]

Additional plumage criteria that may possibly be of use are slightly larger and more contrasting pale loral spots and darker centers to the crown feathers of certain populations of Alder Flycatcher.

Molt—PB: HY/SY partial (Sep-Jan), AHY/ASY complete (Sep-Jan); PA:SY complete (Mar-Apr), ASY partial (Mar-Apr). All molts take place on the winter grounds. More investigation is needed to determine the timing and extent, especially in HY/SYs. Molt strategies may differ between the two species.

Skull—Completes in HY from 15 Oct (may complete as early as 15 Sep in California populations of Willow) thru Dec. Some SYs may retain windows thru spring.

Age—The following is reliable for all autumn birds N of the winter grounds but becomes more difficult to use after completion of the 1st PB. No plumage criteria are known for birds in alternate plumage:

Juv-HY/SY (Jun-Apr): Wing bars wide, bright buffy (thru Dec); eye ring (if present) dull buffy white (thru Dec); flight feathers relatively fresh (thru Nov); rects pointed (fig. 26; rect shape possibly useful thru Oct on some SYs).

AHY/ASY (May-Apr): Wing bars narrow, dull whitish; eye ring (if present) white; flight feathers relatively worn in fall; rects truncate (fig 26).

Sex—♂ = ♀ by plumage. CP/BP (Apr-Aug). Wg: Alder ♂ (n49) 69-77; ♀ (n30) 66-73; Willow ♂ (n50) 68-75, ♀ (n30) 63-71. Also, Phillips *et al.* (1966) report that 90% of Alder Flycatchers can be sexed ysing the following complicated formula: ♂ wg(flat) > 70.9 -.27 × (B-A); ♀ wg(flat) < 40.9 -.27 × (B-A); where B = longest p-p6 and A = p10-p5.

References— DVR,B,R,W,SK,O,BBM; Robbins (1959), Stein (1963), Phillips *et al.* (1964), Phillips *et al.* (1966), Phillips & Lanyon (1970); PRBO data.

LEAST FLYCATCHER
Empidonax minimus

LEFL
Species # 467.0
Band size: 0

Species—From other species of *Empidonax* with caution. Upperparts brownish-olive to grayish; underparts with varying amounts of yellow; ss edged with white or lemon-white; throat whitish; culmen 6.3-8.4; bill width usually > 4.5; bill convex in shape; lower mandible variable, often dusky with a yellow-orange base (fig. 24); wg 57-67; p 10 < to > p5; p9-p5 usually > 5.0; longest p—longest s (wing-tip) < 13.5; p6 emarginated; tail 51-58, slightly notched (outer—central rect usually < 2.5); wg—tail 4-12; legs blackish. From eastern species of *Empidonax* by combination of plumage and leg coloration and smaller measurements. In west most similar to Hammond's Flycatcher (which see for separation from Dusky and Gray flycatchers). From Hammond's Flycatcher by longer wing tip, wider and convexly shaped bill, shorter wg, less notched tail, and whiter color to edging of ss. Check also for larger and more contrasting dark centers to the crown feathers; this species and Alder Flycatcher tend to show this more than other species of *Empidonax*. See also differences in molt strategy for further identification clues.

Molt—PB: HY partial-incomplete (Jul-Oct), AHY complete (Aug-Nov). PA: SY partial-incomplete (Feb-May), ASY limited-partial (Feb-May). 1st PB occurs on the summer grounds and rarely includes a few ss or rects; adult PB occurs on the winter grounds. 1st PA can include 2-3 pairs of ss and some or all rects.

p10 ≈ p5
p9-p5 < 5 mm

Skull—Completes in HY from 15 Oct thru Dec. Some SYs retain windows thru summer.

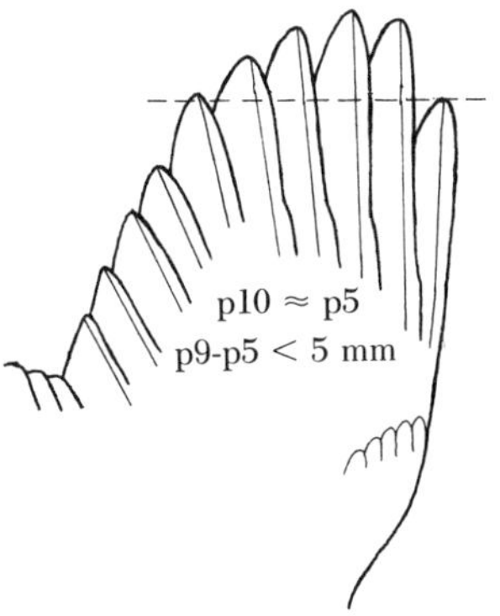

Figure 30. Wing formula of the Least Flycatcher.

Age—In addition to the following, check for contrasts between new and old ss and rects on some spring SYs. Juv (Jun-Sep) resembles HY/SY. A few intermediates between the following may not be reliably aged, especially later in winter; ASYs are probably not reliably distinguished after the PA:

HY/SY (Sep-Aug): Wing bars wide, buffy white (thru Mar); eye ring buffy white (thru Mar); flight feathers fresh in fall; some or all rects tapered (fig. 26; see Molt).

AHY/ASY (Apr-Mar): Wing bars narrow, white; eye ring white; flight feathers relatively worn in fall; rects truncate (fig. 26).

Sex—♂ = ♀ by plumage. CP/BP (May-Aug). Wg: ♂(n80) 60-67, ♀(n80) 57-65. Also, Phillips *et al.* (1966) report that the following formula correctly separated 93% of their sample: ♂ wg(flat) ≥ 61.8 + .13 × (p5-p10); ♀ wg(flat) ≤ 61.8 + .13 × (p5-p10).

References—DVR,B,R,W,SK,O,BBM; Moore (1940), Johnson (1963a, 1963b), Phillips *et al.* (1964), Phillips *et al.* (1966), Phillips & Lanyon (1970), Hussell (1980); PRBO data.

HAMMOND'S FLYCATCHER
Empidonax hammondii

HAFL
Species # 468.0
Band size: 0

Species—From other species of *Empidonax* with caution. Upperparts olive (fall) to grayish (spring) underparts with varying amount of yellow or greenish; throat gray to grayish-white; ss edging buffy white (HY/SY) to grayish (AHY/ASY); outer web of outer rects slightly paler than rest of tail; culmen 6.0-7.9; bill width usually ≤ 4.5; lower mandible dusky with slightly paler base (AHY) to mostly orange (Juv-HY; fig.24); wg 63-75; p10 usually ≥ p5; p9-p5 ≥ 5.0; longest p—longest s (wing tip) ≥ 13.0; p6 emarginated; tail 52-62, markedly notched (outer—central rects usually ≥ 2.5); wg—tail 7-17; legs blackish. From most *Empidonax* species by combination of plumage features, leg color, and wing formula. See Least Flycatcher for separation from that species. From Dusky and Gray flycatchers by larger wg—tail difference, shorter culmen, less contrasting outer webs to outer rects, and wing formula differences. See also differences in molt strategy for further identification clues.

Molt—PB: HY partial (Jul-Oct), AHY complete (Jun-Sep); PA partial-incomplete (Feb-Apr). PBs occur on the summer grounds. PA may include terts and up to two pairs of rects (occasionally all in some SYs).

Skull—Completes in HY from 15 Oct thru Dec. Some SYs retain windows thru summer.

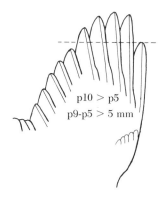

Figure 31. Wing formula of the Hammond's Flycatcher.

Age—Juv (May-Sep) has brownish washed upperparts and buffy wing bars. Some intermediates may not be reliably aged with the following; ASY is probably not reliably distinguished after the PA:

HY/SY (Aug-Jul): Wing bars (thru Mar) and edging to ss and tertials with strong buffy wash; lower mandible mostly orange (thru Nov, possibly later); rects tapered (fig. 26).

AHY/ASY (Apr-Mar): Wing bars and edging to ss and tertials grayish; lower mandible mostly dusky; rects truncate (fig. 26). [This latter criteria possibly useful thru Jun; compare with condition of the pp (see p. 18 and Molt).]

Sex—♂ = ♀ by plumage. CP/BP (May-Aug). Wg: ♂(n47) 67-75, ♀(n55) 63-72.

References—DVR,B,O; Moore (1940), Johnson (1963a, 1963b), Phillips *et al.* (1964), Phillips & Lanyon (1970); PRBO data.

DUSKY FLYCATCHER
Empidonax oberholseri

DUFL
Species # 469.0
Band size: 0

Species—From other species of *Empidonax* with caution. Upperparts grayish-olive to gray-ish-brown; underparts mostly whitish with a varying amount of yellow wash; throat whitish; outeredge of outer rects whitish, contrasting with rest of tail; culmen 6.5-8.9 bill width 4.2-5.3; lower mandible variable, mostly dusky (AHY/ASY) to mostly yellow (Juv-HY), often yellowish with indistinctly defined dusky tip (fig. 24); wg 61-74; p10 < p5, often ≤ p4; p9-p5 usually ≤ 5.0; p6 emarginated; tail 57-68, slightly notched (outer—central rect usually ≤ 2.0); wg—tail 0-8; legs blackish. From most *Empidonax* species by combination of plumage features, leg color, and wing formula. See Hammond's Flycatcher for separation from this species and Least. From Gray Flycatcher with caution, especially with HYs in autumn. Useful criteria include slightly darker coloration, shorter bill and wg—tail differences, relationship of p10 and p4, and indistinctly defined color pattern of lower mandible. See also differences in molt strategy for further identification clues.

Molt—PB: HY/SY partial-incomplete (Aug-Jan), AHY complete (Aug-Dec); PA limited-partial (Mar-May). All molts occur on winter grounds. The 1st PB and/or PA may include some ss.

Skull—Completes in HY from 15 Oct thru Dec. Some SYs occasionally retain windows thru summer/fall.

Age—Intermediates between the following will occur which are not reliably aged by plumage alone, especially without experience:

Juv-HY/SY (Jun-2nd Aug): Wing bars wide, fresh, buffy or yellowish (thru Dec); flight feathers fresh in fall; lower mandible mostly yellow (thru Nov, possibly later); rects tapered (fig. 26), relatively worn in spring. [Some SYs might be reliably aged by rect shape thru Nov, with caution and consideration of molt.]

AHY/ASY (Sep-Aug): Wing bars narrow, abraded (in fall), whitish; flight feathers worn in fall; lower mandible mostly dusky; rects truncate (fig. 26), relatively unabraded in spring.

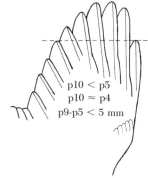

p10 < p5
p10 ≈ p4
p9-p5 < 5 mm

Figure 32. Wing formula of the Dusky Flycatcher.

Sex—♂ = ♀ by plumage. CP/BP (Apr-Aug). Wg: ♂(n63) 65-74, ♀(n64) 61-70.

References—B,O; Moore (1940), Johnson (1963a, 1963b), Phillips & Lanyon (1970); PRBO data.

GRAY FLYCATCHER
Empidonax wrightii

GRFL
Species # 469.1
Band size: 0

Species—From other species of *Empidonax* with caution. Upperparts pale brownish-gray (AHY) to grayish-olive (HY); underparts pale with little (AHY) to some (HY) yellow wash; throat white; outer web of outer rect white, markedly contrasting with rest of tail; culmen 7.6-10.4; bill width 4.4-5.8; lower mandible pale pinkish to yellowish with well defined dark tip (fig. 24); wg 64-76; p10 usually $\geq$ p4; p9-p5 4-10 mm; p6 emarginated; tail 56-66, slightly notched (outer—central rect usually $\leq$ 2.0); wg—tail 6-13; legs blackish. From most *Empidonax* by combination of plumage features, leg color, and bill measurements. Some HYs may be difficult to separate from Dusky Flycatcher (which see). See also differences in molt strategy for further identification clues.

Molt—PB: HY incomplete (Jul-Dec), AHY complete (Jul-Dec); PA SY partial-incomplete (Mar-May), ASY limited-partial (Mar-May). All molts occur on the winter grounds. 1st PB and PA may involve some ss and some or (rarely) all rects.

Skull—Completes in HY from 15 Oct thru Dec. Some SYs may retain windows thru spring.

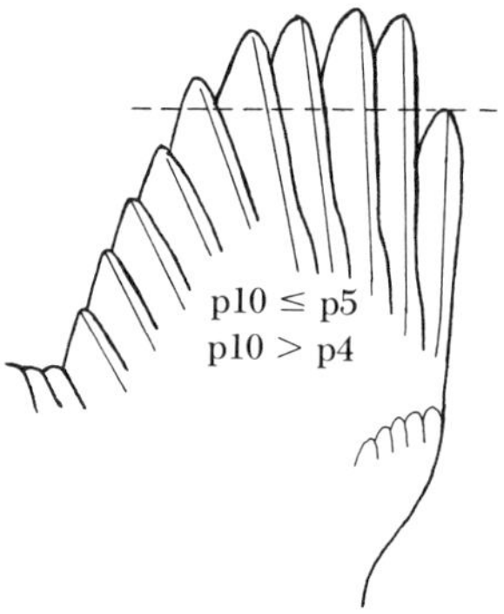

p10 $\leq$ p5
p10 > p4

Figure 33. Wing formula of the Gray Flycatcher.

Age—In addition to the following, Juv/HYs (Jun-Nov) tend to have more green in the upperpart coloration and yellow in the underparts. Autumn AHYs north of the wintering grounds have comparatively faded plumage:

Juv-HY/SY (Jun-2nd Sep): Flight feathers relatively fresh in fall; rects tapered (fig. 26). [Beware of occasional HY/SYs that have replaced all rects; compare with the condition (and shape) of the pp (see p. 18). With caution and consideration of molt, some SYs may be reliably distinguished thru Nov.]

AHY/ASY (Sep-Aug): Flight feathers relatively worn in fall; rects truncate (fig. 26). [See Juv-HY/SY.]

Sex—♂ = ♀ by plumage. CP/BP (May-Jul). Wg: ♂(n52) 67-76, ♀(n53) 64-73.

References—B,O; Moore (1940), Johnson (1963a, 1963b), Phillips & Lanyon (1970); PRBO data.

WESTERN FLYCATCHER
Empidonax difficilis

WEFL
Species # 464.0
Band size: 0

Species—From other species of *Empidonax* with caution. Upperparts greenish-olive (brownish-olive in some Juvs); underparts including throat strongly washed yellow (paler in Juv); eye ring broad, whitish-yellow, tear-drop shaped; bend of wing and underwing covs brownish-yellow to mustard; pp and ss brown in fall, contrasting little with paler edges to ss; culmen 7.7-9.0; bill width ≥ 5/8 culmen; lower mandible entirely yellow; wg 56-74; p10 ≈ p5; p6 emarginated; tail 50-63; wg—tail 3-14; legs gray. From most species of *Empidonax* (including all other western species) by greenish plumage, yellow lower mandible, and gray legs; and for Juvs, eye ring shape, wing formula features, and gray legs. From Acadian Flycatcher by shorter wing and emargination of p6. Closest in plumage and structure to Yellow-bellied Flycatcher, which see for separating charac-

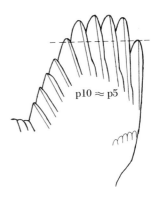

Figure 34. Wing formula of the Western Flycatcher.

teristics. Pine Flycatcher (*E. affinis*), a possible vagrant from Mexico, can be separated from Western by having bill width ≤ 4.5 mm (< 5/8 culmen) and p10 ≤ p5. See also differences in molt strategy for further identification clues.

Subspecies—The A.O.U is currently considering splitting the coastal Pacific and interior western populations into separate species. The separation is based mainly on differences in vocalizations and habitat. No difinitive, in-hand separating criteria are now known, although coastal forms have, on the average, shorter wgs and narrower bills than interior forms. See Johnson (1980) for more information.

Molt—PB: HY partial-incomplete (Sep-Nov), AHY complete (Aug-Nov); PA partial (Mar-May). Most molting occurs on winter grounds. 1st PB can include terts and some or (rarely) all rects.

Skull—Completes in HY from 15 Oct (as early as 15 Sep in some California populations) thru Dec. Some SYs may retain windows thru spring.

Age—The following is reliable for all autumn birds N of the winter grounds; intermediates may occur in spring that are not reliably aged:

Juv-HY/SY (May-2nd Aug): Upperparts brownish-olive, underparts with slight to moderate yellow wash, wing bars wide and buffy brown, and flight feathers relatively fresh (these good thru Oct only); rects tapered (fig. 26), tipped buffy when fresh. [Look also for contrasting new and old rects in spring, and beware of occasional HY/SYs that have replaced all rects; compare with condition and shape of the pp (see p. 18).]

AHY/ASY (Jul-Jun): Upperparts greenish-olive; underparts with moderate to extensive yellow wash; wing bars narrow, whitish; flight feathers relatively worn; rects truncate (fig. 26), without buffy tips. See Juv-HY/SY.

Sex—♂ = ♀ by plumage. CP/BP (Mar-Aug). Wg: ♂ (n30) 60-74, ♀ (n30) 56-70; W > E (excludes the paler Channel Island population, which averages much larger).

References—B,O; Phillips & Lanyon (1970), Johnson (1974, 1980); DeSante *et al.* (1985); PRBO data.

BUFF-BREASTED FLYCATCHER
Empidonax fulvifrons

BBFL
Species # 470.0
Band size: 0

Molt—PB: HY partial (Aug-Sep), AHY complete (Aug-Sep); PA limited (Mar-Apr). PBs occur mostly on summer grounds.

Skull—Completes in HY from 1 Oct thru Dec.

Age—Juv (Jun-Sep) is duller brown above and has distinct, buffy wing bars. Intermediates between the following may be difficult or impossible to age:

HY/SY (Sep-Aug): Breast relatively rich buff; rects tapered (fig. 26).

AHY/ASY (Sep-Aug): Breast relatively pale buff; rects truncate (fig. 26).

Sex—♂ = ♀ by plumage. CP/BP (Apr-Aug). Wg ♂(n30) 58-64, ♀(n30) 55-60.

References—B; Phillips *et al.* (1964), Phillips & Lanyon (1970); R. Bowers (*pers. comm.*).

BLACK PHEOBE
Sayornis nigricans

BLPH
Species # 458.0
Band size: 1

Molt—PB: HY partial (Jun-Sep), AHY complete (Jul-Aug); PA absent. PBs occur primarily on the summer grounds. The 1st PB includes some to all gr covs.

Skull—Completes in HY/SY from 31 Aug thru Jan. Some SYs may retain windows thru spring.

Age—Juv (Apr-Sep) has cinnamon tipping to upperpart feathers and cinnamon wing bars. Intermediates between the following may be difficult or impossible to age:

HY/SY (Aug-Jul): One or more gr cov often (not always) tipped buffy-cinnamon; flight feathers brownish-black to brownish; rects tapered (fig. 35), tipped buffy when fresh.

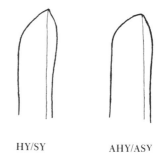

HY/SY   AHY/ASY

Figure 35. Rectrix shape by age in phoebes.

AHY/ASY (Aug-Jul): Gr covs without buffy-cinnamon tips; flight feathers blackish to grayish-black; rects truncate (fig. 35), tipped whitish when fresh.

Sex—♂ = ♀ by plumage. CP/BP (Mar-Aug). Wg: ♂(n30) 84-96, ♀(n30) 81-92.

References—DVR,B,O; PRBO data.

EASTERN PHEOBE
Sayornis phoebe

EAPH
Species # 457.0
Band size: 0

Species—Wing bars lacking or indistinct; lower mandible entirely black; wg 77-91; tail 63-78. These features should separate this from *Empidonax* flycatchers and wood-pewees.

Molt—PB: HY partial (Jul-Aug), AHY complete (Jul-Aug); PA absent. PBs occur on the summer grounds; 1st PB includes some to all gr covs.

Skull—Completes in HY from 1 Oct (as early as 15 Sep in southern populations) thru Nov. Some SYs retain windows thru spring.

Age—Juv (Jun-Aug) has a brownish wash to upperparts and buffy wing bars. Intermediates between the following may be difficult or impossible to age:

HY/SY (Aug-Jul): One or more gr cov often tipped buffy; rects tapered (fig. 35), tipped buffy when fresh.

AHY/ASY (Aug-Jul): Gr covs without buffy tips; rects truncate (fig. 35).

Sex—♂ = ♀ by plumage. CP/BP (Mar-Jul). Wg: ♂(n30) 81-91, ♀(n30) 77-88.

References—B,R,W,O; Yunick (1984); PRBO data.

SAY'S PHOEBE
Sayornis saya

SAPH
Species # 457.0
Band size: 1

Molt—PB: HY partial (Jul-Sep), AHY complete (Jul-Sep); PA absent-partial (Feb-Apr). PBs occur on summer grounds; 1st PB normally includes all gr covs. The extent of the PAs requires further investigation.

Skull—Completes in HY from 30 Aug thru Dec. Some SYs may retain windows thru spring.

Age—Juv (Apr-Aug) has wide, buffy wing bars. Look for retention of one or more gr cov in some HY/SYs, as in the other phoebes. Intermediates may not be reliably aged by the following:

HY/SY (Aug-Jul): Flight feathers brownish-black to brownish; rects tapered (fig.35).

AHY/ASY (Aug-Jul): Flight feathers blackish; rects truncate (fig. 35).

Sex—♂ = ♀ by plumage. CP/BP (Feb-Aug). Wg: ♂(n30) 99-109, ♀(n30) 95-105.

References—B,O; PRBO data.

VERMILLION FLYCATCHER
Pyrocephalus rubinus

VEFL
Species # 471.0
Band size: 0

Molt—PB: HY complete (Aug-Oct), AHY complete (Jul-Sep); PA limited-partial (Feb-Apr). PBs occur on breeding grounds. PA may be more extensive in SY ♂ than other age/sex classes.

Skull—Completes in HY from 1 Aug thru Dec. Some SYs may retain windows thru spring.

Age/Sex—CP/BP (Feb-Aug). Wg: ♂(n40) 75-87, ♀(n40) 73-84; E > W. Juv (Apr-Aug) has scaly brown upperparts and white underparts with oval spotting (♂ = ♀). Rect shape not useful for ageing after the 1st PB. Some intermediates between HY/SY and AHY/ASY (especially ♀ ♀) may occur, mostly in spring, which are not reliably aged by the following:

AHY/ASY ♂ (Aug-Jul): Underparts and crown uniformly bright red.

HY/SY ♂ (Aug-2nd Aug): Crown and/or breast with varying amounts of red, from a few feathers on a brown streaked background, to almost entirely dull red with some pale mottling; lower belly and vent strongly washed salmon-pink to orangish-red.

AHY/ASY ♀ (Aug-Jul): Upperparts grayish-brown; crown and breast without red feathers; lower belly and vent washed with pale salmon-pink.

HY/SY ♀ (Aug-2nd Aug): Like Ad ♀ but lower belly and vent washed pale yellowish.

References—B,O.

DUSKY-CAPPED FLYCATCHER
Myiarchus tuberculifer

DCFL
Species # 455.0
Band size: 1B

Species—From other species of *Myiarchus* with caution. Upperparts brownish-olive; breast gray; belly and vent brightish lemon yellow; rects with very little rufous or (Juv) rufous confined to narrow edging (fig. 36); culmen 11.0-13.5; lower mandible blackish-brown with slightly paler base (fig. 36); wg 74-86; p10 ≤ p4; tail 68-81. [Measurements pertain to Arizona populations; may show considerable geographic variation further south.] Combination of small size, wing formula, and relative lack of rufous in the tail should separate this from other *Myiarchus* species.

Molt—PB: HY complete (Aug-Nov), AHY complete (Aug-Oct); PA: partial (Mar-Apr). PBs probably occur entirely on winter grounds.

Skull—Completes in HY from 15 Oct thru Dec.

Age—The following is reliable for all autumn birds N of winter grounds. Otherwise, rect shape is not useful and no reliable plumage criteria are known after completion of the PBs:

   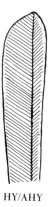 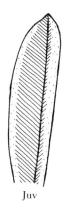

HY/AHY   Juv

Figure 36. Relative bill shape and size, and adult and juvenal rectrix pattern in the Dusky-capped Flycatcher.

Juv-HY (Jun-Nov): Gr and mid covs, ss, and outer web of rects (fig. 36) broadly edged rufous; uppertail covs mostly rufous; flight feathers relatively fresh.

AHY (Jan-Oct): Wing covs and outer web of rects (fig. 36) without rufous; ss narrowly edged rufous; uppertail covs mostly brown with narrow, rufous edging; flight feathers relatively worn.

Sex—♂ = ♀ by plumage. CP (May-Jun); BP (May-Jul) may occur in both sexes but probably more extensively in ♀♀. Wg: ♂(n30) 76-86, ♀(n10) 72-80.

References—DVR,B,O.

ASH-THROATED FLYCATCHER
Myiarchus cinerascens

ATFL
Species # 454.0
Band size 1B

Species—From other species of *Myiarchus* with caution. Upperparts grayish-brown; breast pale gray; belly and vent pale yellow; rects with broad rufous edges on inner webs (brown medial stripe extending < 1 mm from shaft) but tipped brown (fig 37); culmen 13.0-15.5; bill width 5.0-6.5; lower mandible dark brown, sometimes slightly paler at base (fig. 37); mouth lining flesh-colored; wg 88-105; p10 > p5; p9 = p6; tail 82-98. From other N.A. *Myiarchus* by combination of paler plumage, rect color pattern, measurements, and color of lower mandible. Nutting's Flycatcher (*M. nuttingi*), a possible vagrant from Mexico, can be separated with caution by orange-yellow mouth lining, slightly smaller wing (83-99), wing formula (p9 = p5), and rect color pattern (brown expanding less abruptly at tip). See Lanyon (1961) for further means of separation.

Molt—PB: HY complete (Aug-Nov), AHY complete (Aug-Oct); PA limited (Mar-Apr). PBs sometimes begin on the summer grounds but occur mostly on the winter grounds.

Skull—Completes in HY from 1 Sep thru Dec.

Age—The following is reliable for all autumn birds N of winter grounds. Otherwise, rect shape is not useful and no reliable plumage criteria are known after completion of the PBs:

bill width 5.0-6.5

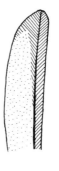 

HY/AHY   Juv

Figure 37. Relative bill shape and size, and adult and juvenal rectrix pattern in the Ash-throated Flycatcher.

Juv-HY (May-Nov): Ss and outer webs of rects (fig. 37) broadly edged pale rufous; uppertail covs mostly cinnamon-rufous; flight feathers relatively fresh (but can become worn quite quickly).

AHY (Jan-Oct): Ss (except outermost) narrowly edged white or grayish-white; uppertail covs brown, narrowly edged rufous-cinnamon; outer web of rects without rufous (fig. 37); flight feathers relatively worn.

Sex—♂ = ♀ by plumage. CP (Mar-Jul); BP (Apr-Aug) may occur in both sexes but is more extensive in ♀♀. Wg useful: ♂(n100) 94-105, ♀(n100) 88-99.

References—B,O,C; Lanyon (1961), Phillips *et al.* (1966), Phillips & Lanyon (1970); PRBO data.

GREAT-CRESTED FLYCATCHER
Myiarchus crinitus

GCFL
Species # 452.0
Band size: 1A-1B

Species—From other species of *Myiarchus* with caution. Upperparts olive; breast gray; belly and vent bright yellow; inner web of rects mostly rufous (brown of outer web extends < 2 mm from shaft), the rufous extending all the way to tip (fig 38); culmen 14.2-16.1; bill width 6.4-7.4; lower mandible brownish, horn-colored to yellow-orange at base (fig. 38); mouth lining yellow-orange; wg 94-110; p10 > p5; tail 82-96. From other *Myiarchus* by brighter plumage, rect color pattern, measurements, and color of lower mandible.

Molt—PB: HY complete (Aug-Nov), AHY complete (Jul-Aug); PA partial-incomplete (Feb-Apr). 1st PB suspended, with flight feather molt occurring on the winter grounds. Adult PB occurs on breeding grounds. A few HY/SYs may retain some juvenal flight feathers until the 1st PA.

Skull—Completes in HY from 15 Oct (possibly as early as 15 Sep in southern U.S. populations) thru Dec.

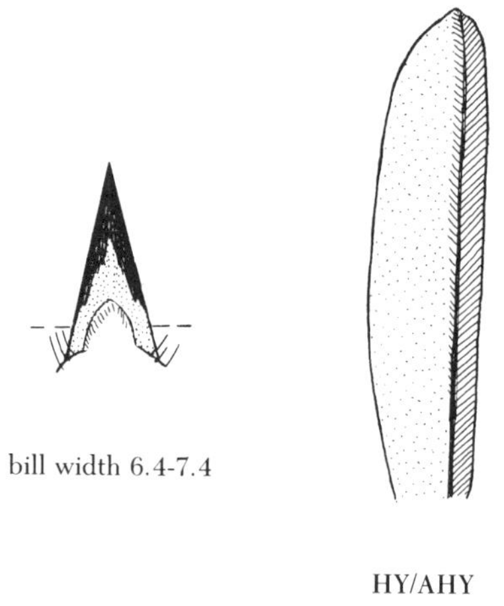

bill width 6.4-7.4

Age—Rect shape is not useful after completion of the 1st PB. The following is reliable on all autumn birds N of the winter grounds:

HY/AHY

Figure 38. Relative bill shape and size, and adult rectrix pattern in the Great-crested Flycatcher.

Juv-HY (Apr-Nov): Wing covs edged cinnamon-buff; outer web of central rects edged rufous; flight feathers relatively fresh. [Look for retained juvenal flight feathers on occasional HY/SYs thru Apr.]

AHY (Jan-Oct): Wing covs brown, without cinnamon edging; outer web of central rects without rufous edging; flight feathers relatively worn. [No reliable plumage criteria known to distinguish AHY/ASYs after completeion of the PBs.]

Sex—♂ = ♀ by plumage. CP (Mar-Jul); BP (Mar-Aug) acquired by both sexes but is usually more extensive in ♀ ♀. Wg: ♂(n30) 100-110, ♀(n30) 94-104.

References—DVR,B,R,W,O; Parkes (1953), Phillips *et al* (1966), Phillips & Lanyon (1970).

BROWN-CRESTED FLYCATCHER
Myiarchus tyrannulus

BCFL
Species # 453.0
Band size: 1A

Species—From other species of *Myiarchus* with caution. Upperparts grayish-brown to olive-brown; breast pale gray; belly and vent pale yellow; inner web of rects with moderate amount of rufous (brown of outer web extends 2-6 mm from shaft) the rufous extending to feather tip (fig 39); culmen 17.1-19.7; bill width 7.5-9.1; lower mandible black, slightly paler at base (fig. 39); mouth lining flesh-colored; wg 96-114; tail 93-105. Larger measurements and rect color pattern should separate this from all other *Myiarchus*.

Molt—PB: HY complete (Aug-Nov), AHY complete (Aug-Oct); PA partial (Feb-Mar). 1st PB probably suspended, with flight feather molt occurring on the winter grounds. Adult PBs occur on the winter grounds.

Skull—Completes in HY from 15 Sep thru Dec.

Age—The following is reliable on all autumn birds N of winter grounds. Otherwise, rect shape is not useful and no reliable plumage criteria known after completion of the PBs:

Juv-HY (May-Nov): Outer webs of central rects broadly edged rufous; flight feathers relatively fresh.

AHY (Jan-Oct): Outer web of central rects without rufous; flight feathers relatively worn.

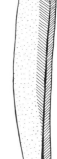

bill width 7.5-9.1

HY/AHY

Figure 39. Relative bill shape and size, and adult rectrix pattern in the Brown-crested Flycatcher.

Sex—♂ = ♀ by plumage. CP/BP (Mar-Aug); BP may occur in both sexes but is probably more developed in ♀ ♀. Wg: ♂(n30) 99-114, ♀(n30) 96-108; Ariz. > Tex.

References—B,O; Phillips & Lanyon (1970).

GREAT KISKADEE
Pitangus sulphuratus

GRKI
Species # 449.0
Band size: 2

Molt—PB: HY partial (Jul-Sep), AHY complete (Jul-Sep); PA limited (Feb-Mar).

Skull—Completes in HY from 1 Oct thru Dec.

Age—Juv (May-Aug) resembles HY/SY but has no yellow in crown and has plumage generally washed brownish.

HY/SY (Aug-2nd Aug): Crown patch with few (Aug-Feb) to many (Mar-Aug) yellow feathers; outer webs of central rects with rufous > 2 mm wide; rects tapered, pattern on outer rects as shown (fig. 40).

AHY/ASY (Aug-Jul): Crown patch extensive, consisting of many yellow feathers; outer webs of central rects with rufous < 2 mm wide; rects truncate, pattern on outer rects as shown (fig. 40).

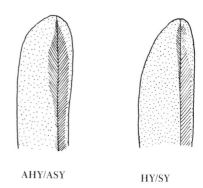

AHY/ASY   HY/SY

Figure 40. Outer rectrix shape by age in the Great Kiskadee.

Sex—♂ = ♀ by plumage. CP/BP (Feb-Aug). Wg: ♂(n30) 117-127, ♀(n30) 113-123.

References—DVR,B,O.

SULPHER-BELLIED FLYCATCHER
Myiodynastes luteiventris

SBFL
Species # 451.0
Band size: 1B

Species—Outer rects with narrow streaks < 3 mm wide (see fig. 41); lower mandible with little or no pale base; culmen 17-19. Streaked Flycatcher (*M. maculatus*), a possible vagrant to N.A., has wider (> 3 mm) and less distinct black streaks on outer rects, an extensive pale base to the lower mandible, and a larger culmen: 19-22.

Molt—PB: HY complete (Aug-Dec), AHY complete (Jul-Nov). PBs occur primarily on the winter grounds. The occurrence and extent of the PA is unknown.

Skull—Completes in HY/SY from 1 Nov thru at least Jan.

Age—The following is reliable for all autumn birds N of the winter grounds; some of the Juv-HY characteristics may be retained until spring. Otherwise, no reliable plumage criteria known after completion of the 1st PB:

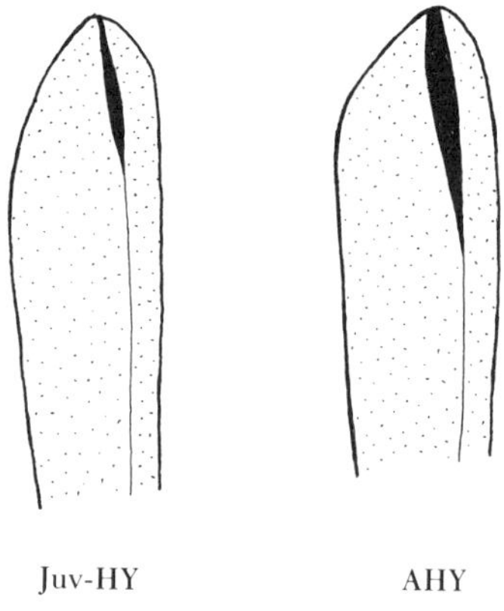

Juv-HY   AHY

Figure 41. Juvenal and adult outer rectrices in the Sulpher-bellied Flycatcher.

Juv-HY (Jun-Dec): Yellow crown patch lacking or restricted to the bases of feathers; ss and wing covs edged cinnamon; outer rects tapered, with narrow black streaks (fig. 41).

AHY (Jan-Nov): Yellow crown patch concealed but extensive; ss and wing covs edged pale grayish or yellowish-white; outer rects truncate, with broader black streaks (fig. 41).

Sex—♂ = ♀ by plumage. CP/BP (Jun-Sep). Wg: ♂(n20) 111-120, ♀(n19) 108-114.

References—DVR,B.

TROPICAL KINGBIRD
Tyrannus melancholicus

TRKI
Species # 446.0
Band size: 1A

Species—Head gray; back grayish-green; tail brownish-black; outer rects unicolored (ad; fig. 42) or with buffy outer edge (Juv); bill width ≥ 10; tail notched, outer—central rect ≥ 5. The combination of these characteristics will separate this species from Western and Cassin's kingbirds.

Tropical and Couch's kingbirds should be separated with care. Tropical Kingbird is a slightly smaller bird but with a relatively longer bill such that the ratio of culmen/wg provides a good identification guide (table 3). Tropical Kingbird also has a slightly less pointed wing than Couch's Kingbird (fig. 42). A scatter diagram plotting culmen/wg against a wing formula (fig. 43) provides the best means for separating the two species. As with the *Empidonax* flycatchers, determination of sex can assist with species separation (see Traylor 1979). See also differences in molt strategy for further identification clues. The measurements (table 3) and scatter diagram (fig. 43) are derived from Traylor (1979).

TABLE 3.
Some measurement ranges (in mm) of Tropical and Couch's kingbirds (derived from Traylor 1979).

	Tropical	Couch's
Sample	148	156
Wing chord	108–122	115–131
Culmen	16.3–21.7	14.2–18.3
Culmen/wg	0.143–0.183	0.128–0.147
longest p–p5/ longest p–p4.	0.51–1.63	0.19–0.75

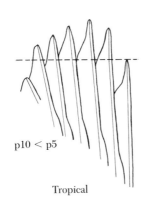
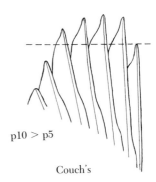

p10 < p5

Tropical

p10 > p5

Couch's

Figure 42. Outer rectrix pattern (for identification) and wing formulas (for separation) of Tropical and Couch's kingbirds.

Molt PB: HY incomplete-complete (Sep-Dec), AHY complete (Jul-Oct); PA: partial-incomplete (Feb-Apr). PB molts occur on winter grounds. HY/SY birds usually (but not always) replace all flight feathers by spring. [This molting sequence applies only to the northwest race of the species, which regularly occurs in N.A.]

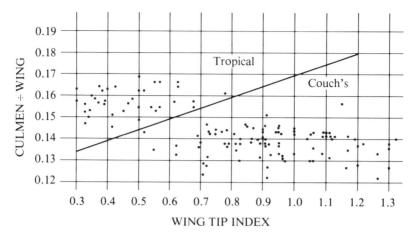

Figure 43.   Scatter diagram of culmen ÷ wing against wing tip index (longest p-p5 ÷ longest p-p4) for U.S. and central Mexican populations of Tropical and Couch's kingbirds (derived from Traylor 1979).

Skull—Completes in HY from 15 Oct thru Dec.

Age—The following is reliable in basic plumage only; no reliable plumage criteria is known in alternate plumage except to distinguish occasional SYs (see below):

Juv-HY/SY (Jun-Apr): Crown without red feathers; some or all outer pp not notched (fig. 44; thru at least Oct, often thru Mar-Apr); flight feathers relatively fresh (Jun-Oct); rects tapered (fig. 45; thru at least Oct), edged buffy when fresh. [Look for juvenal pp and/or rects on a few SYs thru Sep; these should be easily separated from those of HYs (Jun-Sep) by being extremely worn at that time of year.]

AHY/ASY (Apr-Mar): Crown with concealed red feathers; p6-10 substantially notched (fig. 44); flight feathers relatively worn (Jun-Oct); rects truncate (fig. 45), without buffy edging.

Sex—♂ = ♀ by plumage. CP/BP (Apr-Jul). Wg: ♂(n100) 109-122, ♀(n60) 108-118; The following is reliable only after the juvenal primaries have been molted (usually Nov-Apr on HY/SYs). Look for slight differences in the shape of pp 6-10 on HY/SYs previous to the 1st PB, as with Cassin's Kingbird. Otherwise, no plumage criteria known for sexing birds with juvenal primaries:

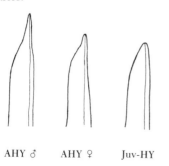

AHY ♂   AHY ♀   Juv-HY

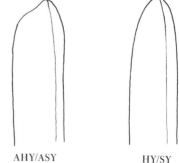

AHY/ASY   HY/SY

Figure 44. The shape of the outer primaries by age and sex in Tropical and Couch's kingbirds. See species accounts for the timing of usefulness of this criterion.

Figure 45. Juvenal and adult rectrix shapes in kingbirds.

AHY ♂: Notches on pp 6-10 ≥ 8 mm from tip (fig. 44).

AHY ♀: Notches on pp 6-10 < 8 mm from tip (fig. 44).

References—DVR,B,O,C; Rea (1969), Traylor (1979).

COUCH'S KINGBIRD
Tyrannus couchii

COKI
Species # 446.1
Band size: 1B-1A

Species—See Tropical Kingbird.

Molt—PB: HY partial-incomplete (Jul-Sep), AHY complete (Jul-Sep); PA: SY partial-complete (Feb-Apr), ASY partial (Feb-Apr). PBs occur on the summer grounds. The 1st PB rarely includes a few flight feathers; 1st PA extremely variable.

Skull—Completes in HY from 15 Oct thru Dec.

Age—Juv (May-Aug) has brownish washed upperparts, and buffy tipped uppertail and gr covs. As with Tropical Kingbird, look for occasional SYs to retain juvenal flight feathers thru the 2nd PB. Otherwise, no reliable criteria known for ageing alternate-plumaged birds:

HY/SY (Jun-Mar): Crown without red feathers; some or all outer pp not notched (fig. 44; possibly good on some SYs thru Aug); rects tapered (fig. 45), tipped buffy when fresh.

AHY/ASY (Jun-Mar): Crown with concealed red feathers; pp 6-10 substantially notched (fig. 44); rects truncate (fig. 45), without buffy tipping.

Sex—♂ = ♀ by plumage. CP/BP (Mar-Aug). Wg: ♂(n100) 118-131, ♀(n62) 115-122. The following is useful only after the juvenal primaries have been molted (see Tropical Kingbird):

AHY ♂: Notches on pp 6-10 ≥ 8 mm from tip (fig. 44).

AHY ♀: Notches on pp 6-10 < 8 mm from tip (fig. 44).

References—B,O,C; Rea (1969), Traylor (1979).

CASSIN'S KINGBIRD
Tyrannus vociferans

CAKI
Species # 448.0
Band size: 1A

Species—Head and breast dark gray; back dark grayish-olive; throat white; tail blackish; outer web of outer rects with narrow buffy edging, not reaching shaft (fig. 46); bill width ≤ 9 mm. p10 < p6; tail slightly notched, longest—central rect < 5 mm. The combination of these features should separate this from Tropical, Couch's and Western kingbirds.

Molt—PB: HY partial-complete (Sep-Dec), AHY complete (Sep-Oct); PA partial (Mar-Apr). PBs occur on the winter grounds. 1st PB can include none to all flight feathers.

Skull—Completes in HY/SY from 1 Oct thru Jan.

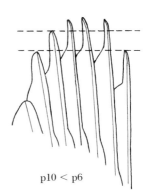

p10 < p6

Figure 46. Outer rectrix pattern and wing formula of Cassin's Kingbird, for identification.

Age/Sex—CP/BP (Apr-Aug). Wg: ♂(n40) 125-138, ♀(n40) 116-132. Some Juv/HY/SYs may be difficult to sex by the following (compare with wg):

AHY/ASY ♂ (Apr-Mar): Crown with at least some concealed orange or red feathers; notches on pp 6-10 > 8 mm from feather tip (fig. 47); rects truncate (fig. 45), without buffy tips. [No reliable plumage criteria known for distinguishing ASY in alternate-plumaged birds.]

Juv-HY/SY ♂ (Jun-2nd Sep): Crown without concealed orange or red feathers (thru Mar); pp 6-10 tapered (fig. 47; thru Oct-Dec, 2nd Sep on some); rects tapered (fig. 45), tipped buffy when fresh.

AHY/ASY ♀ (Apr-Mar): like AHY/ASY ♂ but notches on pp 6-10 < 5 mm from feather tip (fig. 47).

Juv-HY/SY ♀: like HY/SY ♂ but pp 6-10 blunt (fig. 47).

References—B,O,C; Rea (1969).

AHY/ASY ♂ AHY/ASY ♀ Juv-HY/SY ♂ Juv-HY/SY ♀ some HY/SY ♂ some HY/SY ♀

Figure 47. The shape of the outer primaries by age and sex in Cassin's Kingbird. See the species account for the timing of usefulness of this criterion.

THICK-BILLED KINGBIRD
Tyrannus crassirostris

TBKI
Species # 445.1
Band size: 1A

Molt—PB: HY partial (Jul-Sep), AHY complete (Jul-Sep); PA partial (Mar-Apr). PBs occur on the summer grounds.

Skull—Completes in HY from 15 Sep thru Dec.

Age—Juv (May-Aug) has rufous edged flight feathers, wing covs and uppertail covs.

HY/SY (Aug-Jul): Crown without concealed yellow feathers (thru Mar); pp 8-10 not notched (fig. 48); ss and rects edged rufous; rects tapered (fig. 45).

AHY/ASY (Aug-Jul): Crown with at least some concealed yellow feathers; pp 8-10 slightly notched (fig. 48); ss and rects not edged with rufous; rects truncate (fig. 45).

AHY/ASY ♂   AHY/ASY ♀   HY/SY

Sex—♂ = ♀ by plumage. CP/BP (Mar-Jul). Wg: ♂(n30) 124-135, ♀(n26) 118-127. See fig. 48 for differences in shape of pp 8-10 which, with experience, is reliable for sexing most AHY/ASY birds.

Figure 48. The shape of the outer primaries by age and sex of the Thick-billed Kingbird.

References—C; Rea (1969).

WESTERN KINGBIRD
Tyrannus verticalis

WEKI
Species # 447.0
Band size: 1A

Species—Head, breast, and throat gray; back olive-gray; tail black; outer web of outer rect white to shaft (fig. 49); bill width ≤ 9.0; p10 > p6; tail not markedly notched, longest—central rect < 5 mm. Combination of the above features should separate this from Tropical, Couch's and Cassin's kingbirds.

Molt—PB: HY incomplete-complete (Oct-Dec), AHY complete (Aug-Oct); PA partial-incomplete (Mar-Apr). 1st PB occurs on the winter grounds, adult PBs occur on the summer grounds or are suspended. All flight feathers are usually replaced by completion of the 1st PA.

Skull—Completes in HY/SY from 15 Sep thru Jan.

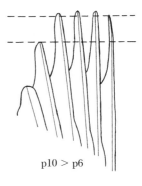

p10 > p6

Figure 49. Wing formula and outer rectrix pattern of Western Kingbird, for identification.

Age—The following is reliable in basic plumage only; no reliable plumage criteria known for ageing alternate-plumaged birds:

Juv-HY/SY (May-Apr): Crown without concealed red or orange feathers; pp 6-10 not notched (fig. 50; thru at least Nov, thru Apr an some birds), flight feathers relatively fresh in fall; rects tapered (fig. 45; thru at least Nov).

AHY/ASY (Apr-Mar): Crown with at least a few concealed, red or orange feathers; pp 6-10 distinctly notched or pointed (fig. 50); flight feathers relatively worn in fall; rects truncate (fig. 45).

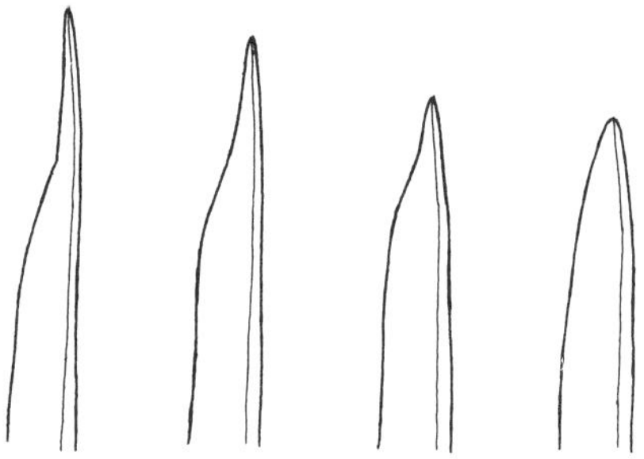

Figure 50. The shape of the outer primaries as a means of sexing and ageing Western Kingbird. See the species account for the timing of the usefulness of this criterion.

AHY ♂   AHY ♀   Juv-HY ♂   Juv-HY ♀

Sex—♂ = ♀ by plumage. CP/BP (Apr-Aug). Wg: ♂(n40) 120-135, ♀(n40) 112-128. Birds subseqent to the 1st primary molt can be reliably sexed with the following; see fig. 50 for slight differences in the shape of p10 which, when combined with wg, may be reliable for sexing many Juv-HY/SY birds:

AHY ♂: p10 notch ≥ 15 mm from tip (fig. 50); pp 7-9 distinctly notched.

AHY ♀: p10 notch < 10 mm from tip (fig. 50), pp 7-9 slightly notched or pointed.

References—DVR,B,R,O,C; Rea (1969); PRBO data.

EASTERN KINGBIRD
Tyrannus tyrannus

EAKI
Species # 444.0
Band size: 1B

Molt—PB: HY incomplete-complete (Aug-Nov), AHY complete (Aug-Oct); PA partial-incomplete (Mar-Apr). PBs are suspended, with flight feather molt occurring on the winter grounds. All flight feathers are usually replaced by HY/SYs during the 1st winter.

Skull—Completes in HY/SY from 15 Oct thru Jan.

Age—The following is reliable in basic plumage; no plumage criteria known for ageing alternate-plumaged birds:

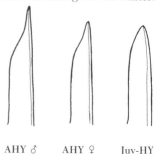

AHY ♂   AHY ♀   Juv-HY

Figure 51. The shape of the outer primaries as a means of sexing and ageing Eastern Kingbird. See the species account for the timing of the usefulness of this criterion.

Juv-HY/SY (Jun-Apr): Crown without concealed red or orange feathers; pp 9-10 blunt or pointed, not notched (fig. 51;

thru Oct only on many, thru Apr on some); rects tapered (fig. 45;), tipped buffy white (thru Oct-Apr); mouth lining yellow (thru Sep).

AHY/ASY (Apr-Mar): Crown with at least some concealed, red or orange feathers; pp 9-10 distinctly or slightly notched (fig. 51); rects truncate (fig. 45), tipped white; mouth lining flesh-colored or white.

Sex—♂ = ♀ by plumage. CP/BP (Apr-Aug). Wg: ♂(n50) 116-129, ♀(n50) 109-119. Birds subsequent to the 1st primary molt (usually after Oct-Nov) may be sexed with the following; some HY/SYs previous to this might be sexable by pp shape as in Western Kingbird (see fig. 50) but this needs further investigation:

♂: Notches on pp 9-10 > 8 mm from tip (fig. 51).

♀: Notches on pp 9-10 < 8 mm from tip (fig. 51).

References—DVR,B,R,W,O,C; Rea (1969).

GRAY KINGBIRD
Tyrannus dominicensis

GYKI
Species # 445.0
Band size 1A

Molt—PB: HY partial-incomplete (Aug-Dec), AHY complete (Aug-Oct); PA partial-incomplete (Feb-Apr). PBs occur mostly on winter grounds. The 1st PB and the 1st PA include a variable number of flight feathers (but usually not all).

Skull—Completes in HY/SY from 15 Sep thru Jan.

Age—The following is possibly reliable for ASY thru Sep; more study is needed:

Juv-HY/SY (May-2nd Sep): Crown without concealed orange feathers (thru Mar); pp 6-10 usually not notched (fig. 52); some or all rects usually tapered (fig. 45) and edged or tipped buffy when fresh. [SYs are separated from HYs in summer-fall by usually having at least a few extremely worn flight feathers.]

AHY/ASY (Apr-Mar): Crown with at least some concealed orange feathers; pp 6-10 at least slightly notched (fig. 52); all rects truncate (fig. 45), without buffy tips or edging.

Sex—♂ = ♀ by plumage. CP/BP (Apr-Aug). Wg: ♂(n8) 114-121, ♀(n13) 107-117. Birds subsequent to the 1st flight feather molt (usually not until 2nd Sep but sometimes earlier) may be sexed as follows:

♂: pp 6-10 notch about 8 mm from tip (fig. 52).

♀: pp 6-10 notch about 5 mm from tip (fig. 52).

References—B,C; Rea (1969).

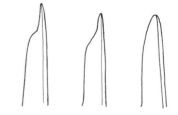

AHY/ASY ♂ AHY/ASY ♀ Juv-HY/SY
some HY/SY ♂ some HY/SY ♀

Figure 52. The shape of the outer primaries as a means of sexing and ageing Gray Kingbird. See the species account for the timing of usefulness of this criterion.

SCISSOR-TAILED FLYCATCHER
Tyrannus forficatus

STFL
Species # 443.0
Band size: 1A

Molt—PB: HY/SY incomplete-complete (Oct-Jan), AHY/ASY complete (Aug-Jan); PA partial-incomplete (Mar-Apr). PBs occur on winter grounds. All flight feathers are usually replaced during the 1st winter.

Skull—Completes in HY/SY from 15 Sep thru Jan.

Age/Sex—CP/BP (Mar-Aug). Wg: ♂(n40) 110-129, ♀(n40) 105-120 (HYs average significantly shorter than AHYs). Rect shape probably of little use for ageing. The timing of the following flight feather criteria for ageing HY/SYs may vary considerably (see Molt); care should be taken in early spring. No reliable plumage criteria known for ageing alternate plumaged birds although the length of the tail for each sex may prove reliable:

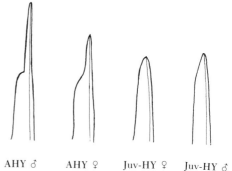

AHY ♂   AHY ♀   Juv-HY ♀   Juv-HY ♂

Figure 53. The shape of the outer primaries as a means of sexing and ageing Scissor-tailed Flycatcher. See the species account for the timing of usefulness of this criterion.

AHY/ASY ♂ (Apr-Mar): Crown with many concealed red or yellow feathers; flanks, undertail covs, and underwing covs strongly washed pink; p10 notch 19-22 mm from tip (fig. 53). Tail 200-256.

Juv-HY/SY ♂ (May-Apr): Crown without concealed red or yellow feathers (probably good thru Mar); underparts with little or no pink (thru Dec); p10 not notched, narrow and pointed (fig. 53; thru Dec-Mar); tail short and notched or as AHY/ASY ♂ (but usually < 235).

AHY/ASY ♀ (Apr-Mar): Crown usually with a few concealed red or yellow feathers; flanks, undertail covs, and underwing covs moderately washed pink; p10 notch 10-15 mm from tip (fig. 53); tail 125-182.

Juv/HY/SY ♀ (May-Apr): Like Juv/HY ♂ in plumage but p10 blunt (fig. 53); tail usually < 166.

References—B,O.

ROSE-THROATED BECARD
Pachyramphus aglaiae

RTBE
Species # 441.1
Band size: 1

Species—♀♀ from Gray-collared Becard (*P. major*), a possible vagrant from Mexico, by outer—central rect usually < 5 vs. > 15 in Gray-collared Becard.

Molt—PB: HY partial (Jul-Aug), AHY complete (Jul-Aug); PA absent-partial (Mar-Apr). PBs occur on the summer grounds. PA possibly partial in SY, absent in ASY.

Skull—Completes in HY from 1 Oct thru Dec.

Age/Sex—CP/BP (Apr-Jul). Wg: ♂(n30) 83-97, ♀(n30) 81-95. Juv (May-Jul) resembles ♀♀ but are more rufous above and buffier below. Some Juv ♂♂ may possibly show a few rose feathers on throat or breast, and are reliably sexed.

AHY/ASY ♂ (Aug-Jul): Upperparts blackish or slate gray; flight feathers gray; breast gray with extensive rose patch; p9 abbreviated, 1/2–1/3 the length of p10.

HY/SY ♂ (Jul-2nd Aug): Upperparts rufous brown or mixed rufous and gray (Mar-Aug); flight feathers rufous; breast and/or throat with one or more rose feathers; p9 full-lengthed.

AHY/ASY ♀ (Aug-Jul): Upperparts rufous brown; underparts pale buffy, without any rose feathers; rects truncate (see HY/SY ♀); p9 full-lengthed.

HY/SY ♀ (Jul-2nd Aug) Like AHY/ASY ♀ but rects tapered. [Intermediates may not be reliably aged by rect shape alone. Molting Juvs in this plumage can be sexed ♀♀ after replacement of the breast feathers.]

References—DVR,B,O.

LARKS   *ALAUDIDAE*

One species. Family characteristics include long wings, a small bill, and short legs and tail. It has 10 primaries (10th spurious), 9 secondaries and 12 rectrices. The first prebasic molt is complete and occurs on the summer grounds. Plumage usually does not allow separation of age classes but is reliable for separation of sexes, in most cases.

HORNED LARK   HOLA
Eremophila alpestris   Species # 474.0
                                                     Band size: 1B

Molt—PB: HY complete (Jul-Sep), AHY complete (Jul-Aug); PA absent. PBs occur on the summer grounds.

Skull—Completes in HY/SY from 30 Aug thru Jan; most populations from 15 Oct thru Dec.

Age—Rect shape not useful and no reliable plumage criteria known for ageing after the 1st PB. HY/SYs, however, average duller than AHY/ASYs in both sexes and extremes may be separable, with experience. Juv (Apr-Aug) has white flecks on the upperparts and lacks black on the head and breast ($\eth = \female$).

Sex—CP/BP (Feb-Aug). Wg: $\eth$(n68) 92-111, $\female$(n59) 87-103; useful in many populations, with little or no overlap between $\eth$ and $\female$ (e.g. see R. Davis 1969a) but ranges of local populations must be determined as wg shows extensive geographic variation. Intermediates occur between the following, especially in fresh plumage (Aug-Nov) which may not be safely sexed:

   $\eth$: Black areas of chest and head distinct and more extensive (fig. 54), contrasting markedly with paler areas; "horns" prominent; nape pinkish, unstreaked; les and mid covs mostly pinkish, usually without prominent shaft streaks.

   $\female$: Black areas of chest and head indistinct and less extensive (fig. 54), often mixed with yellow, whitish, or buffy; "horns" short or lacking; nape cinnimon, indistinctly streaked brownish; les and mid covs mostly brown with some pink in outer webs, and usually with indistinct to prominent shaft streaks.

References—B,R,O,Sv; R. Davis (1969a).

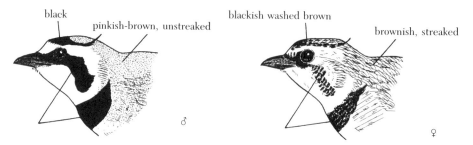

Figure 54. Head patterns in $\eth$ and $\female$ Horned Larks.

SWALLOWS

HIRUNDINIDAE

Eight species. Family characteristics include very long wings, short, wide bills, and short legs. They have 9 visible primaries, 9 secondaries and 12 rectrices. The first prebasic molt is complete, often takes place on the winter grounds and, in some species, is several months later than the adult PB. SYs often show windows in skull pneumatization through the spring. Plumage patterns among the age/sex classes are variable.

PURPLE MARTIN
Progne subis

PUMA
Species # 611.0
Band size: 1A - 2

Species—Juv from other swallows by longer wg (135-153).

Molt—PB: HY complete (Aug-Dec), AHY complete (Jul-Oct); PA partial (Feb-Apr). PBs suspended over fall migration. 1st flight feather molt occurs entirely on winter grounds; birds molting flight feathers on the summer grounds or showing contrasts between new and old feathers during autumn migration are AHY. The 1st PB may be continuous with the 1st PA.

Skull—Completes in HY/SY from 15 Sep thru Feb. Some SYs may retain windows thru spring. An Aug SY with unossified skull (Niles 1972b) was probably abnormal.

Age/Sex—CP/BP (Mar-Jul); most SY ♀♀ may not develop BPs. Wg useful: ♂(n30) 137-153, ♀(n30) 132-145. Rect shape not useful for ageing. Juv (Apr-Aug) Like HY/SY ♀ (below) but has fresher flight feathers, outer - central rect usually < 10, and mouth lining yellow. In addition to the following, see Molt for useful flight feather related ageing criteria:

AHY/ASY ♂ (Sep-Aug): Upperparts and underparts entirely blackish-purple.

HY/SY ♂ (Aug-2nd Sep): Upperparts steel blue to dusky black, often mixed with gray; underparts grayish, almost always with one or more blackish-purple feather; undertail covs without dusky centers (fig. 55).

AHY/ASY ♀ (Sep-Aug): Like HY/SY ♂ but underparts without any purplish-black feathers; undertail covs with distinct dusky centers (fig. 55).

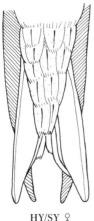
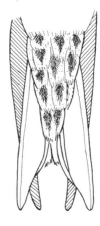

HY/SY ♀
HY/SY ♂

AHY/ASY ♀

Figure 55. Undertail covert patterns in ♀♀ and HY/SY ♂ Purple Martins.

HY/SY ♀ (Sep-2nd Sep): Upperparts brown with slight bluish tinge; underparts without purlple feathers; outer—central rect usually > 10 (Nov-Sep; see Juv); mouth lining horn colored; undertail covs without dusky centers (fig. 55). [Caution is advised in sexing HY ♀ on the summer grounds; be sure contour molt has completed. Compare also with wg.]

References—B,R,W,O,BBM; Niles (1972a, 1972b).

TREE SWALLOW
Tachycineta bicolor

TRSW
Species # 614.0
Band size: 1

Species—Wg 98-125. Juv from Bank Swallow by indistinctness of breast band, lack of feathering on hind tarsus, and generally longer wg; from Juv Purple Martin by shorter wg.

Molt—PB: HY complete (Jul-Dec), AHY complete (Jul-Nov); PA absent. PBs occur primarily on the summer grounds but flight feather molt may not complete until birds have reached the winter grounds (HY and AHY).

Skull—Completes in HY from 1 Oct thru Dec. Some SYs retain windows thru spring.

Age/Sex—CP/BP (Apr-Jul); BP developed by both sexes but is more swollen in ♀ ♀. Wg: ♂(n50) 104-125, ♀(n40) 98-120; E > W. Rect shape not useful for ageing after the 1st PB. Juv (May-Sep) has sooty upperparts and whitish underparts with dusky wash most prominent across breast (♂ = ♀). Intermediates between the following age/sex classifications occur which may not be reliably aged and/or sexed, especially without experience with this species; combine all ageing and sexing criteria. Color of both new and old feathers should be carefully considered on molting birds:

  ♂ ♂, some AHY/ASY ♀ (Oct-Sep): Upperparts including forehead and feathers at base of nostrils steel blue. Birds in this category are not reliably sexed by plumage alone. [Known HY/SYs (by skull), however, can be reliably sexed as ♂ ♂. AHY/ASY ♀ ♀ and HY/SY ♂ ♂ probably average slightly duller than AHY/ASY ♂ ♂. See also Cohen (1984) for methods of sexing birds in this plumage prior to capture at a nest box.]

  Some AHY/ASY ♀ (Oct-Sep): Upperparts mostly blue with 10-50 % brown feathers; forehead and base of nostrils brown.

  HY/SY ♀ (Oct-Sep): Upperparts entirely or mostly brown with 0-50% blue feathers; underparts usually without dusky wash. [May-Sep SYs are separated from Juvs by more faded plumage and worn flight feathers.]

References—B,R,W,SK,O,C,BBM; Hussel (1983), Cohen (1984), Stutchbury & Robertson (1987); PRBO data.

VIOLET-GREEN SWALLOW
Tachicineta thalassina

VGSW
Species # 615.0
Band size: 1

Species—From other swallows in all plumages by distinct white patches on sides of rump.

Molt—PB: HY complete (Sep-Oct), AHY complete (Aug-Sep); PA absent. PBs occur primarily on the summer grounds.

Skull—Completes in HY from 1 Oct thru Dec. Some SYs retain windows thru spring.

Age—Juv (May-Oct) has gray-brown upperparts and gray washed underparts (♂ = ♀). Rect shape not useful for ageing and no reliable plumage criteria known after 1st PB, although some HY/SYs, especially ♀♀, may show duller or more brownish upperparts (especially rump) as in Tree Swallow (this deserves further investigation).

Sex—CP/BP (Apr-Jul); BP may develop in both sexes but is more pronounced in ♀♀. Wg: ♂(n50) 104-121, ♀(n50) 99-115; Juv averages about 8 mm shorter than adult.

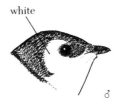

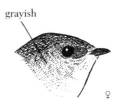

Figure 56. Face pattern differences between ♂ and ♀ Violet-green Swallows.

♂: Upperparts entirely irridescent green and purple (rump); post ocular area and cheek bright white, contrasting markedly with darker crown (fig. 56).

♀: Upperparts usually dull green and purple mixed with brownish; post ocular area and cheek dusky gray-brown, contrasting gradually with darker crown (fig. 56).

References—B,SK,O,C,BBM; PRBO data.

NORTHERN ROUGH-WINGED SWALLOW
Stelgidopteryx serripennis

RWSW
Species # 617.0
Band size: 0

Species—From Juvs of all other swallows by dusky brown throat.

Molt—PB: HY/SY complete (Jul-Jan), AHY complete (Jul-Dec); PA absent. PBs occur primarily during southward migration and/or on the winter grounds.

Skull—Completes in HY/SY from 1 Oct thru Jan. Most SYs retain windows thru spring and (rarely) thru fall.

Age—The following is reliable for all autumn birds N of the wintering grounds. Also, see under Sex for ageing of some SY males. Otherwise, rect shape is not useful and no reliable plumage criteria are known after the 1st PB but look for relatively buffier tips to the terts on spring SYs:

Juv-HY (May-Dec): Upperpart feathers, wing covs and terts edged cinnamon; flight feathers relatively fresh; outer edge of p9 usually without distinct barbs (♂ = ♀).

AHY (Jan-Oct): Upperpart feathers, wing covs and terts without cinnamon edging; flight feathers relatively worn in summer/fall; barbs of outer edge of p9 relatively long, sometimes strongly hooked (fig. 57; see Sex).

Sex—♂ = ♀ by plumage. CP/BP (Apr-Jul). Wg: ♂(n30) 101-117, ♀(n30) 97-110.

♂: Barbs of outer web of p9 strongly hooked (fig. 57).

♀, some HY/SY ♂♂: Outer edge of p9 without distinct barbs or with small, straight barbs (fig. 57). [These are not reliably sexed on this feature alone; known ♂♂ of this category (by CP or wg), however, can be aged SY.]

References—B,W,SK,O,BBM;   Ricklefs (1972); PRBO data.

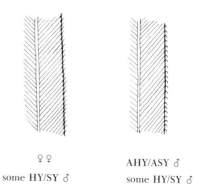

♀♀
some HY/SY ♂

AHY/ASY ♂
some HY/SY ♂

Figure 57. The barbs of the outer web of the outer primary in Rough-winged Swallows, to assist with ageing and sexing.

BANK SWALLOW
Riparia riparia

BKSW
Species # 616.0
Band size: 0

Species—From Juv Tree Swallow by feathering on posterior of tarsus and generally shorter wg (86-107).

Molt—PB: HY/SY complete (Nov-Jan), AHY complete (Jul-Nov); PA partial (Feb-Apr). 1st PB occurs entirely on the winter grounds and is probably continuous with 1st PA. Adult PBs occur primarily on the winter grounds but may be suspended over fall migration, with the inner 2-4 pp sometimes replaced on the summer grounds (the timing of flight feather molt useful for ageing). The PA in SY vs. ASY requires further study.

Skull—Completes in HY from 1 Oct thru Dec. Some SYs (20% reported) retain windows thru spring.

Age—Relative wear of flight feathers may be useful for separating SY and ASY in spring (see Molt). The following is reliable on fall birds N of the winter grounds. Otherwise, rect shape is not useful and no reliable plumage criteria known after the 1st PB:

Juv-HY (Jun-Dec): Upperpart feathers, wing covs and terts edged with rufous-buff; chin and throat washed pinkish (thru Sep), sometimes with faint, dusky spotting; flight feathers relatively fresh in summer/fall.

AHY (Jan-Nov): Upperpart feathers, wing covs and terts without rufous-buff edging; chin and throat white; flight feathers relatively worn in summer/fall.

Sex—♂ = ♀ by plumage. CP/BP (Apr-Aug). Wg: ♂(n100) 96-107, ♀(n100) 93-104.

References—B,R,W,SK,O,BBM,Sv; Yunick (1970a), Freer & Belanger (1981); R. Yunick data.

CLIFF SWALLOW
Hirundo pyrrhonota

CLSW
Species # 612.0
Band size: 1

Species—Forehead buffy or reddish (southwestern U.S. populations); blackish or brownish throat patch variable but present in all plumages and useful for separation from Cave Swallow.

Molt—PB: HY/SY complete (Oct-Apr), AHY complete (Jul-Dec); PA absent. 1st PB occurs on the winter grounds; adult PBs may commence on the summer grounds or during migration but occur primarily on the winter grounds. The timing of the PB is useful for ageing.

Skull—Completes in HY/SY from 1 Oct thru Jan. Some SYs retain windows thru spring.

Age—Rect shape probably not useful for ageing. Relative wear of flight feathers may be useful for separating SY and ASY in spring (see Molt). The following is reliable on fall birds N of winter grounds; no plumage criteria known after completion of the PB, however, the edges of the terts average whiter on ASYs, grayer on SYs, and this may prove useful for ageing thru early summer, before the edges wear off:

Juv-HY/SY (Jun-Mar): Upperparts (except rump) basally brownish-gray; cheeks grayish-brown; tertials with buffy-rufous edging; flight feathers relatively fresh in fall.

AHY (Jan-Dec): Upperparts (except rump) basally steel blue; cheeks reddish; tertials without rufous edging; flight feathers relatively worn in fall.

Sex—♂ = ♀ by plumage. CP/BP (Apr-Aug). Wg: ♂(n30) 98-115, ♀(n30) 95-112. N & E > SW.

References—DVR,B,R,W,SK,O,BBM; R. Yunick data, PRBO data.

CAVE SWALLOW
Hirundo fulva

CASW
Species # 612.1
Band size: 1

Species—Forehead reddish; throat buffy orange, without any blackish.

Molt—The extent and timing of molt in this species probably parallels that of Cliff Swallow, except that the timing of the 1st PB may be earlier. Further investigation is needed.

Skull—Completes in HY from 1 Oct thru Dec; some SYs probably retain windows thru spring.

Age—Ageing criteria for Cliff Swallow probably apply, although the timing of usefulness may be slightly different (see Molt).

Sex—♂ = ♀ by plumage. CP/BP (Mar-Sep). Wg: ♂(n13) 105-115, ♀(n9) 104-113.

References—DVR,O; Walters (1983).

BARN SWALLOW
Hirundo rustica

BASW
Species # 613.0
Band size: 0-1

Molt—PB/PA: HY/SY complete (Oct-May); AHY/ASY complete (Sep-Apr). Molt seems continuous, and occurs primarily away from the summer grounds.

Skull—Completes in HY/SY from 15 Oct thru Jan. Some SY birds retain windows thru spring/summer (up to 29% of all birds in Europe).

Age—Rect shape not useful for ageing after the 1st molt. The following is reliable on autumn birds N of the winter grounds but should thereafter be used with caution, and consideration of molt:

Juv-HY/SY (May-Feb): Upperparts mixed steel blue and brownish; wing covs edged reddish-brown (May-Nov) or buff (Nov-Feb, later if not worn off); throat pale, reddish-brown; breast band incomplete, dusky; tail usually < 68; outer—central rect < 25 mm. ♂ = ♀

AHY (Jan-Dec): Upperparts deep, glossy blue; wing covs without reddish brown or buffy edging; throat deep chestnut; breast band complete, deep blue; tail ≥ 68 mm; outer—central rect > 32 mm.

Sex—CP/BP   (Apr-Aug).   Wg   ♂(n60) 115-127, ♀(n60) 111-122; N > S. The following criteria are useful for birds subsequent to the 1st molt; some intermediates may not be reliably sexed especiallywithout previous experience (combine with skull; these are possibly all SY ♂ ♂):

AHY ♂: Upperparts relatively glossy blue; breast relatively dark cinnamon; tail 79-107; tail plus difference between outer and adjacent rects usually ≥ 104 mm (check both sides of tail). These criteria good for most N.A. populations; beware of large females of northern populations.

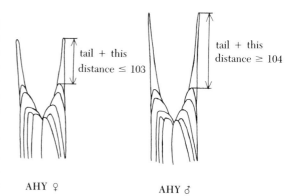

tail + this distance ≤ 103

tail + this distance ≥ 104

AHY ♀

AHY ♂

Figure 58. ♀ vs. ♂ Barn Swallow tails, after completion of the first tail molt (see Molt).

AHY ♀: Upperparts relatively dull blue; breast relatively pale cinnamon; tail 68-84 mm; tail plus difference between outer and adjacent rect usually ≤ 103 mm.

References—B,R,W,SK,O,BBM,Sv; Schaeffer (1968), Patterson (1981); PRBO data; G. Wallace (*pers. comm.*).

JAYS and CROWS

Fifteen species. Family characteristics include rounded wings, long and rounded tails, and powerful bills and legs. They have 10 primaries (10th spurious), 9 secondaries, and 12 rectrices. The first prebasic molt is almost always partial (incomplete in a few southern populations). Sexes are alike in plumage but often may be separated by measurements. Corvids are reliably aged through the 2nd PB; it has been stated, in fact, that "any work on the systematics of corvids in which first year specimens are not distinguished from adults is at once suspect" (Pitelka 1945). Wing covert contrasts, the shape of the rectricies (fig. 59), and the color of the roof of the mouth (fig. 60) are useful with all species and should be combined for reliable age determinations. Look also for rectrix length differences in all species, as is found in Scrub Jay and Clark's Nutcracker.

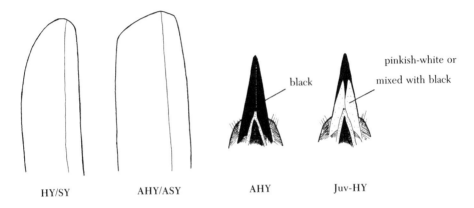

HY/SY   AHY/ASY   AHY   Juv-HY

black

pinkish-white or mixed with black

Figure 59. Rectrix shape by age in corvids.   Figure 60. The color of the roof of the mouth of young and old corvids.

GRAY JAY
Perisoreus canadensis

GRJA
Species # 484.0
Band size: 3-2

Molt—PB: HY partial (Jul-Sep), AHY complete (Jul-Aug); PA absent.

Skull—Completes in HY from 15 Sep thru Dec. May be difficult or impossible to see.

Age—Juv (Apr-Aug) has slate colored or brownish-gray crown, throat, and breast. As in other corvids, color of the roof of the mouth (fig. 60) is probably useful at least thru fall; covert contrasts, however, seem not to be as prominent in this species:

HY/SY (Aug-Jul): Rects tapered (fig. 59).

AHY/ASY (Aug-Jul): Rects truncate (fig. 59).

Sex—♂ = ♀ by plumage. CP/BP (Mar-May). Wg: ♂(n50) 135-158, ♀(n50) 129-151; W > E & NW Coast.

References—B,R.

STELLER'S JAY
Cyanocitta stelleri

STJA
Species # 478.0
Band size: 3-2

Molt—PB: HY partial (Jul-Sep), AHY complete (Jul-Aug); PA absent.

Skull—Completes in HY/SY from 15 Oct thru Jan. May be difficult or impossible to see.

Age—Juv (May-Aug) has upperparts washed brownish or grayish, underparts grayish without blue tones, and roof of mouth grayish-white:

HY/SY (Aug-Jul): Pp covs and possibly some gr covs heavily washed brownish or sooty, contrasting with brighter blue inner gr and mid covs; rects tapered (fig. 59); roof of mouth mixed black and grayish-white (fig. 60; thru Oct-Apr).

AHY/ASY (Aug-Jul): Wing covs uniformly bright blue; rects truncate (fig. 59); color of roof of mouth usually black (fig. 60).

Sex—♂ = ♀ by plumage. CP/BP (Mar-Jul). Wg: ♂(n30) 140-165, ♀(n30) 136-157. Also, for birds of the southern Rocky Mountains (*C. s. macrolopha*) the bill length has been shown to be useful for sexing as follows: ♂ exposed culmen ≥ 27.5 mm, ♀ exposed culmen < 27.5 mm. Bill length seems not as useful in other populations, however.

References—B,O; Pitelka (1958, 1961), Pustmueller (1975); PRBO data.

BLUE JAY
Cyanocitta cristata

BLJA
Species # 477.0
Band size 2-3

Molt—PB: HY partial-incomplete (Jun-Oct), AHY complete (Jun-Sep); PA absent. PBs occur on the breeding grounds. 1st PB can include the terts and central rects, sometimes other rects (southern populations only?).

Skull—Completes in HY/SY from 1 Nov (possibly as early as 1 Oct in Florida populations) thru Feb. May be difficult or impossible to see.

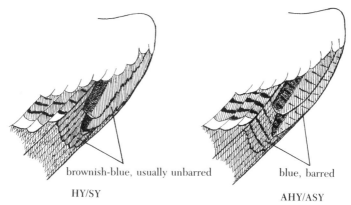

brownish-blue, usually unbarred   blue, barred

HY/SY   AHY/ASY

Figure 61. Wing pattern differences between first-year and adult Blue Jays.

Age—Juv (May-Aug) has upperparts relatively grayish, lores gray, gr covs dull blue-gray with thin white tipping and roof of mouth whitish. Most birds should be reliably aged using the following plumage criteria but beware of intermediates, especially young birds showing adult features (rect shape should be reliable except for occasional Florida and S.Texas HY/SYs that may have replaced all rects at the 1st PB):

HY/SY (Aug-Jul): Alula, pp covs, and sometimes (10-15% of birds) 1-5 outer gr covs grayish-blue and usually unbarred, contrasting with brighter, barred, blue and white (inner) gr and blue mid covs (fig. 61); rects tapered (fig. 59); roof of mouth whitish or mixed white and black (fig. 60; thru Oct-Apr); iris often with gray edge (thru fall).

AHY/ASY (Aug-Jul): Alula and wing covs uniformly bright blue, usually distinctly barred with black (fig. 61); all gr covs tipped white; rects truncate (fig. 59); roof of mouth black (fig. 60); iris usually uniform brown, without grayish edge.

Sex—♂ = ♀ by plumage. CP/BP (Mar-Sep). Wg: ♂(n30) 119-148, ♀(n30) 116-139; N > S.

References—B,R,W,SK,O,BBM; Pitelka (1946), Nichols (1955), Laskey (1958), Dater (1970), Gebhardt (1971), Briggs (1975), Olyphant (1977), Lamb *et al.* (1978), Bancroft & Woolfenden (1982); C. Thompson (*pers. comm.*).

GREEN JAY
Cyanocorax yncas

GNJA
Species # 483.0
Band size: 2

Molt—PB: HY partial (Jun-Sep), AHY complete (Jun-Sep); PA absent.

Skull—Completes in HY from 1 Oct thru Dec. May be difficult or impossible to see.

Age—Juv (May-Jul) has brownish head, chin and throat, relatively dull green upperparts, relatively pale yellow underparts, undertail covs washed with buffy, and white roof of mouth:

HY/SY (Jul-Jun): Pp covs and possibly some outer gr covs brownish-green and faded, contrasting with relatively fresher and brighter inner gr and mid covs; rects tapered (fig. 59); roof of mouth probably mixed grayish and white (fig. 60; thru Oct-Apr).

AHY/ASY (Jul-Jun): Wing covs uniformly bright green (pp covs slightly darker); rects truncate (fig. 59); roof of mouth black (fig. 60).

Sex—♂ = ♀ by plumage. CP/BP (Mar-Jun). Wg: ♂(n30) 110-122, ♀(n30) 104-115.

References—B,O.

SCRUB JAY
Aphelocoma coerulescens

SCJA
Species # 481.0
Band size: 3-2

Species—From Gray-breasted Jay by smaller size: wg 105-141.

Molt—PB: HY partial-incomplete (Jun-Oct), AHY complete (Jun-Sep); PA absent. 1st PB may include terts and central rects (Florida populations only?).

Skull—Completes in HY/SY from 15 Oct (possibly as early as 1 Sep in some California populations) thru Jan. May be difficult or impossible to see.

Age—Juv (Mar-Aug) has relatively grayish upperparts with only slight blue tones, underparts washed sooty and roof of mouth grayish-white. The following covert contrast and rect shape differences can be subtle; a few intermediates may not be reliably aged:

HY/SY (Jul-Jun): Pp covs and most or all gr covs blue with slight brownish cast contrasting with brighter blue mid covs; rects tapered (fig. 59); longest rect—r5 (2nd from outside) usually 3-15; roof of mouth mixed grayish and black (fig. 60; thru Oct-Apr).

AHY/ASY (Jun-May): Wing covs uniformly bright blue; rects truncate (fig. 59); longest rect— r5 usually 10-20; roof of mouth black (fig. 60).

Sex—♂ = ♀ by plumage. CP/BP (Feb-Aug). Wg: ♂(n100) 114-141, ♀(n100) 105-134; W > Florida.

References—B,O; Pitelka (1945), Bancroft & Woolfenden (1982); PRBO data.

GRAY-BREASTED JAY
Aphelcoma ultramarina

GBJA
Species # 482.0
Band size: 3B

Species—From Scrub Jay by larger size: wg 142-173 mm.

Molt—PB: HY partial (Jul-Oct), AHY complete (Jul-Oct); PA absent.

Skull—Completes in HY from 1 Oct thru Dec. May be difficult or impossible to see.

Age—Juv (May-Sep) as in Juv Scrub Jay plus has entirely or mostly yellow bill. The following covert contrast and rect shape differences can be subtle:

HY/SY (Sep-Aug): Pp covs and most or all gr covs blue with slight brownish cast contrasting with brighter blue mid covs; rects tapered (fig. 59); lower mandible entirely yellow or with ≥ 10 mm yellow at base (thru at least Mar); roof of mouth grayish-white or mixed white and black (fig. 60; thru Oct-Apr).

AHY/ASY (Aug-Jul): Wing covs uniformly blue; rects truncate (fig. 59); bill entirely black or with < 10 mm yellow at base; roof of mouth black (fig. 60).

Sex—♂ = ♀ by plumage. CP/BP (Feb-Aug). Wg: Texas ♂(n30) 146-160, ♀(n30) 142-154; Arizona ♂(n30) 157-175, ♀(n30) 151-167.

References—B,O; Pitelka (1945).

PINYON JAY
Gymnorhinus cyanocephalus

PIJA
Species # 492.0
Band size: 3-2

Molt—PB: HY partial-incomplete (Jun-Sep), AHY complete (May-Sep); PA absent. 1st PB can include up to 6 inner ss; adult PBs are sometimes suspended over late summer breeding.

Skull—Completes in HY from 15 Aug thru Dec. May be difficult or impossible to see.

Age—Juv (Mar-Aug) has ash gray underparts without bluish cast and color of roof of mouth probably whitish.

HY/SY (Aug-Jul): All or most pp and ss brown, some birds with contrasting brown and blue ss; pp covs and some or all gr covs brownish-gray, contrasting with bluer inner gr covs; rects tapered (fig. 59); roof of mouth probably mixed gray and black (fig. 60).

AHY/ASY (Jun-May): Pp, ss, and wing covs uniformly blue; rects truncate (fig. 59); color of roof of mouth probably black (fig. 60).

Sex—♂ = ♀ by plumage. CP/BP (Feb-Jul); ♂♂ probably develop a partial BP. Wg: ♂(n100) 142-161, ♀(n100) 136-154.

References—B,O; Bateman & Balda (1973), Ligon & White (1974).

CLARK'S NUTCRACKER
Nucifraga columbiana

CLNU
Species # 491.0
Band size: 3B

Molt—PB: HY/SY partial (Jul-Jan), AHY complete (Mar-Oct); PA absent. Timing of molt useful for ageing.

Skull—Completes in HY from 15 Sep thru Dec. May be difficult if not impossible to see.

Age—Juv (Apr-Sep) has plumage generally washed with brownish, white eye ring and superciliary indistinct or lacking, and roof of mouth probably grayish-white. Protraction of PB molt should be considered in ageing summer and fall birds by the following:

HY/SY (Aug-2nd Sep): Pp covs, all or most gr covs, and sometimes some mid covs dull black or brownish, contrasting with blacker (glossier) mid and les covs; rects tapered, outer—

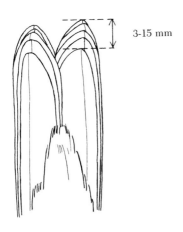

3-15 mm

15-35 mm

HY/SY

AHY/ASY

Figure 62. Tail formula differences by age in Clark's Nutcrackers. Check other corvids for a similar usefulness of tail formula.

central rect usually 3-15 (fig. 62); roof of mouth probably mixed gray and black (fig. 60; thru Oct-Apr).

AHY/ASY (Jun-May): Wing covs uniformly black; rects truncate, outer—central rect usually 15-35 (fig. 62); roof of mouth probably black (fig. 60).

Sex—♂ = ♀ by plumage. CP (Feb-Jun); BP (Mar-Jul) developed by both sexes, slightly more fully in ♀♀, but it should probably not be used alone for sexing. Wg: ♂(n100) 180-202, ♀(n100) 173-196.

References—B,R,O,C (D. Tomback); Mewaldt (1952, 1958).

BLACK-BILLED MAGPIE
Pica pica

BBMA
Species # 475.0
Band size: 4

Molt—PB: HY partial (Jul-Oct), AHY complete (Jul-Oct); PA absent.

Skull—Completes in HY from 15 Sep thru Nov (completion by 15 Aug reported for this species in Europe). May be difficult if not impossible to see.

Age—Juv (May-Sep) has brownish washed upperparts, creamy underparts, and roof of mouth grayish-white.

HY/SY (Sep-2nd Sep): P10 broadly shaped at tip (fig. 63); white of p9 indistinctly defined, tip of white to tip of feather usually > 20 mm (fig. 64); outer rects tapered (fig. 59); roof of mouth probably mixed gray and black (fig 60; thru Oct-Apr).

AHY/ASY (Sep-Aug): P10 attenuated (fig. 63); white of p9 sharply defined, tip of white to tip of feather usually < 20 mm (fig. 64); outer rects truncate (fig. 59); roof of mouth probably black (fig. 60).

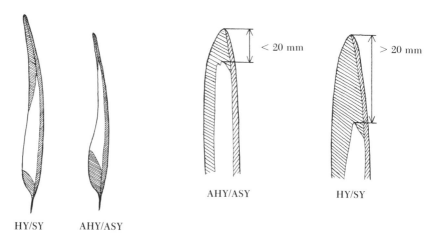

Figure 63. The tenth primary of magpies, by age.

Figure 64. The ninth primary of magpies, by age.

Sex—♂ = ♀ by plumage. CP/BP (Mar-Jul). Wg: ♂(n100) 191-216, ♀(n100) 177-209; tail: ♂(n30) 245-302, ♀(n30) 231-283; tail varies geographically, N > S > NW coast (beware of Juvs, which are free flying and can resemble adults before reaching full size). Also, the following formula successfully separated 95% of adults of a Utah population (Reese & Kadlec 1982); similar formulas are probably reliable with other populations:

AHY ♂: [Wt (gms) × 0.043] + (wg × 0.122) + (exposed culmen × 0.264) > 40.95.

AHY ♀: (Wt × 0.043) + (wg × 0.122) + (exposed culmen × 0.264) ≤ 40.95. [Excludes ♀♀ with eggs in the oviduct, which should also have brood patches.]

References—B,R,O,Sv; Linsdale (1937), Erpino (1968), Reese & Kadlec (1982).

YELLOW-BILLED MAGPIE
Pica nuttalli

YBMA
Species # 476.0
Band size: 3A

Molt—PB: HY partial (Aug-Nov), AHY complete (Aug-Nov); PA absent.

Skull—Completes in HY from 15 Sep thru Nov. May be difficult if not impossible to see.

Age—See Black-billed Magpie.

Sex—♂ = ♀ by plumage. CP/BP (Feb-Jul). Wg: ♂(n30) 182-197, ♀(n30) 173-186; beware of Juvs which are free flying and can resemble adults before reaching full size.

References—B,O,C(Verbeek); Linsdale (1937), Verbeek (1973a).

AMERICAN CROW
Corvus brachyryncos

AMCR
Species # 488.0
Band size: 5

Species—Bases of neck and breast feathers gray; wg 273-350, p5 > p9; tail 153-210; exposed culmen 43-53.5; depth of bill (from anterior end of nostrils) 15-20.5; tarsus 53-66.5; length of throat feathers ≤ 25 mm. The combination of these measurements should separate this from other *Corvus* species in almost all cases, especially when sex is known (see below).

Molt—PB: HY partial (Jul-Sep), AHY complete (Jul-Sep); PA absent.

Skull—Completes in HY from 1 Sep thru Dec. Very difficult if not impossible to see.

Age—Juv (Apr-Aug) has a brownish cast (lacking gloss) to plumage and a pinkish roof of mouth. With the following, the color of the roof of the mouth may be useful for separating SY from ASY through at least the fall, with experience:

HY/SY (Aug-Jul): Pp covs and some or all gr covs brownish, contrasting in color with blacker (glossier) mid and lesser covs (fig. 65); rects tapered (fig. 59); roof of mouth mixed pinkish and black (fig. 60; thru at least Jan-Apr).

AHY/ASY (Aug-Jul): Wing covs uniformly glossy-black (fig. 65); rects truncate (fig. 59); roof of mouth black (fig. 60).

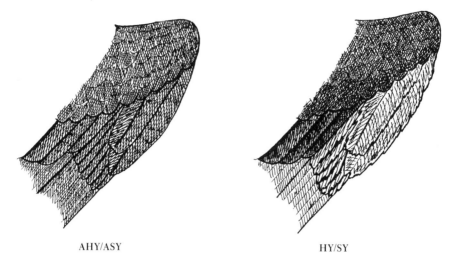

AHY/ASY   HY/SY

Figure 65. Covert contrast in the wings of crows.

Sex—♂ = ♀ by plumage. CP/BP (Feb-Aug). Wg: ♂(n30) 281-350, ♀(n30) 273-326; E > W & Florida.

References—B,R,W,O; Emlen (1936), Pitelka (1945), Rea (1967), Rea & Kanteena (1968), Saiza (1968); C. Caffrey (*pers. comm.*).

NORTHWESTERN CROW
Corvus caurinus

NOCR
Species # 489.0
Band size: 4-4A

Species—Wg 256-292; tail 144-170; exposed culmen 41.5-49.0; depth of bill (ant. nostrils) 15.0-17.5; tarsus 45-53. The combination of smaller measurements should separate this species from almost all American Crows but beware of hybrid forms where the ranges overlap.

Molt—PB: HY partial (Jul-Sep); AHY complete (Jul-Sep); PA absent.

Skull—completes in HY from 15 Oct thru Dec. Very difficult, if not impossible to see.

Age—See American Crow.

Sex—♂ = ♀ by plumage. CP/BP (Apr-Jul). Wg: ♂(n30) 269-294, ♀(n21) 256-285.

References—B; Rea & Kanteena (1968).

FISH CROW
Corvus ossifragus

FICR
Species # 490.0
Band size: 4A

Species—Wg 264-320; tail 137-180; exposed culmen 41.5-48.5; depth of bill (ant. nostrils) 13.5-15.5; tarsus 44.5-50. Combination of smaller measurements, especially those of bill and tarsus, should separate this species from American Crow. Mexican Crow (*C. imparatus*), a non-breeding visitor to Texas, is considerably glossier and smaller: wg < 260.

Molt—PB: HY partial (Jul-Sep); AHY complete (Jul-Sep); PA absent.

Skull—Completes in HY from 15 Oct thru Dec. Very difficult if not impossible to see.

Age—See American Crow.

Sex—♂ = ♀ by plumage. CP/BP (Apr-Jul). Wg: ♂(n30) 274-320, ♀(n30) 264-282.

References—B,O; Rea & Kanteena (1968).

CHIHUAHUAN RAVEN
Corvus cryptoleucos

CHRA
Species # 487.0
Band size: 5

Species—Bases of neck and breast feathers whitish; wg 327-379, p5 usually ≤ p9; tail 181-214; exposed culmen 49.5-59.0; depth of bill (ant. nostrils) 20.0-22.5; tarsus 55.5-68.5; length of throat feathers usually ≥ 25 mm. Plumage differences can be subtle, particularly without direct comparison or experience; the combination of measurements, especially those of the bill, should separate this species from American Crow and Common Ràven.

Molt—PB: HY partial (Sep-Nov), AHY complete (Sep-Nov); PA absent.

Skull—Completes in HY from 15 Sep thru Dec. Very difficult if not impossible to see.

Age—See American Crow; combine ageing criteria with the slightly later timing of molt in this species.

Sex—♂ = ♀ by plumage. CP/BP (Mar-Jul). Wg: ♂(n35) 337-379, ♀(n35) 327-360.

References—B,O; Rea & Kanteena (1968), Saiza (1968).

COMMON RAVEN
Corvus corax

CORA
Species # 486.0
Band size: 6-7A

Species—Bases of neck and breast feathers grayish; wg 380-464; tail 208-259; exposed culmen 65-92; depth of bill (ant. nostrils) 23-31.5; tarsus 63-74. The combination of measurements should separate this from the other *Corvus* species.

Molt—PB: HY partial (Jun-Oct), AHY complete (May-Oct); PA absent.

Skull—Completes in HY from 1 Sep thru Nov. Very difficult if not impossible to see.

Age—See American Crow; combine ageing criteria with differences in the timing of molt for this species.

Sex—♂ = ♀ by plumage. CP/BP (Feb-Jul). Wg: ♂(n30) 396-464, ♀(n30) 380-432; E > W.

References—B,R,W,O,Sv; Rea & Kanteena (1968).

TITMICE   *PARIDAE*

Nine species. Family characteristics include small size, short wings, small and sharp beaks, and strong legs. They have 10 primaries (10th spurious), 9 secondaries, and 12 rectrices. The first prebasic molt is partial to incomplete, usually including the tertials and/or some or all rectrices when incomplete. All plumages (including juvenal) are generally the same. The color of the roof of the mouth may be helpful in ageing some or all species; this should be further examined.

BLACK-CAPPED CHICKADEE
Parus atricapillus

BCCH
Species # 735.0
Band size: 0

Species—Bib often indistinctly contrasting with breast; ss, terts, and gr covs broadly edged white when fresh; flanks washed with pinkish-brown, contrasting distinctly with gray belly and breast; wg 58-69. From all chickadees except Carolina by plumage and range. Best separated from Carolina by plumage combined with wing and tail lengths. In range of overlap, tail length most useful character: 57-67 in Black-capped, 48-58 in Carolina. The tail/wg ratio may then provide further means for separation: 0.886-1.032 for Black-capped, 0.819-0.922 (most ≤ 0.9) for Carolina. See also scatter diagram of wing vs tail (fig. 66, derived from Simon 1960, from eastern populations of the two species). A very few individuals may not be reliably separated with these criteria; also beware of hybrids, especially where breeding ranges overlap.

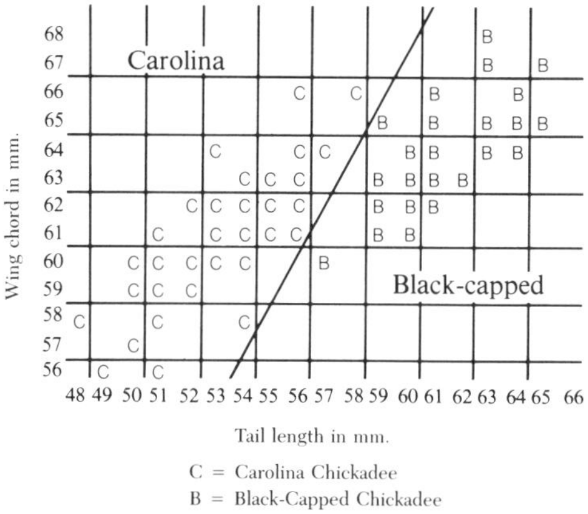

Figure 66. A scatter diagram of wing chord vs. tail in Maryland populations of Black-capped and Carolina chickadees (from Simon 1960).

Molt—PB: HY partial-incomplete (Jul-Oct), AHY complete (Jun-Oct); PA absent. 1st PB sometimes includes terts.

Skull—Completes in HY/SY from 1 Oct thru Jan.

Age—Juv (May-Aug) differs only in having more loosely textured contour feathers, especially undertail covs. In addition to the following, check the width of the pp covs; this has been found useful for ageing in European Parids, narrower feathers

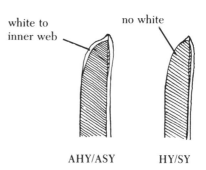

Figure 67. Outer rectrix shape and pattern by age in Black-capped Chickadees.

being found on HY/SY birds (Svensson 1984). Contrast between paler pp covs and darker gr covs (Svensson 1984), however, appears to be difficult to use with N.A. species:

HY/SY (Aug-Jul): Outer rects tapered and pointed, white edge of outer web does not extend onto inner web (fig. 67).

AHY/ASY (Aug-Jul): Outer rects truncate, white edge of outer web usually extends onto inner web (fig. 67).

Sex—♂ = ♀ by plumage. CP/BP (Apr-Aug). Wg: ♂(n100) 60-69, ♀(n100) 58-66. Shape of bib and cap can possibly be used, with experience, to assist in separating the sexes (see Mosher & Lane 1972, but see also Gochfield 1977).

References—B,R,W,SK,O,Sv; Lunk (1952), Tanner (1952), Simon (1960), Blake (1965a), Wiseman (1969), Hubbard (1970), Taylor (1970), Mosher & Lane (1972), Gochfield (1977), Yunick (1980), Meigs *et al.* (1983); Robbins *et al.* (1983); R. Yunick data.

CAROLINA CHICKADEE
Parus carolinensis

CACH
Species # 736.0
Band size: 0

Species—Bib contrast with breast distinct; ss, terts, and gr covs without marked white edging; flanks gray or brownish-gray, not contrasting markedly with remainder of underparts; wg 53-69. From other chickadees except Black-capped by plumage and range. See Black-capped Chickadee for separation from that species.

Molt—PB: HY partial-incomplete (Jul-Sep), AHY complete (Jul-Aug); PA absent. 1st PB can include the terts and some or all rects in southern populations.

Skull—Completes in HY from 1 Oct (possibly as early as 15 Aug in Texas populations) thru Dec.

Age—See Black-capped Chickadee. Birds of southern populations may not be reliably aged AHY/ASY after Sep (see Molt). Otherwise, the rect shape criteria is the same but the amount of white on both HY/SY and AHY/ASY birds is less (fig. 68).

Sex—♂ = ♀ by plumage. CP/BP (Feb-Jun). Wg: ♂(n100) 57-69, ♀(n100) 53-66.

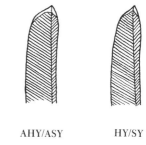

AHY/ASY   HY/SY

Figure 68. Outer rectrix shape and pattern by age in Carolina and Mountain chickadees.

References—B,W,O; Lunk (1952), Tanner (1952), Simon (1960), Blake (1965a), Wiseman (1969), Hubbard (1970), Robbins *et al.* (1983); C. Thompson (*pers. comm.*).

MEXICAN CHICKADEE
Parus sclateri

MECH
Species # 737.0
Band size: 0

Molt—PB: HY partial (Jul-Sep), AHY complete (Jul-Aug); PA absent. Look for some flight feather replacement during the 1st PB, as in Carolina Chickadee.

Skull—Completes in HY from 1 Oct thru Dec.

Age—See Black-capped Chickadee. The rect shape criteria is the same but little or no white is present in either age class (fig. 69).

Sex—♂ = ♀ by plumage. CP/BP (Mar-Jun). Wg: ♂(n30) 64-72, ♀(n26) 61-69.

References—B.

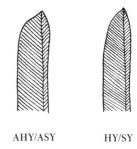

AHY/ASY   HY/SY

Figure 69. Outer rectrix shape in Mexican, Boreal, and Chestnut-backed chickadees, by age.

MOUNTAIN CHICKADEE
Parus gambeli

MOCH
Species # 738.0
Band size: 0

Molt—PB: HY partial (Jul-Aug), AHY complete (Jul-Aug); PA absent. 1st PB may include the terts.

Skull—Completes in HY/SY from 1 Oct thru Jan.

Age—See Black-capped Chickadee. The rect shape criteria is the same but the amount of white on both HY/SY and AHY/ASY birds is less (fig. 68). Also, Juv-HY birds may be separable from AHY thru fall by dark gray vs. white inside of upper mandible. This needs further study, in this and other species of parids.

Sex—♂ = ♀ by plumage. CP/BP (Mar-Aug). Wg: ♂(n30) 67-74, ♀(n30) 64-72;

References—B,O; Felt (1967), Taylor (1970).

BOREAL CHICKADEE
Parus hudsonicus

BOCH
Species # 740.0
Band size: 0

Molt—PB: HY partial (Aug-Sep), AHY complete (Jun-Aug); PA absent.

Skull—Completes in HY from 1 Nov thru Dec.

Age—See Black-capped Chickadee. The rect shape criteria is the same but little or no white is present in either age class (fig. 69).

Sex—♂ = ♀ by plumage. CP/BP (May-Jul). Wg: ♂(n30) 63-71, ♀(n30) 60-67; W > E.

References—B,R; Cherry & Cannell (1984).

CHESTNUT-BACKED CHICKADEE
Parus rufescens

CBCH
Species # 741.0
Band size: 0

Molt—PB: HY partial (Aug-Sep), AHY complete (Aug-Sep); PA absent.

Skull—Completes in HY from 1 Sep thru Dec.

Age—See Black-capped Chickadee. The rect shape criteria is the same but little or no white is present in either age class (fig. 69).

Sex—♂ = ♀ by plumage. CP/BP (Mar-Jul). Wg: ♂(n30) 58-66, ♀(n30) 55-62.

References—B; PRBO data.

BRIDLED TITMOUSE
Parus wollweberi

BRTI
Species # 734.0
Band size: 1

Molt—PB: HY incomplete (Jul-Aug), AHY complete (Jul-Aug); PA absent. 1st PB probably includes at least the rects and terts, as in other titmice.

Skull—Completes in HY/SY from 1 Oct thru Jan.

Age—Rect shape probably not useful for ageing after the 1st PB. Juv (Apr-Aug) has more loosely textured undertail covs. Check the color of the roof of the mouth, as in Tufted Titmouse. Otherwise, no plumage criteria known.

Sex—♂ = ♀ by plumage. CP/BP (Mar-Jun); ♂ may develop a partial BP. Wg: ♂(n30) 61-67, ♀(n30) 58-65.

References—B.

PLAIN TITMOUSE
Parus inornatus

PLTI
Species # 733.0
Band size: 1

Molt—PB: HY incomplete (Jul-Sep), AHY complete (Jul-Aug); PA absent. 1st PB includes the rects, terts, and sometimes up to all ss and pp 1 & 2.

Skull—Completes in HY/SY from 1 Dec (as early as 1 Oct in some California populations) thru Feb.

Age—Rect shape not useful for ageing after the 1st PB. Juv (Apr-Aug) has more loosely textured undertail covs. Otherwise, no reliable plumage criteria known, but look for contrasts in the ss and pp, indicating HY/SY thru Jul (see Molt), and for differences in the color of the roof of the mouth, as with Tufted Titmouse.

Sex —♂ = ♀ by plumage. CP/BP (Mar-Aug); ♂ may develop a partial BP. Wg: ♂(n30) 67-75, ♀(n30) 66-72; W > E.

References—B,O; Dixon (1962).

TUFTED TITMOUSE
Parus bicolor

TUTI
Band size: 1

Tufted Titmouse (TUTI)   Species # 731.0
Black-crested Titmouse (BCTI)   Species # 732.0

Molt—PB: HY incomplete-complete (Jul-Sep), AHY complete (Jul-Aug); PA absent. 1st PB includes the rects and occasionally the terts in Tufted Titmouse, and may normally be complete in Black-crested Titmouse.

Skull—Completes in HY/SY from 1 Dec thru Feb.

Age—Juv (May-Aug) has more loosely textured undertail covs. Rect shape not useful for ageing after the 1st PB. Roof of mouth potentially useful for ageing some birds thru Nov (possibly later): gray in HY, gray or black in AHY (more study needed). Otherwise, no plumage criteria known, but look for contrasting flight feathers in HY/SYs (see Molt).

Sex—♂ = ♀ by plumage. CP/BP (Mar-Jul); ♂ may develop a partial BP. Wg: Tufted Titmouse ♂(n30) 77-85, ♀(n30) 72-82, N > S; Black-crested Titmouse ♂(n30) 68-78, ♀(n30) 65-75; N > S.

References—B,R,W,O,SK; Katholi (1966), Leberman (1973), Woodward (1975); C. Thompson (pers. comm.).

VERDINS   *REMIZIDAE*

One species. Family characteristics include very small size, short wings, and a longish tail. It has 10 primaries (10th spurious), 9 secondaries, and 12 rectrices. The first prebasic molt is incomplete. Ageing and sexing by plumage is subtle; more study is needed on its reliability (especially for ageing).

VERDIN   VERD
Auriparus flaviceps   Species # 746.0
                                             Band size: 0

Species—Juvs possibly confused with Juv Bushtit; best separated by bill shape (fig. 70) and shorter tail: 43-50 when fully grown.

Molt—PB: HY incomplete (Jul-Sep), AHY complete (Jul-Sep); PA absent. The 1st PB usually includes the rects and all remiges except the inner 3-5 pp.

Skull—Completes in HY from 15 Aug thru Nov.

Age—Rect shape not useful for ageing after the 1st PB. Juv (Apr-Aug) lacks yellow feathers on the head, or has mixed yellow and gray on molting birds (♂ = ♀). Many intermediates may be difficult or impossible to age with the following; compare also with intensity of yellow on the head (HY/SYs average duller yellow than AHY/ASYs, within each sex):

HY/SY (Aug-Jul): Pp covs and 1-5 inner pp brownish and faded, contrasting with grayer and fresher gr covs and ss.

AHY/ASY (Aug-Jul): Wing covs, pp, and ss uniformly gray.

Sex—CP/BP (Feb-Jul). Wg: ♂(n30) 49-57, ♀(n30) 46-54; E > W. The following is very subtle and probably unreliable for sexing many intermediate birds (compare with age), especially without previous experience:

♂: Yellow of head relatively bright; les covs relatively rich reddish-brown.

♀: Yellow of head relatively dull, washed brownish; les covs relatively pale reddish-brown or tawny.

References—B,O; Taylor (1970), Austin & Rea (1971).

Verdin   Bushtit

Figure 70. Head and bill shapes of Verdin and Bushtit, for the separation of juveniles.

BUSHTITS   *AEGITHALIDAE*

One species. Family characteristics include very small size, a long tail, and a very small beak. It has 10 primaries (10th spurious), 9 secondaries, and 12 rectrices. The first prebasic molt is complete, after which birds of most populations cannot be aged by plumage. Sexing is accomplished by eye color and plumage.

BUSHTIT   BUSH
Psaltriparus minimus   Species # 743.0
                                                     Band size: 0

Species—Juvs possibly confused with Juv Verdin. Best separated by bill shape (fig. 70) and by longer tail: 46-52 when fully grown.

Molt—PB: HY complete (Jul-Oct), AHY complete (Jul-Oct); PA absent.

Skull—Completes in HY from 15 Aug thru Dec. May be difficult to see due to darkish skin.

Age—Rect shape not useful after the 1st PB. Juv (Apr-Aug) has loosely textured undertail covs and a spurious p10 > 10 mm and rounded (fig. 71). Black in the ear covs (for ♂♂) and eye color (for ♀♀) may be useful for sexing some Juvs (see Sex). Otherwise, no plumage criteria known for ageing although presence of black in the ear coverts of ♂♂ of certain populations may indicate HY/SY; see Sex.

Sex—CP/BP (Apr-Aug). Wg: ♂(n30) 47-55, ♀(n30) 44-52; E > W. In addition to the following, some ♂♂ of certain southern U.S. populations can be separated by the presence of at least some black in the ear coverts. This occurs mostly on Juvs, and Juv ♀♀ of certain W. Texas populations may also show some black. Conversely, any individuals retaining black after the 1st PB (N. of Mexico) are ♂♂. See Raitt (1967) for more information.

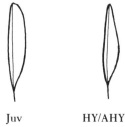

Juv   HY/AHY

Figure 71. The shape of the tenth primary of juvenile and non-juvenile Bushtits.

♂: Throat white; flanks (when fresh) washed pinkish; iris entirely dark brown. [Iris reliable for sexing HY ♂♂ only after completion of 1st PB; the iris is initially dark in Juvs of both ♂ and ♀.]

♀: Throat gray; flanks grayish-white; iris pale grayish, white, or yellow.

References—B,O; van Rossem (1935), Phillips *et al.* (1964), Raitt (1967), Radke *et al.* (1968), Ervin (1975); PRBO data.

NUTHATCHES   *SITTIDAE*

Four species. Family characteristics include slender, sharp bills and short tail and legs. They have 10 primaries (10th spurious), 9 secondaries, and 12 rectrices. The first prebasic molt is partial, yet age related differences in the shape of the rectrices are not apparent. Plumage is reliable for sexing two of the species. More investigation is needed into the usefulness of covert contrasts for ageing (see Norris 1958a, p. 247) for all of the nuthatch species.

RED-BREASTED NUTHATCH   RBNU
Sitta canadensis   Species #728.0
                                          Band size: 0

Molt—PB: HY partial (Jul-Sep), AHY complete (Jun-Oct); PA absent-limited (Mar-Apr). PBs occur primarily on the summer grounds.

Skull—Completes in HY from 15 Sep thru Dec. Occasional birds may show persistant windows (up to 4 mm across) throughout adulthood. Birds found with these during Jan-Sep are probably not reliably aged as SY.

Age—Rect shape seems unhelpful for ageing despite retention of the juvenal tail. Juv (Jun-Aug) has relatively pale crown, black speckling on the head and throat in some birds, and a yellow base to the lower mandible, changing to white after 2-4 weeks. Most Juvs can be sexed by color of crown (see Sex). Otherwise, no reliable plumage criteria known for ageing.

Sex—CP/BP (Apr-Aug); ♂♂ can develop a partial BP. Wg: ♂(n100) 64-73, ♀(n100) 60-70. A few intermediates may not be reliably sexed by the following, especially without experience (compare these with wg and age, if known):

♂: Crown dull (Juv) to glossy black, contrasting markedly with gray back.

♀: Crown gray (Juv), lead colored or dull black, contrasting little to moderately with gray back.

References—B,R,W,SK,O,BBM; Banks (1970, 1978), Yunick (1980); R. Yunick data, PRBO data.

WHITE-BREASTED NUTHATCH   WBNU
Sitta carolinensis   Species # 727.0
                                          Band size: 1B

Molt—PB: HY partial (Jul-Aug), AHY complete (Jun-Sep); PA absent.

Skull—Completes in HY/SY from 15 Sep thru Feb.

Age—Rect shape seems unhelpful for ageing despite retention of juvenal tail. Juv (Apr-Jul) is relatively paler, especially on the crown (see Sex), and has more pronounced wing bars and loosely textured undertail covs.Otherwise, no reliable plumage criteria known.

Sex—CP/BP (Mar-Aug); ♂♂ can develop partial BPs. Wg: ♂(n100) 85-97, ♀(n100) 80-94; E > W. Intermediates of the following occur, especially in southeastern U.S. populations, which may not be reliably sexed on plumage alone; compare with wg and age:

♂: Crown dull black (Juv) or glossy black; upperparts bluish-gray when fresh.

♀: Crown lead colored (Juv) or dull black; upperparts dull gray.

References—B,R,W,SK,O,BBM; Banks (1978); R. Yunick data, PRBO data.

PYGMY NUTHATCH
Sitta pygmaea

PYNU
Species # 730.0
Band size: 0

Molt—PB: HY partial (Jul-Aug), AHY complete (Jul-Aug); PA limited (Feb-Apr).

Skull—Completes in HY from 15 Sep thru Nov.

Age—Rect shape seems unhelpful for ageing, despite retention of juvenal tail. Juv (May-Aug) has relatively drab and grayer crown and relatively browner upperparts. Otherwise, no reliable plumage criteria known, but check for slight contrasts between worn pp covs and new gr covs in HY/SYs thru Jul.

Sex—♂ = ♀ by plumage. CP/BP (Apr-Aug). Wg: ♂(n30) 60-69, ♀(n30) 57-65.

References—B,O; Norris (1958a), Banks (1978); PRBO data.

BROWN-HEADED NUTHATCH
Sitta pusilla

BHNU
Species #729.0
Band size: 0

Molt—PB: HY partial (Jul-Aug), AHY complete (Jul-Aug); PA limited (Feb-Apr).

Skull—Completes in HY from 1 Sep thru Dec.

Age—Rect shape seems unhelpful for ageing despite retention of juvenal tail. Juvs (Apr-Jul) are relatively paler with grayer crowns. Otherwise, no reliable plumage criteria known (see Pygmy Nuthatch).

Sex—♂ = ♀ by plumage. CP/BP (Feb-Aug). Wg: ♂(n30) 60-69, ♀(n30) 58-68; N > Fla.

References—B,O; Norris (1958a), Banks (1978).

CREEPERS   *CERTHIIDAE*

One species. Family characteristics include a slender, curved beak; short legs; and a long tail, with individual rectrices being stiff and pointed. It has 9 visible primaries, 9 secondaries, and 12 rectrices. The first prebasic molt is incomplete, the rectrices being replaced. No plumage related ageing or sexing criteria are known, although the shape of the outer primaries may be of use in ageing. A good study for banders.

BROWN CREEPER   BRCR
Certhia americana   Species # 726.0
                                                Band size: 0

Molt—PB: HY incomplete (Aug-Sep), AHY complete (Aug-Sep); PA absent. PBs occur on the summer grounds. The 1st PB includes the rects.

Skull—Completes in HY from 1 Oct (as early as 1 Sep in west coast populations) thru Dec.

Age—Rect shape not useful for ageing. Juvs (May-Aug) are relatively buffier, with buffy edging to wing covs on some birds. Otherwise, no reliable plumage criteria known.

Sex—♂ = ♀ by plumage. CP/BP (Mar-Aug). Wg: ♂(n30) 60-67, ♀(n30) 57-65; E > W.

References—B,R,W,SK,O,Sv; PRBO data.

WRENS   *TROGLODYTIDAE*

Nine species. Family characteristics include generally small size; slender bills; and short, rounded wings. They have 10 primaries (10th spurious), 9 secondaries, and 12 rectrices. The extent of molt is quite variable in this family, with different species showing partial, incomplete, or complete first prebasic molts. Two species have extensive prealternate molts as well. There are few plumage differences between the age and sex classes.

CACTUS WREN
Camphylorhincus brunneicapillus

CSWR
Species # 713.0
Band size: 1

Molt—PB: HY incomplete-complete (Aug-Sep), AHY complete (Aug-Sep); PA absent. The 1st PB includes a variable number of flight feathers, often the outer 3-5 pp and some but not all rects.

Skull—Completes in HY/SY from 1 Sep thru Jan.

Age—Juv (Apr-Aug) has relatively buffier upperparts, less distinct spotting on the throat and upperbreast, loosely textured undertail covs, and a gray iris. The following will separate many HY/SYs; AHY/ASYs are not reliably distinguished after completion of the 1st PB (although the color of the iris might be reliable thru at least Nov, with experience):

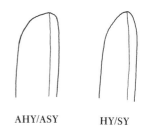

AHY/ASY   HY/SY

Figure 72. The shape of the rectrices by age in the Cactus Wren.

HY/SY (Sep-Aug): outer pp often broadly rounded and contrastingly fresher than more pointed inner pp; some or all rects tapered and relatively worn (fig. 72); iris gray to reddish-brown (thru Nov).

AHY (Jan-Sep): all pp uniformly rounded and showing no contrasts in wear; rects uniformly truncate (fig. 72); iris reddish-brown.

Sex—♂ = ♀ by plumage. CP/BP (Feb-Aug). Wg: ♂(n30) 80-92, ♀(n30) 78-88; E > W.

References—B,O; Selander (1964).

ROCK WREN
Salpinctes obsoletus

ROWR
Species # 713.0
Band size: 1

Molt—PB: HY partial (Aug-Sep), AHY complete (Jul-Sep); PA absent.

Skull—Completes in HY from 15 Sep (as early as 15 Jul in S California populations) thru Dec.

Age—Rect shape seems unhelpful despite retention of juvenal tail. Juv (Mar-Aug) has less streaking on upperparts and breast and loosely textured undertail covs. Otherwise, no plumage criteria known, but check lower mandible color for flesh in Juv-HY (Mar-Oct?) and gray or blackish with yellow base in AHY (Jan-Aug).

Sex—♂ = ♀ by plumage. CP/BP (Jan-Aug). Wg: ♂(n30) 69-77, ♀(n30) 66-73.

References—DVR,B,O; PRBO data.

CANYON WREN
Catherpes mexicanus

CNWR
Species # 717.0
Band size: 1

Molt—PB: HY partial (Aug-Sep), AHY complete (Aug-Sep); PA absent.

Skull—Completes in HY/SY from 1 Sep thru Jan.

Age—Rect shape seems unhelpful despite retention of juvenal tail. Juv (Apr-Aug) is distinguished by having relatively less or no white spotting on back, rump, and belly, and loosely textured undertail covs. Otherwise, no plumage criteria known.

Sex—♂ = ♀ by plumage. CP/BP (Feb-Aug). Wg: ♂(n30) 55-67, ♀(n30) 53-64; S > N.

References—B,O.

CAROLINA WREN
Thryothorus ludovicianus

CAWR
Species # 718.0
Band size: 0

Molt—PB: HY incomplete-complete (Aug-Sep), AHY complete (Aug-Sep); PA absent. 1st PB varies from complete (southern populations) to just the rects and occasionally some ss and/or pp (northern populations).

Skull—Completes in HY/SY from 1 Oct (as early as 1 Sep in southern U.S. populations) thru Jan.

Age—Rect shape not useful for ageing after the 1st PB. Juv (Apr-Aug) is separated by relatively paler plumage, buffy tips to the wing covs, and loosely textured and unbarred undertail covs. Otherwise, no plumage criteria known.

Sex—♂ = ♀ by plumage. CP/BP (Mar-Aug). Wg: ♂(n30) 56-67, ♀(n30) 52-62; Florida > N.

References—B,R,W,SK,O,BBM; C. Thompson (*pers. comm.*).

BEWICK'S WREN
Thryomanes bewickii

BEWR
Species # 719.0
Band size: 1

Molt—PB: HY incomplete-complete (Aug-Sep), AHY complete (Aug-Sep); PA absent. PBs occur on the summer grounds. The 1st PB includes the rects in northern populations and may normally be complete in southern populations.

Skull—Completes in HY from 1 Sep thru Dec.

Age   Rect shape not useful after the 1st PB. Juv (Apr-Aug) has relatively paler plumage, often with dusky edging to the underpart feathers, and loosely textured undertail covs. Otherwise, no plumage criteria known.

Sex—♂ = ♀ by plumage. CP/BP (Mar-Aug). Wg: ♂(n30) 51-62, ♀(n30) 47-59; E > W.

References—B,R,W,O; C. Thompson *pers. comm.*; PRBO data.

HOUSE WREN   HOWR
Troglodytes aedon   Species # 721.0
                                                        Band size: 0

Species—From Winter Wren by longer tail: 38-48.

Molt—PB: HY partial (Aug-Sep), AHY complete (Jul-Aug); PA absent.

Skull—Completes in HY from 1 Oct (possibly as early as 1 Sep in some California populations) thru Dec.

Age—Rect shape seems unhelpful for ageing despite retention of juvenal tail. Juv (May-Aug) has dusky mottling on the breast and less distinct barring on the flanks, vent, and undertail covs (the latter also loosely textured). Otherwise, no plumage criteria known.

Sex—♂ = ♀ by plumage. CP/BP (Apr-Aug). Wg: ♂(n30) 48-54, ♀(n30) 46-52.

References—B,R,W,SK,O,BBM; Fisk (1972); PRBO data.

WINTER WREN   WIWR
Troglodytes troglodytes   Species # 722.0
                                                        Band size: 0

Species—From House Wren by shorter tail: 25-34.

Molt—PB: HY partial (Aug-Sep), AHY complete (Jul-Aug); PA absent.

Skull—Completes in HY from 1 Oct (as early as 1 Sep in coastal California populations) thru Dec.

Age—Juv (May-Aug) has breast mottled indistinctly with dusky and less distinct barring on flanks, vent, and undertail covs (the latter also loosely textured). Rect shape seems unhelpful for ageing despite retention of juvenal tail. The following criteria have been found useful for separating some HY/SYs of European populations of this species. Reliability for the various N.A. populations requires further investigation (it is difficult to use with W Coast forms, at least):

HY/SY (Sep-Aug): 1-8 inner gr covs brown to grayish-brown, often with white tips, contrasting with uniformly rufous brown outer gr covs but not with mid covs in color; alula without white edging; upper mandible brown to brownish-black, lower mandible yellowish to pale brown (thru Oct-Nov?).

AHY (Jan-Aug): Gr covs uniformly brown to grayish-brown, some or many with whitish tips; alula often edged white; upper mandible black; lower mandible brown.

Sex—♂ = ♀ by plumage. CP/BP (Mar-Aug). Wg: ♂(n30) 44-52, ♀(n30) 40-48. E > W.

References—B,R,W,O,Sv; Hawthorn (1972); PRBO data.

SEDGE WREN
Cistothorus platensis

SEWR
Species # 724.0
Band size: 0

Molt—PB: HY partial-incomplete (Aug-Sep), AHY complete (Jul-Aug); PA incomplete-complete (Mar-Apr). The 1st PB sometimes includes the terts. The PA is poorly understood but involves all contours and some to all flight feathers. The extent of the PA may differ between SY and ASY.

Skull—Completes in HY/SY from 15 Oct thru Jan.

Age—Rect shape seems unhelpful for ageing despite retention (until spring) of the juvenal tail. Juv (Jun-Aug) has less white streaking to upperparts, especially crown; relatively paler underparts; and loosely textured undertail covs. Otherwise, no plumage criteria known.

Sex—♂ = ♀ by plumage. CP/BP (May-Aug). Wg: ♂(n30) 42-48, ♀(n30) 40-46.

References—B,R,W,O.

MARSH WREN
Cistothorus palustris

MAWR
Species # 723.0
Band size: 1

Molt—PB: HY complete (Aug-Sep), AHY complete (Jul-Aug); PA complete (Feb-Apr).

Skull—Completes in HY/SY from 1 Oct (as early as 1 Sep in coastal Pacific populations) thru Jan.

Age—Rect shape not useful for ageing. Juv (May-Aug) is separated by relatively darker crown, less distinct or no white streaking on back, less distinct superciliary, and loosely textured undertail covs. Otherwise, no plumage criteria known.

Sex—♂ = ♀ by plumage. CP/BP (Mar-Sep). Wg: ♂(n30) 45-57, ♀(n30) 43-54.

References—B,R,W,O; Kale (1966).

DIPPERS   *CINCLIDAE*

One species. Family characteristics include stocky porportions, strong legs, and a short tail. It has 10 primaries (10th spurious), 9 secondaries, and 12 rectrices. The first prebasic molt is partial. Sexes are alike, plumagewise. The usefulness of ageing criteria begs further investigation.

AMERICAN DIPPER
Cinclus mexicanus

AMDI
Species # 701.0
Band size: 2-1A

Molt—PB: HY partial (Aug-Oct), AHY complete (Jul-Aug); PA absent.

Skull—Completes in HY from 15 Sep thru Dec.

Age—Rect shape seems unhelpful for ageing but shape of pp covs (fig. 73) has been found useful thru late fall, at least. Juv (May-Sep) is separated by pale grayish throat, mottled underparts, pale edging to the gr covs, and entirely or mostly yellow bill. The extent of yellow in the bill is probably useful for separating HY/SY from AHY thru winter. Otherwise, no reliable plumage criteria known after the 1st PB although HY possibly separated by relatively wider and more distinct white edging to the underparts as in European Dipper (*C. cinclus*, see Svensson 1984).

Sex—♂ = ♀ by plumage. CP/BP (Mar-Jul). Wg useful: ♂(n30) 89-100, ♀(n30) 80-92; E > W.

References—B,O,Sv.

AHY/ASY   HY/SY

Figure 73. The shape of the primary coverts by age in the American Dipper.

MUSCICAPIDS

MUSCICAPIDAE

Seventeen species. Family characteristics include generally small and delicate bills, relatively pointed wings, and delicate legs. For convenience, this family is herein divided into subfamilies.

Kinglets and Gnatcatchers

Sylviinae

Five species. Subfamily characteristics include small size and delicate features. They have 10 primaries (10th spurious), 9 secondaries, and 12 rectrices. The first prebasic molt is partial. Because of their small size, skull pneumatization completes relatively early with this group. Sexing is generally possible by plumage; age classes are basically alike.

GOLDEN-CROWNED KINGLET
Regulus satrapa

GCKI
Species # 748.0
Band size: 0

Molt—PB: HY partial (Aug-Sep), AHY complete (Jul-Aug); PA absent. PBs occur on the summer grounds.

Skull—Completes in HY from 1 Oct (as early as 1 Sep in coastal Pacific populations) thru Dec.

Age—Juv (May-Aug) lacks yellow or orange in the crown, and has loosely textured undertail covs ($\delta = \varphi$). The following will reliably separate at least 50% of individuals, especially with experience, but may become difficult to use in spring due to wear:

HY/SY (Aug-Jul): Rects tapered and pointed (fig. 74).

AHY/ASY (Aug-Jul): Rects broader and truncate (fig. 74; may have small point at shaft).

Sex—CP/BP (Apr-Aug). Wg: δ(n100) 54-62, φ(n100) 51-59; E > W. The following is reliable after the 1st PB:

δ: Yellow crown with at least a few orange-red feathers.

φ: Yellow crown with no orange-red feathers. [Occasional birds with one or two orange-red feathers are not reliably sexed by plumage alone. Compare with age; these should either be AHY/ASY $\varphi\varphi$ or HY/SY $\delta\delta$.]

References—B, R, W, SK, O, BBM, Sv; Leberman (1970), Fairfield & Shirkoff (1978), W. Smith (1979), Prescott (1980b); PRBO data.

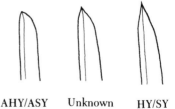

AHY/ASY   Unknown   HY/SY

Figure 74. The shape of the rectrices by age in the kinglets.

RUBY-CROWNED KINGLET
Regulus calendula

RCKI
Species # 749.0
Band size: 0

Species—From Hutton's Vireo by smaller bill; thinner, blackish legs; and shorter tail: 39-45.

Molt—PB: HY partial (Aug-Sep), AHY complete (Jul-Aug); PA absent-limited (Feb-Apr). PBs occur on the summer grounds.

Skull—Completes in HY from 1 Oct thru Nov.

Age—Shape of rects (see Golden-crowned Kinglet) useful for ageing about 35% of individuals (more with experience) thru spring. Juv (May-Aug) has brownish cast to upperparts, buffy-brown wing-bars, and loosely textured undertail covs ($\delta = \female$). Otherwise, no plumage criteria known.

Sex—CP/BP (May-Aug). Wg: δ(n100) 55-63, $\female$(n100) 52-59. The following is reliable after the 1st PB:

δ: Crown with at least a few red or orange-red feathers.

$\female$: Crown with no red or orange-red feathers. [Occasional birds with one or two red or orange-red feathers are not reliably sexed by plumage alone; compare with age.]

References—B,R,W,SK,O,BBM,Sv; Leberman (1970), Fairfield & Shirkoff (1978), W. Smith (1979), Prescott (1980a); PRBO data.

BLUE-GRAY GNATCATCHER
Polioptila caerulea

BGGN
Species # 751.0
Band size: 0

Species—Outer 2 rects with a substantial amount of white including most of the outer webs (fig. 75); p8 > p4; p9-p10 > 15; outer—central rect usually ≤ 9; exposed culmen 9-11. From Black-tailed by pattern of outer rects. From Black-capped Gnatcatcher by wing and tail formulas, bill length, and plumage in breeding $\delta \delta$ (see below).

Molt—PB: HY partial (Jul-Aug), AHY complete (Jul-Aug); PA limited (Jan-Mar). PBs occur on summer grounds.

Skull—Completes in HY from 1 Oct (as early as 15 Sep in southern populations) thru Dec.

Age—Rect shape seems unhelpful for ageing despite retention of juvenal tail. Shape of outer pp possibly of use with experience, being more pointed (and worn) in HY/SY

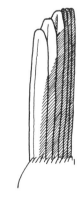

Figure 75. The tail pattern of Blue-gray Gnatcatcher.

thru at least early spring. Juv (May-Jul) is similar to adult ♀ but has loosely textured undertail covs (♂ = ♀). Otherwise, no plumage criteria known.

Sex—CP/BP (Mar-Aug). Wg: ♂(n30) 49-55, ♀(n30) 46-52. The following plumage criterion is reliable with alternate plumaged birds only; no plumage criteria known for sexing basic-plumaged birds:

AHY ♂ (Jan-Aug): Forehead with black superciliary extending from bill behind eye.

AHY ♀ (Mar-Jul): Forehead and superciliary region uniformly blue-gray or whitish.

References—B,R,W,SK,O,C(Collins & Phillips); Fisk (1972), Phillips *et al.* (1973), Rappole *et al.* (1979), Parkes (1985); PRBO data.

BLACK-TAILED GNATCATCHER
Polioptila melanura

BTGN
Species # 752.0
Band size: 0

Species—Outer rects mostly black with white confined to tips and outer webs (fig. 76); exposed culmen 8.6-9.9. These should separate this species from other N.A. gnatcatchers.

Molt—PB: HY partial (Jul-Oct), AHY complete (Jul-Oct); PA limited (Jan-Apr). PBs occur on the summer grounds.

Skull—Completes in HY from 1 Sep thru Nov.

Age—Rect shape seems unhelpful for ageing despite retention of juvenal tail. See Blue-gray Gnatcatcher. Juv (Apr-Aug) is similar to adult ♀ but has loosely textured undertail covs (♂ = ♀). Otherwise, no criteria known but see Sex for possible ageing of some AHY/ASY ♂♂.

Sex—CP/BP (Mar-Aug). Wg: ♂(n30) 43-50, ♀(n30) 41-48. The following plumage criterion is reliable with AHY birds only:

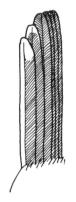

Figure 76. The tail pattern of Black-tailed Gnatcatcher.

AHY ♂ (Jan-Dec): Crown entirely black (Mar-Aug) or with at least some black patches (Aug-Mar; probably AHY/ASYs only).

AHY ♀ (Apr-Aug): Crown without any black. [♀♀ of the nominate "Plumbeous" race of S. California may have dark, dusky foreheads. ♀♀ of all forms not reliably sexed in Sep-Mar]

References—B,O,C(Collins & Phillips); Phillips *et al.* (1964), Phillips *et al.* (1973).

BLACK-CAPPED GNATCATCHER
Polioptila nigriceps

BCGN
Species # 753.1
Band size: 0

Species—Outer 2 rects as with Blue-gray Gnatcatcher (fig. 75); p8 < p4; p9-p10 usually < 15; outer—central rect usually > 9; exposed culmen 11-12. See Blue-gray Gnatcatcher.

Molt—PB: HY partial (Jul-Sep), AHY complete (Jul-Sep); PA partial (Jan-Apr). PBs occur on the summer grounds.

Skull—Completes in HY from 1 Sep thru Dec.

Age—See Black-tailed Gnatcatcher.

Sex—CP/BP (Mar-Jul). Wg: ♂(n8) 46-50, ♀(n5) 44-48. The following criteria is reliable with AHY birds only:

AHY ♂ (Jan-Dec): Crown entirely black (Mar-Aug) or with forecrown mixed black and gray (Aug-Mar); upperparts bluish-gray.

AHY ♀ (Apr-Aug): Crown without black; upperparts pale grayish without blue tinge. [♀ ♀ are not reliably sexed in Sep-Mar.]

References—C(Collins & Phillips); Phillips *et al.* (1973).

Thrushes

Turdinae

Eleven species. Subfamily chracteristics include a plump posture; a short, medium-statured bill; and, generally, a shortish tail. They have 10 primaries (10th spurious), 9 secondaries, and 12 rectrices. The first prebasic molt is usually partial, with rectrix molt being recorded in only one species. Ageing is generally possible by combining plumage with the shape of the rectrices and primaries. Sexing by plumage is possible with five of the eleven species. Research is needed into ageing by the length and shape of the 10th primary.

EASTERN BLUEBIRD
Sialia sialis

EABL
Species # 766.0
Band size: 1B-1

Species—♀♀ with throat pale chestnut, lower belly and undertail covs white, separated distinctly from chestnut of upper belly. See Western Bluebird.

Molt—PB: HY partial-incomplete (Jul-Oct), AHY complete (Jul-Sep); PA absent. PBs occur on the summer grounds. The 1st PB often includes some to all rects.

Skull—Completes in HY/SY from 1 Nov (as early as 1 Oct in Florida populations) thru Feb. Can be difficult to see through skin.

Age/Sex—CP/BP (Mar-Aug). Wg: ♂(n30) 96-109, ♀(n30) 93-104; Arizona > E. Juv (May-Aug) has mostly brown upperparts streaked white and mottled underparts. Juvs may be sexed by the color of the pp, rects, and wing covs (mostly blue in ♂♂, mostly gray in ♀♀), and the width of the buffy border on the outer rects (< 0.5 mm in ♂♂, > 0.5 mm in ♀♀). Intermediates between HY/SY and AHY/ASY occur (particularly with ♂♂) which may be impossible to reliably age by the following alone:

AHY/ASY   HY/SY

Figure 77. The tenth primary coverts of bluebirds, by age.

AHY/ASY ♂ (Aug-Jul): Upperparts and pp relatively bright blue; gr and pp covs uniformly blue; p10 cov distinctly pointed, showing some blue (fig. 77); underparts relatively deep rufous; rects truncate (fig. 78).

HY/SY ♂ (Aug-Jul): Upperparts and pp relatively dull or faded blue; pp covs blue washed with brownish or dusky, contrasting with brighter blue gr and mid covs; p10 cov rounded, usually without blue (fig. 77); underparts relatively pale rufous; rects tapered or truncate (fig. 78; see Molt).

AHY/ASY ♀ (Aug-Jul): Upperparts grayish with fairly strong blue wash; pp mostly bluish; pp, gr, and mid covs uniformly grayish-blue; p10 cov pointed, usually with some blue (fig. 77); rects truncate (fig. 78).

HY/SY ♀ (Aug-Jul): Upperparts grayish with slight to moderate blue wash; pp faded gray with slight bluish wash; pp covs gray with little or no bluish, contrasting with bluish-gray gr and mid covs; p10 cov rounded, brown (fig. 77); rects tapered or truncate (fig. 78; see Molt).

References—B,R,W,O,BBM; Pinkowski (1974, 1976), Pitts (1985).

WESTERN BLUEBIRD
Sialia mexicana

WEBL
Species # 767.0
Band size: 1B

Species—♀♀ with throat, lower belly, and undertail covs grayish; merging gradually with chestnut of upper belly.

Molt—PB: HY partial (Jul-Sep), AHY complete (Aug-Sep); PA absent. PBs occur on the summer grounds. Look for some replacement of the rects during the 1st PB, as with Eastern Bluebird.

Skull—Completes in HY/SY from 1 Oct thru Jan. Can be difficult to see through skin.

Age/Sex—CP/BP (Mar-Aug). Wg: ♂(n30) 102-117, ♀(n30) 97-110; W Coast > W Mts. Rect shape (fig. 78) is useful for separating most if not all HY/SYs (see Molt). Otherwise, age and sex criteria (including those of Juv) follow that of Eastern Bluebird.

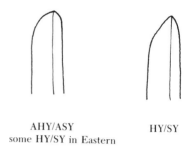

AHY/ASY   HY/SY
some HY/SY in Eastern

Figure 78. The shape of the outer rectrices by age in bluebirds.

References—B,O; PRBO data.

MOUNTAIN BLUEBIRD
Sialia currucoides

MOBL
Species # 768.0
Band size: 1B-1A

Molt—PB: HY partial (Jul-Sep), AHY complete (Jul-Sep); PA absent. PBs occur on the summer grounds.

Skull—Completes in HY/SY from 1 Oct thru Jan. Can be difficult to see through skin.

Age/Sex—CP/BP (Mar-Aug). Wg: ♂(n30) 110-121, ♀(n30) 103-116. Juv (May-Aug) has grayish upperparts with white streaking and underparts with dusky mottling. Juvs can be sexed by the color of the pp (bright bluish in ♂♂, dull turquoise in ♀♀). Rect shape and covert contrasts can be quite subtle and many intermediates (especially between HY/SY and AHY/ASY ♀♀) occur which are not reliably aged by the following alone:

AHY/ASY ♂ (Aug-Jul): Plumage bright turquois; pp, gr and mid covs uniformly blue; alula bluish; rects truncate (fig. 78).

HY/SY ♂ (Aug-Jul): Like AHY/ASY ♂ but pp covs and some outer or all gr covs relatively grayish and pale (faded), contrasting with bluer mid covs and inner gr covs; alula blue washed brownish; rects tapered (fig. 78).

AHY/ASY ♀ (Aug-Jul): Plumage dull bluish-gray; pp, gr, and mid covs uniformly bluish-gray; alula blue washed brownish; rects truncate (fig. 78).

HY/SY ♀ (Aug-Jul): Like AHY/ASY ♀ but pp covs and some outer or all gr covs brownish or pale (faded) grayish, contrasting with bluish-gray mid covs and inner gr covs; alula brownish; rects tapered (fig. 78).

References—B,O.

TOWNSEND'S SOLITAIRE
Myadestes townsendi

TOSO
Species # 754.0
Band size: 1B

Molt—PB: HY partial (Jul-Sep), AHY complete (Jul-Sep); PA absent. PBs occur on the summer grounds.

Skull—Completes in HY/SY from 1 Nov thru Feb.

Age—Shape of rects seems unhelpful for ageing despite retention of juvenal tail. Juv (Jun-Sep) easily separated (well into the 1st PB) by heavily spotted upperparts and heavily scaled underparts. Otherwise, no reliable plumage criteria known.

Sex—♂ = ♀ by plumage. CP/BP (Apr-Sep). Wg: ♂(n30) 112-123, ♀(n30) 107-116.

References—B,R,O.

VEERY
Catharus fuscescens

VEER
Species # 756.0
Band size: 1B

Species—Upperparts and tail uniformly reddish to reddish-brown; cheeks grayish, without distinct buffy eyering; underparts with indistinct reddish-brown spotting confined primarily to upperbreast, otherwise mostly white; flanks gray; p10 usually < pp covs (fig. 79, see Age); p9 > p6; p6 slightly emarginated. From Gray-cheeked and Swainson's thrushes by combination of plumage features and slight emargination of p6. From Hermit Thrush by upperpart/tail coloration and wing formula.

Molt—PB: HY partial (Jul-Sep), AHY complete (Jul-Aug); PA absent. PBs occur on the summer grounds.

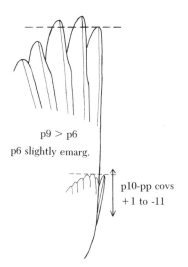

p9 > p6
p6 slightly emarg.

p10-pp covs
+1 to -11

HY/SY variations (juvenal covs)

adult covs

Figure 79. The wing formula of the Veery.

Figure 80. Variations of juvenal and adult greater coverts in the *Catharus* thrushes.

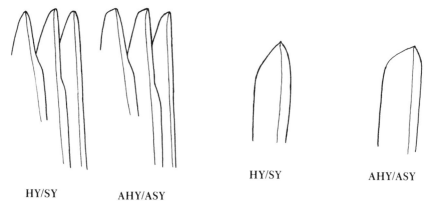

Figure 81. Primary and rectrix shapes in thrushes, by age.

Skull—Completes in HY from 15 Oct thru Dec. Some SYs may retain windows thru spring.

Age—Juv (Jun-Aug) has upperpart feathers with buffy tipping. In addition to the following, the length and shape of p10 may be of use in ageing being longer and more rounded in HY/SY than AHY/ASY (compare with fig. 79); this deserves further study:

HY/SY (Aug-Jul): At least one gr cov usually with terminal, buffy shaft streak or spot (fig. 80, lacking in about 5% of fall HY/SYs); rects and pp tapered (fig. 81).

AHY/ASY (Aug-Jul): No gr covs with buffy shaft streaks or spots (fig. 80); rects and pp truncate (fig. 81).

Sex—♂ = ♀ by plumage. CP/BP (Apr-Jul). Wg: ♂(n100) 95-106, ♀(n40) 89-103.

References—B,R,W,O,BBM; Robbins (1975).

GRAY-CHEEKED THRUSH
Catharus minimus

GCTH
Species # 757.0
Band size: 1B

Species—Upperparts and tail uniformly brownish or grayish-olive; cheeks grayish, without distinct buffy eyering; auriculars streaked whitish; throat white; upper and lower breast with distinct blackish spotting; flanks brownish-gray; p10 < pp covs (fig. 82, see Age); p9 > p6; p6 emarginated (occasionally only slightly). From Swainson's Thrush (with caution) and other *Catharus* by combination of plumage features and wing formula. The "Bicknell's" race of New England most closely resembles Swainson's Thrush in plumage but has a generally shorter wg (see Sex).

Molt—PB: HY partial (Aug-Sep), AHY complete (Jul-Aug); PA absent. PBs occur on the summer grounds.

Skull—Completes in HY from 1 Nov thru Dec. Some SYs retain windows thru spring.

Age—Juv (Jul-Aug) has upperpart feathers with pale grayish or buffy tipping and a distinct, buffy eye ring. In addition to the following, the shape and length of p10 in relation to the pp covs may be useful for ageing (see Veery; compare with fig. 82):

HY/SY (Aug-Jul): At least one gr cov with terminal, buffy shaft streak or spot (fig. 80; lacking in about 15% of fall HY/SYs); rects and pp tapered (fig. 81).

AHY/ASY (Aug-Jul): No gr covs with buffy shaft streaks or spots (fig. 80); rects and pp truncate (fig. 81).

Sex—♂ = ♀ by plumage. CP/BP (May-Aug). Wg: ♂(n30) 100-109, ♀(n30) 97-106; for "Bicknell's" race: ♂ (n30) 88-98, ♀(n22) 85-93.

References—B, R, W, O, BBM; Robbins (1975).

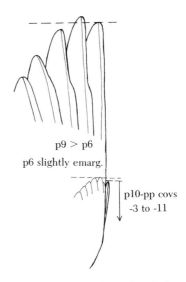

p9 > p6
p6 slightly emarg.

p10-pp covs
-3 to -11

Figure 82. The wing formula of the Gray-cheeked Thrush.

SWAINSON'S THRUSH
Catharus ustulatus

SWTH
Species # 758.0
Band size: 1B

Species—Upperparts and tail uniformly olive-brown to grayish-olive; cheeks buffy or whitish with distinct, buffy eyering; auriculars streaked buffy; throat tinged buffy; upper and lower breast with fairly distinct, large brownish spotting; flanks brownish or olive-brown; p10 < or > pp covs (fig. 83; see Age); p9 > p6; p6 not emarginated. From Gray-cheeked Thrush (with caution) and other *Catharus* by combination of plumage features and wing formula.

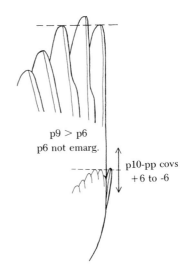

p9 > p6
p6 not emarg.

p10-pp covs
+6 to -6

Molt—PB: HY partial (Aug-Sep), AHY complete (Jul-Sep); PA absent. PBs occur on the summer grounds and/or during the early part of fall migration.

Skull—Completes in HY from 1 Nov (as early as 1 Oct in California populations) thru Dec. Some SYs (and possibly some AHY/ASYs) retain windows thru spring.

Age—Juv (May-Aug) has upperpart feathers with buffy tipping. In addition to the

Figure 83. The wing formula of the Swainson's Thrush.

following, the shape and length of p10 in relation to the pp covs may be useful for ageing (see Veery; compare with fig. 83):

HY/SY (Aug-Jul): At least one gr cov often with terminal, buffy shaft streak or spot (fig. 80; lacking in about 25% of fall HY/SYs); rects and pp tapered (fig. 81).

AHY/ASY (Aug-Jul): No gr covs with buffy shaft streaks or spots (fig. 80); rects and pp truncate (fig. 81).

Sex—♂ = ♀ by plumage. CP/BP (Mar-Aug). Wg: ♂(n100) 92-104, ♀(n100) 88-100; E > W.

References—B,R,W,O,BBM; Stewart (1971, 1972a), Robbins (1975), Cherry (1985); PRBO data.

HERMIT THRUSH
Catharus guttatus

HETH
Species # 759.0
Band size: 1B-1

Species—Upperparts brown to grayish-brown, contrasting with rufous uppertail covs and tail; p10 > pp covs; p9 < p6 (fig. 84). From other *Catharus* thrushes by combination of upperpart/tail color and wing formula.

Molt—PB: HY partial (Aug-Oct), AHY complete (Aug-Sep); PA absent. PBs occur on summer grounds.

Skull—Completes in HY/SY from 1 Nov thru Jan. Some SYs retain windows thru spring.

Age—Juv (May-Aug) has upperpart feathers with buffy tipping. In addition to the following, the shape and length of p10 in relation to the pp covs may be useful for ageing (see Veery; compare with fig. 84):

HY/SY (Aug-Jul): At least one gr cov usually with terminal, buffy shaft streak or spot (fig. 80; lacking in about 10% of HY/SYs); rects and pp tapered (fig. 81).

AHY/ASY (Aug-Jul): No gr covs with buffy shaft streaks or spots (fig. 80); rects and pp truncate (fig. 81).

p9 < p6
p6 emarg.
p10 > pp covs

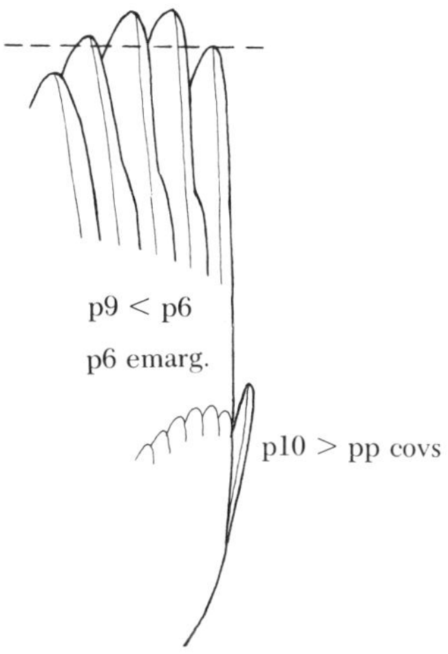

Figure 84. The wing formula of the Hermit Thrush.

Sex—♂ = ♀ by plumage. CP/BP (Apr-Sep). Wg: ♂(n100) 85-110, ♀(n100) 79-101; W Mts > E > W Coast.

References—B,R,W,O,BBM; Aldrich (1968), Stewart (1972a), Robbins (1975); PRBO data.

WOOD THRUSH
WOTH
Hylocichla mustelina
Species # 755.0
Band size: 1A

Molt—PB: HY partial (Jul-Aug), AHY complete (Jul-Aug); PA absent-limited (Feb-Apr). PBs occur on the summer grounds. The occurrence and extent of the PA in the wild requires more investigation.

Skull—Completes in HY/SY from 15 Oct thru Jan. Some SYs may retain windows thru summer. May be difficult to see skull through skin.

Age—Juv (Jun-Aug) has buffy spotting to the upperparts. Rect shape not as reliable as with *Catharus* thrushes; a few HY/SYs may be distinguished thru spring by very tapered rects. Check for usefulness of pp shape (see fig. 80). Also, a few HY/SYs retain 1-4 outer gr covs and may be separated with caution by a contrast of these with darker, less buffy, and fresher molted feathers. Otherwise, no plumage criteria known.

Sex—♂ = ♀ by plumage. CP/BP (Apr-Aug); Wg: ♂(n30) 101-119, ♀(n30) 92-112.

References—B,R,W,SK,O,BBM; Norris (1958b).

AMERICAN ROBIN
AMRO
Turdus migratorius
Species # 761.0
Band size: 2

Molt—PB: HY partial-incomplete (Aug-Oct), AHY complete (Aug-Sep); PA absent. PBs occur on the summer grounds; 1st PB sometimes includes the terts.

Skull—Completes in HY/SY from 15 Oct thru Jan. Some SYs probably retain windows thru spring. Can sometimes be difficult to see skull through skin.

Age—Juv (May-Sep) is distinguished (well into the 1st PB) by the presence of at least some buffy spotting to the upperparts and black spotting to the underparts (♂ = ♀). In addition to the following, HY/SYs of both sexes average paler and duller than AHY/ASYs; this may prove reliable for ageing thru spring when combined with sexing criteria. Also, look for a few black (juvenal) spots on the breast in occasional HY/SYs thru spring/summer:

HY/SY (Sep-Aug): Rects grayish; rects and pp tapered (fig. 80).

AHY/ASY (Sep-Aug): Rects blackish; rects and pp truncate (fig. 80).

Sex—CP/BP (Mar-Aug). Wg: ♂(n30) 124-146, ♀(n30) 121-142; NW > SE. The following criteria should be used with caution and in combination with ageing criteria and wg; intermediates (especially HY/SY ♂♂ & AHY/ASY ♀♀) occur which are not reliably sexed by plumage alone:

♂: Crown black; upperparts deep grayish to dark brown; underparts rich cinnamon-rufous, feathers of upperbreast without paler edging.

♀: Crown dark brown; upperparts light brown or pale grayish; underparts medium to pale rufous-orange, feathers of upperbreast with paler edging.

References—B,R,W,SK,O; PRBO data.

VARIED THRUSH
Ixoreus naevius

VATH
Species # 763.0
Band size: 2

Molt—PB: HY partial (Aug-Sep), AHY complete (Aug-Sep); PA absent. PBs take place on the summer grounds.

Skull—Completes in HY/SY from 1 Oct thru Feb.

Age/Sex—CP/BP (Mar-Aug). Wg: ♂(n30) 123-136, ♀(n30) 120-133. Juv (May-Aug) has heavy dusky mottling on the upperbreast, not forming a breast band. Juvs can be sexed by color of rects (see below). In addition to the following, HY/SYs average duller in both sexes (see American Robin); a few intermediates may occur which are not reliably aged and/or sexed by plumage alone (combine all criteria):

AHY/ASY ♂ (Aug-Jul): Upperparts deep bluish-gray; breast band black, distinctly defined (fig. 85); rects and pp truncate (fig. 80), rects entirely deep bluish-gray.

HY/SY ♂ (Aug-Jul): Upperparts bluish-gray, often tinged brownish; breast band blackish, distinctly defined (fig. 85); rects and pp tapered (fig. 80), rects often gray washed brownish, bluer at base.

AHY/ASY ♀ (Aug-Jul): Upperparts brownish-olive to brownish-gray; breast band brownish, indistinct (fig. 85); rects and pp truncate (fig. 80), rects mostly brown with a bluish tinge.

HY/SY ♀ (Aug-Jul): Upperparts brown; breast band brownish, indistinct (fig. 85), or nearly obscure; rects and pp tapered (fig. 80); rects entirely brown.

References—B,C(B. Sorrie); PRBO data.

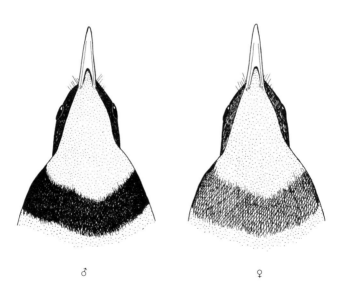

♂   ♀

Figure 85. ♂ vs. ♀ breast bands in the Varied Thrush.

Wrentits   *Timaliinae*

One species. Subfamily characteristics include very short wings and a long tail. It has 10 primaries (10th spurious), 9 secondaries, and 12 rectrices. The first prebasic molt is complete. Except for skull and iris color, no reliable, in-hand ageing or sexing criteria are known for this species.

WRENTIT   WREN
Chamea fasciata   Species # 742.0
                                                              Band size: 1

Molt—PB: HY complete (Jul-Sep), AHY complete (Jul-Sep); PA absent.

Skull—Completes in HY/SY from 1 Sep thru Jan.

Age—Rect shape not useful for ageing after the 1st PB. Juv (May-Aug) resembles adult in plumage. The feathers around the eye should be gently pulled back when using the following. Otherwise, no plumage criteria known for ageing:

Juv/HY (Apr-Sep): Outer iris brownish-gray to brown, sometimes with reddish flecking.

AHY (Jan-Aug): Outer iris reddish-brown to maroon.

Sex—This species is probably not reliably sexed in the hand. ♂ = ♀ by plumage. CP/BP (Feb-Aug) not reliably used for sexing as both sexes develop both breeding conditions. Subtle differences in the shape of the CP (Mar-Jul) may be of some use, with experience. No differences occur in the BP. Wg: ♂(n30) 54-63, ♀(n30) 53-61.

References—B; PRBO data.

MOCKINGBIRDS AND THRASHERS   *MIMIDAE*

Ten species. Family characteristics include longish, curved beaks; short, rounded wings; and long tails. They have 10 primaries (10th spurious), 9 secondaries, and 12 rectrices. The first prebasic molt tends to be partial but can be incomplete to complete in most species, especially with juveniles of earlier clutches. Iris color and flight feather condition are the main ageing criteria; no reliable plumage differences are known for sexing.

GRAY CATBIRD
Dumetella carolinensis

GRCA
Species # 704.0
Band size: 1A

Molt—PB: HY partial (Aug-Sep), AHY complete (Jul-Sep); PA absent. PBs occur on the summer grounds. Abnormal retention of juvenal undertail covs thru 1st PB has been recorded.

Skull—Completes in HY/SY from 1 Nov thru Feb.

Age—Juv (Jun-Aug) has upperparts with brownish wash, undertail covs relatively pale rufous and loosely textured, iris gray to gray-brown, and pale whitish mouth lining. Experience with the following is required to age birds accurately after late fall, and many intermediate individuals may not be reliably aged, even with experience. Also beware of abnormal AHY/ASYs with gray irides:

HY/SY (Aug-Jul): Flight feathers relatively brownish; pp covs brownish, contrasting subtly with more slaty gr and mid covs; rects tapered (fig. 86); iris grayish-brown to reddish-brown (thru Dec-Mar); mouth lining mixed whitish and/or pale gray and black (thru Nov-Mar).

AHY/ASY (Aug-Jul): Flight feathers black with slate inner webs; wing covs uniformly slate; rects truncate (fig. 86); iris maroon; mouth lining mostly black, paler at base.

Sex—♂ = ♀ by plumage. CP/BP (Apr-Sep). Wg: ♂(n100) 85-102, ♀(n100) 80-97.

References—B,R,W,SK,O,BBM; Parkes & Leberman (1967), Fisk (1972), Carpenter (1979), Raynor (1979), Prescott (1982).

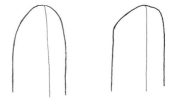

HY/SY   AHY/ASY

Figure 86. Rectrix shape by age in mimids.

NORTHERN MOCKINGBIRD
Mimus polyglottos

NOMO
Species # 703.0
Band size: 2-1A

Molt—PB: HY partial-complete (Aug-Nov), AHY complete (Jul-Oct); PA absent. PBs occur primarily on the summer grounds. 1st PB variable; may occasionally be complete but more often includes some to most pp and ss and a variable number (none to all) of rects.

Skull—Completes in HY/SY from 1 Oct (as early as 15 Aug in southern populations) thru Feb.

Age—Juv (Apr-Sep) has dusky spotting on throat and breast and gray to grayish-olive iris. Except in very young birds, iris color should not be used for reliable ageing without consultation of other criteria. The pattern and amount of white in the flight feathers and pp covs are possibly of some use for ageing (AHY/ASY genarally has more than HY/SY), but this varies considerably with the individual (see Michener 1953) and, perhaps, the population. Watch also for contrasts in wear and shape between new and old rects on some HY/SYs:

HY/SY (Aug-Jul): Iris usually grayish to greenish-gray (thru Feb); rects tapered or truncate (fig. 86; see Molt).

AHY/ASY (Aug-Jul): Iris usually greenish-yellow to yellowish-orange; rects truncate (fig. 86).

Sex—♂ = ♀ by plumage. CP/BP (Feb-Sep); ♂ may develop partial BP. Wg: ♂(n100) 103-122, ♀(n100) 100-118; tail ♂(n30) 109-134, ♀(n30) 100-127.

References—B,R,W,SK,O,BBM; Michener (1953), Fisk (1973a), Prescott (1972); C. Thompson (*pers. comm.*), PRBO data.

SAGE THRASHER
Oreoscoptes montanus

SATH
Species # 702.0
Band size: 1B-1A

Species—Culmen 11.0-13.5; p10 > pp covs by 6-10 mm; p9 ≥ p5 (fig. 87). These should separate this from other thrashers.

Molt—PB: HY partial-incomplete (Aug-Sep), AHY complete (Aug-Sep); PA absent. PBs occur on the summer grounds; 1st PB may include some rects.

Skull—Completes in HY/SY from 15 Oct thru Jan.

Age—Shape of rects (fig. 86) possibly of some use, but very subtle and probably not reliable after Feb/Mar, when feathers become quite worn. Juv (May-Aug) is distinguished by browner and streaked back, and broad, buffy white edging to the terts. Otherwise, no plumage criteria known.

Sex—♂ = ♀ by plumage. CP/BP (Apr-Aug); ♂ ♂ may develop a partial BP. Wg: ♂(n30) 96-103, ♀(n30) 93-100.

References—B,O; PRBO data.

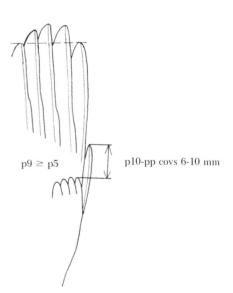

p9 ≥ p5   p10-pp covs 6-10 mm

Figure 87. The wing formula of the Sage Thrasher.

BROWN THRASHER
Toxostoma rufum

BRTH
Species # 705.0
Band size: 2-3

Species—Undertail covs buffy, occasionally with indistinct dusky centers (fig. 88); wing tip (longest p—longest s) 10-20 (fig. 89). See Long-billed Thrasher.

Molt—PB: HY partial-incomplete (Jul-Sep), AHY complete (Jul-Aug); PA absent. PBs occur on the summer grounds; 1st PB occasionally includes some rects.

Skull—Completes in HY/SY from 1 Nov (as early as 1 Oct in Florida populations) thru Jan. May be difficult to see through skin.

Age—Juv (May-Aug) has upperparts usually with indistinct buffy spotting, loosely textured undertail covs, and a gray to grayish-olive iris. The following plumage criteria become increasingly difficult to use in spring/summer, as the feathers become more worn:

HY/SY (Aug-Jul): Flight feathers relatively pale rufous-orange with browner inner webs; terts tipped buffy (thru Oct-Feb); wing-bars pale dirty-buff; rects tapered (fig. 86); iris brownish to grayish-yellow (thru Mar).

AHY/ASY (Aug-Jul): Flight feathers uniformly deep rufous and glossy; terts without buffy tips; wing-bars white to buffy cream; rects truncate (fig. 86); iris yellow to yellowish-orange.

Sex—♂ = ♀ by plumage. CP/BP (Mar-Aug); ♂♂ may develop a partial BP and sometimes have a reduced CP. Wg: ♂(n60) 99-116, ♀(n46) 95-113; W > E.

References—B,R,W,SK,O,BBM, Nichols (1953b).

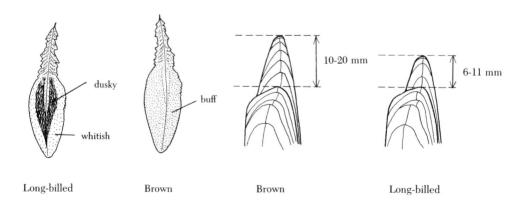

Figure 88. The greater undertail covert patterns of Brown vs. Long-billed thrashers.

Figure 89. Differences in the wing tips of Brown and Long-billed thrashers.

LONG-BILLED THRASHER
Toxostoma longirostre

LBTH
Species # 706.0
Band size: 2

Species—Undertail covs whitish with distinct, dusky centers (fig. 88); wing tip 6-11 (fig. 89). See Brown Thrasher.

Molt—PB: HY partial-incomplete (Jul-Sep), AHY complete (Jul-Aug); PA absent. 1st PB may occasionally include some (rarely all) rects.

Skull—Completes in HY/SY from 15 Oct thru Jan. May be difficult to see through skin.

Age—Rect shape (fig. 86) probably useful for ageing many birds thru summer; check also for contrasts between new and old rects in some HY/SYs. Juv (May-Aug) has dusky streaking to the rump and loosely textured and relatively buffy undertail covs. Otherwise, no reliable plumage criteria known, although those of Brown Thrasher likely apply to this species as well.

Sex—♂ = ♀ by plumage. CP/BP (Mar-Jul); ♂♂ probably develop partial BPs, as in Brown Thrasher. Wg: ♂(n27) 96-105, ♀(n12) 92-102.

References—B,O.

BENDIRE'S THRASHER
Toxostoma bendirei

BETH
Species # 708.0
Band size: 2

Species—Upperbreast with distinctly defined spots, darker than back; p10—longest pp cov > 15, p9 ≤ p5 (fig. 90); culmen 17.5-19.5 when fully grown; lower mandible with pale base, gonydeal angle (under lower mandible) rounded (fig. 91). From Sage Thrasher by longer culmen and wing formula. From Curve-billed Thrasher (especially Juv) by plumage, shorter culmen, and lower mandible features.

Molt—PB: HY partial-incomplete (Jun-Sep), AHY complete (Jul-Aug); PA absent. PBs occur on the summer grounds. 1st PB may include the terts and some or all rects. [This species has an extended breeding season that usually includes two well spaced clutches. The timing and probably the extent of the PB in 1st clutch Juvs varies significantly from that of 2nd clutch juvs. This deserves further investigation.]

Skull—Completes in HY/SY from 15 Aug thru Feb. May be difficult to see through skin.

Age—Rect shape probably not useful after fall due to rapid fading and wear in all

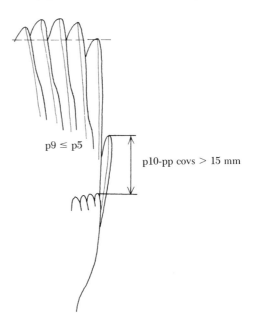

p9 ≤ p5

p10-pp covs > 15 mm

Figure 90. The wing formula of the Bendire's Thrasher.

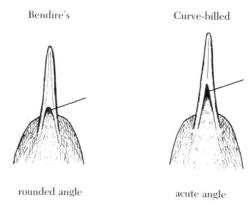

Bendire's   Curve-billed

rounded angle   acute angle

Figure 91. The underside of the bills of Bendires vs. Curve-billed thrashers.

ages of this species. Juv (Mar-Aug) has a slightly reddish-brown wash to upperparts and buffy or cinnamon-buff edging to the gr covs and terts. Otherwise, no reliable plumage criteria known after the 1st PB although color and pattern of the white on the rect tips may be of some use when fresh (see Curve-billed Thrasher). Also check for grayer irides in younger birds.

Sex—♂ = ♀ by plumage. CP/BP (Feb-Aug); ♂ ♂ may develop a partial BP as in other thrashers. Wg: ♂(n22) 99-110, ♀(n13) 97-105.

References—B; Phillips *et al.* (1964).

CURVE-BILLED THRASHER
Toxostoma curvirostre

CBTH
Species # 707.0
Band size: 3

Species—Upperbreast with indistinctly defined spotting, usually lighter or the same color as the back; culmen 20.0-25.5; lower mandible entirely black, gonydeal angle acute (fig. 91). These features should separate this species from Bendire's Thrasher. Care should be taken in separating Juvs, which may not have fully grown bills.

Molt—PB: HY partial-complete (Jun-Sep), AHY complete (Jul-Aug); PA absent. 1st PB may include some or all rects; see note under Bendire's Thrasher.

Skull—Completes in HY/SY from 1 Sep thru Feb. May be difficult to see through skin.

Age—Juv (Apr-Aug) has upperparts and upperbreast washed rufous, undertail covs loosely textured, and rects as in HY/SY. The following becomes increasingly difficult to use thru spring as tail rapidly becomes faded and bedraggled. Also, beware of some HY/SYs which have replaced rects during 1st PB:

HY/SY (Aug-Jul): Outer rects with pale, buffy-gray tip, indistinctly defined and mostly confined to the inner web (fig. 92); rects tapered (fig. 86); iris gray, cream, or yellowish (thru Oct).

AHY (Jan-Sep): Outer rects with distinctly defined white tip, broader on outer web but extending to inner web (fig. 92); rects truncate (fig. 86); iris orange-yellow. [Most Oct-Aug birds with these features are probably AHY/ASY; see Molt.]

Sex—♂ = ♀ by plumage. CP/BP (Mar-Aug); ♂♂ may develop partial, or nearly complete BP. Wg: ♂(n100) 101-115, ♀(n100) 98-111; S > N. Tail: ♂(n71) 115-130, ♀(n37) 111-120.

References—B,O; Phillips *et al.* (1964), Walters & Lamm (1986).

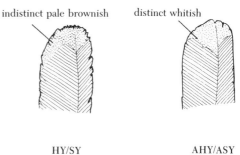

Figure 92. The pattern of the outer rectrices for ageing Curve-billed Thrasher.

CALIFORNIA THRASHER

Toxostoma redivivum

CATH
Species # 710.0
Band size: 3

Species—Superciliary fairly distinct; malar stripe indistinct; undertail covs and lower belly tan; exposed culmen 35-40. See Crissal Thrasher.

Molt—PB: HY partial-incomplete (May-Aug), AHY complete (Jul-Aug); PA absent. 1st PB possibly includes some or all rects on some birds; see note under Bendire's Thrasher.

Skull—Completion in HY/SY may occur as early as 1 Jul but generally takes place from 15 Sep thru Jan. May be difficult to see through skin.

Age—Rect shape (fig. 86) probably useful for ageing some HY/SYs with experience. Juv (Feb-Aug) has buffy-cinnamon edging to gr covs and terts and loosely textured undertail covs. Otherwise, no plumage criteria known.

Sex—♂ = ♀ by plumage. CP/BP (Dec-Jul); ♂♂ may develop partial or perhaps nearly complete BP. Wg: ♂(n30) 97-108, ♀(n30) 94-105; N > S.

References—B.

CRISSAL THRASHER

Toxostoma dorsale

CRTH
Species # 712.0
Band size: 1A-2

Species—Superciliary indistinct or lacking; malar stripe distinct; undertail covs rufous, contrasting with grayish-white lower belly; exposed culmen 32-38. See California Thrasher.

Molt—PB: HY partial (Jun-Sep), AHY complete (Jul-Aug); PA absent. 1st PB may include some or all rects; see note under Bendire's Thrasher.

Skull—Completes in HY/SY from 1 Sep thru Jan. May be difficult to see through skin.

Age—Rect shape (fig. 86) possibly useful for ageing some HY/SYs thru winter/spring. Juv (Mar-Aug) has buffy-cinnamon edging to gr covs and terts and relatively paler and loosely textured undertail covs. Otherwise, no plumage criteria known.

Sex—♂ = ♀ by plumage. CP/BP (Feb-Aug) ♂♂ probably develop partial and perhaps nearly complete BP as in other thrashers. Wg: ♂(n30) 97-105, ♀(n30) 93-101.

References—B,O.

LE CONTE'S THRASHER

Toxostoma leconti

LCTH
Species # 711.0
Band size: 2

Molt—PB: HY partial (May-Sep), AHY complete (Jul-Aug); PA absent. 1st PB may include some or all rects; see note under Bendire's Thrasher.

Skull—Completes in HY/SY from 1 Aug thru Jan. May be difficult to see through skin.

Age—Rect shape (fig. 86) and wear possibly useful for ageing some HY/SYs thru winter/spring. Juv (Feb-Aug) is slightly darker brown above (compared with faded AHYs) with relatively paler and loosely textured undertail covs. Otherwise, no plumage criteria known.

Sex—♂ = ♀ by plumage. CP/BP (Jan-Aug) ♂♂ develop partial and perhaps nearly complete BPs. Wg: ♂(n30) 94-102, ♀(n30) 91-98.

References—B.

PIPITS   *MOTACILLIDAE*

Two species. Family characteristics include slender bills, pointed wings, and long hind claws. They have 10 primaries (10th spurious), 9 secondaries, and 12 rectrices. The first prebasic molt is partial, however, shape of rectrices does not appear useful for ageing. Sexes are alike in plumage.

WATER PIPIT   WAPI
Anthus spinoletta   Species # 697.0
                                           Band size: 1

Species—Upperparts grayish to brownish-olive, indistinctly streaked dusky; white of 5th rect usually extends only 25-40 mm from tip (fig. 93; N.A. populations); outer rect mixed brown and white; legs black or brownish-black; hind toe and claw shorter than central toe and claw; tail 58-70. These criteria should readily separate this species from Sprague's Pipit. Red-throated Pipit (*A. cervinus*), a rare migrant to western N.A., is distinguished by its conspicuously streaked back and pale brown to flesh colored legs.

Molt—PB: HY partial (Jul-Sep), AHY complete (Jul-Sep); PA partial-incomplete (Mar-Apr). PBs occur primarily on the summer grounds. PAs include the central rects on some birds.

Skull—Completes in HY/SY from 1 Nov thru Jan.

Age—Rect shape seems unhelpful but relative wear may be of use. Juv (Jun-Aug) has brownish washed upperparts and relatively pale underparts. The following has been found useful in Europe and seems to apply to N.A. populations as well. Intermediates will occur, especially later in spring, that are not reliably aged; compare with wear of flight feathers:

HY/SY (Aug-Jul): Gr and mid covs relatively faded, with grayish centers contrasting indistinctly with whitish edging; gr covs without indentations on corner of outer web and mid covs with pronounced points extending from tip of dark centers (fig. 94). [Some birds may molt a few inner gr covs during the 1st PB; these should appear as described for AHY/ASY, and should contrast with those retained.]

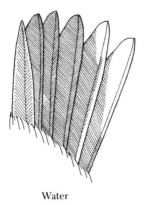
Water

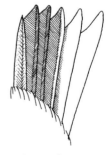
Sprague's

Figure 93. Tail patterns of Water vs. Sprague's pipits.

AHY/ASY (Aug-Jul): Gr and mid covs uniformly fresh, with glossy blackish centers contrasting distinctly with pale brownish to buffy edging; gr covs with distinct indentations on corner of outer web and mid covs with no or small points extending from tips of dark centers (fig. 94).

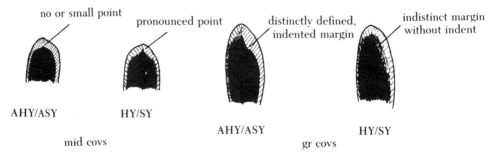

Figure 94. The middle and greater covert patterns by age in Water Pipits. Check for the usefulness of these criteria on Sprague's Pipit.

Sex—♂ = ♀ by plumage. CP/BP (May-Aug). Wg ♂(n40) 78-92, ♀(n40) 74-86; W Mts > E & W Coast.

References—B,R,W,O,Sv; Shortt (1951), Verbeek (1973b).

SPRAGUE'S PIPIT
Anthus spragueii

SPPI
Species # 700.0
Band size: 1

Species—Upperparts buffy brown, broadly streaked with dusky; white of 5th rect extends > 40 mm from tip (fig. 94); outer rects entirely white; legs pale brownish or yellow; hind toe and claw longer than central toe and claw; tail 52-61. See Water Pipit. From Red-throated Pipit also by amount of white in the outer rects (Red-throated Pipit has a similar amount and pattern as Water Pipit).

Molt—PB: HY partial (Aug-Sep), AHY complete (Aug-Sep); PA partial (Mar-Apr). PBs occur on the summer grounds.

Skull—Completes in HY from 15 Oct thru Dec.

Age—Rect shape seems unhelpful for ageing although relative wear of flight feathers may be more useful. Juv (Jun-Aug) has dull black spotting (rather than streaking) to upperparts and pale tips to some or all back feathers. Otherwise, no reliable plumage criteria known but those listed for ageing Water Pipit may apply in this species as well.

Sex—♂ = ♀ by plumage. CP/BP (May-Aug). Wg: ♂(n25) 78-88, ♀(n16) 75-84.

References—B,R,O; Shortt (1951).

WAXWINGS   *BOMBYCILLIDAE*

Two species. Family characteristics include plump postures, crests, short legs, and waxy appendages to the secondaries (rarely the greater coverts) in adult birds. They have 9 visible primaries, 9 secondaries, and 12 rectrices. The first prebasic molt is partial. Most birds should be reliably aged and sexed when all criteria are combined.

BOHEMIAN WAXWING   BOWX
Bombycilla garrulus   Species # 618.0
                                                            Band size: 1A

Species—From Cedar Waxwing in all plumages by chestnut undertail covs and longer wg: 109-121.

Molt—PB: HY partial (Aug-Nov), AHY complete (Aug-Nov); PA absent. PBs usually occur in the vicinity of the summer grounds or during post-breeding wandering.

Skull—Completes in HY/SY from 1 Nov thru Feb.

Age—Juv (Jun-Oct) has a white throat, and underparts indistinctly streaked with dusky (♂ = ♀ but see table 4). The following should be compared with the information provided in table 4, especially on known-sexed birds:

HY/SY (Oct-Sep): pp without white tips to inner webs (fig. 95); yellow tips to rects often dull or washed with dusky; rects tapered (fig. 96; compare with wear and molt on Aug-Oct birds).

AHY/ASY (Oct-Aug): At least some pp (often pp 4-7) with white extending to tips of inner webs (fig. 95); yellow tips to rects usually bright; rects truncate (fig. 96).

Sex—CP/BP (May-Sep); ♂ may develop partial BP. Wg: ♂(n30) 111-121, ♀(n30) 109-119. A few intermediates between the following may occur which are not reliably sexed by this feature alone (see fig. 97 for Cedar Waxwing). Compare with ageing criteria and information provided in table 4:

TABLE 4.
Number and length of waxy appendages and length of yellow to the tips of the central and outer most rectrices of Bohemian Waxwing (all in mm; derived from Svensson 1984).

	AHY/ASY M	HY/SY M	AHY/ASY F	HY/SY F
# of waxy appendages to ss	6–8	4–8	5–7	0–5
length of longest waxy appendage	6.0–9.5	3.5–5.5	3.0–7.5	0.0–3.5
Length of yellow at tip of central rect	5.5–8.5	5.0–8.0	4.0–6.0	2.0–6.0
length of yellow at tip of 5th rect	7.0–11.0	7.0–10.5	5.0–8.0	3.0–6.0

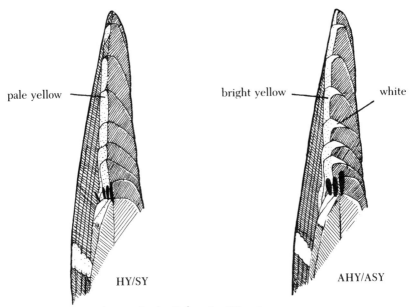

pale yellow

bright yellow

white

HY/SY

AHY/ASY

Figure 95. Wing patterns by age in the Bohemian Waxwing.

♂: Throat patch full, black, and contrasting sharply with breast.

♀: Throat patch relatively restricted, washed grayish or brownish, and contrasting indistinctly with breast.

References—B,R,O,Sv.

CEDAR WAXWING
Bombycilla cedrorum

CEWX
Species # 619.0
Band size: 1B

Species—From Bohemian Waxwing by white or pale buffy undertail covs and shorter wg (89-100).

Molt—PB: HY partial (Sep-Dec), AHY complete (Aug-Nov); PA absent. PBs occur primarily on the winter grounds but may commence during migration or post-breeding wandering.

Skull—Completes in HY/SY from 15 Oct thru Feb.

Age—Juv (Jun-Nov) has a whitish chin with distinct malars, underparts with heavy dusky streaking and a grayish iris (♂ = ♀ but see fig. 96). The following should be compared with the information provided in table 5, especially on known-sexed birds:

HY/SY (Oct-2nd Oct): Iris grayish-brown to reddish-brown (thru early spring); rects tapered, usually with dusky-washed and shorter (by sex) yellow tips (fig. 96; compare shape with wear and molt on Aug-Oct birds).

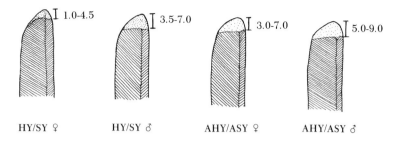

| HY/SY ♀ | HY/SY ♂ | AHY/ASY ♀ | AHY/ASY ♂ |

Figure 96. Typical amounts and shading of yellow at the tip of the tails by age and sex in the Cedar Waxwing.

Figure 97. Throat patterns of ♂ and ♀ Cedar Waxwings.

AHY/ASY (Sep-Aug): Iris deep reddish; rects truncate, usually with bright and longer (by sex) yellow tips (fig. 96).

Sex—CP/BP (May-Oct); ♂ may develop partial BP. Wg: ♂(n30) 91-100, ♀(n30) 89-99. Intermediates between the following should be compared with the information provided in fig. 96 and table 5, especially with known-aged birds:

♂: Chin glossy black, base of black patch 7-15 mm wide (fig. 97).

♀: Chin dull or brownish-black, base of patch 2-8 mm wide (fig. 97). [A few individuals with intermediate patches, 7-8 mm wide at the base should not be sexed using this criterion alone. These are probably HY/SY ♂♂ or AHY/ASY ♀♀; combine with age criteria.]

References—B,R,W,SK,O,BBM; Yunick (1970c); PRBO data.

TABLE 5.
Range and mean number of waxy appendages on one wing of Cedar Waxwings by age and sex (derived from Yunick 1970c, PRBO data, and museum skin examination).

	AHY/ASY M	HY/SY M	AHY/ASY F	HY/SY F
Sample	60	73	60	69
Range	3–9	0–7	1–7	0–3
Mean	6.2	0.4	5.3	0.1

SILKY-FLYCATCHERS   *PTILOGONATIDAE*

One species. Family characteristics include a crest, short legs, and a long tail. It has 10 primaries (10th spurious), 9 secondaries, and 12 rectrices. The first prebasic molt is variable but usually not complete. Sexes are distinguishable by plumage. Reliable ageing by plumage is possible with all males and most females.

PHAINOPEPLA   PHAI
Phainopepla nitens   Species # 620.0
                                             Band size: 1B

Molt—PB: HY partial-complete (Jun-Nov), AHY complete (Jun-Oct); PA absent. 1st PB extremely variable, involving none to (rarely) all flight feathers. HYs with near complete molt will often retain ss 1-3 and the central rects. PBs are often suspended in migratory populations.

Skull—Completes in HY from 15 Aug thru Dec.

Age/Sex—CP/BP (Feb-Aug); ♂ may develop partial BP. Wg: ♂(n30) 85-98, ♀(n30) 82-94; SW > Calif. Juv (Mar-Sep) is like HY/SY ♀ (see below) but has relatively buffy wingbars and brownish washed upperparts (♂ = ♀). Some ♀♀ are probably not reliably aged by the following:

AHY/ASY ♂ (Aug-Jul): Contours and flight feathers uniformly glossy black; gr and undertail covs without distinct white edging (may show traces of white tipping when fresh); rects truncate (fig. 98).

HY/SY ♂ (Aug-2nd Aug): Contours mottled gray and black, or if entirely black, gr and undertail covs with distinct white tipping; flight feathers grayish or with contrasting gray and black feathers (rarely all black); some or all rects tapered (fig. 98). [Jul-Aug SYs in this plumage should have very worn flight feathers and pneumatized skulls, to separate them from molting HYs.]

AHY/ASY ♀ (Aug-Jul): Contours and flight feathers entirely and uniformly gray; indistinct wing bars (if not worn off) pale grayish to white; rects truncate (fig. 98).

HY/SY ♀ (Aug-Jul): Like AHY/ASY ♀ but flight feathers often showing clearly contrasting dark and faded gray feathers; some gr covs often with buffy tips; some or all rects tapered (fig. 98).

References—B,O; Miller (1933).

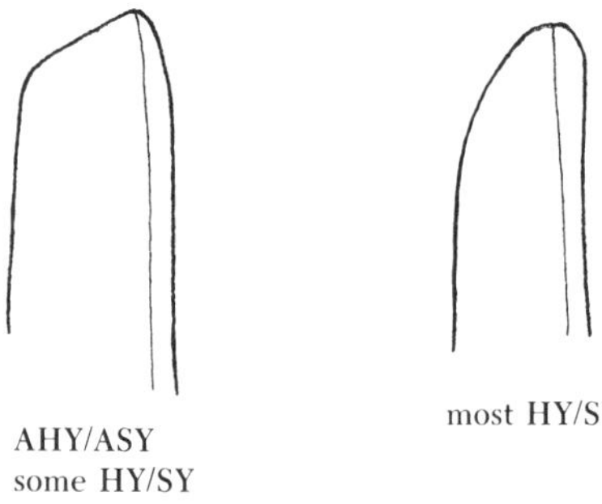

AHY/ASY
some HY/SY

most HY/SY

Figure 98. Outer rectrix shapes in Phainopeplas, by age.

SHRIKES

LANIIDAE

Two species. Family characteristics include large heads, heavy and hooked beaks, short legs, and rounded tails. They have 10 primaries (10th spurious), 9 secondaries, and 12 rectrices. The first prebasic molt is partial to incomplete. Ageing is accomplished with molt related criteria. The sexes, however, are basically alike.

NORTHERN SHRIKE
Lanius excubitor

NOSH
Species # 621.0
Band size: 2

Species—From Loggerhead Shrike by more extensive barring to the underparts (moderate on AHY, heavy on HY) and longer wg (106-121), tail (104-118), and culmen (13.0-14.3; fig. 99).

Molt—PB: HY partial (Oct-Dec), AHY complete (Jul-Sep); PA absent-limited (Mar-Apr). 1st PB occurs on the winter grounds; adult PB occurs on the summer grounds.

Skull—Completes in HY/SY from 15 Oct thru Jan. May be difficult to see through skin.

Age—In addition to the following, see molt for age-related differences in timing and location of the PBs:

Juv-HY/SY (Aug-2nd Aug): Face mask brownish, indistinct; upperparts washed rufous-brown (thru Nov) to dull olive-gray; underparts brownish (thru Nov) to grayish, heavily barred; flight feathers and some or all gr covs dull, brownish-black, contrasting markedly with blacker inner gr covs and mid covs; base of p6 as shown (fig. 100); rects tapered (fig.101).

AHY/ASY (Aug-Jul): Face mask black, distinct; upperparts pearly gray; underparts white, indistinctly barred; flight feathers and wing covs uniformly glossy black; base of p6 as shown (fig. 100); rects truncate (fig. 101).

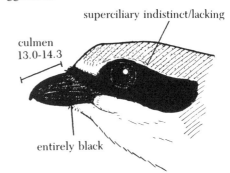

Loggerhead

superciliary indistinct/lacking

culmen
13.0-14.3

entirely black

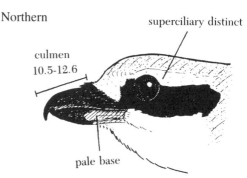

Northern

superciliary distinct

culmen
10.5-12.6

pale base

Figure 99. Head patterns and bill sizes in Northern vs. Loggerhead Shrike.

Sex—CP/BP (May-Aug). Wg: ♂(n30) 110-121, ♀(n30) 106-117; W > E. HY/SY ♀♀ average slightly browner than HY/SY ♂♂, and AHY/ASY ♀♀ have slightly duller black flight feathers (on the average) than AHY/ASY ♂♂ but these are not reliable on their own. Otherwise, no plumage criteria known for sexing.

References—B,R,W,SK,O,Sv; Miller (1931).

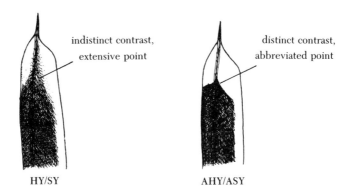

indistinct contrast,
extensive point

distinct contrast,
abbreviated point

HY/SY   AHY/ASY

Figure 100. The base of the sixth primary in Northern Shrikes, by age. Check for this on Loggerhead Shrikes, as well.

LOGGERHEAD SHRIKE
Lanius ludovicianus

LOSH
Species # 622.0
Band size: 1A

Species—From Northern Shrike by less extensive barring to the underparts (none on AHY/ASY, slight on HY/SY), and shorter wg (88-106), tail (86-104), and culmen (10.5-12.6; fig. 99).

Molt—HY partial-incomplete (Jun-Nov), AHY complete (Jun-Oct); PA limited (Feb-Apr). PBs occur mostly on the summer grounds. 1st PB variable, often including most or all rects and some outer pp and inner ss.

Skull—Completes in HY/SY from 15 Sep (as early as 1 Aug in southern populations) thru Jan. May be difficult to observe through skin.

Age—Juv (Mar-Sep) has contour feathers with indistinct barring and buffy tipped les covs. In addition to the following, check the base of p6 for age related differences, as in Northern Shrike (see fig. 100):

HY/SY (Aug-Jul): Gr covs (often inner 1-4 ss and outer 4-6 pp as well) black, contrasting with browner outer ss, inner pp, and pp covs; inner pp covs with white or buffy white tips, fairly broad when fresh; rects tapered (fig. 101) or truncate.

AHY/ASY (Aug-Jul): Ss, pp and wing covs fairly uniformly black (inner ss tend to be darker but without distinct contrasts between adjacent feathers); inner pp covs entirely black or (when fresh) with small white spots; rects truncate (fig. 101).

Sex—♂ = ♀ by plumage. CP/BP (Feb-Aug). Wg: ♂(n30) 92-106, ♀(n30) 88-104; N & W > SE & California.

References—B,R,W,SK,O; Miller (1928, 1931); PRBO data.

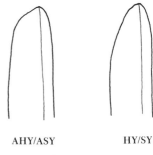

AHY/ASY   HY/SY

some HY/SY
Loggerhead

Figure 101. Juvenal vs. adult outer rectrix shapes in Shrikes.

STARLINGS   *STURNIDAE*

One species. Family characteristics include a robust body, strong legs, and a short tail. It has 10 primaries (10th vestigial), 9 secondaries, and 12 rectrices. The first prebasic molt is complete, or nearly so. Almost all birds should be reliably aged and sexed when all of many criteria are combined.

EUROPEAN STARLING   EUST
Sturnus vulgaris   Species # 493.0
                                                  Band size: 2

Molt—PB: HY complete (Jul-Nov), AHY complete (Jun-Oct); PA absent. The alula and a few ss may occasionally be retained during the 1st PB.

Skull—Completes in HY/SY from 1 Dec thru Mar. May be difficult to see through skin.

Age—Rect shape useful despite complete 1st PB. Juv (May-Oct) has entirely gray-brown plumage, or mixed gray-brown and blackish when molting (many Juvs can be sexed by eye color; see below):

HY/SY (Sep-Aug): Length of irridescence of throat feathers 2-12 (fig. 103; compare with sex); rects relatively rounded, central rect with indistinct black subterminal and buffy terminal edging (fig. 102); outer rect with narrow or indistinct cinnamon edging; toungue often with at least some yellow (thru Nov).

AHY/ASY (Aug-Jul): Length of irridescence on throat feathers 7-23 (fig. 103; compare with sex); rects relatively pointed, central rect with distinctly defined black subterminal and cinnamon terminal edging (fig. 102); outer rect with wide, distinct cinnamon edging; tongue without yellow coloration.

AHY/ASY   HY/SY

Sex—CP/BP (Mar-Sep); ♂♂ may develop a partial BP. Wg: ♂(n40) 125-138, ♀(n35) 122-135. With the following, beware of occasional non-Juvs (1-3%) showing conflicting iris and bill color characteristics. Always combine with length of irridescence on the throat feathers which, with other ageing criteria, should allow reliable sexing of most of these:

Figure 102. Differences in the shape and pattern of the central rectrices of first-year vs. adult European Starlings.

♂: Length of irridescence on throat feathers 6-23 (fig. 103; compare with age); iris usually entirely brown (> 6 wks old) or dark brownish-gray (Juv); base of lower mandible blue or bluish-gray (Jan-Jun, possibly Jul-Nov).

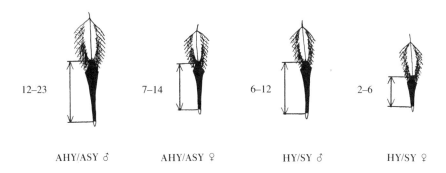

12–23   7–14   6–12   2–6

AHY/ASY ♂   AHY/ASY ♀   HY/SY ♂   HY/SY ♀

Figure 103. Lengths of irridesence on the throat feathers of European Starling, by age and sex.

♀: Length of irridescence on throat feathers 2-14 (fig. 103; compare with age); iris usually brown with distinct (occasionally indistinct) yellow outer ring (> 6 wks) or pale grayish with yellow tint (Juv); base of lower mandible pinkish (Jan-Jun, possibly Jul-Dec).

References—B,R,W,O,Sv; Kessel (1951), D. Davis (1960), Parks (1962), Lloyd (1965), Schwab & Marsh (1967); PRBO data.

VIREOS   *VIREONIDAE*

Eleven species. Family characteristics include stout, hooked beaks; spectacles on most species; and shortish tails. They have 10 primaries (10th spurious in 8 species, full-lengthed in three), 9 secondaries, and 12 rectrices. The first prebasic molt is usually partial. Windows in the pneumatization of the skull are often retained into the first spring. Otherwise, ageing is generally difficult, with shape of the rectricies and eye color helping in certain species. Only one species shows difinitive sex related plumage characters; wing length is not as useful for sexing as it is in most other passerine groups.

WHITE-EYED VIREO

Vireo griseus

WEVI
Species # 631.0
Band size: 0

Molt—PB: HY incomplete (Jul-Sep); AHY complete (Jun-Sep); PA absent. PBs occur on the summer grounds. The 1st PB usually includes the rects, terts, and 5-6 outer pp, but is variable.

Skull—Completes in HY/SY from 1 Sep (southern U.S. populations) thru Jan. Check for windows in spring, indicating SY.

Age—Juv (Apr-Aug) has brownish-buff head plumage, including lores and eye ring; buffy wing bars; and a grayish-brown iris. In the following, caution is advised with the use of eye color, especially in southern populations (adults with gray irides have been reported in Florida). Rect shape can also be subtle:

HY/SY (Aug-Jul): Iris brownish-gray (thru Jan); outer 5-6 pp often contrastingly fresher and more truncate than inner pp (see Molt); rects sometimes tapered (fig. 104). [Most birds are probably not reliably aged SY in spring/summer.]

AHY (Jan-Nov): Iris usually white, or white with slight grayish wash; pp uniformly shaped and worn; rects truncate (fig. 104). [No criteria known for reliably ageing AHY/ASY after Nov.]

Sex—♂ = ♀ by plumage. CP/BP (Mar-Aug); ♂♂ develop a partial BP. Wg: ♂(n30) 55-65, ♀(n30) 54-63; N > S.

References—B,R,W,SK,O;   Fisk   (1972), George (1973), Thompson (1973), Lloyd-Evans (1983).

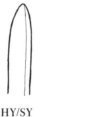

HY/SY   AHY/ASY
(many HY/SY White-eyed)

Figure 104. Outer rectrix shape by age in White-eyed, Bell's, and Hutton's vireos.

BELL'S VIREO

Vireo bellii

BEVI
Species # 633.0
Band size: 0

Species—White lores and eye ring present but indistinct; upper wing bar very indistinct; wg 51-59; p10 about 1/3 p9, 6.5-11.0 mm longer than pp covs (fig. 105); tail 41-54. Combination of plumage, shorter measurements, and wing formula will separate this from the other vireo species.

Molt—PB: HY partial (Jul-Aug), AHY complete (Jul-Aug); PA absent. PBs occur on the summer grounds.

Skull—Completes in HY from 1 Oct (as early as 1 Sep in California populations) thru Dec. Windows may occur in some spring SYs.

Age—Juv (May-Aug) has brownish wash to upperparts, whiter underparts, and relatively distinct wing-bars. The following can be very subtle; intermediates will

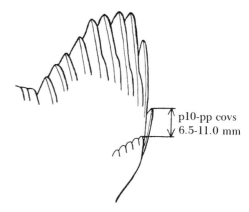

Figure 105. The wing formula of the Bell's Vireo.

occur that can not be reliably aged. Check also for contrasts in wing covs, as in Hutton's Vireo:

HY/SY (Aug-Jul): Rects tapered (fig. 104).

AHY/ASY (Aug-Jul): Rects truncate (fig. 104).

Sex—♂ = ♀ by plumage. CP/BP (Mar-Aug); ♂ may develop a partial BP. Wg: ♂ (n30) 52-59, ♀ (n29) 51-57.

References—B,R,O.

BLACK-CAPPED VIREO
Vireo atricapillus

BCVI
Species # 630.0
Band size: 1

Species—Drab individuals may be confused with other vireo species. From Bell's Vireo by distinct white lores and eye ring; from all other species, including Solitary Vireo, by short wg: 51-58.

Molt—PB: HY partial (Jul-Aug), AHY complete (Jul-Aug); PA limited (Feb-Mar). PBs occur on the summer grounds. PA may occur in SYs only.

Skull—Completes in HY from 15 Sep thru Dec. Windows may occur in some spring SYs.

Age/Sex—CP/BP (Mar-Aug); ♂ may develop a partial BP. Wg: ♂ (n16) 53-58, ♀ (n8) 51-55. Juv (May-Jul) has plumage washed with buffy and lores and eye ring light buff (♂ = ♀). Rect shape (fig. 104) seems unhelpful for ageing despite retention of juvenal tail. Intermediates between the following may occur which are not reliably aged or sexed by plumage alone:

Basic Plumage

AHY/ASY ♂ (Aug-Mar): Crown and nape glossy black.

AHY/ASY ♀ (Aug-Feb): Crown and nape slate gray to dull black, uniform in coloration, and contrasting fairly markedly with olive-green back; underparts (except lemon-yellow flanks) white or whitish.

HY/SY (Jul-Feb): Crown and nape dull brownish-gray, showing little or no marked contrast with brownish-olive back; underparts, especially upperbreast, washed with buffy or yellow. ♂ = ♀. [Compare carefully with AHY ♀.]

Alternate Plumage

AHY ♂ (Mar-Aug): Crown and nape glossy black. [Birds in this plumage are probably reliably aged ASY thru Jul.]

SY ♂ (Mar-Aug): Crown and nape gray with patches of glossy black. [Aug SYs should have very worn flight feathers to distinguish them from molting HYs.]

♀ (Mar-Aug): Crown and nape uniformly slate gray to dull black.

References—B,O; P. Ashman (*pers. comm.*).

GRAY VIREO
Vireo vicinior

GRVI
Species # 634.0
Band size: 1

Species—From the plumbeous form of Solitary Vireo by wing formula (p9 < p5; fig 106) and shorter wg: 61-68. From Bell's Vireo by longer wing, and tail: 53–61.

Molt—PB: HY partial (Jul-Sep), AHY complete (Jul-Sep); PA absent. PBs occur on the summer grounds.

Skull—Completes in HY from 15 Sep thru Dec. Windows may occur in some spring SYs.

Age—Rect shape seems unhelpful, despite retention of juvenal tail. Juv (May-Aug) has brown washed plumage and relatively distinct wing bars. Otherwise, no reliable plumage criteria known, although wing cov contrasts, as in Hutton's Vireo, may prove useful for ageing.

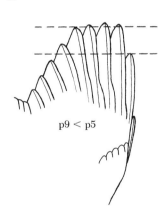

p9 < p5

Figure 106. The wing formula of the Gray Vireo.

Sex—♂ = ♀ by plumage. CP/BP (Apr-Aug); ♂ develops a partial BP. Wg: ♂(n30) 62-68, ♀(n19) 61-67.

References—B,O.

SOLITARY VIREO
Vireo solitarius

SOVI
Species # 629.0
Band size: 1

Species—Lores and eye ring bold; yellowish or white wing-bars distinct; wg 70-85; p9 > p5; p10 (spurious) > or < pp covs (see fig. 107). Plumage should eliminate most other vireo species. Plumbeous form separated from Gray Vireo and West Coast form from Hutton's Vireo by wing formula and longer wg.

Molt—PB: HY partial (Jul-Sep), AHY complete (Jul-Aug); PA absent-limited (Mar-Apr). PBs occur on the summer grounds. The extent and variation of the PA needs further investigation.

Skull—Completes in HY from 15 Sep thru Dec. Windows may be retained by SYs thru spring.

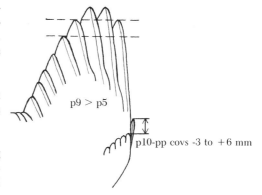

p9 > p5

p10-pp covs -3 to +6 mm

Age—Rect shape seems unhelpful for ageing despite retention of juvenal tail. Juv (May-Aug) averages browner and drabber in all populations. Otherwise, no reliable plumage criteria known.

Figure 107. The wing formula of the Solitary Vireo.

Sex—♂ = ♀ by plumage. CP/BP (Mar-Aug); ♂ develops a partial BP. Wg not very helpful due to geographical variation and little size dimorphism: ♂ (n30) 71-85, ♀ (n30) 70-84.

References—B,R,W,O; PRBO data.

YELLOW-THROATED VIREO
Vireo flavifrons

YTVI
Species # 628.0
Band size: 1

Molt—PB: HY partial (Jul-Aug), AHY complete (Jul-Aug); PA absent. PBs occur on the summer grounds.

Skull—Completes in HY/SY from 1 Oct thru Jan. Windows occur on some spring SYs.

Age—Rect shape seems unhelpful for ageing despite retention of juvenal tail. Juv (May-Aug) is separated by brownish washed upperparts, and pale, buffy-yellow throat. Otherwise, no reliable plumage criteria known.

Sex—♂ = ♀ by plumage. CP/BP (Apr-Aug); ♂ may develop a partial BP. Wg: ♂ (n30) 71-80, ♀ (n30) 70-78.

References—B,R,W,O.

HUTTON'S VIREO
Vireo huttoni

HUVI
Species # 632.0
Band size 0

Species—Wg 58-72; p9 < p5; p10 9-12 mm > pp covs (fig. 108); tail 47-55. From Bell's Vireo by more distinct facial pattern and longer wg; from western Solitary Vireo by wing formula and shorter wg; from Ruby-crowned Kinglet by thicker vireo-type bill, thicker bluish-gray legs, and longer tail.

Molt—PB: HY partial (Jul-Sep), AHY complete (Jul-Sep); PA absent. PBs occur on the summer grounds.

Skull—Completes in HY from 15 Aug thru Dec. Some SYs retain windows thru spring.

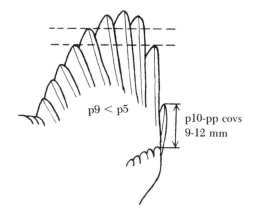

Figure 108. The wing formula of the Hutton's Vireo.

Age—Juv (Apr-Aug) has upperparts relatively paler and washed brownish, and relatively distinct buffy wing bars. The following is subtle but appears reliable:

HY/SY (Aug-Mar): Pp covs brownish, faded, without green edging, contrasting in coloration with slightly glossier and green-edged gr covs; rects tapered (fig. 104).

AHY/ASY (Aug-Mar): Wing covs uniform in coloration, slightly glossy with green edges; rects truncate (fig. 104).

Sex—♂ = ♀ by plumage. CP/BP (Feb-Aug); ♂ may develop a partial BP. Wg: ♂(n30) 61-72, ♀(n30) 58-69; SW > W Coast.

References—B,O; PRBO data.

WARBLING VIREO
Vireo gilvus

WAVI
Species # 627.0
Band size: 1

Species—Lores pale grayish; underparts with little to some yellow, usually confined to sides of breast and flanks; superciliary indistinct to moderately distinct, bordered on top by grayish; wg 64-75; p10 spurious, 3-8 mm longer than the pp covs (fig. 109). From Philadelphia and Red-eyed vireos by plumage and wing formula.

Molt—PB: HY partial (Jul-Sep), AHY complete (Jul-Sep); PA limited (Feb-Apr). 1st PBs occur on the summer grounds; adult PBs may normally be suspended, as with Red-eyed Vireo; more study is needed.

Skull—Completes in HY/SY from 1 Oct (as early as 15 Sep in California populations) thru Jan. Some SYs retain windows thru spring.

Age—Rect shape seems unhelpful despite retention of juvenal tail. Juv (May-Aug) distinguished by cinnamon-buff tipping to the gr covs. Otherwise, no reliable plumage criteria known.

Sex—♂ = ♀ by plumage. CP/BP (Mar-Jul); ♂ may develop a partial BP. Wg: ♂(n30) 66-75, ♀(n30) 64-73.

References—DVR, B, R, W, O; PRBO data.

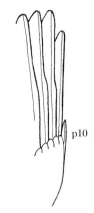

Figure 109. The wing formula of the Warbling Vireo.

PHILADELPHIA VIREO
Vireo philadelphicus

PHVI
Species # 626.0
Band size 0

Species—Lores dark brownish; underparts with substantial yellow, uniformly distributed on center and sides of breast; p10 full-lengthed (a short "remical", < pp covs, is sometimes present; fig. 110); wg 61-70. From Warbling Vireo by plumage and wing formula; from Red-eyed Vireo by shorter wg.

Molt—PB: HY partial (Jul-Aug), AHY complete (Jul-Aug); PA absent. PBs occur on the summer grounds.

Skull—Completes in HY/SY from 15 Oct thru Jan. Windows may be retained by some spring SYs.

Age—Rect shape seems unhelpful despite retention of juvenal tail. Juv (Jun-Aug) is generally drabber with a brownish wash to the plumage and more distinct wing bars. Otherwise, no reliable plumage criteria known.

Sex—♂ = ♀ by plumage. CP/BP (May-Aug); ♂ may develop a partial BP. Wg: ♂(n30) 63-70, ♀(n30) 61-67.

References—B, R, W, O; PRBO data.

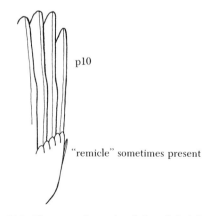

p10

"remicle" sometimes present

Figure 110. The wing formula of the Philadelphia Vireo.

RED-EYED VIREO
Vireo olivaceus

REVI
Band size: 1-0

Red-eyed Vireo (REVI)
Yellow-green Vireo (YGVI)

Species # 624.0
Species # 625.0

Species—Superciliary distinct, bordered on top by black (Red-eyed form); malar streak lacking; p10 full lengthed; wg 72-85; culmen 8.4-10.4. From Warbling Vireo by plumage and wing formula; from Philadelphia Vireo by longer wg; from Black-whiskered Vireo by plumage and shorter culmen.

Subspecies—Yellow-green Vireo is readily separated by green upperparts, yellower underparts and less distinct superciliary features.

Molt—PB: HY partial-incomplete (Jul-Sep), AHY incomplete-complete (Jul-Oct); PA: SY absent? ASY absent-incomplete (Feb-Apr). 1st PB occurs on the summer grounds and sometimes includes the terts. In some (possibly all) AHYs the PB appears to be suspended over migration, with some flight feathers not renewed until the PA. This should be further investigated.

Skull—Completes in HY/SY from 1 Oct thru Feb. Windows may be retained thru spring by some SYs.

Age—Rect shape seems unhelpful for ageing, despite retention of juvenal tail. Juv (May-Aug) has brownish tinged plumage, indistinct wing bars, and a brown iris. Ageing of some SYs thru spring, by brownish cast to the iris, may be possible with experience; compare with skull and shape and wear of flight feathers. Check also for contrasting new and old flight feathers on some AHYs during fall migration. Otherwise, no reliable plumage criteria known:

HY/SY (Aug-Feb): Iris brown to gray-brown.

AHY (Jan-Nov): Iris bright red.

Sex—♂ = ♀ by plumage. CP/BP (Apr-Aug); ♂ may develop a partial BP. Wg: ♂(n100) 75-85, ♀(n100) 73-81.

References—DVR,B,R,W,SK,O,BBM; Goodpasture (1963), Wood & Wood (1972), J. Baird *in* Lloyd-Evans (1983), Cannell *et al.* (1983); PRBO data.

BLACK-WHISKERED VIREO
Vireo altiloquus

BWVI
Species # 623.0
Band size: 1

Species—From Red-Eyed Vireo by the presence of indistinct malar streaks and a longer culmen: 10.7-12.3.

Molt—PB: HY partial (Jul-Aug), AHY complete (Jun-Aug); PA absent. PBs occur on the summer grounds. The timing and occurrence of molt in this species needs confirmation.

Skull—Completes in HY from 1 Oct thru Dec. Some SYs probably retain windows through spring.

Age/Sex—The same criteria apply as in Red-eyed Vireo. Wg: ♂(n20) 77-82, ♀(n16) 73-83.

References—B,O.

EMBERIZIDS   *EMBERIZIDAE*

One hundred and thirty species. A varied family, it is broken down into subfamilies in this guide.

Wood-Warblers   *Parulinae*

Fifty-two species. Subfamily characteristics include generally small size, delicate features, and slender bills. They have 9 primaries, 9 secondaries, and 12 rectrices. The first prebasic molt is generally partial but can be incomplete or complete in a few of the species, especially in southern populations. Plumages are generally bright, and vary considerably by species as to differentiation between the seasons and the age and sex classes. Different species show as many as nine different plumages, as few as one. Many species can be aged and sexed in both spring and fall, when all criteria are considered.

BACHMAN'S WARBLER   BMWA
Vermivora bachmanii   Species # 640.0
                                                   Band size: 0

Species—♀ ♀ separated from most warbler species by the presence of white or pale patches in the outer rects; from female Hooded Warbler by the presence of an eye ring, a grayer crown, and a shorter tail (41-48).

Molt—PB: HY partial (Jun-Aug), AHY complete (Jun-Aug); PA limited (Feb-Mar). PBs occur on the summer grounds.

Skull—Completes in HY from 1 Sep thru Nov.

Age/Sex—CP/BP (Mar-Jul). Wg: ♂(n19) 59-65, ♀(n7) 56-59. Juv (May-Jul) has brownish washed plumage and distinct, buffy wing bars; Juvs may be sexed by the amount of white in the rects (see below). With the following, some intermediates may not be reliably aged, especially in spring:

AHY/ASY ♂ (Jul-Jun): Black of breast extensive (reaching across breast), feathers with narrow yellow tipping; forecrown with distinct black patch; rects and outer pp truncate (fig. 112); white and gray in outer rects contrasting distinctly. [Spring SY and ASY ♂ ♂ (Mar-Jul) probably differ in the extent of black on the breast and forecrown but this needs further study; compare with the flight feather criteria.]

HY/SY ♂ (Jul-Jun): Black of breast restricted to center, feathers with broad yellow tipping and forecrown with little or no black (these plumage criteria reliable thru Mar; see AHY/ASY ♂); rects and outer pp tapered (fig. 112); outer rects with diffuse white patches, contrasting indistinctly with the gray.

AHY/ASY ♀ (Jul-Jun): Breast and forecrown without black feathering; rects and outer pp truncate (fig. 112); outer rect with diffuse white patches.

HY/SY ♀ (Jul-Jun): Like AHY/ASY ♀ but rects and outer pp tapered (fig. 112); outer rect usually with very indistinct pale spots.

References—B; Robbins (1964).

BLUE-WINGED WARBLER
Vermivora pinus

BWWA
Species # 641.0
Band size: 0

Molt—PB: HY partial (Jul-Aug), AHY complete (Jun-Aug); PA absent. PBs occur on the summer grounds.

Skull—Completes in HY from 1 Oct thru Nov.

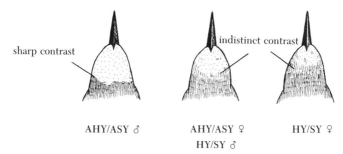

Figure 111. Typical head color patterns in Blue-winged Warblers by age and sex. The same basic pattern applies to the Prothonotary Warbler, as well.

Age/Sex—CP/BP (May-Aug). Wg useful for sexing: ♂(n30) 58-64, ♀(n30) 54-61. Juv (Jun-Jul) is like adults but drabber, lores and eye line less distinct, wing bars washed or tinged with yellow (♂ = ♀). The following should be used only in conjunction with other age/sex criteria, especially in fall, when feather tipping creates greener crowns in all age/sex classes:

AHY/ASY ♂ (Jul-Jun): Forehead and crown bright yellow, contrasting with darker green nape and back (fig. 111); eye line black; rects and outer pp truncate (fig. 112).

HY/SY ♂ (Jul-Jun): Forehead and crown moderately yellow, grading into green of nape and back (fig. 111); eye line dusky to dull blackish; rects and outer pp tapered (fig. 112).

AHY/ASY ♀ (Jul-Jun): like HY/SY ♂ but rects and outer pp truncate (fig. 112).

HY/SY ♀ (Jul-Jun): Forehead and crown greenish, sometimes with a diffuse patch of yellow (fig. 111); eye line dusky; rects and outer pp tapered (fig. 112).

References—B,R,W,O; Robbins (1964).

BLUE-WINGED X GOLDEN-WINGED WARBLER

Brewster's Warbler (BRWA)   Species # 641.2
Lawrence's Warbler (LAWA)   Species # 641.3

The information found in the accounts of Blue-winged and Golden-winged warblers should be carefully combined when ageing or sexing a hybrid between the two species. Generally, the most useful plumage criteria on hybrids are the amount of yellow in the crown (Brewster's and Lawrence's) and the coloration of the throat and auriculars (Lawrence's). The molt and flight feather related ageing criteria should all apply, as well. It should be kept in mind that intergrades can show any combination of characteristics between the two species, and that the ageing and sexing criteria should be weighted accordingly. For more information on these hybrids, see Parkes (1951) and Short (1963).

GOLDEN-WINGED WARBLER
Vermivora chrysoptera

GWWA
Species # 642.0
Band size: 0

Molt—PB: HY partial (Jul-Aug), AHY complete (Jul-Aug); PA absent. PBs occur on the summer grounds.

Skull—Completes in HY from 1 Oct thru Nov.

Age—Juv (Jun-Jul) has a strong olive wash to the upperparts and yellowish underparts ($\male = \female$; beware of hybrids, which might also have this plumage). In addition to the following, it is possible that some HY/SY $\male\male$ may be separated from some AHY/ASY $\male\male$ by having relatively less black in the throat and auriculars and less yellow in the mid covs. This should be further investigated. Some intermediates may be difficult to age with the following:

HY/SY (Jul-Jun): Rects and outer pp tapered (fig. 112).

AHY/ASY (Jul-Jun): Rects and outer pp truncate (fig. 112).

Sex—CP/BP (May-Jul). Wg $\male$(n30) 59-66, $\female$(n24) 56-64.

$\male$: Throat and cheeks black (tipped gray in fall), contrasting markedly with adjoining white; crown relatively bright yellow; gr covs with bright yellow margins to outer webs.

$\female$: Throat and cheeks dusky, not showing marked contrast with adjoining white; crown yellow, suffused with green; gr covs with greenish-yellow margins on outer webs.

References—B,R,W,O; Robbins (1964).

TENNESSEE WARBLER
Vermivora peregrina

TEWA
Species # 647.0
Band size: 0

Species—From Orange-crowned Warbler by upperparts green, undertail covs white, short tail (39-46), and longest pp—longest ss $\geq$ 15. [Old World warblers (*Phylloscopus*), potential vagrants to N.A. which resemble this species, can always be identified by the presence of a reduced p10, which the wood-warblers lack. See Svensson (1984).]

Molt—PB: HY partial (Jul-Aug), AHY complete (Jul-Aug); PA limited (Jan-Apr). PBs occur primarily on the summer grounds although AHY may sometimes suspend flight feather molt over migration.

Skull—Completes in HY from 1 Oct thru Nov.

Age—Juv (Jun-Jul) has distinct yellow wing bars ($\male = \female$). The following can be subtle and should always be combined with all other age/sex criteria. Also, see Sex for some plumage related indicators:

HY/SY (Aug-Jul): Rects and outer pp tapered (fig. 112).

AHY/ASY (Aug-Jul): Rects and outer pp truncate (fig. 112)

Sex—CP/BP (May-Aug). Wg useful: ♂(n100) 62-68, ♀(n100) 58-64. The following is reliable with alternate-plumaged birds only and should be combined with wg and age criteria, especially on intermediates (probably HY/SY ♂ ♂ or AHY/ASY ♀ ♀):

Alternate Plumage

AHY ♂ (Mar-Jul): Crown pale bluish-gray; auriculars and superciliary grayish-white; upperparts green; underparts mostly white with small amounts of yellowish wash, confined mostly to the sides.

AHY ♀ (Mar-Jul): Crown grayish washed with olive; auriculars and superciliary washed yellow or greenish; upperparts olive-green; underparts white with moderate to extensive yellow wash, especially on upper breast.

Basic Plumage

In basic plumage (Jul-Mar) ♂ ♂ (especially AHY/ASY) tend to have a more distinct superciliary and eye line, and whiter (as opposed to yellower) underparts than ♀ ♀ (especially HY/SY), but considerable overlap occurs. With experience and by combining this with wg and age criteria, some individuals may be reliably sexed.

References—DVR,B,R,W,SK,O; Goodpasture (1963), Robbins (1964), Raveling (1965), Raveling & Warner (1965), Baird (1967), Sealey (1985); PRBO data.

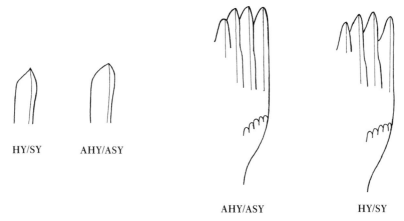

HY/SY   AHY/ASY

AHY/ASY   HY/SY

Figure 112. Rectrix and outer primary shape by age in the *Vermivora* warblers.

ORANGE-CROWNED WARBLER
Vermivora celata

OCWA
Species # 646.0
Band size: 0

Species—From Tennessee Warbler by upperparts olive to yellowish, undertail covs yellow, longer tail (45-54), and longest pp—longest ss ≤ 15.

Molt—PB: HY partial-incomplete (Jun-Sep), AHY complete (Jul-Sep); PA absent-limited (Feb-May). PBs occur primarily on the summer grounds. 1st PB occasionally includes some terts or ss and/or some (rarely all) rects.

Skull—Completes in HY from 1 Oct (as early as 15 Aug in California populations) thru Nov.

Age—Juv (Apr-Aug) has a brownish or grayish wash to the upperparts and relatively distinct buffy-yellow wing bars (♂ = ♀).

HY/SY (Aug-Jul): Rects and outer pp tapered (fig. 112), often tinged brownish, relatively worn, especially in spring. [Occasional HY/SYs may have some or all rects truncate; see molt.]

AHY/ASY (Aug-Jul): Rects and outer pp truncate (fig. 112), glossier green, relatively unworn.

In western races, no additional plumage criteria are known following the 1st PB except, perhaps, the amount of orange in the crown with known sexed birds (see Sex). In the eastern race (*V. c. celata*) the following is helpful in basic-plumaged birds but should be used in conjunction with other ageing criteria and sex:

HY/SY (Sep-Feb): Crown and nape grayish, contrasting with greenish back; throat grayish-white; eye ring and superciliary whitish; streaking on breast relatively indistinct.

AHY/ASY (Sep-Feb): Crown and nape greenish, uniform in coloration with rest of upperparts; throat, eye ring, and superciliary yellowish; streaking on breast relatively distinct.

Sex—CP/BP (Mar-Aug). Wg ♂ (n45) 55-66, ♀(n37) 51-61; E > W; for the Pacfic race (*V. c. lutescens*): ♂(n30) 55-61, ♀(n30) 51-57. The following has been found reliable in *lutescens* after the 1st PA and is probably so in the other races as well:

AHY ♂: Length of concealed crown patch ≥ 14.

AHY ♀: Length of concealed crown patch ≤ 5.

AHY birds with crown patch 6-13 are not reliably sexed by plumage alone but compare with age; SY birds are probably ♂♂ and ASY birds, ♀♀. Also, a small percentage of known, basic-plumaged HY/SY (Aug-Feb) ♂ *lutescens* have at least a small amount of orange in the crown and are reliably sexed. HY/SYs (Aug-Mar) without orange should not be sexed.

References—B,R,W,O,C,BBM; Robbins (1964), Foster (1967a, 1967b), Bohlen & Kleen (1976); PRBO data.

NASHVILLE WARBLER
Vermivora ruficapilla

NAWA
Species # 645.0
Band size: 0

Species—Extremely dull ♀♀ separated from HY/SY ♂ Virginia's Warbler by at least a slight yellowish wash to the throat and flanks, not contrasting sharply with the yellow of the breast.

Molt—PB: HY partial (Jul-Sep), AHY complete (Jul-Sep); PA limited-partial (Feb-Apr). PBs occur on the summer grounds.

Skull—Completes in HY from 1 Oct thru Dec.

Age/Sex—CP/BP (Apr-Aug). Wg useful: ♂(n30) 58-66, ♀(n30) 53-61. Juv (May-Aug) has browner upperparts, buffier underparts, and relatively distinct wing bars (♂ = ♀). Some birds (especially in alternate plumage) may be difficult to age with the following:

Basic Plumage

AHY/ASY ♂ (Aug-Mar): Crown patch dark rufous, well defined, 9-16 mm (obscured by feather tipping in fall); crown ashy gray, contrasting markedly with brightish green back; underparts, especially chin and throat, bright yellow; rects and outer pp truncate (fig. 112).

HY/SY ♂ (Aug-Mar): As AHY/ASY ♂ but plumage generally duller and browner; crown patch dark rufous and usually well defined but 2-12 mm; underparts moderately yellow, paler on chin and throat; rects and outer pp tapered (fig. 112).

AHY/ASY ♀ (Aug-Mar): As HY/SY ♂ (Aug-Mar) but crown with an indistinctly defined patch, usually containing one to a few pale rufous feathers measuring 0-10 mm; rects and outer pp truncate (fig. 112).

HY/SY ♀ (Aug-Mar): Crown usually with no rufous, grayish-olive, not contrasting markedly with brownish-olive back; underparts pale buffy yellow; chin and throat whitish; rects and outer pp tapered (fig. 112).

Alternate Plumage

ASY ♂ (Mar-Jul): Plumage generally bright; crown patch dark rufous, well defined, 9-16 mm; crown ashy gray, contrasting markedly with brightish green back; underparts, especially chin and throat, bright yellow; rects and outer pp truncate (fig. 112).

SY ♂ (Mar-Aug): As ASY ♂ but rects and outer pp tapered (fig. 112). [HY/SY ♂♂ also average slightly duller in plumage than AHY/ASY ♂♂, but this is not reliable for ageing.]

ASY ♀ (Mar-Jul): Plumage relatively dull; crown with an indistinctly defined patch, usually containing one to a few pale rufous feathers measuring 0-10 mm; rects and outer pp truncate (fig. 112).

SY ♀ (Mar-Aug): As ASY ♀ but rects and outer pp tapered (fig. 112).

References—B,R,W,O; Robbins (1964); PRBO data.

VIRGINIA'S WARBLER
Vermivora virginiae

VIWA
Species # 644.0
Band size: 0

Species—From Colima Warbler by the relative lack of brown in the plumage, especially the flanks; the presence of yellow on the breast of most birds; and by smaller tail (45-51) and exp. culmen (8.9-10.9). HY/SY ♂ from dull ♀ Nashville Warblers by the lack of yellow in the throat or flanks, this contrasting markedly with the yellow breast.

Molt—PB: HY partial (Jul-Aug), AHY complete (Jul-Aug); PA limited-partial (Feb-May). PBs occur on the summer grounds.

Skull—Completes in HY from 15 Oct thru Dec.

Age/Sex—CP/BP (May-Aug). Wg: ♂(n30) 58-67, ♀(n30) 54-63. Juv (Jun-Jul) has brownish washed plumage, lacks rufous in crown and yellow on breast, and has distinct buffy wing bars (♂ = ♀). With the following, alternate-plumaged birds become increasingly difficult to age due to wear of the flight feathers. Many May-Aug birds may be impossible to age reliably:

Basic Plumage

AHY/ASY ♂ (Aug-Mar): Crown patch deep rufous, 8-13 mm, rufous of individual feathers usually measuring > 5 mm from bases (fig. 113); yellow patch on underparts extensive, spanning width of breast; rects and outer pp truncate (fig. 112).

HY/SY ♂ (Aug-Mar): Crown patch rufous to deep rufous, 6-10 mm (often scattered individual feathers), rufous of individual feathers usually measuring < 5 mm from base (fig. 113); yellow patch on breast reduced, usually confined to center of breast; rects and outer pp tapered (fig. 112).

AHY/ASY ♂   HY/SY ♂

Figure 113. Crown feathers in ♂ Virginia's Warblers, by age.

AHY/ASY ♀ (Aug-Mar): Like HY/SY ♂ but crown patch variable, pale orange in coloration, 2-10 mm; rects and outer pp truncate (fig. 112).

HY/SY ♀ (Aug-Mar): Crown patch absent or reduced to one or two feathers (0-4 mm), pale orangeish; yellow on breast reduced to small patch on center of breast, or lacking; rects and outer pp tapered (fig. 112).

Alternate Plumage

ASY ♂ (Mar-Jul): Crown patch deep rufous, 8-13 mm; yellow patch on underparts extensive, spanning width of breast; rects and outer pp truncate (fig. 112).

SY ♂ (Mar-Aug): Like ASY ♂ but rects and outer pp tapered (fig. 112). [SY ♂ ♂ probably also average slightly duller overall than ASY ♂ ♂.]

ASY ♀ (Mar-Jul): Crown patch variable, pale orange in coloration, 2-10 mm; yellow of breast reduced, confined to center; rects and outer pp truncate (fig. 112).

SY ♀ (Mar-Aug): Like ASY ♀ but rects and outer pp tapered (fig. 112).

References—B,O; PRBO data.

COLIMA WARBLER
Vermivora crissalis

CLWA
Species # 647.1
Band size: 1

Species—Upperparts grayish-brown; flanks strongly washed brown; breast with little or no yellow; tail 51-58, exp culmen 10.7-11.9. Plumage and larger measurements should separate this from Virginia's Warbler.

Molt—PB: HY partial (Jul-Aug), AHY complete (Jun-Aug); PA limited (Feb-Apr). PBs occur on the summer grounds. The timing and extent of all molts need confirmation.

Skull—Completes in HY from 1 Oct thru Nov.

Age/Sex—CP/BP (Apr-Aug). Wg: ♂(n11) 62-68, ♀(n9) 57-65. Rect and pp shape (fig. 112) probably useful for ageing, as with other *Vermivora* warblers. Juv (Jun-Jul) is drab with two buffy wing bars present (♂ = ♀). Otherwise, no reliable plumage criteria are known for this species although relative size and color of crown patch is probably useful, as in Virginia's Warbler.

References—B,O; Bangs (1925).

LUCY'S WARBLER
Vermivora luciae

LUWA
Species # 643.0
Band size: 0

Molt—PB: HY partial (Jul-Aug), AHY complete (Jul-Aug); PA absent. PBs occur on the summer grounds. A limited PA may occur in some individuals.

Skull—Completes in HY from 1 Sep thru Nov.

Age—Because of extensive wearing, rect and pp shape (fig. 112) seem not as useful as in other *Vermivora*, at least in spring. Look for significantly more faded flight feathers on HY/SYs, however. Juv (May-Jul) lacks the crown patch entirely, is generally pale, and has relatively distinct, buffy-white wing bars (♂ = ♀). Otherwise, no reliable plumage criteria known although HY/SYs have a heavier yellow wash, on the average, than AHY/ASYs. The extent of the crown patch may also be of limited use, when combined with sex and flight feather condition.

Sex—CP/BP (Apr-Aug). Wg useful: ♂(n30) 55-61, ♀ (n30) 49-56. In addition, the following plumage criteria, although subtle, seem reliable for sexing. Some overlap occurs (probably only between HY/SY ♂♂ and AHY/ASY ♀♀); compare with age criteria and wg:

♂: Crown patch well defined, deep rufous, 9-13 mm; rump deep rufous.

♀: Crown patch lacking or relatively diffuse, pale rufous washed orange, 0-10 mm; rump rufous with orangish tinge.

References—B,O.

NORTHERN PARULA
Parula americana

NOPA
Species # 648.0
Band size: 0

Molt—PB: HY partial (Jul-Aug), AHY complete (Jul-Aug); PA limited (Feb-Apr). PBs occur on the summer grounds.

Skull—Completes in HY from 1 Oct (as early as 15 Sep in SE populations) thru Nov.

Age—Juv (May-Jul) as adult ♀ but relatively pale all over, underparts with yellow confined to throat, flanks washed gray (♂ = ♀). The following is reliable with most birds but may become difficult, especially with ♀♀ in spring/summer; see also Sex for further plumage indications:

  HY/SY (Aug-Jul): Alula brownish, edged greenish or grayish; pp covs pale brownish, contrasting in coloration with darker and blacker centers to gr and mid covs; flight feathers edged greenish; rects and outer pp tapered (fig. 112).

  AHY/ASY (Aug-Jul): Alula black with blue edging; pp covs black, more uniform in coloration with centers of gr and mid covs; flight feathers edged blue; rects and outer pp truncate (fig. 112).

Sex—CP/BP (Mar-Aug). Wg: ♂(n30) 54-65, ♀(n30) 51-60:

  ♂: Tawny and slate breast bands distinct or (in some HY/SYs) breast with a wide tawny band and little or no black.

  ♀: Breast usually uniformly yellow, without slate, sometimes with a slight tawny wash (AHY/ASYs).

References—B,R,W,O,SK,BBM; Robbins (1964); PRBO data.

TROPICAL PARULA
Parula pitiayumi

TRPA
Species # 649.0
Band size: 0

Molt—PB: HY partial (Jul-Aug), AHY complete (Jul-Aug); PA partial (Feb-Apr). PBs occur on the summer grounds.

Skull—Completes in HY from 15 Sep thru Nov.

Age—The ageing criteria for Northern Parula (which see) is applicable to this species as well. In addition, ♂♂ with complete black lores and cheek patches can be aged AHY/ASY thru Feb (see Sex).

Sex—CP/BP (Apr-Aug). Wg: ♂(n12) 50-55, ♀(n6) 46-50 (Texas populations). The following is reliable with AHY/ASY birds only. HY/SY birds (thru the 1st PA) are not reliably sexed by plumage, except possibly some ♂♂ that may develop partially adult plumage during the 1st PB (compare with wg). This should be further investigated:

AHY/ASY ♂: Cheeks black; breast with a strong tawny band.

AHY/ASY ♀: Cheeks blue; breast with little or no tawny.

References—B,O.

Ageing and Sexing *Dendroica* Warblers

Ageing and sexing *Dendroica* warblers is generally complicated by much plumage overlap between the age/sex classes and the fact that most species change plumage at the prealternate molt. By combining plumage and skull with flight feather condition, wing covert contrasts, and the amount of white in the 4th rectrix (r4 or 3rd from the outside), however, many individuals of this genus should be reliably aged and sexed in both basic and alternate plumages.

Fig. 114 illustrates typical differences in the shape and the amount of wear of the rectrices in both spring and fall. With experience, the shape of the outer primaries is probably also of use, as in *Vermivora* warblers (fig. 112), and both these and the rectrices will appear browner in HY/SY birds and blacker in AHY/ASYs. Only in a few species (e.g. Yellow-rumped, Palm, and Cerulean warblers) do shape of the rectricies appear difficult to use for ageing.

In many species, the primary coverts are browner, with pale brownish edging in HY/SYs and blacker, with grayer edging in AHY/ASYs. In HY/SYs, these retained coverts will often contrast markedly in color and wear with the centers of molted lesser, middle, and greater coverts, providing a good indicator of age. This contrast may be more apparent in spring, when the juvenal primary coverts have become more abraded, but is probably of use in fall, as well. In some species, however, the secondary coverts may be replaced during the prealternate molt by both SY and ASY birds, creating a contrast in both age classes. On these, the color alone of the primary coverts will have to be relied on to a greater extent. Careful examination of the covert contrast is encouraged in both fall and spring, so that the usefulness and timing of this criteria and the extent of the prealternate molts in SY and ASY birds can be better understood. [In the species accounts, note that the contrast refers to the color of the centers of the coverts, disregarding the presence of wing bars or paler edging.]

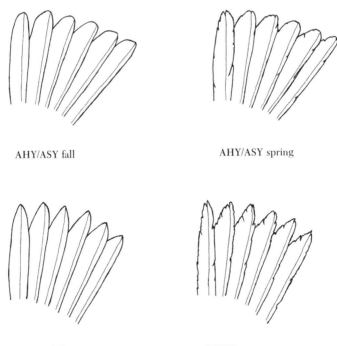

AHY/ASY fall   AHY/ASY spring

HY/SY fall   HY/SY spring

Figure 114. Typical shapes, and amounts of abrasion, in *Dendroica* warblers (and other passerines) by age and season.

The amount of white in the 4th rectrix (2nd in Magnolia Warbler) will provide a final clue for both ageing and sexing most *Dendroica*. Generally, AHY/ASY ♂♂ have a significantly larger spot than both HY/SY ♂♂ and AHY/ASY ♀♀, which in turn, have a larger spot than HY/SY ♀♀. The usefulness of the size of this spot for ageing varies from species to species and in certain species (e.g. Chestnut-sided, Bay-breasted, and Blackpoll warblers) it seems a nearly useless criterion. In all species, there is also significant individual variation within each age/sex class. As a rule, the size of the spot should not be relied upon alone. When combined with other age/sex criteria, however, it can be quite useful. In the fall, for instance, when skull condition can provide the age, the amount of white in the 4th rectrix should assist with sexing. In the spring, most *Dendroica* warblers are readily sexed by plumage, during which time the 4th rectrix criterion can help with ageing. As with the covert contrasts, a better understanding of how the amount of white varies with age and sex is needed—a good statistical analysis project for banders.

The criteria presented in the species accounts should coincide with each other in most cases. Individuals will be found with conflicting characteristics, however, and these are best left unaged and/or unsexed, especially without experience with the species.

YELLOW WARBLER
Dendroica petechia

YEWA
Species # 652.0
Band size: 0

Species—From all similar warblers by the presence of yellow in the outer rects.

Molt—PB: HY partial (Jun-Aug), AHY complete (Jun-Aug); PA partial-incomplete (Feb-Apr). PBs occur primarily on the summer grounds; some AHYs possibly suspend flight feather molt over fall migration. PAs sometimes include the terts and may or may not include gr covs.

Skull—Completes in HY from 15 Oct (as early as 15 Sep in California populations) thru Dec.

Age/Sex—CP/BP (Apr-Aug). Wg: ♂(n100) 58-72, ♀(n100) 55-65. Juv (May-Aug) is brownish and obscurely streaked above, and has distinct buffy wing bars (♂ = ♀ but some ♂♂ may be distinguished by the amount of yellow in rects; fig. 115). Intermediates between the following, and birds showing conflicting characteristics will occur which are not reliably aged and/or sexed; rect shape criteria, especially, can be subtle. Also, the usefulness of wing covert contrast in spring seems good but needs confirmation:

Basic Plumage

AHY/ASY ♂ (Aug-Mar): Crown and nape bright yellow washed moderately with green; underparts brightish yellow with moderately distinct red streaking on breast and flanks; flight feathers and pp covs brightish yellow; rects truncate (fig. 114); outer rects with substantial yellow contrasting with dark brown (fig. 115).

HY/SY ♂ (Aug-Mar): Crown and nape dull to moderately bright yellow, washed heavily with greenish; underparts pale to brightish yellow often with a few (but sometimes no) very indistinct reddish streaks on the upperbreast; flight feathers and pp covs dull yellow; rects tapered (fig. 114); outer rects dull brown with a variable amount of yellow (fig. 115). [These can overlap in plumage with HY/SY ♀ (check wg); known HY/SYs in this plumage with streaks are reliably sexed ♂.]

AHY/ASY ♀ (Aug-Mar): Like HY/SY ♂ in plumage but flight feathers and pp covs brightish yellow; rects truncate (fig. 114); outer rects darkish brown, usually with substantial yellow (fig. 115). [Known AHY/ASYs in this plumage without streaks are reliably sexed ♀.]

HY/SY ♀ (Aug-Mar): Upperparts dull greenish-yellow or grayish-yellow; underparts pale yellow without reddish streaks; flight feathers and pp covs dull yellow; rects tapered (fig. 114); outer rects dull brown usually with relatively little yellow (fig 115). [Birds in this plumage are probably not reliably sexed, except in comparison with wg; see HY/SY ♂.]

Alternate Plumage

ASY ♂ (Mar-Aug): Crown and nape bright yellow, contrasting in coloration with greener back; red streaking of breast and flanks distinct and wide; flight feathers and pp covs brightish yellow, fairly uniform in coloration with gr covs; rects truncate (fig. 114); outer rects darkish brown with substantial yellow (fig. 115).

SY ♂ (Mar-Aug): Like ASY ♂ but flight feathers and pp covs dull or brownish-yellow, often contrasting with brighter gr covs; rects tapered (fig. 114); outer rects dull brown with a variable amount of yellow (fig. 115).

ASY ♀ (Mar-Aug): Crown and nape yellow washed greenish, not showing a marked contrast with back coloration; red streaking of underparts narrow and indistinct; flight feathers and wing covs as ASY ♂; rects truncate (fig. 114); outer rects darkish brown, usually with substantial yellow (fig. 115).

SY ♀ (Mar-Aug): Like ASY ♀ but reddish streaks sometimes lacking; flight feathers and pp covs dull or brownish-yellow, contrasting with brighter gr covs; rects tapered (fig. 114); outer rects dull brown usually with relatively little yellow (fig. 115).

References—DVR,B,R,W,SK,O,BBM; Southern (1961), Robbins (1964), Stewart (1972a), Raveling & Warner (1978), Yunick (1984); PRBO data.

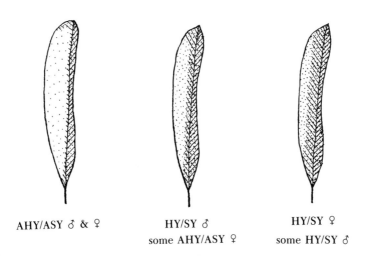

AHY/ASY ♂ & ♀   HY/SY ♂   HY/SY ♀
                       some AHY/ASY ♀   some HY/SY ♂

Figure 115. Typical outer rectrix patterns in Yellow Warblers, by age and sex.

CHESTNUT-SIDED WARBLER
Dendroica pensylvanica

CSWA
Species # 659.0
Band size: 0

Molt—PB: HY partial (Jun-Aug), AHY complete (Jun-Aug); PA partial (Feb-Apr). PBs occur on the summer grounds. The PA may or may not include the gr covs.

Skull—Completes in HY from 15 Oct thru Dec.

Age/Sex—CP/BP (May-Aug). Wg useful: ♂(n30) 60-68, ♀(n30) 57-64. Juv (Jun-Jul) has brownish-olive upperparts, buffy yellow wing bars, and dull white underparts (♂ = ♀). The amount of white in the 4th rect is not as useful as in other *Dendroica* but may show some age/sex related variation, and the covert contrast criteria in spring seems useful but needs confirmation. Intermediates between the following (especially between HY/SY ♂ and ♀ in basic plumage) and birds showing conflicting characteristics will occur which are not reliably aged and/or sexed:

Basic Plumage

AHY/ASY ♂ (Aug-Mar): Chestnut on flanks distinct, relatively extensive; wing bars whitish; uppertail covs with bold black centers (fig. 116); flight feathers and pp covs black; rects truncate (fig. 114).

HY/SY ♂ (Aug-Mar): Chestnut on flanks indistinct and limited, if present at all; wing bars yellowish; uppertail covs with indistinct to distinct but relatively narrow blackish centers (fig. 116); flight feathers and pp covs dull black; rects tapered (fig. 114). [Many of these may not be safely distinguished from HY/SY ♀ ♀, however known HY/SYs with any chestnut on flanks can reliably be sexed ♂.]

AHY/ASY ♀ (Aug-Mar): Like HY/SY ♂ but wing bars white or with a slight yellow wash; flight feathers and pp covs blackish; rects truncate (fig. 114). [Known AHY/ASYs with very little or no chestnut present on the flanks are safely sexed ♀.]

HY/SY ♀ (Aug-Mar): No chestnut present on flanks; wing bars yellowish; uppertail covs with indistinct dusky streaks (fig. 116); flight feathers and pp covs brownish-black; rects tapered (fig. 114). [Most of these are probably not reliably sexed, except in combination with short wg.]

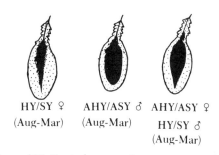

HY/SY ♀   AHY/ASY ♂   AHY/ASY ♀
(Aug-Mar)   (Aug-Mar)   HY/SY ♂
                                          (Aug-Mar)

Figure 116. Typical uppertail covert patterns by age and sex in basic-plumaged Chestnut-sided Warblers.

Alternate Plumage

ASY ♂ (Mar-Aug): Crown bright yellow, without streaking, contrasting with blackish nape; lores and moustache deep black, distinct; chestnut on sides relatively bold and extensive, usually extending beyond the base of the legs; flight feathers and wing covs fairly uniformly blackish; rects truncate (fig. 114).

SY ♂ (Mar-Aug): Like ASY ♂ but plumage averages duller; flight feathers and pp covs brownish-black, often contrasting with blacker gr covs; rects tapered (fig. 114). [Some overlap may occur between these and ASY ♀♀; use all criteria to separate.]

ASY ♀ (Mar-Aug): Crown greenish-yellow, often with some black streaking, not contrasting with greenish nape; lores and moustache dull black; chestnut on sides relatively indistinct and restricted, usually not reaching base of legs; flight feathers and wing covs fairly uniformly blackish; rects truncate (fig.114).

SY ♀ (Mar-Aug): Like ASY ♀ but plumage averages duller; lores and moustache relatively indistinct; flight feathers and pp covs brownish, often contrasting with blacker gr covs; rects tapered (fig. 114).

References—B,R,W,SK,O; Robbins (1964); PRBO data.

MAGNOLIA WARBLER

Dendroica magnolia

MAWA
Species # 657.0
Band size: 0

Molt—PB: HY partial (Jul-Aug), AHY complete (Jul-Aug); PA partial-incomplete (Feb-Apr). PBs occur on the summer grounds. PAs sometimes include some terts and may or may not include the gr covs.

Skull—Completes in HY from 15 Oct thru Dec.

Age/Sex—CP/BP (May-Aug). Wg: ♂(n30) 57-64, ♀(n30) 54-60. Juv (Jun-Aug) has brownish washed plumage, buffy wing bars, and no streaking on the undersides (sexing sometimes possible by the amount of white on r2; fig. 118). Intermediates between the following or birds with conflicting characteristics will occur that are not reliably aged and/or sexed:

Basic Plumage

AHY/ASY ♂ (Aug-Mar): Back feathers with large and distinct black centers (fig. 117); streaks on flanks wide and distinct; flight feathers and pp covs black; rects truncate (fig. 114); whitepatch on r2 relatively large (fig. 118).

AHY/ASY ♀ (Aug-Mar): Back feathers with small but distinct black centers (fig. 117); streaks on flanks narrow, moderately indistinct; flight feathers and pp covs blackish; rects truncate (fig. 114); white patch on r2 moderate in size (fig. 118).

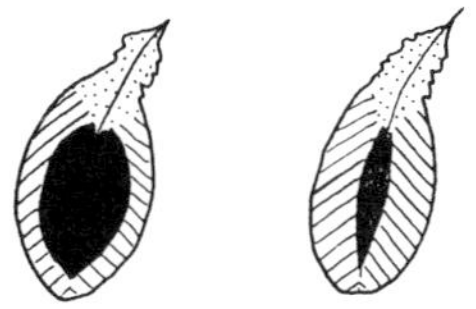

AHY/ASY ♂   AHY/ASY ♀

(Aug-Mar)

HY/SY (Aug-Mar): Back feathers with (or without) indistinct, dusky centers; streaks on flanks indistinct; flight

Figure 117. Typical back feather patterns in basic-plumaged Magnolia Warblers, by age and sex.

feathers and pp covs dull black; rects tapered (fig. 114); white patch on r2 relatively small (fig. 118). [♂♂ may average slightly brighter plumage than ♀♀ and have slightly larger white patches on r2 but HY/SYs are generally not reliably sexed except, perhaps, by wg.]

Alternate Plumage

AHY/ASY ♂ (Mar-Aug): Crown bluish-gray; upperback black; lores and auriculars black; streaking on underparts wide and distinct; flight feathers and wing covs uniformly blackish; rects truncate (fig. 114); white patch on r2 relatively large (fig. 118).

SY ♂ (Mar-Aug): Like ASY ♂ but plumage averages duller; upperback feathers sometimes edged greenish; flight feathers and pp covs brownish-black, often contrasting with blacker gr covs; rects tapered (fig. 114); white patch on r2 smaller (fig. 118).

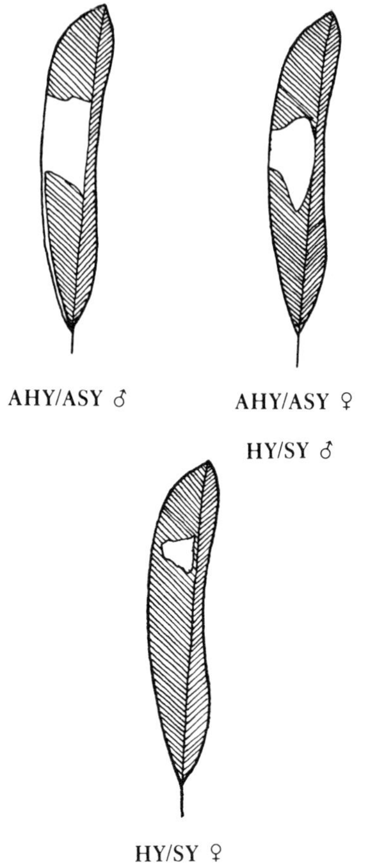

ASY ♀ (Mar-Aug): Crown grayish to greenish-gray; upperback greenish, feathers with small black centers; lores and auriculars grayish or blackish; streaking on underparts narrow, relatively indistinct; flight feathers and wing covs fairly uniformly blackish; rects truncate (fig. 114); white patch on r2 moderately sized (fig. 118).

SY ♀ (Mar-Aug): Like ASY ♀ but plumage averages duller; flight feathers and pp covs brownish, often contrasting with blacker gr covs; rects tapered (fig. 114); white on r2 relatively small (fig. 118).

AHY/ASY ♂   AHY/ASY ♀

HY/SY ♂

HY/SY ♀

Figure 118. Typical patterns in the fourth rectrices of Magnolia Warblers, by age and sex.

References—DVR,B,R,W,SK,O; Goodpasture (1963), Robbins (1964).

CAPE MAY WARBLER
Dendroica tigrina

CMWA
Species # 650.0
Band size: 0

Species—HY/SY ♀ from HY/SY Yellow-rumped Warbler by generally greener tones to the plumage, less distinct yellow rump patch, some yellow present in auriculars, and shorter tail: 43-50.

Molt—HY partial (Jul-Aug), AHY complete (Jul-Aug); PA partial (Feb-Apr). PBs occur on the summer grounds.

Skull—Completes in HY from 15 Oct thru Dec.

Age/Sex—CP/BP (May-Aug). Wg: ♂(n30) 63-72, ♀(n30) 61-70. Juv (Jun-Aug) has upperparts brown tinged olive; and underparts grayish, mottled, and with dusky streaking (sexing sometimes possible by the amount of white in r4; fig. 120). Intermediates and birds showing conflicting characteristics between the following may occur that are not reliably aged; birds are readily sexed in all plumages by the gr and mid covs (fig. 119):

Basic Plumage

AHY/ASY ♂ (Aug-Mar): Auriculars with at least some chestnut; gr and mid covs with broad and distinct white edging (fig. 119); flight feathers and pp covs black; rects truncate (fig. 114); white patch on r4 relatively large (fig. 120).

HY/SY ♂ (Aug-Mar): Auriculars usually without chestnut; gr and mid covs with indistinct white edging (fig. 119); flight feathers and pp covs dull black; rects tapered (fig. 114); white patch on r4 relatively small (fig. 120).

AHY/ASY ♀ (Aug-Mar): Upperparts and underparts washed brownish; auriculars washed yellow; gr and mid covs with narrow whitish edging (fig. 119); flight feathers and pp covs blackish; rects truncate (fig. 114); white patch on r4 small or lacking (fig. 120).

HY/SY ♀ (Aug-Mar): Upperparts and underparts washed grayish; auriculars grayish with little or no yellow; gr and mid covs with narrow pale edging (fig. 119); flight feathers and pp covs brownish-black; rects tapered (fig. 114); r4 usually without white (fig. 120).

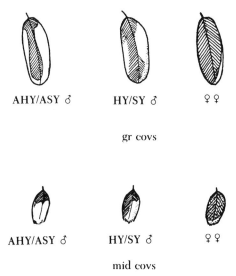

AHY/ASY ♂   HY/SY ♂   ♀♀

gr covs

AHY/ASY ♂   HY/SY ♂   ♀♀

mid covs

Figure 119. Patterns of white in the greater and middle coverts of ♂ (by age) and ♀ Cape May Warblers.

Alternate Plumage

ASY ♂ (Mar-Aug): Cap heavily streaked black; chestnut auricular patch extensive, without yellow suffusion; gr covs with broad and distinct white edging (fig. 119); flight feathers and pp covs blackish; rects truncate (fig. 114); white patch on r4 relatively large (fig. 120).

SY ♂ (Mar-Aug): Cap grayish-green, moderately streaked black; chestnut auricular patch restricted, suffused with yellow; gr covs with indistinct or distinct white edging (fig. 119); flight feathers and pp covs brownish-black; rects tapered (fig. 114); white patch on r4 relatively small (fig. 120). [Some SYs may replace some or all gr covs during the 1st PA, which will show distinct patterns as in ASY.]

ASY ♀ (Mar-Aug): Auriculars yellowish, without chestnut; gr and mid covs without broad white edging (fig. 119); flight feathers and wing covs fairly uniformly blackish; rects truncate (fig. 114); white patch on r4 restricted or lacking (fig. 120).

SY ♀ (Mar-Aug): Like ASY ♀ but flight feathers and pp covs brownish, often contrasting with blacker gr covs; rects tapered (fig. 114); r4 usually without white (fig. 120).

Refernces—B,R,W,SK,O; Robbins (1964).

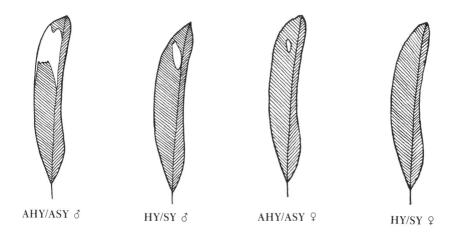

AHY/ASY ♂   HY/SY ♂   AHY/ASY ♀   HY/SY ♀

Figure 120. Typical patterns in the fourth rectrices of Cape May Warblers, by age and sex.

BLACK-THROATED BLUE WARBLER
Dendroica caerulescens

BTWA
Species # 654.0
Band size: 0

Molt—PB: HY partial (Jul-Sep), AHY complete (Jul-Aug); PA limited (Feb-Apr). PBs occur on the summer grounds.

Skull—Completes in HY from 15 Oct thru Dec.

Sex—CP/BP (Apr-Aug). Wg useful: ♂(n30) 62-68, ♀(n30) 57-63. The following is useful on all birds except Juvs:

♂: Upperparts blue; throat black; underparts white.

♀: Upperparts olive; underparts yellowish-olive.

Age—Juv (Jun-Aug) is like ♀ (above) but plumage heavily washed with brownish. Sexing possible by the amount of white in the rects (fig. 121) and pp; see below and also see wg:

AHY/ASY ♂ (Aug-Jul): Upperparts blue, feathers without green; alula and wing covs uniformly blackish with blue edging; white at base of pp extends 9-14 mm from pp covs (closed wing); rects truncate (fig. 114), white on outer rect relatively distinct (more so than in fig. 121).

HY/SY ♂ (Aug-Jul): Upperpart feathers blue with green tipping; alula and pp covs brownish edged green, often contrasting with blacker and blue-edged ss covs; flight feathers brownish-black; white at base of pp entends 5-10 mm from pp covs; rects tapered (fig. 114), white of outer rect less distinct (fig. 121).

AHY/ASY ♀ (Aug-Jul): Alula, pp covs and ss covs uniformly greenish in coloration and wear; flight feathers green; white at base of pp distinct, extending 4-8 mm from pp covs; rects tapered (fig. 114); white of outer rect as with HY/SY ♂ (see fig 121).

HY/SY ♀ (Aug-Jul): Alula and pp covs washed dusky, contrasting in coloration with greener ss covs; flight feathers dull green washed brownish; white at base of pp extends 0-5 mm from pp covs; rects tapered (fig. 114), pale patch of outer rect very indistinct or lacking (fig. 121).

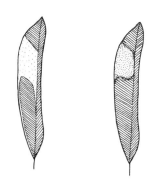

Juv-HY/SY ♂   Juv-HY/SY ♀

Figure 121. Pattern of white in the outer rectrices of ♂ and ♀ Black-throated Blue Warblers for sexing juvenals. Note also that adult birds of both sexes will have larger and more distinct patches than these, which are retained until the second prebasic molt (2nd August).

References—B,R,W,SK,O,BBM; Robbins (1964), Parkes (1979); PRBO data.

YELLOW-RUMPED WARBLER

YRWA

Dendroica coronata

Band size: 0

Myrtle Warbler (MYWA)

Species # 655.0

Audubon's Warbler (AUWA)

Species # 656.0

Species—HY from HY ♀ Cape May Warbler by lack of olive in the plumage, a more distinct yellow rump patch, lack of yellow in the auriculars, and longer tail: 50-64.

Subspecies—Myrtle and Audubon's Warblers can almost always be separated when a combination of criteria are considered. Intergrades occur, however, showing any and all combinations of the following characteristics. Combine with ageing and sexing criteria:

Myrtle Warbler: Throat white or buffy-white, never showing yellow; auriculars blackish or dusky, contrasting with paler nape and crown; pale lores and superciliary, and black eye line and auriculars fairly distinct; gr covs with reduced paler tips on both webs (fig. 122); white in rects reduced by age and sex (fig. 123); wg 63-78 (see Sex).

Audubon's Warbler: Throat usually with some yellow (none in some HY/SYs); auriculars, lores, superciliary and eyeline uniformly grayish, not contrasting markedly with nape and crown and giving face a very plain appearance; gr covs with extended pale tips to outer web (fig. 122); rects with relatively much white by age and sex class (fig. 123); wg 68-83 (see Sex).

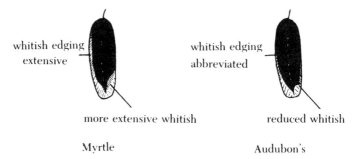

whitish edging extensive

whitish edging abbreviated

more extensive whitish

reduced whitish

Myrtle

Audubon's

Figure 122. Greater covert pattern in Myrtle vs. Audubon's warblers.

Molt—PB: HY partial (Jul-Sep), AHY complete (Jul-Sep); PA partial (Feb-Apr). PBs occur on the summer grounds.

Skull—Completes in HY/SY from 15 Oct thru Dec in Myrtle Warbler, 15 Sep thru Jan in Audubon's Warbler.

Age/Sex—CP/BP Myrtle (May-Aug), Audubon's (Apr-Aug). Wg: Myrtle ♂(n30) 68-78, ♀(n30) 63-75; Audubon's ♂(n30) 71-83, ♀(n30) 68-78, W Mts > W Coast. Juv (May-Aug) has heavily streaked underparts (sexing sometimes possible by the amount of white in the tail; fig. 124). The plumages of this species are variable and complex such that (except for sexing in spring) all criteria should coincide before reliable determinations are made. Rect shape (fig. 114) does not seem as useful for ageing in this species as in other *Dendroica* but may be helpful with extremes or with experience by the handler:

Basic Plumage

AHY/ASY ♂ (Aug-Mar): Upperparts with noticeable grayish wash; back and some breast feathers with large black centers; yellow crown and side patches distinct; uppertail covs with broad, bluish edging and large black centers (fig. 123); flight feathers and pp covs blackish; rects with relatively much white by subspecies (fig. 124).

HY/SY ♂ (Aug-Mar): As AHY/ASY ♂ but usually averages duller in all aspects; upperparts slightly (sometimes without) grayish; yellow side patches usually present but relatively small; black centers to back feathers and uppertail covs (fig. 123) smaller but usually distinct, edging brown or mixed bluish and brown; flight feathers and pp covs dull black; rects with a moderate amount of white by subspecies (fig. 124). [Many intermediates occur between these and ♀ ♀; combine with all age criteria and wg for each race before sexing.]

AHY/ASY ♀ (Aug-Mar): Like HY/SY ♂ but flight feathers and wing covs uniformly blackish; white in rects as illustrated by subspecies (fig. 124). [Some ♀ ♀ may not be reliably aged, except by skull.]

HY/SY ♀ (Aug-Mar): Upperparts without gray; yellow crown and side patches very small or lacking; back and breast feathers usually with narrow, indistinct centers; uppertail covs with narrow dusky centers (fig. 123) and brown edges; flight feathers and pp covs brownish-black; white in rects as illustrated by subspecies (fig. 124).

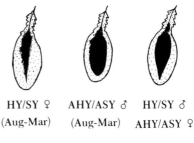

HY/SY ♀   AHY/ASY ♂   HY/SY ♂
(Aug-Mar)   (Aug-Mar)   AHY/ASY ♀

(Aug-Mar)

Figure 123. Indicative uppertail covert patterns, by age and sex, in basic (an alternate?) plumages of the Yellow rumped Warbler. Much overlap may occur with this criterion.

Alternate Plumage

ASY ♂ (Mar-Aug): Upperparts bluish-gray; auriculars black (Myrtle) or dark bluish-gray (Audubon's); breast with wide, complete black band; flight feathers and wing covs fairly uniformly blackish; white in rects as illustrated (fig. 124); rects usually showing relatively less wear (fig. 114).

SY ♂ (Mar-Aug): Like ASY ♂ but plumage usually duller; flight feathers and pp covs brownish-black, often contrasting with blacker gr covs; rects with less white (fig. 124); and usually more worn (fig. 114).

ASY ♀ (Mar-Aug): Upperparts and auriculars brownish to brownish-gray; breast with distinct black streaking but no complete black band; flight feathers and wing covs fairly uniformly blackish; white in rects as illustrated (fig 124); rects usually showing relatively less wear (fig. 114).

SY ♀ (Mar-Aug): Like ASY ♀ but plumage usually slightly duller; flight feathers and pp covs brownish, often contrasting with blacker gr covs; rects with less white (fig. 124) and usually showing more wear (fig. 114).

References—DVR,B,R,W,SK,O; Robbins (1964), Hubbard (1969), Fisk (1970, 1973c), Prescott (1981); PRBO data.

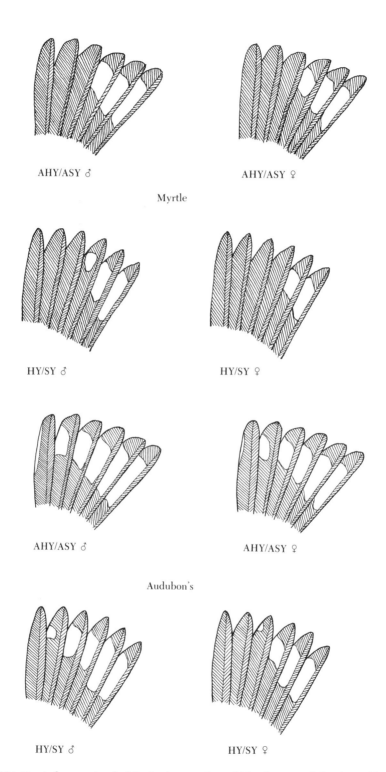

AHY/ASY ♂   AHY/ASY ♀

Myrtle

HY/SY ♂   HY/SY ♀

AHY/ASY ♂   AHY/ASY ♀

Audubon's

HY/SY ♂   HY/SY ♀

Figure 124. Typical amounts of white in the rectrices of Myrtle vs. Audubon's warblers, by age and sex.

BLACK-THROATED GRAY WARBLER
Dendroica nigrescens

BYWA
Species # 665.0
Band size: 0

Molt—PB: HY partial (Jul-Aug), AHY complete (Jul-Aug); PA limited (Feb-Apr). PBs occur on the summer grounds.

Skull—Completes in HY from 1 Oct thru Dec.

Age/Sex—CP/BP (Apr-Aug). Wg: ♂(n30) 60-69, ♀ (n30) 56-64. Juv (May-Aug) is similar to HY/SY ♀ (see below) but has considerably browner upperparts (a few Juvs may be sexed by the amount of white on r4; fig. 127). Birds showing conflicting characteristics and intermediates between the following occur which are not reliably aged and/or sexed. The usefulness of the mid cov pattern as in Townsends Warbler (fig. 128), needs to be determined:

Basic Plumage

AHY/ASY ♂ (Aug-Mar): Chin and throat entirely black, feathers with narrow gray tips or edging; cheeks black or blackish; crown mostly black; back feathers with distinct black centers (fig. 125); flight feathers and pp covs black; rects truncate (fig. 114), white patch of r4 relatively large (fig. 127).

HY/SY ♂ (Aug-Mar): Chin mostly white; throat mixed black and white; cheeks gray to blackish; crown mixed gray and black; back feathers with moderate and fairly distinct black centers (fig. 125); flight feathers and pp covs dull black; rects tapered (fig. 114), white patch on r4 relatively small (fig. 127).

AHY/ASY ♀ (Aug-Mar): Like HY/SY ♂ in plumage but flight feathers and wing covs blacker; rects truncate (fig. 114), white patch on r4 possibly averages larger (fig. 127).

HY/SY ♀ (Aug-Mar): Chin and throat white with little or no black; cheeks dull, dusky gray; crown and back feathers gray with indistinct, narrow, dusky centers (fig. 125); flight feathers and pp covs brownish-black; rects tapered (fig. 114); white patch on rect 4 variable but usually more reduced than HY/SY ♂ (fig. 127).

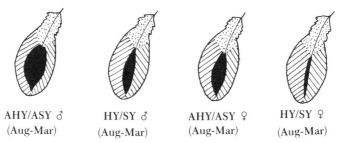

| AHY/ASY ♂ | HY/SY ♂ | AHY/ASY ♀ | HY/SY ♀ |
| (Aug-Mar) | (Aug-Mar) | (Aug-Mar) | (Aug-Mar) |

Figure 125. Indicative back feather patterns by age and sex in basic-plumaged Black-throated Gray Warblers.

Alternate Plumage

ASY ♂ (Mar-Aug): Crown, cheeks, chin, and throat black (fig. 126); streaking on flanks wide and distinct; flight feathers and wing covs fairly uniformly blackish; rects truncate (fig. 114); white on r4 large (fig. 127).

SY ♂ (Mar-Aug): Like ASY ♂ but flight feathers and pp covs brownish-black, often contrasting with blacker gr covs; rects tapered (fig. 114); white on r4 reduced (fig. 127).

ASY ♀ (Mar-Aug): Crown and cheeks dusky gray to blackish, chin usually white, throat black suffused with white (fig. 126); streaking on flanks narrow and indistinct; flight feathers and wing covs fairly uniformly blackish; rects truncate (fig. 114); white patch on r4 moderately large (fig. 127).

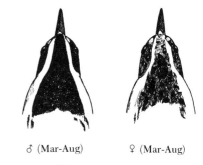

♂ (Mar-Aug)   ♀ (Mar-Aug)

Figure 126. Throat patterns of ♂ and ♀ Black-throated Gray Warblers in alternate plumage.

SY ♀ (Mar-Aug): Like ASY ♀ but flight feathers and pp covs brownish, often contrasting with blacker gr covs; rects tapered (fig. 114); white patch on r4 averages smaller (fig. 127).

References—B,O; Robbins (1964); PRBO data.

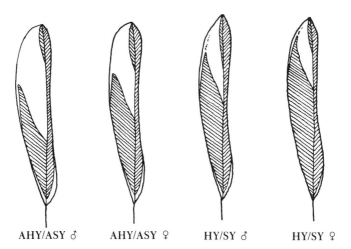

AHY/ASY ♂   AHY/ASY ♀   HY/SY ♂   HY/SY ♀

Figure 127. Typical fouth rectrix pattern by age and sex in the Black-throated Gray Warbler.

TOWNSEND'S WARBLER
Dendroica townsendi

TOWA
Species # 668.0
Band size: 0

Species—From the three similar species in all plumages by a well defined auricular patch and by vent and lower belly without yellow.

Molt—PB: HY partial (Jul-Aug), AHY complete (Jul-Aug); PA limited (Feb-Apr). PBs occur on the summer grounds.

Skull—Completes in HY from 15 Oct thru Dec.

Age/Sex—CP/BP (May-Aug). Wg: ♂(n30) 62-71, ♀(n30) 59-68; W Mt > W Coast. Juv (Jun-Aug) has upperparts and head washed considerably with brownish (sexing often possible by the amount of white on r4; fig. 129). Birds showing conflicting characteristics and intermediates between the following occur which are not reliably aged and/or sexed. The r4 criteria may be slightly more reliable with mountain forms than with coastal forms:

Basic Plumage

AHY/ASY ♂ (Aug-Mar): Crown, auriculars, chin, and throat black, feathers narrowly edged with yellow or green; back feathers and uppertail covs with large, distinct black centers; mid covs bright white proximally, without black streaks (fig. 128); flight feathers and pp covs black; rects truncate (fig. 114); white patch on r4 usually large (fig. 129).

HY/SY ♂ (Aug-Mar): Crown and auriculars dull blackish, feathers moderately edged green; chin usually yellow; throat mottled black and yellow; back feathers with fairly distinct, largish black centers; mid covs with narrow black streaks through white tips (fig. 128); flight feathers and pp covs dull black; rects tapered (fig. 114); white patch on r4 relatively small to moderate (fig. 129).

AHY/ASY ♀ (Aug-Mar): Like HY/SY ♂ but flight feathers and wing covs blacker; rects truncate (fig. 114); white patch on r4 may average larger (fig. 129).

AHY/ASY ♂   AHY/ASY ♀   HY/SY ♀
                HY/SY ♂

HY/SY ♀ (Aug-Mar): Crown and auriculars mostly olive; chin and throat mostly yellow; back feathers with small and indistinct black centers; mid covs usually with wide black streaks through white tips (fig. 128); flight feathers and pp covs brownish-black, contrasting with blacker gr covs; rects tapered (fig. 114); white patch on r4 small (fig. 129) or lacking.

Figure 128. Middle covert pattern by age and sex in Townsend's, Hermit, and Black-throated Green warblers. Look for the usefulness of this criterion in other species of *Dendroica*.

Alternate Plumage

ASY ♂ (Mar-Aug): Chin and throat usually entirely black; flight feathers and wing covs fairly uniformly blackish; mid covs bright white proximally, without black streaks (fig. 128); rects truncate (fig.114); white patch on r4 relatively large (fig. 129).

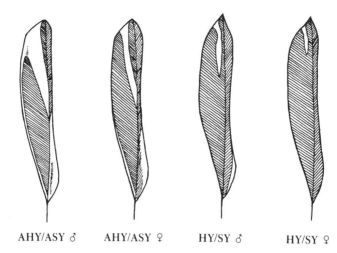

AHY/ASY ♂   AHY/ASY ♀   HY/SY ♂   HY/SY ♀

Figure 129. Typical patterns of the fouth rectrix in Townsend's Warbler, by age and sex.

SY ♂ (Mar-Aug): Chin and throat entirely or mostly black, often with a little yellow mixed in; flight feathers and pp covs brownish-black, often contrasting with blacker gr covs; mid covs with narrow black streaks through white tips (fig. 128); rects tapered (fig. 114); white patch on r4 small to moderate (fig. 129). [SYs may molt some or all mid covs during the 1st PA, which would resemble those of ASY; more study is needed on the extent of this.]

ASY ♀ (Mar-Aug): Chin yellow; throat mottled yellow and black; flight feathers and wing covs fairly uniformly blackish; mid covs with narrow black streaks through white tips (fig. 128); rects truncate (fig. 114); white patch on r4 small to moderate (fig. 129).

SY ♀ (Mar-Aug): Chin and throat usually entirely yellow; flight feathers and pp covs brownish, contrasting with blacker gr covs; mid covs usually with wide black streaks through white tips (fig. 128); rects tapered (fig. 114); white patch on r4 small (fig. 129) or lacking. [See SY ♂ concening mid covs.]

References—B,O; Robbins (1964); PRBO data.

HERMIT WARBLER
Dendroica occidentalis

HEWA
Species # 669.0
Band size: 0

Species—From the three similar *Dendroica* warblers by the lack of strong yellow coloration to the underparts (none in vent area), and the lack of black streaking to the sides of the central and lower breast. HY/SY ♀♀ from Olive Warbler by lack of white at the base of the pp, shorter wing (60-66), and a squarer tail (outer—central rects ≤ 3.5 mm).

Molt—PB: HY partial (Jul-Aug), AHY complete (Jul-Aug); PA limited (Feb-Apr). PBs occur on the summer grounds.

Skull—Completes in HY from 1 Oct thru Dec.

Age/Sex—CP/BP (Apr-Aug). Wg: ♂(n30) 63-72, ♀(n30) 60-68. Juv (Jun-Aug) resembles HY/SY ♀ (see below) but is washed brownish above and buffy below, and has less yellow in the face

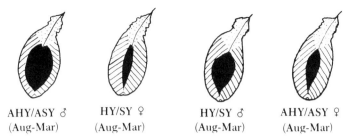

AHY/ASY ♂   HY/SY ♀   HY/SY ♂   AHY/ASY ♀
(Aug-Mar)   (Aug-Mar)   (Aug-Mar)   (Aug-Mar)

Figure 130. Back feather pattern by age and sex in basic-plumaged Hermit Warblers.

(sexing sometimes possible by the amount of white on r4; fig. 131). Birds showing conflicting characteristics and intermediates between the following will occur which are not reliably aged and/or sexed:

Basic Plumage

AHY/ASY ♂ (Aug-Mar): Chin and throat black with thin, yellowish or whitish tips; forehead and auriculars mostly yellow with little or no blackish or olive; back feathers and uppertail covs with large black centers (fig. 130); mid covs tipped pure white (fig. 128); flight feathers and pp covs black; rects truncate (fig. 114); white patch on r4 relatively large (fig. 131).

HY/SY ♂ (Aug-Mar): Chin buffy white or yellowish; throat buffy, usually noticeably mottled with black; forehead and auriculars indistinctly washed olive; back feathers and uppertail covs with relatively distinct blackish centers (fig. 130); white tipping of mid covs with thinnish black shaft streaks (fig. 128); flight feathers and pp covs dull black; rects tapered (fig. 114); white patch on r4 small to moderate (fig. 131). [Some overlap may occur with HY/SY ♀; the black centers to the upperpart feathers seems the most reliable criterion; compare with pattern of white in the rects and wg.]

AHY/ASY ♀ (Aug-Mar): Plumage like HY/SY ♂ but back feathers and uppertail covs with smaller black centers (fig. 130); flight feathers and pp covs blackish; rects truncate (fig. 114); white patch on r4 possibly averages larger (fig. 131).

HY/SY ♀ (Aug-Mar): Chin and throat buffy white with very little if any black mottling; forehead and auriculars extensively washed olive; back feathers and uppertail covs with very indistinct or no dusky centers (fig. 130); white tipping of mid covs with black triangular centers (fig. 128); flight feathers and pp covs brownish-black; rects tapered (fig. 114); white patch on r4 reduced (fig. 131) or lacking. [See HY/SY ♂.]

Alternate Plumage

ASY ♂ (Mar-Aug): Chin and throat black; flight feathers and wing covs fairly uniformly blackish; mid covs tipped pure white (fig. 128); rects truncate (fig. 114); white patch on r4 relatively large (fig. 131).

SY ♂ (Mar-Aug): Like ASY ♂ but throat sometimes with a little yellow; flight feathers and pp covs brownish-black, often contrasting with blacker gr covs; white tipping of mid covs with thinnish black shaft streaks (fig. 128); rects tapered (fig. 114); white patch on r4 small to moderate (fig. 131). [See note under SY ♂ Townsend's Warbler concerning mid covs.]

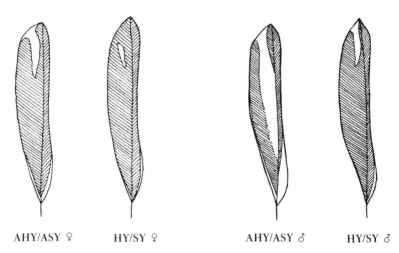

AHY/ASY ♀   HY/SY ♀   AHY/ASY ♂   HY/SY ♂

Figure 131. Typical patterns of the fourth rectrices in Hermit Warbler, by age and sex.

ASY ♀ (Mar-Aug): Chin and throat mottled yellow and black; flight feathers and wing covs uniformly dull black; white tipping of mid covs with thinnish black shaft streaks (fig. 128); rects truncate (fig. 114); white patch on r4 small to moderate (fig. 131).

SY ♀ (Mar-Aug): Like ASY ♀ but flight feathers and pp covs brownish, often contrasting with blacker gr covs; white tipping of mid covs with black triangular centers (fig. 128); rects tapered (fig. 114); white patch on r4 reduced (fig. 131) or lacking.

References—B,O; Robbins (1964); PRBO data.

BLACK-THROATED GREEN WARBLER
Dendroica virens

BNWA
Species # 667.0
Band size: 0

Species—From the three similar warblers by the lack of a distinct auricular patch or eyeline, relatively greener upperparts, the presence of yellow in the vent area, and distinct streaking to the sides of the mid and lower breast.

Molt—PB: HY partial (Jul-Aug); AHY complete (Jul-Aug); PA limited (Feb-Apr). PBs occur on the summer grounds.

Skull—Completes in HY from 1 Oct (as early as 15 Sep in southeastern populations) thru Dec.

Age/Sex—CP/BP (Apr-Aug). Wg: ♂(n30) 60-69, ♀(n30) 56-64. Juv (Jun-Aug) resembles HY/SY ♀ (see below) but is washed brownish above and buffy below, and has less yellow in the face (sexing sometimes possible by the amount of white in r4; fig. 132). Birds showing conflicting characteristics and intermediates between the following will occur which are not reliably aged and/or sexed; check also for the usefulness of the mid cov pattern, as in Townsend's and Hermit warblers:

Basic Plumage

AHY/ASY ♂ (Aug-Mar): Chin, throat, and upperbreast black with narrow yellow tipping;back feathers green with small but distinct black centers; flight feathers and pp covs black; rects truncate (fig. 114); white patch on r4 relatively large (fig. 132).

HY/SY ♂ (Aug-Mar): Chin and throat usually yellow, without black mottling; upperbreast with obscured but noticeable black mottling; back feathers greenish-olive with indistinct or no dusky centers; flight feathers and pp covs dull black; rects tapered (fig. 114); white patch on r4 small to moderate (fig. 132).

AHY/ASY ♀ (Aug-Mar): Like HY/SY ♂ in plumage but flight feathers and pp covs blackish; rects truncate (fig. 114); white patch in r4 averages larger (fig. 132).

HY/SY ♀ (Aug-Mar): Chin, throat, and upperbreast with little or no black mottling; upperparts brownish-olive, feathers without dusky centers; flight feathers and pp covs brownish-black; rects tapered (fig. 114); white patch in r4 relatively small (fig. 132).

Alternate Plumage

ASY ♂ (Mar-Aug): Chin, throat, and upperbreast extensively black; flight feathers and wing covs fairly uniformly blackish; rects truncate (fig. 114); white patch on r4 large (fig. 132).

SY ♂ (Mar-Aug): Like ASY ♂ but flight feathers and pp covs brownish-black, often contrasting with blacker gr covs; rects tapered (fig. 114); white patch on r4 relatively reduced (fig. 132).

ASY ♀ (Mar-Aug): Chin and throat yellowish-white, upperbreast mottled yellow and black; flight feathers and wing covs fairly uniformly blackish; rects truncate (fig. 114); white patch on r4 as shown (fig. 132).

SY ♀ (Mar-Aug): Like ASY ♀ but flight feathers and pp covs brownish, usually contrasting with blacker gr covs; rects tapered (fig. 114); white patch on r4 reduced (fig. 132).

References—B,R,W,SK,O; Robbins (1964); PRBO data.

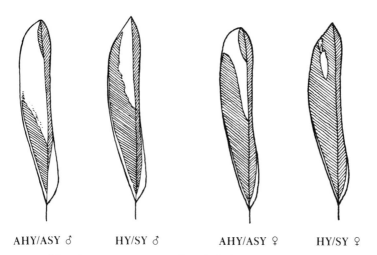

AHY/ASY ♂   HY/SY ♂   AHY/ASY ♀   HY/SY ♀

Figure 132. Typical fourth rectrix pattern in the Black-throated Green Warbler, by age and sex.

GOLDEN-CHEEKED WARBLER
Dendroica chrysoparia

GCWA
Species # 666.0
Band size: 0

Species—From the three similar warblers by the complete lack of an auricular patch but the presence of a distinct, black or blackish eye line in all plumages, and the lack of yellow to the underparts (including vent area).

Molt—PB: HY partial (Jun-Aug), AHY complete (Jun-Aug); PA limited (Feb-Apr). PBs occur on the summer grounds.

Skull—Completes in HY from 1 Sep thru Nov.

Age/Sex—CP/BP (Mar-Aug). Wg: ♂(n15) 62-68, ♀(n8) 58-63. Rect shape (fig. 114), pattern of mid covs (fig. 128, possibly), color of flight feathers and pp covs, and pattern of white in rects are probably useful for ageing as in other *Dendroica*. Otherwise ageing and sexing is basically the same as Black-throated Green Warbler but note lack of yellow on the underparts and blacker back color; black centers to back feathers probably parallel those of Hermit Warbler (fig. 130).

References—B,O.

BLACKBURNIAN WARBLER
Dendroica fusca

BLWA
Species # 662.0
Band size: 0

Molt—PB: HY partial (Jul-Aug), AHY complete (Jul-Aug); PA partial-incomplete (Feb-Apr). PBs occur on the summer grounds. PAs may sometimes include the terts.

Skull—Completes in HY from 15 Oct thru Dec.

Age/Sex—CP/BP (May-Aug). Wg: ♂(n30) 65-73, ♀(n30) 63-71. Juv (Jun-Aug) resembles HY/SY ♀ (see below) but is washed brownish, has buffy wing bars, and little or no orange in the face (some Juvs may be sexed by amount of white on r4; fig. 134). All birds should be reliably sexed and most reliably aged by the following; the pattern and timing of the gr cov criterion (especially for HY/SY ♂♂, and ♀♀ in spring) needs verification:

Basic Plumage

AHY/ASY ♂ (Aug-Mar): Nape, auriculars, and shoulder black, feathers edged yellowish; inner gr covs broadly edged white (fig. 133) forming, with mid covs, a wing patch; flight

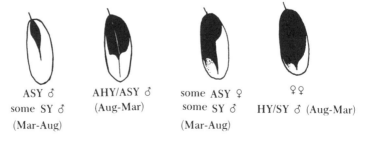

ASY ♂
some SY ♂
(Mar-Aug)

AHY/ASY ♂
(Aug-Mar)

some ASY ♀
some SY ♂
(Mar-Aug)

♀♀
HY/SY ♂ (Aug-Mar)

Figure 133. The inner greater coverts by age and sex in Blackburnian Warblers. This criterion may need further study.

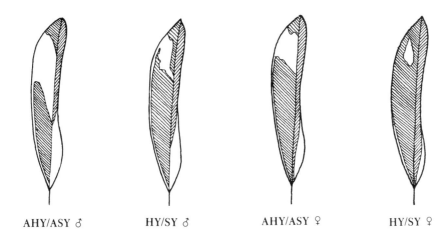

AHY/ASY ♂   HY/SY ♂   AHY/ASY ♀   HY/SY ♀

Figure 134. Typical pattern of the fourth rectrix, by age and sex, in the Blackburnian Warbler.

feathers and pp covs black; rects truncate (fig. 114); white patch on r4 relatively large (fig. 134).

HY/SY ♂ (Aug-Mar): Nape and auricular patch mixed black and brown; shoulder patch dull black; inner gr covs moderately edged white (fig. 133); flight feathers and pp covs dull black; rects tapered (fig. 114); white patch on r4 moderately small (fig. 134).

AHY/ASY ♀ (Aug-Mar): Nape, auricular patch, and shoulder grayish-olive to dusky brown; inner gr covs moderately edged white (fig. 133) forming, with mid covs, two wing bars; flight feathers and pp covs blackish; rects truncate (fig. 114); white patch on r4 moderate (fig. 134).

HY/SY ♀ (Aug-Mar): Like AHY/ASY ♀ but nape, auricular patch and shoulder dull olive-brown; flight feathers and pp covs brownish-black; rects tapered (fig. 114); white patch on r4 reduced (fig. 134) or lacking.

Alternate Plumage

ASY ♂ (Mar-Aug): Nape, auricular patch, and shoulder black; superciliary and throat bright orange; inner gr covs mostly white (fig. 133); flight-feathers and pp covs blackish, fairly uniform in color with upperparts; rects truncate (fig. 114); white patch on r4 large (fig. 134).

SY ♂ (Mar-Aug): Like ASY ♂ but flight feathers and pp covs brownish-black, contrasting much with black of upperparts; inner gr covs often with less white (fig. 133); rects tapered (fig. 114); white patch on r4 smaller (fig. 134).

ASY ♀ (Mar-Aug): Nape, auricular patch, and shoulder olive-gray to gray; superciliary and throat yellowish; inner gr covs moderately or broadly edged white (fig. 133); flight feathers and wing covs fairly uniformly blackish; rects truncate (fig. 114); white patch on r4 moderate (fig.134).

SY ♀ (Mar-Aug): Like ASY ♀ but flight feathers and pp covs brownish, contrasting with blacker gr covs; rects tapered (fig. 114); white patch on r4 smaller (fig. 134) or lacking.

References—B,R,W,SK,O; Robbins (1964); PRBO data.

YELLOW-THROATED WARBLER
Dendroica dominica

YTWA
Species # 663.0
Band size: 0

Molt—PB: HY partial (Jun-Aug), AHY complete (Jun-Aug); PA absent. PBs occur on the summer grounds.

Skull—Completes in HY from 1 Sep thru Nov.

Age/Sex—CP/BP (Mar-Jul). Wg: ♂(n30) 62-72, ♀(n30) 59-69; N ("White-lored") > S ("Yellow-lored"). Juv (Apr-Aug) has grayish to olive-brown upperparts with indistinct, dusky streaking and buffier wing bars and underparts (♂ = ♀). The amount of white in the rects shows some age/sex related variation but does not seem quite as useful as with other *Dendroica* (this should be further investigated). All criteria should coincide before birds are reliably aged and/or sexed with the following:

AHY/ASY ♂ (Aug-Jul): Plumage generally bright; crown heavily streaked black (fig. 135); upperparts with little to no brown wash; auriculars black; flank streaking wide; flight feathers and wing covs uniformly blackish; rects truncate (fig. 114), relatively unworn.

HY/SY ♂ (Aug-Jul): Like AHY/ASY ♂ but plumage slightly duller; crown moderately to heavily streaked black (fig. 135); upperparts slightly washed brown; flight feathers and pp covs brownish-black, often contrasting with blacker gr covs; rects tapered (fig. 114), relatively worn, especially in spring.

AHY/ASY ♀ (Aug-Jul): Plumage generally duller; crown lightly to moderately streaked black (fig. 135); upperparts slightly washed brown; auriculars dull black, less extensive; flank streaking moderately narrow, indistinct; flight feathers and wing covs uniformly blackish; rects truncate (fig. 135), relatively unworn.

HY/SY ♀ (Aug-Jul): Like AHY/ASY ♀ but plumage slightly duller; crown lightly streaked black (fig. 135); upperparts moderately washed brown; flight feathers and pp covs brownish, often contrasting with blacker gr covs; rects tapered (fig. 114), relatively worn, especially in spring.

References—B,W,SK,O.

AHY/ASY ♂   some AHY/ASY ♀   ♀ ♀
some HY/SY ♂   some HY/SY ♂

Figure 135. Crown patterns of Yellow-throated Warblers, by age and sex.

GRACE'S WARBLER
Dendroica graciae

GRWA
Species # 664.0
Band size: 0

Molt—PB: HY partial (Jun-Aug), AHY complete (Jul-Aug); PA absent. PBs occur on the summer grounds.

Skull—Completes in HY from 1 Oct thru Nov.

Age/Sex—CP/BP (Apr-Aug). Wg: ♂(n100) 63-70, ♀(n30) 59-66. Juv (Apr-Aug) has grayish to olive-brown upperparts with indistinct, dusky streaking and buffier and indistinctly spotted underparts (♂ = ♀). All criteria should coincide before birds are reliably aged and/or sexed with the following:

AHY/ASY ♂ (Aug-Jul): Plumage generally bright; back feathers with large and distinct black centers (fig. 136); flank streaking wide, distinct; flight feathers and wing covs uniformly black; rects truncate (fig.114); white patch on r4 relatively large (fig. 137).

HY/SY ♂ (Aug-Jul): Like AHY/ASY ♂ but plumage with more brownish wash; back feathers with distinct but slightly smaller black centers (fig. 136); flight feathers and pp covs brownish-black, often contrasting with blacker gr covs; rects tapered (fig.114); white patch on r4 reduced (fig. 137).

AHY/ASY ♀ (Aug-Jul): Plumage moderately dull; back feathers with small and indistinct blackish centers (fig. 136); flank streaking narrow, indistinct; flight feathers and wing covs uniformly blackish; rects truncate (fig. 114). [See HY/SY ♀ concerning the white patch on r4.]

HY/SY ♀ (Aug-Jul): Like AHY/ASY ♀ but plumage with more brownish wash; back feathers usually without darker centers (see fig. 136); flight feathers and pp covs brownish, often contrasting with blacker gr covs; rects tapered (fig. 114). [The white patch on r4 may average slightly smaller on HY/SY ♀ than AHY/ASY ♀, but seems generally to be about the same size as that of the HY/SY ♂; fig. 137).]

References—B,O; Webster (1961).

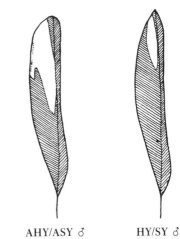

AHY/ASY ♂   HY/SY ♂

Figure 137. Rectrix four patterns by age in ♂ Grace's Warblers, ♀♀ typically show as much as HY/SY ♂, perhaps averaging less in HY/SY ♀ than AHY/ASY ♀.

AHY/ASY ♂   AHY/ASY ♀   HY/SY ♂   HY/SY ♀

Figure 136. Typical back feather patterns in the Grace's Warbler, by age and sex.

PINE WARBLER
Dendroica pinus

PIWA
Species # 671.0
Band size: 0

Species—From Bay-breasted and Blackpoll warblers by lack of any black or dusky centers to the upperpart feathers; longest undertail cov to longest rect 19-26 mm; soles of feet dark blackish, without bluish-gray. From HY/SY ♀ Prairie Warbler by longer wg (65-78).

Molt—PB: HY partial-incomplete (Jun-Aug), AHY complete (Jun-Aug); PA absent. PBs occur on the summer grounds. 1st PB can include some or all rects.

Skull—Completes in HY from 1 Oct (as early as 1 Sep in populations S of Virginia-Missouri) thru Nov.

Age/Sex—CP/BP (Mar-Aug). Wg: ♂(n30) 68-78, ♀(n30) 65-74. Juv (Apr-Jul) has completely brown upperparts, buffy underparts, and buffy wing-bars (♂ = ♀). The amount of white in the rects does not appear useful for ageing or sexing. The following characteristics are relative, and many intermediates may not be reliably aged and/or sexed. With rect shape, beware of HY/SYs that have molted the tail during the 1st PB. In all age/sex classes, birds are more heavily washed with brownish and buffy in fall than in spring:

AHY/ASY ♂ (Aug-Jul): Back greenish with little or no brownish wash; breast bright yellow with little or no buffy wash, belly and vent white; flight feathers and wing covs fairly uniformly blackish; rects truncate (fig. 114).

HY/SY ♂ (Aug-Jul): Back mostly brownish, often washed with green; breast yellow washed buffy; belly and vent washed buffy (this wears off by spring); flight feathers and pp covs brownish, often contrasting with blacker gr covs; rects tapered (fig. 114). [These may be difficult to separate from HY/SY ♀; compare with wg.]

AHY/ASY ♀ (Aug-Jul): Back dull greenish; breast yellow washed greenish; belly and vent white, often washed lightly with buff; flight feathers and wing covs fairly uniformly dull black; rects truncate (fig. 114).

HY/SY ♀ (Aug-Jul): Back brownish with little or no green; breast buffy lightly washed yellow; belly and vent buffy; flight feathers and pp covs brown, contrasting with blacker gr covs; rects tapered (fig. 114).

References—B,R,W,SK,O; Norris (1952), Robbins (1964), Whitney (1983).

KIRTLAND'S WARBLER
Dendroica kirtlandii

KIWA
Species # 670.0
Band size: 1

Molt—PB: HY partial (Jul-Sep), AHY complete (Jul-Sep); PA limited-partial (Feb-Apr). PBs occur primarily on the summer grounds but may complete on migration or the winter grounds.

Skull—Completes in HY from 1 Oct thru Nov.

Age/Sex—CP/BP (May-Aug). Wg: ♂(n14) 69-75, ♀(n12) 64-71. Juv (Jun-Aug) has completely brown upperparts, buffy wing bars, and distinct black speckling on the throat and chin

($\delta = \mathbb{Q}$). The following plumage criteria are most useful in basic plumage. In alternate plumage (Mar-Aug) use covert contrast and rectrix criteria to age, and plumage to sex:

AHY/ASY δ (Aug-Jul): Forecrown and lores black; upperparts grayish-blue with slight brown wash; underparts relatively bright yellow; flank streaking black, distinct; flight feathers and wing covs uniformly blackish; rects truncate (fig. 114).

HY/SY δ (Aug-Jul): Forecrown and lores blackish; upperparts grayish washed moderately (Aug-Mar) to lightly (Mar-Jul) with brown; underparts moderately bright yellow; flank streaking blackish, indistinct (Aug-Mar) to distinct (Mar-Jul); flight feathers and pp covs brownish-black, contrasting with blacker gr covs; rects tapered (fig. 114).

AHY/ASY $\mathbb{Q}$ (Aug-Jul): Like HY/SY δ but forecrown and lores mostly gray; flight feathers and wing covs uniformly blackish; rects truncate (fig. 114).

HY/SY $\mathbb{Q}$ (Aug-Jul): Forecrown and lores brownish-gray; upperparts mostly brown (Aug-Mar) to brownish-gray (Mar-Aug); underparts relatively faded yellow and washed buffy; flank streaking dusky, indistinct (Aug-Mar) to moderately distinct (Mar-Jul); flight feathers and pp covs brownish, contrasting with blacker gr covs; rects tapered (fig. 114).

References—B,R; Mayfield (1960).

PRAIRIE WARBLER

Dendroica discolor

PRWA
Species # 673.0
Band size: 0

Species—HY/SY $\mathbb{Q}$ from Pine Warbler by shorter wg (50-55).

Molt—PB: HY partial (Jul-Aug), AHY complete (Jul-Aug); PA limited (Dec-Apr). PBs occur primarily on the summer grounds.

Skull—Completes in HY from 15 Sep thru Nov.

Age/Sex—CP/BP (Apr-Aug). Wg: δ(n100) 53-61, $\mathbb{Q}$(n100) 50-57. Juv (Jun-Aug) has brownish washed upperparts and buffy wing bars (sexing often possible by the amount of white in r4; fig. 139). Birds showing conflicting characteristics and intermediates between the following will occur which are not reliably aged and/or sexed:

Basic Plumage

AHY/ASY δ (Aug-Mar): Eye line and crescent-shaped cheek patch black, without gray (obscured by yellow feather tipping in fall); back feathers with large and distinct chestnut centers (fig 138); black streaking on flanks broad and distinct; flight feathers and pp covs blackish; rects truncate (fig. 114); white patch on r4 relatively large (fig. 139).

HY/SY δ (Aug-Mar): Cheeks with some grayish or whitish; eye line relatively distinct, blackish; back feathers with fairly distinct chestnut patches (fig. 138); flight feathers and pp covs dusky; rects tapered (fig. 114); white patch on r4 moderately small (fig. 139).

AHY/ASY $\mathbb{Q}$ (Aug-Mar): Eye line dusky or dull black; crescent-shaped cheek patch dusky, indistinct, or lacking but without gray; back feathers with little (sometimes no) chestnut in the center (fig. 138); flank streaking narrow and indistinct; flight feathers and pp covs blackish; rects truncate (fig. 114); white patch on r4 moderate to large (fig. 139).

HY/SY ♀ (Aug-Mar): Cheeks largely grayish or whitish; eye line dusky, quite indistinct; back feathers with no chestnut (fig. 138); flank streaking very indistinct; flight feathers and pp covs dusky; rects tapered (fig. 114); white patch on r4 relatively small (fig. 139).

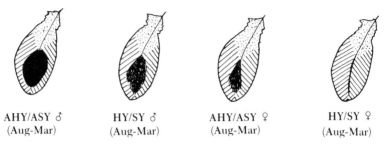

AHY/ASY ♂	HY/SY ♂	AHY/ASY ♀	HY/SY ♀
(Aug-Mar)	(Aug-Mar)	(Aug-Mar)	(Aug-Mar)

Figure 138. Typical amounts of chestnut in the back feathers of basic-plumaged Prairie Warblers, by age and sex.

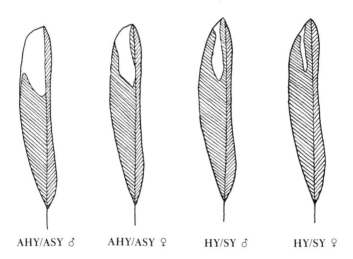

AHY/ASY ♂   AHY/ASY ♀   HY/SY ♂   HY/SY ♀

Figure 139. Typical patterns of the fourth rectrices, by age and sex, in Prairie Warblers.

Alternate Plumage

ASY ♂ (Mar-Aug): Eye line and cheek patch black; back feathers with moderate to large reddish centers (fig. 138; this may vary with age); flank streaking wide, distinct; rects dull black, truncate (fig. 114); r4 with a large white patch (fig. 139).

SY ♂ (Mar-Aug): Like ASY ♂ but plumage genarally slightly duller; rects brownish-dusky, tapered (fig.114); r4 with smaller white patch (fig. 139).

ASY ♀ (Mar-Aug): Eye line dusky or dull black; crescent-shaped cheek patch dusky, indistinct, or lacking; back feathers with little or no chestnut in the center (fig. 138; this may vary with age); flank streaking narrow and indistinct; rects dull black, truncate (fig. 114); white patch on r4 moderately large (fig. 139).

SY ♀ (Mar-Aug): Like ASY ♀ but rects grayish, tapered (fig. 114); white patch on r4 reduced or lacking (fig. 139).

References—DVR,B,W,SK,O; Robbins (1964), Nolan & Mumford (1965), Nolan (1978); PRBO data.

PALM WARBLER
Dendroica palmarum

PAWA
Band size: 0

Yellow Palm Warbler (YPWA)   Species # 672.0
Western Palm Warbler (WPWA)   Species # 672.9

Subspecies—The races are easiest to separate by the color of the lower breast and belly: yellow in Yellow Palm Warbler, not contrasting with the color of the undertail covs or upperbreast; whitish in Western, markedly contrasting with yellow undertail covs and upperbreast or throat.

Molt—PB: HY partial (Jul-Sep), AHY complete (Jul-Sep); PA limited (Jan-Apr). PBs occur on the summer grounds.

Skull—Completes in HY from 15 Oct thru Dec.

Age—Juv (Jun-Aug) has brown upperparts, cinnamon wing bars, and dull whitish underparts with dusky spotting. Use caution with the following; differences (especially with the shape of the rects) are generally more subtle than in other *Dendroica*:

HY/SY (Aug-Jul): Flight feathers and pp covs brownish-black, contrasting with blacker gr covs; rects tapered (fig. 114).

AHY/ASY (Aug-Jul): Flight feathers and wing covs uniformly blackish; rects truncate (fig. 114).

Sex—CP/BP (May-Aug). Wg: Western ♂(n30) 60-68, ♀(n30) 57-64; Yellow ♂(n30) 62-71, ♀(n30) 60-68. With HY/SYs, look for a yellower tinge to the breast and one or two reddish feathers in the crowns of some ♂♂, and little to no yellow tinge and no reddish feathers in ♀♀. Otherwise, ♂ = ♀ by plumage.

References—B,R,W,SK,O; Goodpasture (1963), Robbins (1964); PRBO data.

BAY-BREASTED WARBLER
Dendroica castanea

BBWA
Species # 660.0
Band size: 0

Species—In basic plumage, upperparts yellowish-green, feathers with indistinct to distinct blackish centers; flanks often with some chestnut; undertail covs usually tinged buffy; p6 at least slightly emarginated; longest undertail cov to tip of tail 16-26 mm; soles of feet dark bluish-gray. The combination of these criteria should separate this species from Pine and Blackpoll warblers (which see) in fall-winter.

Molt—PB: HY partial (Jul-Aug), AHY complete (Jul-Aug); PA partial (Feb-Apr). PBs occur on the summer grounds.

Skull—Completes in HY from 15 Oct thru Dec.

Age/Sex—CP/BP (May-Aug). Wg: ♂(n100) 70-78, ♀(n100) 67-74. Juv (Jun-Aug) has grayish-olive upperparts, buffy wing bars, and dusky spotting on the underparts (♂ = ♀). The size of the white patch on r4 does not seem as useful for ageing and/or sexing as with other *Dendroica* but there may be some age/sex related variation; differences in rect shape and wing covert contrast in spring are also difficult to use, possibly because the gr covs are molted during the PA. With the following, birds with conflicting characteristics or intermediates will occur which are not reliably aged and/or sexed; extreme caution should be used:

Basic Plumage

AHY/ASY ♂ (Aug-Mar): Crown and throat with some chestnut feathers; back feathers with large, distinct black centers (fig. 140); rump gray with little or no green; flanks with a moderate amount of chestnut; flight feathers and pp covs black; rects truncate (fig. 114).

HY/SY ♂ (Aug-Mar): Crown and throat occasionally with some chestnut feathers; back feathers with small but distinct blackish centers (fig. 140); rump gray, strongly washed green; flanks usually with some indistinct chestnut; flight feathers and pp covs brownish-black; rects tapered (fig. 114).

AHY/ASY ♀ (Aug-Mar): Crown and throat without chestnut feathers; back feathers with indistinct blackish centers (fig. 140); rump gray with little or no green; flanks usually with some indistinct chestnut; flight feathers and pp covs blackish; rects truncate (fig. 114).

HY/SY ♀ (Aug-Mar): Crown, throat, and flanks without chestnut; back feathers with indistinct dusky centers (fig. 140); rump mostly green; flight feathers and pp covs brownish-black; rects tapered (fig. 140).

Alternate Plumage

ASY ♂ (Mar-Aug): Forehead, lores, and auriculars black; crown and nape chestnut, without black streaking; chestnut on breast and flanks extensive; flight feathers and pp covs blackish; rects truncate (fig. 114).

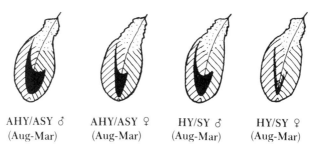

AHY/ASY ♂   AHY/ASY ♀   HY/SY ♂   HY/SY ♀
(Aug-Mar)   (Aug-Mar)   (Aug-Mar)   (Aug-Mar)

Figure 140. Indicative amounts of black in the back feathers of basic-plumaged Bay-breasted and Blackpoll warblers, by age and sex.

SY ♂ (Mar-Aug): Like ASY ♂ but plumage usually duller (lores often washed buffy); flight feathers and pp covs brownish; rects tapered (fig. 114).

ASY ♀ (Mar-Aug): Forehead mixed black and green; auriculars dusky; crown and nape grayish-olive with black and chestnut streaking; chestnut on breast and flanks indistinct, mixed with buffy; flight feathers and pp covs blackish; rects truncate (fig. 114).

SY ♀ (Mar-Aug): Like ASY ♀ but plumage averages duller; flight feathers and pp covs brownish; rects tapered (fig. 114).

References—B,R,W,SK,O; Blake (1954a), Robbins (1964), Howard (1968), Stiles & Campos (1983), Whitney (1983).

BLACKPOLL WARBLER

Dendroica striata

BPWA
Species # 661.0
Band size: 0

Species—In basic plumage: upperparts grayish-green, feathers usually with at least indistinct, to moderate blackish centers; flanks without chestnut; undertail covs white, often tinged lemon-yellow; p6 not emarginated; longest undertail cov—longest rect 12-15 mm; soles of feet yellowish. The combination of these criteria should separate this species from Pine and Bay-breasted warblers (which see) in fall-winter.

Molt—PB: HY partial (Jul-Aug), AHY complete (Jul-Aug); PA partial (Feb-Apr). PBs occur on the summer grounds.

Skull—Completes in HY from 15 Oct thru Dec.

Age/Sex—CP/BP (May-Aug). Wg: ♂(n100) 71-78, ♀(n100) 66-74. Juv (Jun-Aug) has upperparts grayish-brown mottled black, and heavily mottled underparts (♂ = ♀). Besides the following, the size of the white patch on r4 may relate somewhat to age and sex but much overlap occurs. Differences in rect shape and wing covert contrast in spring are also difficult to use, possibly because the gr covs are molted during the PA. With the following, birds with conflicting characteristics or intermediates will occur which are not reliably aged and/or sexed; extreme caution, especially with basic-plumaged birds, should be used:

Basic Plumage

AHY/ASY ♂ (Aug-Mar): Back feathers with large black centers (see fig. 140); rump grayish; breast brightish yellow, contrasting with white undertail covs; upperbreast and flanks with distinct streaking; flight feathers and pp covs blackish; rects truncate (fig. 114).

AHY/ASY ♀ (Aug-Mar): Like AHY/ASY ♂ but distinct black centers on back (fig. 140) and streaks to upperbreast and flanks average smaller and less distinct; undertail covs sometimes tinged yellow. [Combine with wg for reliable separation of AHY/ASY ♂ from ♀.]

HY/SY (Aug-Jul): Back feathers with little or no dark centers (fig. 140); rump olive to grayish-olive; upperbreast and flanks with indistinct, dusky streaking; flight feathers and pp covs brownish-black to brownish; rects tapered (fig. 114). [HY/SY ♂ ♂ and ♀ ♀ are not reliably separated, except, perhaps, by wg.]

Alternate Plumage

ASY ♂ (Mar-Aug): Crown and nape black, without streaking, contrasting sharply with white cheeks; flight feathers and pp covs blackish; rects truncate (fig. 114).

SY ♂ (Mar-Aug): Like ASY ♂ but plumage may average duller; flight feathers and pp covs brownish; rects tapered (fig. 114).

ASY ♀ (Mar-Aug): Crown and nape grayish-olive with distinct black streaking; no distinct contrast between crown and cheeks; flight feathers and pp covs blackish; rects truncate (fig. 114).

SY ♀ (Mar-Aug): Like ASY ♀ but plumage probably averages duller; flight feathers and pp covs brownish; rects tapered (fig. 114).

References— B,R,W,SK,O; Blake (1954a), Nisbet *et al.* (1963), Robbins (1964), Howard (1968), Stiles & Campos (1983), Whitney (1983); PRBO data.

CERULEAN WARBLER   CEWA
Dendroica cerulea   Species # 658.0
                                                          Band size: 0

Species—HY/SY ♀ from similar species by combination of distinct, whitish wing bars and short tail (38-43).

Molt—PB: HY partial (Jul-Aug), AHY complete (Jul-Aug); PA partial (Feb-Apr). PBs occur on the summer grounds.

Skull—Completes in HY from 1 Oct thru Dec.

Age/Sex—CP/BP (May-Aug). Wg useful: ♂(n30) 62-70, ♀(n26) 58-64. Juv (Jun-Aug) has brownish-gray upperparts, a pale median crown stripe, and entirely white underparts (sexing may be possible by the color of the edging of the flight feathers; see below). Rect shape and the size of the white patch on r4 seems not as useful in this species as in other *Dendroica*. The following, however, should lead to reliable ageing and sexing of most birds:

Basic Plumage

AHY/ASY ♂ (Aug-Mar): Upperparts largely blue, feathers with distinct black centers; sides of upperbreast with distinct black streaking; alula and pp covs black; flight feathers black edged blue.

HY/SY ♂ (Aug-Mar): Upperparts greenish distinctly washed blue (especially on rump), back feathers often with indistinct blackish streaking; underparts mostly white, tinged yellow on throat; flanks with indistinct black streaking; alula and pp covs brownish-black; flight feathers brownish-black, edged grayish-green.

AHY/ASY ♀ (Aug-Mar): Like HY/SY ♂ but upperpart feathers without blackish streaking; underparts washed yellowish; alula and pp covs blackish; flight feathers blackish, edged bluish-green.

HY/SY ♀ (Aug-Mar): Upperparts olive with little or no blue, back feathers without streaks; streaking on flanks very obscure; alula and pp covs brownish; flight feathers brownish, edged greenish-yellow.

Alternate Plumage

ASY ♂ (Mar-Aug): Superciliary absent; upperparts blue; alula and wing covs fairly uniformly blackish; flight feathers blackish edged blue.

SY ♂ (Mar-Aug): Like ASY ♂ but alula and pp covs brownish, often contrasting with blacker gr covs; flight feathers brownish edged grayish-green.

ASY ♀ (Mar-Aug): Yellow superciliary distinct; upperparts grayish tinged green; alula and wing covs fairly uniformly blackish; flight feathers blackish edged bluish-green.

SY ♀ (Mar-Aug): Like ASY ♀ but alula and pp covs brownish, often contrasting with blacker gr covs; flight feathers brownish edged greenish-yellow.

References—B,R,W,SK,O; Robbins (1964).

BLACK-AND-WHITE WARBLER
Mniotitla varia

BAWA
Species # 636.0
Band size: 0

Molt—PB: HY partial (Jul-Aug), AHY complete (Jul-Aug); PA partial (Feb-Apr). PBs occur on the summer grounds.

Skull—Completes in HY from 1 Oct thru Dec.

Age/Sex—CP/BP (Apr-Jul). Wg: ♂(n100) 64-74, ♀(n100) 59-69. Juv (Jun-Aug) resembles HY/SY ♀ (see below) but is buffier with entire underparts spotted or streaked dusky (♂ = ♀).

Basic Plumage

AHY/ASY ♂ (Aug-Mar): Auriculars black or blackish; undertail covs and flanks with bold, black streaking; flight feathers and pp covs black; rects truncate as in *Dendroica* warblers (fig. 114).

HY/SY ♂ (Aug-Mar): Auriculars grayish or whitish; undertail covs and flanks with fairly bold blackish streaking, often blurred but distinct; flight feathers and pp covs brownish-black; rects tapered (fig. 114).

AHY/ASY ♀ (Aug-Mar): Like HY/SY ♂ but undertail covs and flanks with indistinct, dusky streaking; flight feathers and pp covs blackish; rects truncate (fig. 114).

HY/SY ♀ (Aug-Mar): Auriculars buffy whitish; undertail covs and flanks with very indistinct dusky streaking; flight feathers and pp covs brownish-black; rects tapered (fig. 114).

Alternate Plumage

ASY ♂ (Mar-Aug): Chin, throat, and auriculars black or blackish; flight feathers and wing covs fairly uniformly blackish; rects truncate (fig.114).

SY ♂ (Mar-Aug): Like ASY ♂ but flight feathers and pp covs brownish, contrasting with blacker gr covs; rects tapered (fig. 114).

ASY ♀ (Mar-Jul): Chin and throat white; auriculars grayish; flight feathers and wing covs fairly uniformly blackish; rects truncate (fig. 114).

SY ♀ (Mar-Aug): Like ASY ♀ but flight feathers and pp covs brownish, contrasting with blacker gr covs; rects tapered (fig. 114).

References—B,R,W,SK,O,BBM; Robbins (1964).

AMERICAN REDSTART
Setophaga ruticilla

AMRE
Species # 687.0
Band size: 0

Molt—PB: HY partial (Jul-Aug), AHY complete (Jul-Aug); PA: limited (Dec-Apr). PBs occur on the summer grounds. Limited, continuous molt occurs on the winter grounds, which is probably more extensive in SY ♂♂.

Skull—Completes in HY/SY from 15 Oct thru Jan.

Age/Sex—CP/BP (May-Aug). Wg: ♂(n40) 59-69, ♀(n40) 55-66. Rect shape seems unhelpful in ageing but may be useful with extremes. Juv (Jun-Aug) has brownish upperparts, grayish underparts, and two whitish wing bars (some Juvs may be sexed by amount of yellow in the rects; fig 141). Most birds should be reliably aged and sexed with the following:

AHY/ASY ♂ (Aug-2nd Aug): Upperparts, throat, and breast entirely black; flight feathers black and orange.

HY/SY ♂ (Aug-2nd Aug): Upperparts grayish-olive (Aug-Dec) or grayish-olive with some black mottling (Jan-Aug); underparts mostly white (Aug-Dec); or white with some black

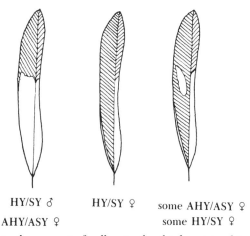

HY/SY ♂   HY/SY ♀   some AHY/ASY ♀
AHY/ASY ♀   some HY/SY ♀

Figure 141. Variation in the amount of yellow in the third rectrix of American Redstart. The reliability of this criterion, especially for ageing ♀♀, needs further determination.

mottling, especially about throat and breast (Jan-Aug); patches at sides of breast orangish-yellow to salmon colored, contrasting with yellow underwing covs; pp covs brownish-gray; flight feathers brownish-gray and yellow; yellow patch on r3 large (fig. 141). [There may be some overlap with AHY/ASY ♀ ♀ in fall; combine with skull and wg.]

AHY/ASY ♀ (Aug-Jul): Upperparts grayish-olive and underparts mostly white, without black mottling; patches at sides of breast lemon yellow to orange-yellow, not contrasting markedly in color with underwing covs; pp covs gray; flight feathers gray and yellow; r3 usually with large patch of yellow (fig. 141). [Check also for more yellow in the wings of AHY/ASY ♀ (and HY/SY ♂) than in HY/SY ♀.]

HY/SY ♀ (Aug-Jul): Like AHY/ASY ♀ but breast patches paler yellow; pp covs brownish-gray; flight feathers brownish-gray and yellow; yellow patch on r3 reduced and washed dusky or lacking (fig. 141).

References—B,R,W,SK,O,BBM; Robbins (1964), Gray (1973), Foy (1974a, 1974b), Rowher *et al.* (1983); PRBO data.

PROTHONOTARY WARBLER
Protonotaria ctrea

PTWA
Species # 637.0
Band size: 0

Molt—PB: HY partial (Jun-Jul), AHY complete (Jul-Aug); PA absent. PBs occur on the summer grounds.

Skull—Completes in HY from 1 Oct (as early as 15 Sep in Florida populations) thru Nov.

Age/Sex—CP/BP (Apr-Aug). Wg: ♂(n100) 67-76, ♀(n30) 64-72. Juv (May-Jul) has brownish-olive upperparts, grayish-olive underparts, and two olive wing bars (Juvs may be sexed by the amount of white in the outer rects; fig. 142). All birds should be easily sexed by the following, but intermediates will occur which are not reliably aged:

AHY/ASY ♂ (Aug-Jul): Crown and nape bright yellow, contrasting sharply with greenish back (see fig. 111); all rects but central pair with white; outer rects with large white patches (fig. 142); flight feathers and pp covs gray; rects truncate (see fig. 114).

HY/SY ♂ (Aug-Jul): Like AHY/ASY ♂ but hindcrown and nape yellow washed greenish, contrasting moderately with greenish back (fig. 111); flight feathers and pp covs brownish-gray, contrasting with grayer gr covs; rects tapered (fig. 114).

AHY/ASY ♀ (Aug-Jul): Crown and nape greenish-yellow, contrasting slightly with greenish back (fig. 111); outer 2-3

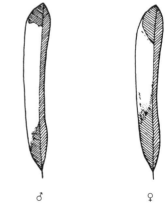

♂   ♀

Figure 142. Outer rectrix pattern in ♂ and ♀ Prothonotary Warblers, particularly useful for sexing juveniles.

rects only with white; outer rects with small white patches (fig. 142); flight feathers and pp covs gray; rects truncate (see fig. 114).

HY/SY ♀ (Aug-Jul): Like AHY/ASY ♀ but crown and nape greenish, blending with the color of the back (fig. 111); flight feathers and pp covs brownish-gray, contrasting with grayer gr covs; rects tapered (fig. 114).

References—B,R,W,SK,O; Robbins (1964), Kowalski (1986).

WORM-EATING WARBLER
Helmitheros vermivorus

WEWA
Species # 639.0
Band size: 1-0

Molt—PB: HY partial (Jun-Aug), AHY complete (Jul-Aug); PA absent. PBs occur on the summer grounds.

Skull—Completes in HY from 1 Oct thru Nov.

Age—Juv (Jun-Jul) is buffier and has two cinnamon wing bars. Intermediates between the following will occur, especially in spring, which are not reliably aged:

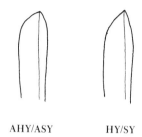

AHY/ASY   HY/SY

HY/SY (Aug-Jul): Upperbreast tawny; terts with rusty tips (usually wearing off between Nov & Mar); rects tapered (fig. 143), relatively worn, especially in spring.

Figure 143. Outer rectrix shape by age in Worm-eating Warblers.

AHY/ASY (Aug-Jul): Upperbreast tan; terts without rusty tips; rects truncate (fig. 143), relatively unworn.

Sex—♂ = ♀ by plumage. CP/BP (Apr-Aug). Wg: ♂(n30) 66-73; ♀(n30) 63-70.

References—B,W,O; Robbins (1964).

SWAINSON'S WARBLER
Limnothlypis swainsonii

SWWA
Species # 638.0
Band size: 1-0

Molt—PB: HY partial (Jun-Aug), AHY complete (Jul-Aug); PA absent. PBs occur on the summer grounds.

Skull—Completes in HY from 1 Oct thru Dec.

Age—Juv (May-Jul) lacks superciliary and has buffy wing bars. The following can be difficult, and should only be used on extremes:

HY/SY (Aug-Jul): Rects and pp tapered (see fig. 112); relatively worn, especially in spring.

AHY/ASY (Aug-Jul): Rects and pp truncate (fig. 112), relatively unworn.

Sex—♂ = ♀ by plumage. CP/BP (Apr-Jul). Wg: ♂(n29) 68-76; ♀(n16) 66-72.

References—B,O.

OVENBIRD
Seiurus aurocapillus

Molt—PB: HY partial-incomplete (Jun-Aug), AHY complete (Jul-Aug); PA limited (Jan-Mar). PBs occur on the summer grounds; 1st PB may occasionally include some or all rects.

Skull—Completes in HY/SY from 1 Nov thru Feb. Check spring birds for windows, indicating SY.

Age—Juv (Jun-Aug) has upperpart feathers edged cinnamon and two buffy wing bars. Intermediates between the following, especially in spring/summer, may not be reliably aged:

HY/SY (Aug-Jul): Terts with narrow rusty tipping (these wear off during Nov-May); rects tapered (fig. 144), usually relatively worn; edges of outer rects without indistinct pale spots.

AHY/ASY (Aug-Jul): Terts without rusty tips; rects truncate (fig. 144), relatively unworn; edges of outer rects occasionally (on about 5% of birds) with indistinct pale spots extending > 1 mm onto the inner webs.

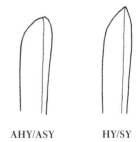

AHY/ASY   HY/SY

Sex—♂ = ♀ by plumage. CP/BP (Apr-Aug). Wg: ♂(n100) 71-82, ♀(n100) 68-78.

References—B,R,W,SK,O,BBM; Eaton (1957b), Robbins (1964), Short & Robbins (1967), Taylor (1972, 1973); PRBO data.

Figure 144. Juvenal and adult outer rectrix shapes in Ovenbird and the waterthrushes.

NORTHERN WATERTHRUSH
Seiurus novaboracensis

Species—Superciliary usually yellowish, tapering behind eye and chin and throat usually with distinct narrow black streaking (fig. 145); flanks and underparts uniformly yellowish or whitish in coloration; all undertail covs with regularly patterned gray bases (fig. 145); wg

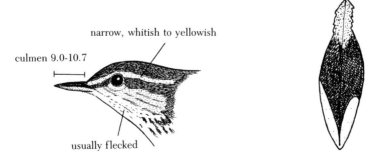

narrow, whitish to yellowish

culmen 9.0-10.7

usually flecked

Figure 145. Head and greater undertail covert pattern for identifying Northern Waterthrush.

68-82; culmen 9.0-10.7. The combination of these features should easily separate this from Louisiana Waterthrush.

Molt—PB: HY partial (Jun-Aug), AHY complete (Jul-Aug); PA absent. PBs occur on the summer grounds; 1st PB may occasionally include the rects.

Skull—Completes in HY/SY from 1 Nov thru Jan. Some SYs retain windows thru spring.

Age—Juv (Jun-Jul) has upperpart feathers tipped cinnamon and distinct buffy wing bars. Intermediates between the following, especially in spring/summer, may not be reliably aged:

HY/SY (Aug-Jul): Terts with narrow rusty tipping; rects tapered (fig. 144), usually relatively worn; edges of outer rects without indistinct pale spots.

AHY/ASY (Aug-Jul): Terts without rusty tipping; rects truncate (fig. 144), relatively unworn; edges of outer rects occasionally (on about 8% of birds) with indistinct whitish spots extending > 1 mm onto the inner webs.

Sex—♂ = ♀ by plumage. CP/BP (Apr-Aug). Wg: ♂(n100) 72-82, ♀(n100) 68-78; W > E > British Columbia (see Eaton 1957a for geographic variation in wg).

References—B,R,W,SK,O,C(Collins and Binford),BBM; Eaton (1957a, 1957b), Robbins (1964), Short & Robbins (1967), Binford (1971); PRBO data.

LOUISIANA WATERTHRUSH
Seiurus motacilla

LOWA
Species # 676.0
Band size: 1

Species—From Northern Waterthrush (which see) by the following: Superciliary white, broad, usually extending to nape and chin and throat usually without streaking (fig. 146); flanks and undertail covs buffy, contrasting with white underparts; largest undertail covs with irregular and restricted gray patches (fig. 146); wg 74-85; culmen 10.2-12.2.

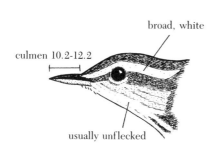
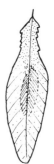

broad, white

culmen 10.2-12.2

usually unflecked

Figure 146. Head and greater undertail covert pattern for identifying Louisiana Waterthrush.

Molt—PB: HY partial (Jun-Jul), AHY complete (Jun-Jul); PA absent. PBs occur on the summer grounds. 1st PB may occasionally include the rects.

Skull—Completes in HY from 1 Oct thru Dec. Some SYs retain windows thru spring.

Age—The same age criteria as Northern Waterthrush apply to this species, except that ASY and SY are reliably separated only through Jun.

Sex—♂ = ♀ by plumage. CP/BP (Mar-Aug). Wg: ♂(n30) 77-85, ♀(n30) 74-81; E > W.

References—B,R,W,SK,O,C(Collins and Binford),BBM; Eaton (1957b, 1958), Robbins (1964), Short & Robbins (1967), Binford (1971), Schaeffer (1974).

KENTUCKY WARBLER
Oporornis formosus

KEWA
Species # 677.0
Band size: 1

Molt—PB: HY partial (Jun-Aug), AHY complete (Jun-Aug); PA limited (Feb-Apr). PBs occur on the summer grounds. PA possibly more extensive in SYs than ASYs.

Skull—Completes in HY/SY from 1 Oct thru Jan.

Age/Sex—CP/BP (Apr-Jul). Wg: ♂(n40) 65-75, ♀(n40) 61-70. Juv (May-Jul) lacks black on the crown and face and has brownish-yellow plumage (♂ = ♀). Intermediates between the following occur which are not reliably aged and/or sexed:

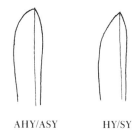

AHY/ASY   HY/SY

Figure 147. Rectrix shape by age in the *Oporornis* warblers.

AHY/ASY ♂ (Aug-Jul): Crown black, feathers tipped gray with little or no brown; black of mask distinct and extensive (fig. 147); rects truncate (fig. 148).

HY/SY ♂ (Aug-Jul): Crown blackish, feathers tipped with dusky brown; mask dull black, suffused with greenish, less extensive (Aug-Mar; fig. 147); or crown like AHY/ASY ♂ but probably averages duller (Mar-Jul); rects tapered (fig. 148). [Aug-Mar birds may be difficult to separate from HY/SY ♀♀; compare with wg.]

AHY/ASY ♀ (Aug-Jul): Crown dull black, feathers tipped gray in fall with little or no brown; black mask restricted (fig.147); rects truncate (fig. 148).

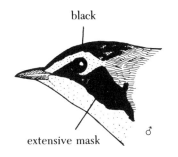

black

extensive mask   ♂

blackish washed olive

reduced mask   ♀

Figure 148. Typical head and face mask patterns in ♂ and ♀ Kentucky Warblers. First-year ♀♀ in basic plumage average even duller.

HY/SY ♀ (Aug-Mar): Crown dusky with extensive olive-brown wash; face mask dusky or olive, restricted (Aug-Mar; see fig. 147); or crown as with AHY/ASY (Mar-Jul); rects tapered (fig. 148).

References—B,W,O; Goodpasture (1963), Robbins (1964).

CONNECTICUT WARBLER
Oporornis agilis

COWA
Species # 678.0
Band size: 1

Species—Eye ring full and distinct; wg 63-75; p9 > p6 by at least 3.5 mm; wg (flat)—tail 19-27 mm. These should readily separate this species from Mourning and MacGillivray's warblers (which see).

Molt—PB: HY partial (Jul-Aug), AHY complete (Jul-Aug); PA limited (Feb-Apr). PBs occur on the summer grounds. PA may occur to a greater extent in SY than ASY; this should be further studied.

Skull—Completes in HY from 1 Nov thru Dec.

Age/Sex—CP/BP (May-Jul). Wg: ♂(n30) 65-75, ♀(n30) 63-73. Juv (Jun-Aug) has entire plumage washed brownish (♂ = ♀). Intermediates between the following occur, which are not reliably aged and/or sexed:

Basic Plumage

AHY/ASY ♂ (Aug-Mar): Forecrown, throat, and upperbreast slate gray, feathers tipped brownish or pale gray; eye ring white; rects truncate (fig. 148).

HY/SY ♂ (Aug-Mar): Forecrown and upperbreast brownish-gray; throat pale whitish; eye ring buffy to buffy-white; rects tapered (fig. 148). [May be difficult to separate from HY/SY ♀; combine with wg.]

AHY/ASY ♀ (Aug-Mar): Like HY/SY ♂ but eye ring white; rects truncate (fig. 148).

HY/SY ♀ (Aug-Mar): Forecrown and upperbreast olive-brown; throat buffy white; eye-ring buffy to buffy-white; rects tapered (fig. 148).

Alternate Plumage

ASY ♂ (Mar-Jul): Forecrown, throat, and upperbreast slate gray, contrasting markedly with yellow underparts; upperparts usually without brownish tinge; rects truncate (fig. 148).

SY ♂ (Mar-Jul): Like ASY ♂ but plumage averages duller; contrast between head and underparts usually less distinct; upperparts often tinged with brownish; rects tapered (fig. 148).

ASY ♀ (Mar-Jul): Forecrown, throat, and upperbreast olive-gray to brownish-gray; rects truncate (fig. 148).

SY ♀ (Mar-Jul): Like ASY ♀ but rects tapered (fig. 148).

References—B,R,W,SK,O,C, Robbins (1964), Lanyon & Bull (1967).

MOURNING WARBLER
Oporornis philadelphia

MOWA
Species # 679.0
Band size: 1-0

Species—AHY/ASY ♂ without eye ring (occasionally with a few white feathers around eye), HY/SYs and ♀♀ with eye ring whitish to yellowish, thin, variable in size, from almost absent to complete (but not as full as Connecticut Warbler; fig. 149); HY/SYs with throat usually strongly washed yellow and breast band usually broken such that yellow continues uninterupted to breast; undertail covs relatively bright yellow; wg 53-65; p9 ≤ p6 or (rarely) p9 > p6 by up to 3.0 mm; tail 43-53; wg (flat)—tail 10-18 mm. Plumage and measurements should separate this species from Connecticut and MacGillivray's warblers (which see). A few may not be seperable from MacGillivray's by wg (flat)—tail (= 10-12, possibly to 15); compare with plumage and tail length. [An analysis of this criterion within each age/sex class is needed.] Also, beware of hybrids.

broad & white   narrow & whitish to yellowish

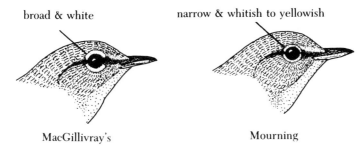

MacGillivray's   Mourning

Figure 149. Head and eye ring features in ♀♀ and HY/SY ♂ Mourning vs. MacGillivray's warblers.

Molt—PB: HY partial (Jul-Aug), AHY complete (Jul-Aug); PA limited (Feb-Apr). PBs occur primarily on the summer grounds. PA is probably more extensive on SYs than ASYs

Skull—Completes in HY from 15 Oct thru Dec.

Age/Sex—CP/BP (May-Aug). Wg: ♂(n30) 56-65, ♀(n30) 53-63. Juv (Jun-Aug) has entire plumage washed brownish (♂ = ♀). Intermediates between the following occur which are not reliably aged and/or sexed:

Basic Plumage

AHY/ASY ♂ (Aug-Mar): Crown and throat gray or blackish lightly washed brownish, upperbreast substantially blackish with some pale mottling, forming the appearance of a complete breast band or hood; eye ring absent; rects truncate (fig. 148).

HY/SY ♂ (Aug-Mar): Crown olive-grayish; lores, throat and upperbreast gray washed yellow, sides of upperbreast with brownish-gray patches and sometimes some black mottling, but not forming complete breast band or hood; partial eye ring yellowish-white; rects tapered (fig. 148). [May be difficult to separate from HY/SY ♀; compare with wg.]

AHY/ASY ♀ (Aug-Mar): Crown, lores, throat and upperbreast pale brownish-gray, throat and center of the upperbreast gray washed buffy-whitish, without black mottling, but maintaining the appearance of a full breast band or hood; partial eye ring whitish; rects truncate (fig.148).

HY/SY ♀ (Aug-Mar): Crown brownish-olive, lores, throat and upperbreast buffy yellow without gray or black mottling, sides of upperbreast with indistinct brownish-olive patches; partial eye ring yellowish; rects tapered (fig. 148).

Alternate Plumage

ASY ♂ (Mar-Aug): Forehead and throat slate gray; upperbreast mottled blackish; upperparts usually without brownish tinge; eye ring absent; rects truncate (fig. 148).

SY ♂ (Mar-Aug): Like ASY ♂ but plumage averages duller; upperparts often tinged brownish; rects tapered (fig. 148).

ASY ♀ (Mar-Aug): Forehead, throat, and upperbreast pale gray to brownish-gray; throat pale, sometimes tinged yellow; narrow, broken, whitish eye ring often present; rects truncate (fig. 148).

SY ♀ (Mar-Aug): Like ASY ♀ but rects tapered (fig. 148).

References—DVR,B,R,W,SK,O,C; Robbins (1964), Lanyon & Bull (1967), Hall (1979), Kowalski (1983); PRBO data.

MACGILLIVRAY'S WARBLER
Oporornis tolmiei

MGWA
Species # 680.0
Band size: 1-0

Species—Wide, broken white eye ring (fig. 149) present in all plumages; HY/SYs with throat and upperbreast grayish washed buffy, occasionally with some yellow; grayish of breast usually forming the appearance of a complete breast band; undertail covs relatively pale yellow; wg 53-67; p9 ≤ p6; tail 47-63; wg (flat)—tail 2-12 (possibly to 15) mm. Plumage and measurements should separate this species from Connecticut and Mourning warblers (which see). A few may not be separable from Mourning by wg (flat)—tail (= 10-12, possibly to 15); compare with plumage and tail length. Also, beware of hybrids.

Molt—PB: HY partial (Jul-Aug), AHY complete (Jul-Aug); PA limited-partial (Feb-Apr). PBs occur on the summer grounds. PA is probably more extensive in SYs than ASYs.

Skull—Completes in HY from 1 Oct thru Dec.

Age/Sex—CP/BP (Apr-Aug). Wg: ♂(n44) 54-67, ♀(n42) 53-63; Rocky Mtn > W Cst. Juv (Jun-Aug) has entire plumage washed brownish (♂ = ♀). Intermediates between the following occur which are not reliably aged and/or sexed:

Basic Plumage

AHY/ASY ♂ (Aug-Mar): Crown and throat gray or blackish, lightly washed with pale brownish; upperbreast substantially blackish with some grayish mottling; rects truncate (fig. 148).

HY/SY ♂ (Aug-Mar): Crown dull brownish-gray; lores grayish; throat and upperbreast pale gray washed slightly with buff; upperbreast sometimes with a few concealed blackish feathers; rects tapered (fig. 148).

AHY/ASY ♀ (Aug-Mar): Like HY/SY ♂ but lores buffy gray; upperbreast without black feathers; rects truncate (fig. 148).

HY/SY ♀ (Aug-Mar): Crown brownish-olive; lores grayish-buff; throat and upperbreast very pale grayish to grayish-buff; rects tapered (fig. 148).

Alternate Plumage

ASY ♂ (Mar-Aug): Forehead and throat slate gray; upperbreast mottled blackish; upperparts without brownish tinge; rects truncate (fig. 148).

SY ♂ (Mar-Aug): Like ASY ♂ but upperparts sometimes tinged brownish; rects tapered (fig. 148).

ASY ♀ (Mar-Aug): Forehead, throat, and upperbreast pale gray to brownish-gray; throat pale, sometimes tinged buffy; rects truncate (fig. 148).

SY ♀ (Mar-Aug): Like ASY ♀ but rects tapered (fig. 148).

References—DVR,B,SK,O,C; Lanyon & Bull (1967), Hall (1979), Kowalski (1983); PRBO data.

COMMON YELLOWTHROAT
Geothlypis trichas

COYE
Species # 681.0
Band size: 0

Species—♀♀ from all other warblers by the lack of rictal bristles.

Molt—PB: HY partial-incomplete (Jul-Aug), AHY complete (Jul-Aug); PA limited (Jan-Apr). PBs occur on the summer grounds; 1st PB can include some (or all?) flight feathers in some southern populations. The PA may occur only in SY ♂♂; this could use further investigation.

Skull—Completes in HY/SY from 1 Oct (as early as 1 Sep in some California populations) thru Jan.

Age/Sex—CP/BP (Mar-Aug). Wg: ♂(n100) 50-62, ♀(n100) 47-57; W > E (generally). Juv (May-Aug) has olive-green upperparts and two cinnamon wing bars (♂ = ♀). The shape of the rects can be extremely subtle and should be used with caution, especially in ageing adults of southern forms (see Molt):

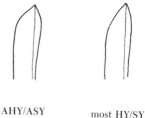

AHY/ASY
some HY/SY

most HY/SY

Figure 150. Rectrix shape by age in the Common Yellowthroat.

AHY/ASY ♂ (Mar-Feb): Forehead, lores and auriculars completely black; eye ring black; rects truncate (fig. 150).

HY/SY ♂ (Aug-Jul): Forehead, lores, and auriculars mixed brown and black (mostly brown in Aug-Mar; completely black or black with some buff in Mar-Jul); eye ring buff, mixed buff and black, or black ; rects tapered (fig. 150).

AHY/ASY ♀ (Aug-Jul): Forehead, lores, and auriculars completely brown; throat and upper breast yellow; rects truncate (fig. 150).

HY/SY ♀ (Aug-Jul): Like AHY/ASY ♀ but throat and upper breast with less (sometimes no) yellow; rects tapered (fig. 150). [Lack of black in the face is probably reliable for ♀ ♀ after the 1st PB. In certain (eastern?) populations, occasional HY/SY ♂ ♂ (Aug-Mar) may not show any black; compare with wg.]

References—DVR,B,R,W,SK,O,BBM; Stewart (1952), Robbins (1964), Ewert & Lanyon (1970), Fisk (1972), Taylor (1976); PRBO data.

HOODED WARBLER
Wilsonia citrina

HOWA
Species # 684.0
Band size: 0

Species—HY/SY ♀ from most other warblers by the presence of white spots in the outer rects; from Bachman's Warbler by the lack of an eye ring or gray in the crown and a longer tail (52-64).

Molt—PB: HY partial-complete (Jun-Aug), AHY complete (Jun-Aug); PA absent.PBs occur on the summer grounds. The 1st PB is variable; it can be partial but usually includes the rects and a variable number of other flight feathers. At least some HYs have a complete molt (see Walters and Lamm 1980).

Skull—Completes in HY from 1 Oct thru Dec.

Sex—CP/BP (Apr-Aug). Wg: ♂(n30) 63-72, ♀(n30) 58-67. The following is reliable after the 1st PB:

♂: Black hood extensive and complete, feathers with narrow yellow tipping in fall. [Birds molting in black during the 1st PB are reliably sexed ♂.]

♀: Crown, nape, throat, and upperbreast with varying amount of black, from none to heavily mottled, but never as extensive as ♂ (see Age).

Age—Juv (May-Aug) has entire plumage washed buffy or brownish, with two buffy wing bars (♂ = ♀ although the amount of white in the rects may provide a clue; more study needed). The extent of black on ♀ ♀ (see Sex) is probably age related. Birds with no black are probably HY/SYs while those with extensive black are probably AHY/ASYs. A good study for banders. Otherwise, the following is reliable for some HY/SYs but AHY/ASYs (especially ♂ ♂) are generally not reliably aged by plumage after completion of the PB:

HY/SY (Aug-Jul): Some or all flight feathers dull green, sometimes with a brownish tinge; some or all rects tapered (see fig. 151).

AHY (Jan-Aug): All flight feathers glossy green; rects truncate (fig. 151).

References—B,W,O; Walters & Lamm (1980); PRBO data.

WILSON'S WARBLER
Wilsonia pusilla

WIWA
Species # 685.0
Band size: 0

Species—HY/SY ♀ from Hooded Warbler by the lack of whitish spots in the outer rects and shorter tail (44-52).

Molt—PB: HY partial (May-Jul), AHY complete (Jun-Aug); PA limited Feb-Apr. PBs occur on the summer grounds. The 1st PB begins immediately after Juvs leave the nest.

Skull—Completes in HY from 15 Oct (as early as 15 Sep in California populations) thru Nov.

Age—Juv (May-Aug) has entire plumage washed brownish or buffy, and two brownish wing-bars (♂ = ♀); birds are rarely caught in this plumage (at least in the west). In addition to the following, the extent and percentage of green in the cap (see Sex) is probably age related for the respective sexes, and the shape of the primaries, as with *Vermivora* warblers (fig. 112), is probably also of use (these need further investigation):

HY/SY (Aug-Jul): Rects tapered (fig. 151).

AHY/ASY (Aug-Jul): Rects truncate (fig. 151).

Sex—CP/BP (Apr-Aug). Wg: ♂(n100) 52-61, ♀(n100) 48-57; W > E. Sexing by extent and percent of green in the black crown patch (fig. 152) is reliable after the 1st PB but varies between populations. For populations E of the Rocky Mts, the following is reliable; on intermediates, compare with wg and age (these are likely HY/SY ♂♂ or AHY/ASY ♀♀):

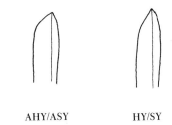

AHY/ASY   HY/SY

Figure 151. Rectrix shape by age in *Wilsonia* warblers.

♂: Black cap shiny, ≥ 11 mm in length.

♀: Black cap absent or obscured by greenish, ≤ 8 mm.

For populations W of the Rockies use the following; again, compare with wg and age for intermediates:

♂: Black cap shiny, with less than 5% greenish tipping and ≥ 11 mm (usually > 14) in length.

♀: Black cap suffused with more than 20% greenish and ≤ 12 mm.

References—B,R,W,SK,O,BBM; Stewart (1972a, 1972c), McNicholl (1977); PRBO data.

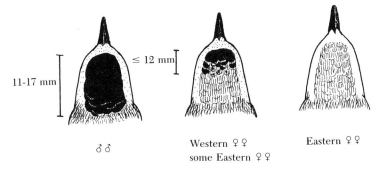

Figure 152. Amounts of black in the crowns of Wilson's Warblers, by sex and population. This may also vary with age (see account).

CANADA WARBLER
Wilsonia canadensis

CAWA
Species # 686.0
Band size: 0

Molt—PB: HY partial (Jun-Aug), AHY complete (Jun-Aug); PA limited (Feb-Apr). PBs occur on the summer grounds.

Skull—Completes in HY from 15 Oct thru Dec.

Age/Sex—CP/BP (May-Jul). Wg: ♂(n100) 61-69, ♀(n55) 58-66. Juv (Jun-Jul) has brown upperparts with buffy wing bars (♂ = ♀). Use caution with the following; many intermediates may not be reliably aged and/or sexed (compare with wg):

Basic Plumage

AHY/ASY ♂ (Aug-Mar): Forehead black to bluish with black flecking; upperbreast with wide (1-2 mm) black streaks; flight feathers and pp covs bluish; rects truncate (fig. 151).

HY/SY ♂ (Aug-Mar): Forehead usually greenish; sometimes flecked with black; upperbreast with small but distinct blackish streaks or spots; flight feathers and pp covs grayish; rects tapered (fig. 151). [May be difficult to separate from HY/SY ♀, especially without experience.]

AHY/ASY ♀ (Aug-Mar): Forehead usually grayish tinged greenish; upperbreast with relatively indistinct, grayish or blackish streaks; flight feathers and pp covs grayish-blue; rects truncate (fig. 151).

HY/SY ♀ (Aug-Mar): Forehead greenish; upperbreast with very indistinct grayish streaking; flight feathers and pp covs grayish; rects tapered (fig. 151).

Alternate Plumage

ASY ♂ (Mar-Aug): Forehead, crown, auriculars, and sides of neck black or mostly black, feathers often edged gray; back bluish, without greenish wash; upperbreast with bold black streaking; flight feathers and wing covs fairly uniformly bluish; rects truncate (fig. 151).

SY ♂ (Mar-Aug): Like ASY ♂ but back sometimes with a slight greenish wash; flight feathers and pp covs brownish-gray, contrasting with bluer gr and mid covs; rects tapered (fig. 151).

ASY ♀ (Mar-Aug): Forehead, crown, auriculars, and sides of neck gray or greenish-gray, sometimes flecked with black; upperbreast with grayish and relatively indistinct streaking; flight feathers and wing covs fairly uniformly grayish-blue; rects truncate (fig. 151).

SY ♀ (Mar-Aug): Like ASY ♀ but flight feathers and pp covs brownish-gray, contrasting with bluer gr and mid covs; rects tapered (fig. 151).

References—B,R,W,O; Rappole (1983).

RED-FACED WARBLER
Cardellina rubrifrons

RFWA
Species # 690.0
Band size: 0

Molt—PB: HY partial (Jun-Jul), AHY complete (Jun-Jul); PA absent. PBs occur on the summer grounds.

Skull—Completes in HY from 1 Oct thru Dec.

Age—Rect shape seems of limited use despite the retention of the juvenal tail. Juv (Jun-Jul) is generally washed brownish and is dull pinkish-orange in the face and breast. Otherwise, no reliable plumage criteria known for AHY/ASYs, however, some HY/SYs (especially ♀♀) may be aged by a paler and pinkish or orange tinge to the face and upperbreast.

Sex—♂ = ♀ by plumage (but see Age). CP/BP (Apr-Jul). Wg useful: ♂(n30) 67-72, ♀(n20) 63-69.

References—B.

PAINTED REDSTART
Myioborus pictus

PARE
Species # 688.0
Band size: 0

Molt—PB: HY partial (Jul-Oct), AHY complete (Jun-Aug); PA absent. PBs occur primarily on the summer grounds.

Skull—Completes in HY from 1 Sep thru Dec.

Age—Juv (May-Sep) has duller black upperparts and lacks red on the belly. Intermediates between the following may not be reliably aged:

HY/SY (Aug-Jul): Flight feathers brownish-black; rects tapered (fig. 153).

AHY/ASY (Aug-Jul): Flight feathers black; rects truncate (fig. 153).

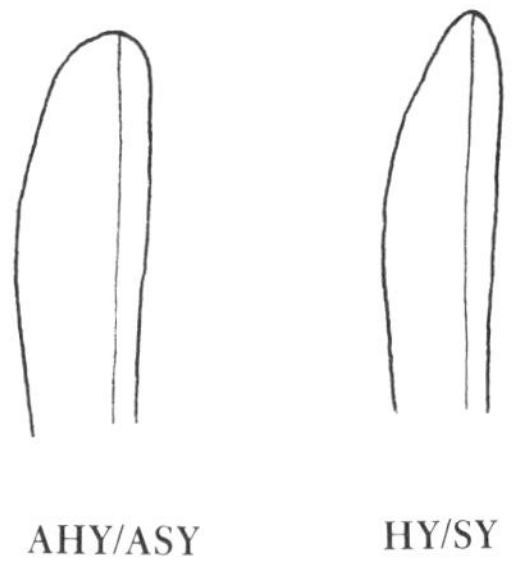

AHY/ASY   HY/SY

Figure 153. Rectrix shape by age in the Painted Redstart.

Sex—♂ = ♀ by plumage. CP/BP (Mar-Aug). Wg: ♂(n30) 68-75, ♀(n30) 66-71. [♀♀ possibly average duller than ♂♂ but this may be complicated by age.]

References—B,O.

YELLOW-BREASTED CHAT
Icteria virens

YBCH
Species # 683.0
Band size: 1B

Molt—PB: HY incomplete (Jul-Oct), AHY complete (Jul-Oct); PA absent. PBs occur on the summer grounds. The 1st PB usually includes 3-6 outer pp, the terts, and probably some or all ss and rects; the completeness and variability in this molt need further investigation.

Skull—Completes in HY from 1 Oct thru Dec. Check for windows in spring and summer, probably indicating SY.

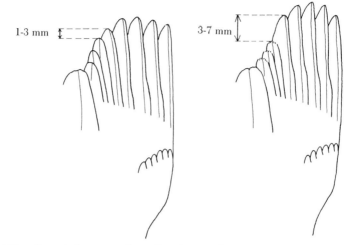

Figure 154. Wing formula by age in the Yellow-breasted Chat. The break between new and old feathers may occur elsewhere within the primaries (see account).

Age—Rect shape possibly of use on some birds after the 1st PB (see Molt); look also for contrasts between new and old rects indicating HY/SY. Juv (May-Aug) has duller grayish-olive or brownish-olive upperparts, no yellow on the underparts, and spotting on the throat and upperbreast ($\eth = ♀$).

HY/SY (Aug-2nd Aug): Outer 3-6 (usually 5) pp relatively fresh and green, contrasting with inner 3-6 (usually 4) pp; distance between the adjacent primaries of these two groups 3-7 mm (fig. 154).

AHY/ASY (Sep-Aug): Pp uniform in coloration and fadedness, the distance between adjacent pp of p3-p7 1-3 mm (fig. 154). [Occasional HY/SYs may molt all the primaries but birds in this category can reliably called AHY/ASYs. Compare with other ageing criteria and plumage (AHY/ASYs average brighter than HY/SYs in the respective sexes).]

Sex—CP/BP (Apr-Aug). Wg: $\eth$(n47) 74-84, ♀(n43) 71-80; W > E. Some intermediates will occur between the following. Compare with age; these are likely HY/SY $\eth \eth$ or AHY/ASY ♀♀:

$\eth$—Lores black or blackish; bill black; mouth black (Apr-Aug, possibly longer).

♀—Lores dark gray; bill brown or blackish-brown; mouth pinkish.

References—B,O,W,SK,WB; Dennis (1958, 1967), Phillips (1974); PRBO data.

OLIVE WARBLER
Peucedramus taeniatus

OLWA
Species # 651.0
Band size: 0

Species—HY/SY ♀ from Hermit Warbler by white patch at the base of the pp (sometimes hidden by pp covs), longer wg (67-73), and greater notch in tail (outer—central rect 4.5 mm).

Molt—PB: HY partial (Jul-Aug), AHY complete (Jul-Aug); PA absent-limited (Feb-Apr). PBs occur on the summer grounds. The PA involves a few throat feathers on some $\eth \eth$ (SY only?).

Skull—Completes in HY from 15 Oct thru Dec.

Age/Sex—CP/BP (May-Aug). Wg useful: ♂(n30) 72-81, ♀(n30) 67-75. Juv (Jun-Jul) has upperparts strongly washed with greenish, and yellowish wing bars (♂ = ♀). The following (and the above) applies to U.S. populations only; more southern subspecies differ in having HY/SY ♂ similar to AHY/ASY ♂ in head coloration, at least:

AHY/ASY ♂ (Aug-Jul): Crown, nape, throat, and upperbreast rich tawny; lores and auriculars black; white at base of pp > 5 mm longer than longest pp cov (closed wing); flight feathers gray; rects truncate (as in *Dendroica* warblers; fig. 114).

HY/SY ♂ (Aug-Jul): Forecrown, throat, and upperbreast yellowish, with a slight tawny wash or with a few bright tawny feathers (Mar-Jul); nape, lores, and auriculars grayish, suffused with yellow or pale tawny; white at base of pp usually 2-5 mm longer than than longest pp cov; flight feathers brownish-gray, tapered (fig. 114).

AHY/ASY ♀ (Aug-Jul): Like HY/SY ♂ but throat usually with less tawny wash and no bright tawny feathers; flight feathers gray; rects truncate (fig. 114).

HY/SY ♀ (Jul-Jun): Crown, nape, and auriculars grayish suffused with buffy; throat and upperbreast pale buffy yellow; white at base of pp covered by, or longer by < 1 mm, than longest pp cov; flight feathers brownish-gray; rects tapered (fig. 114).

References—B; Webster (1958, 1962).

Tanagers   *Thraupinae*

Four species. Subfamily characteristics include a fairly robust posture, bright plumage, and toothed, conical bills. They have 9 primaries, 9 secondaries, and 12 rectrices. The first prebasic molt is partial; the prealternate molts are partial to incomplete, sometimes including the tertials and rectrices on SY birds, at least. The combination of plumage and wing chord should allow ageing and sexing of most birds in both basic and alternate plumages.

HEPATIC TANAGER   HETA
Piranga flava   Species # 609.0
                                                Band size: 1A

Species—Auriculars and flanks gray or strongly washed grayish (both sexes); wing bars indistinct or lacking; wg 94-109; p7 > p6 by < 2mm; p6 ≥ p9; bill blackish or bluish. The combination of these features should separate this from the other tanager species. Juv from Juv Summer Tanager by bill color and grayish-tan rump.

Molt—PB: HY partial (Jul-Aug), AHY complete (Jul-Aug); PA absent-limited (Feb-Mar). PBs occur on the summer grounds. PA may include a few feathers, probably more so in SY ♂♂.

Skull—Completes in HY/SY from 1 Nov thru Jan. Check for windows on SYs thru spring.

Age/Sex—CP/BP (May-Aug). Wg: ♂(n30) 97-109, ♀(n30) 94-103. Juv (Jun-Aug) is like ♀ but is streaked over much of the body plumage (♂ = ♀):

AHY/ASY ♂ (Aug-Jul): Plumage entirely reddish, without any green or yellow feathers; rects reddish, truncate (fig. 155).

SY/TY ♂ (Aug-Jul): Plumage mostly reddish but with at least a few greenish or grayish-yellow feathers or patches of feathers in upperparts and underparts; rects reddish, truncate (fig. 155). [Not all SY/TYs may have this plumage; some attaining the full red plumage of "AHY/ASY".]

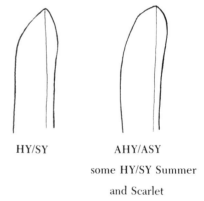

HY/SY   AHY/ASY

some HY/SY Summer

and Scarlet

Figure 155. Rectrix shape by age in the tanagers.

HY/SY ♂ (Aug-Jul): Plumage mostly grayish-yellow and yellow but with one or more reddish feathers or patches which contrast markedly with surrounding plumage; throat and undertail covs often strongly tinged orange; rects yellowish-gray, tapered (fig. 155). [This plumage is found more in Feb-Jun than at other times of year; see HY/SY ♀.]

AHY/ASY ♀ (Aug-Jul): Plumage grayish-yellow and yellow, without any markedly contrasting red feathers; throat and undertail covs often lightly tinged orange; rects yellowish, truncate (fig. 155).

HY/SY ♀ (Aug-Jul): Like AHY/ASY ♀ but throat and undertail covs without orange tinge; rects yellowish-gray, tapered (fig. 155). [These are probably not reliably sexed from Aug-Mar except in conjunction with a short wg. From Mar-Jul they can be reliably sexed ♀.]

References—DVR,B,O,BBM; Eisenmann (1969), Rea (1972).

SUMMER TANAGER   SUTA
Piranga rubra   Species # 610.0
                                                       Band size: 1A

Species—Auriculars and flanks uniform in coloration with surrounding plumage or with a slight brownish wash; wing bars indistinct or lacking; underwing covs uniformly yellow to orangish; wg 86-107; p7 > p6 by ≥ 3 mm; p9 ≥ p6; bill pinkish-tan (Juv) to bright yellow; culmen 12-17; ♀♀ plumage brownish-yellow to orange-yellow. The combination of these features should separate this from other tanager species. Juv from Juv Hepatic Tanager by bill color and rich cinnamon-buff rump.

Molt—PB: HY partial (Jul-Aug), AHY complete (Jul-Aug); PA limited-incomplete (Nov-Mar). PBs occur on the summer grounds. PA highly variable, usually more extensive in SY than ASY, and can include the rects in some SYs (♂♂ only?).

Skull—Completes in HY/SY from 1 Oct thru Jan. Check for windows on SYs thru spring.

Age/Sex—CP/BP (Mar-Aug). Wg: ♂(n100) 91-107, ♀(n100) 86-102; W > E. Juv (May-Aug) resembles ♀♀ but has distinctly paler wing bars, pale buffy underparts, and is streaked throughout (♂ = ♀). Some overlap occurs between the plumages of HY/SY ♂♂ and ♀♀ (especially with HYs in fall) but by comparing the following with wg, most birds should be reliably aged and sexed:

AHY/ASY ♂ (Aug-Jul): Body plumage entirely red; all flight-feathers edged red; rects truncate (fig. 155). [Look for green feathers or patches in occasional birds, possibly indicating SY/TY as in Hepatic Tanager.]

HY/SY ♂ (Aug-Jul): Body plumage varies from rich yellow or brownish-yellow, often with scattered reddish feathers (Aug-Feb); to mostly red with scattered yellow patches, the red and yellow markedly contrasting (Mar-Jul); undertail covs rich yellow to orangeish; flight feathers brownish, some or all edged yellowish; rects tapered (fig. 155). [Some birds may have red-edged and truncate rects in Mar-Jul (see Molt).]

AHY/ASY ♀ (Aug-Jul): Body plumage mostly yellowish, usually washed lightly to heavily with orange or reddish (especially on the throat and undertail covs), the red and yellow not contrasting markedly; flight feathers and pp covs dusky, edged yellow or orangish; rects truncate (fig. 155). [♀♀ of western populations attain less orange in plumage than those of eastern populations.]

HY/SY ♀ (Aug-Jul): Body plumage, including undertail covs, yellowish-olive to brownish-yellow, without orange tinging; flight feathers and pp covs brownish, edged yellow; rects tapered (fig. 155). [Reliable separation of HY/SY ♀ and ♂ in Aug-Mar requires some experience and comparison with wg.]

References—B,R,W,O,C(Rea),BBM; Blake (1965a), Parkes (1967), Eisenmann (1969), Rea (1970, 1972), T. Davis (1971).

SCARLET TANAGER
Piranga olivacea

SCTA
Species # 608.0
Band size: 1B

Species—Wing bars usually absent (whitish if present on ♂♂); underwing covs whitish with dusky or black bar on leading edge; p9 > p6; bill horn-colored; culmen 10.5-12.0; ♀♀ with upperparts, including nape, yellowish-green blending into paler rump. The combination of these features should separate ♀♀ and Juvs from other tanager species. Occasional HY/SY ♀♀ may show yellowish wing bars as in Western Tanager but these can be separated by the color of the back and underwing covs.

Molt—PB: HY partial (Jul-Sep), AHY complete (Jul-Sep); PA partial-incomplete (Feb-May); PBs occur on the summer grounds. PA variable, often includes terts and rects (SY only?).

Skull—Completes in HY/SY from 1 Nov thru Feb. Some SYs retain windows thru spring and even into summer.

Age/Sex—CP/BP (May-Sep). Wg: ♂(n30) 91-100, ♀(n30) 87-95. Juv (Jun-Aug) is like ♀ but has distinct, paler wing bars and streaked plumage (sexes possibly separated by color of flight feathers: darker, grayish-brown in ♂♂, paler brown in ♀♀). Some intermediates between the following may occur, which are not reliably aged and/or sexed; compare with wg:

Basic Plumage

AHY/ASY ♂ (Aug-Mar): Body plumage brightish olive-green; flight feathers and wing covs uniformly glossy black; rects truncate (fig. 155).

HY/SY ♂ (Aug-Mar): As AHY/ASY ♂ but flight feathers brown with moderate greenish edging; pp covs grayish-brown, contasting with black mid and (some or all) gr covs; rects tapered (fig. 155).

AHY/ASY ♀ (Aug-Mar): Body plumage moderately bright yellowish-green; flight feathers and wing covs uniformly darkish brown with green edging; rects truncate (fig. 155).

HY/SY ♀ (Aug-Mar): As AHY/ASY ♀ but body plumage dull or dusky olive; flight feathers and pp covs pale brown with substantial greenish edging, contrasting with darker brown mid and (some or all) gr covs; rects tapered (fig. 155).

Alternate Plumage

ASY ♂ (Mar-Aug): Body plumage red; flight feathers and wing covs fairly uniformly blackish; rects truncate (fig. 155).

SY ♂ (Mar-Sep): As ASY ♂ but flight feathers and pp covs mostly grayish-brown, contrasting with black mid covs and , sometimes, terts; rects tapered (fig. 155) or truncate (and black) on some birds.

ASY ♀ (Mar-Aug): Body plumage fairly bright yellowish-green; flight feathers and wing covs fairly uniformly darkish brown, with a slight greenish wash; rects truncate (fig. 155).

SY ♀ (Mar-Aug): As ASY ♀ but body plumage averages duller; flight feathers and pp covs pale brown with distinct greenish wash, often contrasting with darker brown mid covs and, sometimes, terts; rects tapered (fig. 155) or truncate (and darker brown) in some Mar-Aug birds. [Not all ♀♀ may be reliably aged.]

References—B,R,W,SK,O,BBM; Blake (1965a), T. Davis (1971).

WESTERN TANAGER
Piranga ludoviciana

WETA
Species # 607.0
Band size: 1B

Species—Wing bars always distinct, usually yellowish (can be narrow and whitish in some worn birds); underwing covs bright to pale yellowish; ♀♀ with upperparts grayish-green, often contrasting distinctly with paler yellowish rump and nape. These features should separate dull ♀♀ of this from other tanager species.

Molt—PB: HY partial (Jul-Aug), AHY complete (Jul-Aug); PA limited-partial (Feb-Apr). PBs occur on the summer grounds. PA might sometimes include the terts and is probably more extensive in SY ♂♂ than in other age/sex classes.

Skull—Completes in HY/SY from 1 Nov thru Feb. Some SYs retain windows thru spring.

Age/Sex—CP/BP (Apr-Aug). Wg: ♂(n30) 90-99, ♀(n30) 86-96. Juv (Jun-Aug) is like ♀♀ but has distinctly streaked underparts (♂ = ♀). Some intermediates between the following may occur, which are not reliably aged and/or sexed:

Basic Plumage

AHY/ASY ♂ (Aug-Mar): Head with varying amounts of red; flight feathers and pp covs black; rects truncate (fig. 155).

HY/SY ♂ (Aug-Mar): Head without red; throat and rump brightish yellow, rump contrasting distinctly with greener back; flight feathers and pp covs brown; rects tapered (fig. 155). [Some overlap in plumage occurs with ♀♀; for reliable separation combine plumage with wg.]

AHY/ASY ♀ (Aug-Mar): Head without red; throat and rump moderately yellow, rump not contrasting markedly with back; flight feathers and pp covs brown; rects truncate (fig. 155).

HY/SY ♀ (Aug-Mar): Head without red; throat and rump dull yellow, rump uniform or nearly uniform in color with back; flight feathers and pp covs palish brown; rects tapered (fig. 155).

Alternate Plumage

ASY ♂ (Mar-Aug): Head bright red; flight feathers and wing covs fairly uniformly blackish; rects truncate (fig. 155).

SY ♂ (Mar-Aug): Head brightish red; flight feathers and pp covs brownish, contrasting with black gr and mid covs; rects tapered (fig. 155). [Look for SYs (Mar-Jul) with adult terts and rects, as with other tanager species.]

ASY ♀ (Mar-Aug): Head without red or (sometimes) with a little; flight feathers and wing covs fairly uniformly dark brown; rects truncate (fig. 155).

SY ♀ (Mar-Aug): Head without red; flight feathers and pp covs pale brown, contrasting with darker brown gr and mid covs; rects tapered (fig. 155). [Not all ♀♀ may be reliably aged.]

References—DVR,B,R,O,C(Sheppard and Collins),BBM; T. Davis (1971); PRBO data.

Cardinals, Grosbeaks, and Buntings   *Cardinalinae*

Ten species. Subfamily characteristics include bright and colorful male plumages, and very robust, conical bills. They have 9 primaries, 9 secondaries, and 12 rectrices. The molts show substantial variation as to sequence and extent. Plumages are also variable. Most birds are reliably aged and sexed when all criteria are combined.

NORTHERN CARDINAL
Cardinalis cardinalis

NOCA
Species # 593.0
Band size: 1A

Molt—PB: HY partial-complete (Jun-Nov), AHY complete (Jun-Oct); PA absent. 1st PB variable, and dependent on latitude and date of hatching; it usually includes either all or no pp and a variable amount of ss and rects. It is normally complete in southern populations.

Skull—Completes in HY/SY from 15 Oct thru Feb.

Age—Juv (Apr-Sep) is like ♀ but has duller plumage, little or no red on crest, and a black or dusky bill (presence of red, especially on the crest and breast might indicate ♂; compare with wg; otherwise, ♂ = ♀). In addition to the following, look for contrasts in color and wear of flight feathers in some HY/SYs. The lack of contrasts, along with truncate rects, is probably reliable for AHY/ASY (Aug-Jul) in northern populations; more study is needed into the locality vs. the extent of the 1st PB:

HY/SY (Aug-2nd Sep): Flight feathers and pp covs washed dusky, contrasting with brighter gr covs (more apparent in ♂♂ than ♀♀); some or all rects tapered (fig. 156). [Aug-Sep SYs distinguished from HYs by extremely worn flight feathers.]

AHY (Jan-Aug): Flight feathers and wing covs uniform in coloration; all rects truncate (fig. 156).

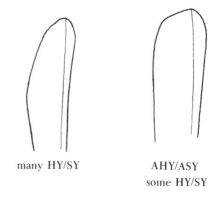

many HY/SY   AHY/ASY
                      some HY/SY

Figure 156. Rectrix shape by age in the cardinals.

Sex—CP/BP (Mar-Sep). Wg: ♂(n100) 88-105, ♀(n100) 83-101; SW > N > SE. The following is reliable after the 1st PB:

♂: Body plumage partially (molting Juvs) or entirely bright red.

♀: Body plumage brown except for red crest. [Beware of Juv ♂♂. Juvs molting brown to brown may be sexed ♀♀.]

References—B,R,W,SK,O,BBM; J. Reese (1975), Scott (1967), Wiseman (1968b, 1977); C. Thompson (*pers. comm.*).

PYRRHULOXIA
Cardinalis sinuatus

PYRR
Species # 594.0
Band size: 1A

Molt—PB: HY partial-complete (Jun-Nov), AHY complete (Jun-Oct); PA absent. 1st PB variable (as with Northern Cardinal).

Skull—Completes in HY/SY from 1 Oct thru Jan.

Age—Juv (May-Sep) is like ♀ but usually lacks red crest and has distinct, pale wing bars (presence of some red on the crest and throat might indicate ♂; compare with wg. Otherwise, ♂ = ♀). The following is indicative but probably not reliable for AHY/ASY beyond Aug:

HY/SY (Aug-Jul): Some or all rects tapered (fig. 156), relatively quite abraded.

AHY (Jan-Aug): All rects truncate (fig. 156), relatively unworn.

Sex—CP/BP (Mar-Sep). Wg: ♂(n30) 89-101, ♀(n30) 86-96. The following is reliable after the 1st PB:

♂: Lores, malar area, chin, and throat red.

♀: Lores, malar area, chin, and throat with little or no red.

Refererences—B,O.

ROSE-BREASTED GROSBEAK
Pheucticus ludovicianus

RBGR
Species # 595.0
Band size: 1A

Species—♀♀ separated from ♀♀ Black-headed Grosbeak (which see) by: superciliary white; underparts (especially throat and flanks) whitish, with little buffy or a relatively light buffy wash to breast and thick dusky streaking spanning across center of breast (fig. 157); underwing lining lemon yellow (most birds), salmon, or mixed yellowish and pink. [Intermediate types may occur, but these should be HY/SY Rose-breasted Grosbeaks or AHY/ASY Black-headed Grosbeaks; compare with age and wg (see Sex). Also, beware of hybrids.]

Molt—PB: HY partial (Jul-Aug), AHY complete (Jul-Oct); PA: SY incomplete (Feb-May), ASY partial (Feb-Apr). PBs occur on the summer grounds or (in some AHYs) are suspended, with some flight feather molt completing on the winter grounds. 1st PA usually includes some or all rects, the terts, and sometimes some inner ss (probably more so in ♂♂ than ♀♀). An incomplete PA may occasionally occur in ASY as well.

Skull—Completes in HY/SY from 1 Nov thru Feb. May be difficult to see through skin.

Age/Sex—CP/BP (May-Sep); a partial BP develops in some ♂♂. Wg: ♂(n30) 97-108, ♀(n30) 93-104. Juv (Jun-Jul) is like ♀♀ but has upperpart feathers distinctly edged tawny, and cinnamon wing-bars (many Juvs can be sexed: ♂ often has mixed pink and yellow underwing linings, yellow in ♀; and also by the length of white at the base of pp; see below). In the following, all birds should be easily sexed (compare also with wg) and ♂♂ should be readily aged, but intermediates between AHY/ASY and HY/SY ♀♀ may not be reliably separated:

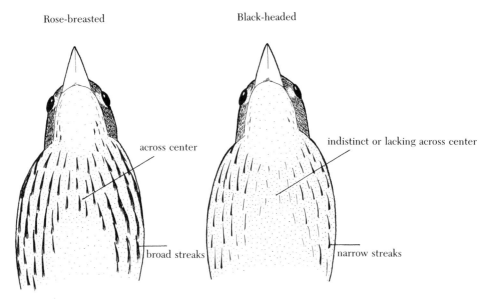

Rose-breasted

Black-headed

across center

indistinct or lacking across center

broad streaks

narrow streaks

Figure 157. Typical patterns to the underparts in ♀ Rose-breasted and Black-headed grosbeaks, Note that, within each species, AHY/ASYs will resemble the Rose-breasted illustration more, while HY/SYs will tend more towards that of Black-headed.

AHY/ASY ♂ (Sep-Aug): Wing linings pink; breast and throat with substantial pink; wing covs and flight feathers uniformly black (gr covs marginally blacker in Mar-Jul); white at base of pp extends 6-15 mm from tips of pp covs (closed wing); rects truncate (fig. 158).

HY/SY ♂ (Aug-2nd Aug): Wing linings pink; breast and throat usually with at least some pink (Aug-Mar) or with almost as much as AHY/ASY ♂ (Mar-Aug); all or most flight feathers, and pp covs dark brown, contrasting distinctly with blacker gr covs; mid covs mostly white; white at base of pp extends 4-8 mm from pp covs; rects tapered (fig. 158), truncate, or a mixture of both (50% of SYs; see Molt). [A few SYs may be distinguished thru fall migration by still retaining a few faded, brown juvenal pp, which contrast markedly with blacker and fresher adult pp.]

AHY/ASY ♀ (Aug-Jul): Wing lining deep salmon or mixed yellow and pink (occasionally entirely pink); underparts relatively whitish, with distinct dusky streaks; breast without pink (occasionally one or two feathers); flight feathers and pp and gr covs uniformly dark brown (gr covs may be marginally darker in spring); mid covs mostly brown with white tipping; white at base of pp extends 3-10 mm from pp covs; rects truncate (fig. 158).

HY/SY ♀ (Aug-Jul): Underwing lining lemon yellow to pale salmon; underparts relatively buffy, with indistinct

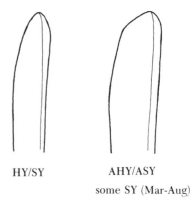

HY/SY

AHY/ASY

some SY (Mar-Aug)

Figure 158. Juvenal and adult rectrix shapes in Rose-breased and Black-headed grosbeaks.

dusky streaks (thru Mar); flight feathers and pp covs pale brown, contrasting with darker brown gr covs; white at base of pp extends 0-4 mm from pp covs; rects tapered (fig. 158). [As with HY/SY ♂♂, the rects may show molt related variation in spring, but probably less so.]

References—DVR,B,R,W,SK,O,BBM; West (1962), C. Smith (1966), Goodpasture (1972), Anderson & Daugherty (1974), Cannell *et al.* (1983), Leberman (1984); PRBO data.

BLACK-HEADED GROSBEAK
Pheucticus melanocephalus

BHGR
Species # 596.0
Band size 1A

Species—♀♀ separated from ♀♀ Rose-breasted Grosbeak (which see) by: superciliary often buffy to buffy-white; underparts (including throat and flanks) strongly washed buffy, especially across breast and with narrow black streaking usually confined to the sides of the breast (fig. 157); underwing lining bright, orange-yellow to brownish-yellow or mustard colored.[Intermediate types may occur; see Rose-breasted Grosbeak.]

Molt—PB: HY partial (Jul-Aug), AHY complete (Jul-Oct); PA: SY incomplete (Feb-May), ASY partial (Feb-Apr). Molt strategies and variation seems to follow that of Rose-breasted Grosbeak, with perhaps a slightly less extensive (partial-incomplete) PA.

Skull—Completes in HY/SY from 1 Oct thru Jan. May be very difficult to see due to thickness of skin.

Age/Sex—CP/BP (Apr-Aug); some ♂♂ may develop a partial BP. Wg: ♂(n30) 97-109, ♀(n30) 94-105. Juv (May-Jul) is like ♀♀ but has upperpart feathers distinctly edged tawny, and cinnamon wing-bars (♂ = ♀; some Juvs sexed by ♀ having a greater amount of streaking to the underparts and by the length of the white at the base of pp; see below). With the following, all birds should be easily sexed (compare also with wg), ♂♂ should be readily aged but intermediates between the ♀♀ may not be reliably separated:

AHY/ASY ♂ (Aug-Jul): Crown and face entirely black (often with an orange superciliary); breast strongly washed tawny; rump cinnamon, unstreaked, contrasting markedly with brown and streaked back; mid covs entirely or mostly white; flight feathers and wing covs uniformly black (gr covs may be marginally blacker in spring); white at base of pp extends 5-15 mm from tips of pp covs (closed wing); rects truncate (fig. 158).

HY/SY ♂ (Aug-2nd Aug): Like AHY/ASY ♂ but plumage duller (fall and spring); crown buffy streaked dark brown (Aug-Mar) or black washed brownish (Mar-Aug); most flight feathers and pp covs brown, contrasting in color with black gr covs; white at base of pp extends 3-10 mm from pp covs; rects tapered (fig. 158). [Some Mar-Aug SYs may show adult or mixed juvenal and adult rects and some may be aged thru the fall migration as in Rose-breasted Grosbeak.]

AHY/ASY ♀ (Aug Jul): Crown dark brown and buffy; face dark brown; underparts pale buffy with narrow dusky streaks usually restricted to the sides of the underparts; rump brown, usually with some streaking, not contrasting markedly with back; flight feathers and pp and gr covs uniformly dark brown; mid covs brown tipped white; white at base of pp extends 3-10 mm from pp covs; rects truncate (fig. 158).

HY/SY ♀ (Aug-Jul): Like AHY/ASY ♀ but plumage generally duller (fall and spring); underparts strongly colored buffy with a larger number of more prominent dusky streaks (found sometimes across center of breast; more prominent in Aug-Mar birds); flight feathers and pp covs paleish brown, contrasting with darker brown gr covs; white at base of pp extends 0-4 mm from pp covs; rects tapered (fig. 158). [A few Mar-Jul SYs may show adult or mixed juvenal and adult rects.]

References—B,O,C(Sheppard and Collins),BBM; Michener & Michener (1951), Anderson & Daugherty (1974); PRBO data.

BLUE GROSBEAK
Guiraca caerulea

BLGR
Species # 597.0
Band size: 1B

Species—From all bunting species by larger wg (79-94).

Molt—PB: HY partial (Jul-Oct), AHY complete (Jul-Oct); PA: SY incomplete (Jan-Apr), ASY absent. The PBs probably occur mostly on the summer grounds but may be suspended over fall migration. 1st PA variable, includes some or all rects, the terts, and sometimes some ss and/or pp, and is probably more extensive in ♂♂ than ♀♀.

Skull—Completes in HY/SY from 1 Oct thru Jan. May be difficult to see through the skin.

Age/Sex—CP/BP (Apr-Aug). Wg: ♂(n30) 82-94, ♀(n30) 79-88; SW > SE. Juv (May-Aug) is like HY/SY but is slightly more heavily streaked (♂ = ♀).

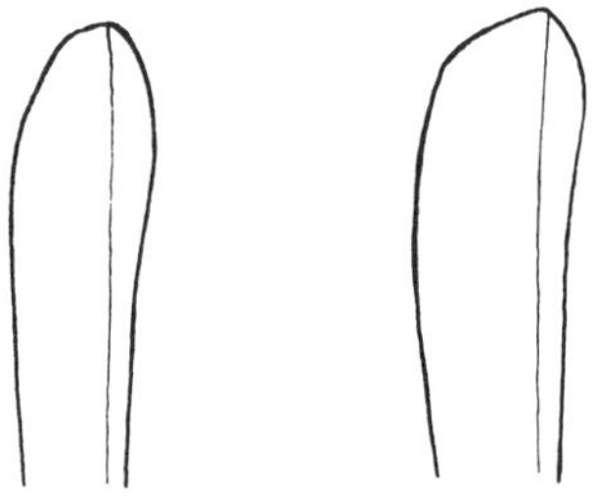

HY/SY   AHY/ASY
               some SY (Mar-Aug)

Figure 159. Rectrix shape in Blue Grosbeaks, by age.

Basic Plumage

AHY/ASY ♂ (Aug-Mar): Body plumage entirely blue, feathers tipped brownish; flight feathers and pp covs dull black; rects truncate (fig. 159).

AHY/ASY ♀ (Aug-Mar): Body plumage brown, sometimes with a few blue feathers in the upperparts, especially the crown, les covs, and rump; flight feathers and pp covs dark brown; rects truncate (fig. 159).

HY/SY (Aug-Feb): Body plumage entirely brown; flight feathers and pp covs pale brown; rects tapered (fig. 159). [A few ♂ may be sexed by the presence of a few blue body feathers or the adventitious replacement of dull black flight feathers, contrasting markedly with adjacent, brown flight feathers. Otherwise, ♂ = ♀ by plumage but compare with wg.]

Alternate Plumage

ASY ♂ (Mar-Aug): Body plumage entirely blue; flight feathers and wing covs fairly uniformly dull black; rects truncate (fig. 159).

SY ♂ (Mar-Sep): Body plumage mixed blue and brown including some blue on the underparts; all or some flight feathers, and pp covs brown, often contrasting with blacker mid covs and, sometimes, some flight feathers; rects tapered (fig.159), mixed tapered and truncate or truncate (see Molt).

ASY ♀ (Mar-Jul): Body plumage brown, usually with some blue in the upperparts but none in the underparts; flight feathers and wing covs fairly uniformly dark brown; rects truncate (fig. 159). [May be difficult to distinguish from SY ♀, without experience.]

SY ♀ (Mar-Aug): Like ASY ♀ but plumage averages less blue; all or most flight feathers and pp covs pale brown, contrasting with darker brown mid covs and, sometimes, other flight feathers; rects tapered (fig. 159). [Some or all rects may be replaced as with SY ♂ but probably less often.]

References—DVR,B,O; Blake (1969b); PRBO data.

LAZULI BUNTING

Passerina amoena

LZBU
Species # 599.0
Band size: 1

Species—HY/SY and ♀ have upperparts brownish, usually contrasting slightly with grayer rump; throat pale buffy, uniform in color with unstreaked (sometimes slightly streaked) breast; edges of terts and gr covs paler, forming distinct wing bars. See also wg by sex (below). A combination of these features should separate this from HY/SY and ♀ Indigo Bunting (which see; Juvs, however, are probably inseparable by plumage). From ♀ Varied Bunting by wing bars and wing formula (p9 > p5; fig. 160).

Molt—PB: HY incomplete (Jul-Dec), AHY complete (Jul-Aug); PA: SY partial (Feb-May), ASY incomplete (Jan-Apr). The molt strategy is probably the same as in Indigo Bunting (which see).

Skull—Completes in HY/SY from 15 Oct (as early as 1 Sep in California populations) thru Jan. Some SYs probably retain windows thru summer/fall.

Age/Sex—CP/BP (Mar-Aug). Wg useful: ♂(n30) 70-78, ♀(n30) 65-73. Juv (May-Aug) resembles HY/SY (below) but has upperpart feathers edged with pale brown and relatively heavy streaking to the underparts (♂ = ♀).

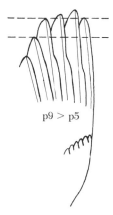

p9 > p5

Figure 160. The wing formula of Lazuli and Indigo buntings.

Basic Plumage

AHY/ASY ♂ (Aug-Mar): Head, throat, and rump mixed brown and blue; pp covs, alula and flight feathers blackish edged blue; rects truncate (fig. 161).

AHY/ASY ♀ (Aug-Mar): Head and throat brown; rump and les covs mostly brown but with some dull blue; flight feathers, pp covs, and alula uniformly brown edged with dull blue or greenish; rects truncate (fig. 161).

HY/SY (Aug-Mar): Plumage, including rump, uniformly brown without blue; flight feathers, pp covs and alula brown without greenish edging (Aug-Nov), or outer 4-6 pp edged green, contrasting with other flight feathers (Dec-Mar); rects tapered (fig. 161). [In Nov-Dec, many HY/SY ♂ ♂ acquire blue feathers in the body plumage (see Molt) and may be separated from ♀ ♀. Otherwise, birds without blue are probably not reliably sexed except, perhaps, by wg.]

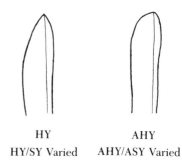

HY   AHY
HY/SY Varied AHY/ASY Varied

Figure 161. Rectrix shape by age in *Passerina* buntings. See accounts for the timing of usefulness of this criterion.

Alternate Plumage

ASY ♂ (Mar-Aug): Head, throat, and rump bright blue; pp covs, alula and flight feathers uniformly blackish edged blue; rects truncate (fig. 161).

SY ♂ (Mar-Aug): Head, throat, and rump mostly blue mixed variably with brown; outer 4-6 pp blackish edged blue, contrasting with brown alula, pp covs, and other flight feathers (some may show uniformly brownish pp); rects tapered (fig. 161). [Some SY ♂ ♂ may molt some or all rects in Dec-Jan, as with Indigo Bunting, and they would then resemble those of ASY ♂ ♂ but would be fresher.]

ASY ♀ (Mar-Aug): Head and throat brown; rump and les covs mixed brown and blue; flight feathers, pp covs, and alula uniformly brown, edged with dull blue or greenish; rects truncate (fig. 161).

SY ♀ (Mar-Aug): Like ASY ♀ but blue of les covs and rump more restricted and greenish; outer 4-6 pp dark brown edged pale greenish, contrasting with paler brown alula, pp covs and other flight feathers; rects tapered (fig. 161). [Some birds may show uniformly brown primaries; others may have molted some or all rects, as in SY ♂.]

References—B,O,C (Sheppard); PRBO data.

INDIGO BUNTING
Passerina cyanea

INBU
Species # 598
Band size: 1

Species—HY/SY and ♀ has upperparts and rump uniformly brownish (or rump tinged bright blue); throat whitish or pale buffy, contrasting with browner and noticeably streaked breast; edges of terts and gr covs indistinctly paler, usually not forming distinct wing bars. See also wg by sex (below). A combination of these features should separate this from HY/SY and ♀ Lazuli Bunting (which see; Juvs, however, are probably inseparable by plumage). From ♀ Varied Bunting by wing formula (p9 > p5; fig. 160).

Molt—PB: HY incomplete (Jun-Dec), AHY complete (Jul-Aug); PA: SY partial (Feb-May), ASY incomplete (Jan-Apr). The 1st PB occurs in two stages. A partial molt occurs on the breeding grounds, afterwhich the terts, 4-6 outer pp, and the rects are molted during Nov-Jan, along with most or all of the contours for a second time, on the winter grounds. This is referred to as a "supplemental" molt (see Rohwer 1986 for more details). The 1st PA occurs mostly on the winter grounds but often completes on the summer grounds. Adult PAs usually include the terts, and occur completely on the winter grounds.

Skull—Completes in HY/SY from 15 Oct thru Feb. Some SYs retain windows thru summer and (rarely) fall.

Age/Sex—CP/BP (Apr-Aug). Wg: ♂(n100) 63-72, ♀(n100) 59-67. Juv (Jun-Aug) resembles HY/SY (below) but is grayer, mottled above, and has heavier streaking below (♂ = ♀). In the following, the basic plumage includes the supplemental, HY/SY plumage which is found in Dec-Mar:

Basic Plumage

AHY/ASY ♂ (Aug-Mar): Body plumage brown mixed substantially with blue (especially in rump); alula, pp covs, and flight feathers blackish edged with blue; rects truncate (fig. 161).

AHY/ASY ♀ (Aug-Mar): Body plumage entirely brown; mid covs with cinnamon edging; alula, wing covs and flight feathers uniformly dark brown edged with greenish-blue; rects truncate (fig. 161).

HY/SY (Aug-Mar): Body plumage and les covs entirely brown; mid covs with pale buffy edging; alula, pp covs and flight feathers entirely brown (Aug-Dec), or outer 4-6 pp blackish with bluish edging, contrasting with other, brown pp (Dec-Mar); rects tapered (fig. 161). [In Nov-Dec, most (if not all) HY/SY ♂♂ acquire blue feathers in the body plumage and blue-based rects, and may be separated from HY/SY ♀♀. Otherwise, birds without blue should probably not be reliably sexed except, perhaps, by wg.]

Alternate Plumage

ASY ♂ (Mar-Aug): Body plumage entirely blue; alula, pp covs, and flight feathers fairly uniformly blue or blackish edged with blue.

SY ♂ (Mar-Aug): Body plumage mostly blue with a variable amount of brown mottling; outer 4-6 pp blackish edged blue, contrasting with paler brown alula, pp covs and other pp.

ASY ♀ (Mar-Aug): Body plumage entirely brown or brown with a few bluish feathers; alula, pp covs and flight feathers uniformly dark brown edged with greenish-blue; rects truncate (fig. 161). [Some ♀♀, especially in worn plumage, may be difficult to age in spring.]

SY ♀ (Mar-Aug): Body plumage entirely brown; outer 4-6 pp dark brown edged greenish, contrasting with paler and entirely brown alula, pp covs and other pp; some or all rects sometimes tapered (fig. 161).

References—DVR,B,R,W,SK,O; Blake (1965b, 1969), D. Johnston (1967), Hamel *et al.* (1983), Rohwer (1986), Quay (1987); PRBO data.

VARIED BUNTING
Passerina versicolor

VABU
Species # 600.0
Band size: 1

Species—HY/SY and ♀ from Lazuli and Indigo buntings by the lack of any wing bars (non Juvs) and by wing formula (p9 < p5; fig. 162).

Molt—PB: HY partial (Jun-Aug), AHY complete (Jun-Aug); PA absent-partial (Jan-Apr). PBs occur on the breeding grounds. A supplemental 1st PB, and age-related variation in the PA, as with Indigo Bunting, could occur with this species.

Skull—Completes in HY/SY from 15 Sep thru Jan. Some SYs probably retain windows thru spring.

Age/Sex—CP/BP (Mar-Aug). Wg: ♂(n30) 63-70, ♀(n30) 58-66; E > W. Juv (May-Aug) is like HY/SY ♀ but has distinct, buffy wing bars (♂ = ♀). Most birds should be reliably aged and sexed by the following:

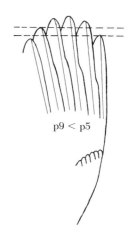

p9 < p5

Figure 162. The wing formula of the Varied Bunting.

AHY/ASY ♂ (Aug-Jul): Crown, cheeks, and rump blue; nape red; underparts and back maroon (most body feathers obscured by brown edging from Aug-Mar); alula, pp covs, and flight feathers uniformly blackish edged with slaty blue; rects truncate (fig. 161).

HY/SY ♂ (Aug-Jul): Upperparts olive-gray, rump extensively bluish-gray; underparts brownish (body plumage washed brown in fall; and sometimes with a few maroon feathers of AHY/ASY ♂ in Mar-Aug); alula, pp covs, and flight feathers uniformly pale brown, without bluish edging; rects tapered (fig. 161). [Look for contrasting flight feathers on Mar-Jul birds, especially outer 4-6 pp, as with other *Passerina* buntings. Combine with wg for reliable separation from HY/SY ♀, especially in Aug-Mar.]

AHY/ASY ♀ (Aug-Jul): Like HY/SY ♂ but alula, pp covs, and flight feathers dark brown with bluish or gray-green edging; rects truncate (fig. 161). [Intermediates may be difficult to distinguish from HY/SY ♂♂; compare with wg.]

HY/SY ♀ (Aug-Jul): Upperparts brownish, with little or no bluish or green; alula, pp covs, and flight feathers uniformly pale brown, without greenish edging (possibly with contrasts in spring; see HY/SY ♂); rects tapered (fig. 161).

References—B,O.

PAINTED BUNTING
Passerina ciris

PABU
Species # 601.0
Band size: 1

Molt—PB: HY incomplete (May-Nov), AHY complete (Aug-Oct); PA limited (Jan-Apr). PBs occur entirely on the summer grounds; 1st PB occurs in two stages, as with Indigo Bunting, and usually includes the rects, terts, at least 3-6 outer pp and their pp covs, and often other flight feathers. The body plumage is molted twice, in Jun-Aug and Sep-Nov. The PA is more limited in ASY ♂ than in other age/sex classes, and can include green (instead of colored) replacement feathers on HY/SY ♂.

Skull—Completes in HY/SY from 1 Nov thru Feb. Some SYs probably retain windows thru spring/summer.

Age/Sex—CP/BP (Mar-Sep). Wg: SE populations ♂(n100) 63-74, ♀(n100) 61-70; SW populations ♂(n100) 68-78, ♀(n100) 64-73. Juv (May-Jul) has nearly uniform, brownish-olive plumage and brown flight feathers (♂ = ♀). Rect shape not useful for ageing after the 1st PB but look for contrasts in other flight feathers (see Molt):

AHY/ASY ♂ (Aug-Jul): Plumage multicolored; all flight feathers edged red.[Molting birds with old flight feathers edged red might be aged ASY thru Sep but beware of adventitiously replaced, *green*-edged flight feathers.]

HY/SY ♂ (Aug-2nd Sep): Upperparts dull (Aug-Oct) to fairly bright (Nov-Sep) green, often with a few blue, red, and green feathers in Mar-Sep; underparts dull (Aug-Oct) to bright (Nov-Sep) greenish-yellow, often with a few red feathers in Mar-Sep; most or all pp covs and some flight feathers brown, without greenish edging. [Aug-Oct HYs may not be reliably separated from ♀♀; compare with wg. Aug-Sep SYs may resemble ASYs but are separated by the presence of brown, very worn, juvenal flight feathers.]

AHY/ASY ♀ (Aug-Jul): Like HY/SY ♂ but plumage without blue, red, or green feathers; all pp covs and flight feathers edged with bright green.

HY/SY ♀ (Aug-Jul): Upperparts dull buffy-green; underparts dull buffy-yellow; no colored feathers of ♂ present; most or all pp covs brown, without greenish edging. [See HY/SY ♂.]

References—B,O; Storer (1951), Fisk (1974b), Tipton & Tipton (1978); C. Thompson (*pers. comm.*).

DICKCISSEL
Spiza americana

DICK
Species # 604.0
Band size: 1B

Molt—PB: HY partial (Jun-Aug), AHY complete (Jun-Aug); PA limited (Feb-Apr). PBs occur on the summer grounds.

Skull—Completes in HY/SY from 1 Nov thru Feb. Some SYs retain windows thru spring.

Age/Sex—CP/BP (Apr-Aug). Wg very useful: ♂(n30) 78-86, ♀(n30) 69-79. Juv (May-Aug) is similar to HY/SY ♀ but is buffier below and has two distinct, pale wing bars (♂ = ♀). All birds should be reliably aged and sexed when wg is combined with the following:

AHY/ASY ♂ (Aug-Jul): Upperbreast with substantial black (may be obscured by yellow feather tips in fall); mid covs broadly edged rufous; alula and pp covs dark brown edged buffy-rufous, uniform in coloration with gr covs; rects truncate (fig. 163).

HY/SY ♂ (Aug-Jul): Upperbreast with little or no black (Aug-Mar), or as AHY/ASY (Mar-Aug); mid covs with moderately broad, pale rufous edging; alula and pp covs pale brown and without buffy-rufous edging, contrasting with darker and buffy-rufous edged gr covs; rects tapered (fig. 163). [Combine with wg for reliable separation from ♀ ♀ in fall/winter.]

AHY/ASY ♀ (Aug-Jul): Upperbreast without black; superciliary and breast usually with some yellow; les covs mostly rufous; mid covs brown tipped pale rufous; alula and pp covs dark brown with narrow, buffy to buffy-rufous edging; rects truncate (fig. 163).

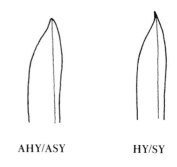

AHY/ASY   HY/SY

Figure 163. Rectrix shape by age in the Dickcissel.

HY/SY ♀ (Aug-Jul): Upperbreast without black; superciliary and breast usually without yellow (thru Mar); les covs brown or brown mixed with some rufous; mid covs with narrow buffy tipping; alula and pp covs brown, usually without buffy-rufous edging; rects tapered (fig. 163).

References—B,R,W,O; PRBO data.

Towhees, Sparrows, and Longspurs   *Emberizinae*

Forty-five species. Subfamily characteristics include generally subdued plumages, thick, seed-eating bills, and short wings. They have 9 primaries, 9 secondaries, and 12 rectrices. The first prebasic molts are variable but generally partial to incomplete. Plumage characteristics are also variable, ages and sexes being alike in most of the species.

OLIVE SPARROW   OLSP
Arremonops rufivirgatus   Species # 586.0
                                                     Band Size: 1

Species—from dull Green-tailed Towhees by smaller wg (58-68).

Molt—PB: HY partial (Jun-Sep), AHY complete (Jun-Sep); PA absent.

Skull—Completes in HY/SY from 15 Sep thru Feb.

Age—Rect shape (fig. 164) seems not as helpful as in towhees. Juv (Apr-Aug) has a brown wash to upperparts, buffy wash to underparts, lacks the crown stripes and has pale brown wing bars. Otherwise, no plumage criteria are known.

Sex—♂ = ♀ by plumage. CP/BP (Mar-Sep). Wg useful: ♂(n21) 62-68, ♀(n19) 58-65.

References—B,O.

GREEN-TAILED TOWHEE   GTTO
Pipilo chlorurus   Species # 590.0
                                                     Band size: 1B-1A

Species—Dull individuals from Olive Sparrow by larger wg (70-81).

Molt—PB: HY partial (Jul-Sep), AHY complete (Jul-Sep); PA limited (Feb-May). PBs occur on the summer grounds.

Skull—Completes in HY/SY from 15 Nov thru Feb. Some SYs may retain windows thru spring/summer.

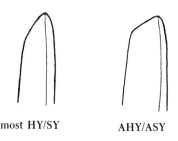

most HY/SY   AHY/ASY

some HY/SY (except Green-tailed)

Figure 164. Rectrix shape in towhees, by age.

Age—Juv (Jun-Aug) is mostly brownish with distinct streaking to upperparts and upperbreast. In addition to the following, HY/SYs (especially ♂ ♂) have duller crowns, on the average than AHY/ASYs; compare with sex (if known):

HY/SY (Aug-2nd Aug): Flight feathers and pp covs greenish-brown, contrasting with greener mid and les covs; rects relatively worn (especially in spring) and tapered (fig. 164).

AHY/ASY (Sep-Aug): Flight feathers and wing covs fairly uniformly greenish; rects relatively unworn, truncate (fig. 164).

Sex—CP/BP (May-Sep). Wg: ♂(n30) 75-84, ♀(n30) 70-79. No reliable plumage criteria known although ♀ averages duller than ♂, especially in the crown; compare with wg and age.

References—B,O,C(J. Davis); PRBO data.

RUFOUS-SIDED TOWHEE
Pipilo erythrophthalmus

RSTO
Band size: 2-1A

Rufous-sided Towhee Species # 587.0
Spotted Towhee (SPTO) Species # 588.0

Molt—PB: HY partial-incomplete (Jul-Sep), AHY complete (Jun-Aug); PA absent. PBs occur on the breeding grounds. 1st PB may include some or all rects in certain populations.

Skull—Completes in HY/SY from 1 Nov thru Feb. Some SYs may retain windows thru spring.

Age/Sex—CP/BP (Apr-Sep). Wg: ♂(n45) 82-94, ♀(n35) 76-90; N > S. Juv (Jun-Aug) has buffy to brown body plumage with distinct blackish streaking on underparts and upperparts; Juvs of eastern populations may be sexed by the color of the flight feathers (see below; probably not reliable with Spotted Towhees but on California birds try the size of the white patch on r4). In the following, the measurements of the white spot on the 4th rect (r4) applies to California populations of the Spotted Towhee. More study is needed on the usefulness and specifics of this criterion with other races:

AHY/ASY ♂ (Aug-Jul): Upperparts, head, and throat glossy black; flight feathers and wing covs fairly uniformly black; rects truncate (fig. 164); white spot on r4 usually 4.0-10.5 mm long (see above); iris bright red.

HY/SY ♂ (Aug-Jul): As AHY/ASY ♂ but pp covs brownish-black, contrasting in coloration with blacker ss covs; flight feathers blackish to dark brown; rects tapered (fig. 164); white spot on r4 usually 0-7.0 mm long (see above); eye gray-brown to dull red (thru Nov, possibly thru spring on some birds). [Some birds, especially of southern populations, may attain adult rects during the 1st PB.]

AHY/ASY ♀ (Aug-May): Upperparts, head, and throat brown (E. populations) to black-ish-gray (W. populations); wing covs and flight feathers fairly uniformly brown or brownish-black; rects truncate (fig. 164); white spot on r4 usually 3.0-10.0 (see above); iris bright red. [Some ♀ ♀ may be impossible to age reliably.]

HY/SY ♀ (Aug-May): As AHY/ASY ♀ but pp covs noticeably pale and worn in contrast to darker and fresher ss covs; flight feathers brown; rects tapered (fig. 164); white spot on r4 usually 0-5.0 mm (see above); iris gray-brown to dull red (thru Nov, possibly thru spring on some birds). [Some birds may show adult rects after the first PB.]

References—B,R,W,O,C(Davis); Nichols (1953a), J. Davis (1957); PRBO data.

BROWN TOWHEE
Pipilo fuscus

BRTO
Species # 591.0
Band size: 2

Molt—PB: HY partial-incomplete (Jun-Oct), AHY complete (Jun-Oct); PA absent. 1st PB sometimes includes some or (rarely?) all rects.

Skull—Completes in HY/SY from 1 Sep thru Feb. Some SYs may retain windows thru spring but these can be difficult to see through skin.

Age— Juv (May-Aug) is paler with distinct streaking in the body plumage. The following may be difficult to use in late spring/summer, when the feathers can become quite worn:

HY/SY (Aug-2nd Aug): Flight feathers brown; rects tapered (fig. 164). [Look also for contrasts between juvenal and adult rects or (rarely) only adult rects in some HY/SYs.]

AHY/ASY (Sep-Aug): Flight feathers blackish-brown; rects truncate (fig. 164). [See HY/SY.]

Sex—♂ = ♀ by plumage. CP/BP (Feb-Sep). Wg useful: ♂(n30) 90-100, ♀(n30) 83-93.

References—B,O,C(Davis); J. Davis (1951); PRBO data.

ABERT'S TOWHEE
Pipilo aberti

ABTO
Species # 592.0
Band size: 2

Molt—PB: HY partial-incomplete (Jun-Oct), AHY complete (Jun-Oct); PA absent. 1st PB may include some or (rarely?) all rects in some birds.

Skull—Completes in HY/SY from 1 Sep thru Feb. Some SYs may retain windows thru spring but these may be difficult to see through skin.

Age—Ageing criteria parallels that of Brown Towhee.

Sex—♂ = ♀ by plumage. CP/BP (Feb-Sep). Wg useful: ♂(n30) 88-97, ♀(n30) 82-91.

References—B,C(Davis); J. Davis (1951).

BACHMAN'S SPARROW
Aimophila aestivalis

BASP
Species # 575.0
Band size: 1

Species—Superciliary distinct; upperparts darkish gray to orangish-rufous, back feathers usually with distinct, black shaft streaks, forming well defined black streaking on the back; uppertail covs with shaft streaks but without anchor-shaped pattern (fig. 165); upperbreast grayish-buff to rich buffy; outer rects with buffy-whitish tips measuring 5-6 mm (fig. 165); central rects without shaft streaks and indistinctly barred; wg 54-65. The combination of these features should separate this from other species of *Aimophila*, including rufous forms of the Cassin's Sparrow (which see).

Molt—PB: HY complete (May-Dec), AHY complete (Jun-Oct); PA partial-incomplete (Mar-Aug). The first PB occurs in two stages: May-Aug including the contours, terts, and

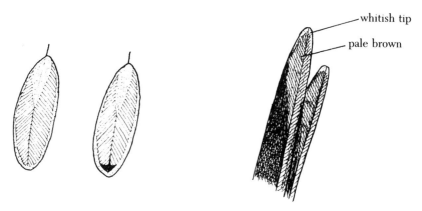

Figure 165. The patterns of the uppertail coverts and outer rectrices in Bachman's Sparrows, as a means of identification.

sometimes some rects, and Sep-Dec complete (those feathers included in the first stage being replaced again). The PA sometimes includes some flight feathers, especially the central rects. Molting is tied in with the timing of breeding.

Skull—Completes in HY/SY from 1 Oct thru Jan.

Age—Juv (May-Sep) has blackish streaking in the crown. Flight feather shape and condition is not useful for ageing, and no criteria are known to reliably distinguish AHY/ASYs after the 1st PB or to age anything after Mar:

HY/SY (Jul-Mar): Breast with one or more distinct, blackish spots.

AHY (Jan-Nov): Breast without spots.

Sex—♂ = ♀ by plumage. CP/BP (Apr-Aug). Wg: ♂(n30) 56-65, ♀(n27) 54-63.

References—B,O; Wolf (1977), Willoughby (1986).

BOTTERI'S SPARROW
Aimophila botterii

BOSP
Species # 576.0
Band size: 1

Species—Superciliary indistinct; uppertail covs with broad shaft streaks but no anchor-shaped pattern (fig. 166); outer rects with slightly paler, brown tips measuring 10-15 mm (fig. 166); central rects without shaft streaks, and indistinctly barred; wg 57-71. These features should separate this from other *Aimophila* species (which see).

Molt—PB: HY complete (Jun-Dec), AHY complete (Jun-Oct); PA partial-incomplete (Feb-Apr). The 1st PB may occur in two stages, as with Bachman's and Cassin's sparrows.

Skull—Completes in HY/SY from 1 Oct thru Jan.

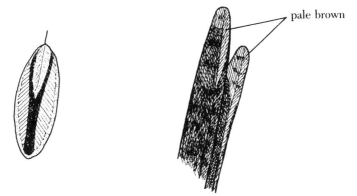

pale brown

Figure 166. Patterns of uppertail coverts and outer rectrices in the Botteri's Sparrow.

Age—Ageing criteria parallels that of Bachman's Sparrow.

Sex—♂ = ♀ by plumage. CP/BP (Apr-Aug). Wg: ♂(n100) 59-71, ♀(n30) 57-68.

References—B,O; Webster (1959); Wolf (1977): Bowers & Dunning (1986).

CASSIN'S SPARROW
Aimophila cassinii

CASP
Species # 578.0
Band size: 1

Species—Upperparts pale brownish-gray to rufous (without orange tinge), back feathers without distinct, black shaft streaks, but irregular, terminal, round or anchor-shaped spots; uppertail covs with black, anchor-shaped patterns (fig. 167); superciliary distinct; upperbreast grayish, sometimes with slight buffy wash; outer rects usually with pale grayish measuring > 15 mm from tips and contrasting with white on terminal 2-5 mm (fig. 167); central rects variable, distinctly barred and with central shaft streaks in some birds (usually western and grayer populations), or without shaft streaks and indistinctly barred (mostly eastern and rufous populations); wg 56-68. The combination of these features should separate this from other species of *Aimophila* (which see).

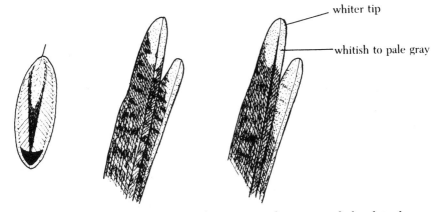

whiter tip

whitish to pale gray

Figure 167. Pattern of the uppertail coverts, and variation in the amount of whitish in the outer rectrices in the Cassin's Sparrow.

Molt—PB: HY complete (Jun-Nov), AHY complete (Aug-Nov); PA incomplete (Feb-Jun). PBs occur on the summer grounds or on post-breeding territories. The 1st PB occurs in two stages, as with Bachman's Sparrow. The PA includes the terts and central rects; sometimes other flight feathers.

Skull—Completes in HY/SY from 15 Sep thru Feb.

Age—Ageing criteria parallels that of Bachman's Sparrow.

Sex—♂ = ♀ by plumage. CP/BP (Apr-Sep). Wg: ♂(n30) 59-68, ♀(n30) 56-65.

References—B,O; Wolf (1977), Bowers & Dunning (1986); Willoughby (1986); PRBO data.

RUFOUS-WINGED SPARROW
Aimophila carpalis

RWSP
Species # 579.0
Band size: 0-1

Species—Non-Juvs from other similar sparrows by the presence of rufous in the les covs. More study is needed into the identification of Juvs.

Molt—PB: HY partial-incomplete (Aug-Nov), AHY complete (Sep-Nov); PA incomplete (May-Jun). 1st PB usually includes the terts, sometimes other flight feathers. The PA is variable, usually including at least some rects (almost always the central pair), sometimes other flight feathers, and may approach being complete. Molts in this species show yearly variation depending on the timing of the breeding season (see Phillips 1951).

Skull—Completion of pneumatization of HY/SYs varies according to breeding season conditions. May complete as early as 1 Oct in wet years. In dry (normal) years, completion occurs from 15 Nov thru Feb.

Age—Rect shape possibly of use thru early spring but excessive wear in both HY/SYs and AHY/ASYs makes it difficult beyond late fall. Check also for symmetrical contrasts of flight feathers in some SYs thru Apr (see Molt). Juv (Jun-Nov) is browner overall and has distinct spotting on the breast; look for occasional spots thru May, indicating HY/SY. Otherwise, no plumage criteria are known for ageing.

Sex—♂ = ♀ by plumage. CP/BP (Apr-Nov; timing variable). Wg: ♂(n30) 58-67, ♀(n30) 55-62.

References—B; Phillips (1951); Wolf (1977).

RUFOUS-CROWNED SPARROW
Aimophila ruficeps

RCSP
Species # 580.0
Band size: 1

Molt—PB: HY incomplete (Jun-Nov), AHY complete (Jun-Nov); PA absent. 1st PB includes a variable amount of flight feathers, usually at least the outer pp, terts, and rects; the extent of the 1st PB varies with the timing and conditions of the breeding season, as with Rufous-winged Sparrow. Look for evidence of a PA in this species, as with other *Aimophila*.

Skull—Completes in HY/SY from 1 Oct thru Feb. Windows may persist in many birds thru the first spring/summer.

Age—Rect shape not useful but symmetrical contrasts in wear between juvenal and adult pp may be useful for ageing some HY/SYs thru spring/summer (see Molt). Juv (May-Oct) lacks a solid rufous crown, has streaking in the upperbreast and has a rufous tail. Otherwise, no reliable plumage criteria are known.

Sex—♂ = ♀ by plumage. CP/BP (Mar-Oct). Wg: ♂(n30) 62-71, ♀(n30) 58-68; SW > W Coast.

References—B,O; Wolf (1977); PRBO data.

AMERICAN TREE SPARROW
Spizella arborea

TRSP
Species # 559.0
Band size: 1-0

Species—From other species of *Spizella* by rusty cap, yellow lower mandible, the presence of a breast spot, and longer wg: 71-82.

Molt—PB: HY partial (Aug-Oct), AHY complete (Aug-Sep); PA limited (Mar-Apr). PBs occur on the summer grounds.

Skull—Completes in HY/SY from 15 Nov thru Jan.

Age—Juv (Jul-Oct) has streaking on the crown, nape and upperbreast; hints of streaking may remain on some birds thru Oct. Intermediates between the following may not be reliably aged; compare with wg and plumage (see Sex):

HY/SY (Sep-Aug): Rects tapered (fig. 168), usually relatively worn, especially in spring.

AHY/ASY (Sep-Aug): Rects truncate (fig. 168), relatively unworn.

Sex—♂ = ♀ by plumage. CP/BP (May-Sep). Wg: ♂(n30) 73-82, ♀(n30) 71-79. [See Heydwieller (1936) for an assessment of relative plumage and other criteria, the combination of which may result in up to 90% reliable ageing and sexing of basic plumaged (Sep-Mar) birds, with much experience.]

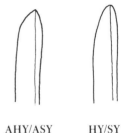

AHY/ASY   HY/SY

Figure 168. Rectrix shape by age in Tree and Field sparrows.

References—B,R,W,SK,O; Heydwieller (1936); PRBO data.

CHIPPING SPARROW
Spizella passerina

CHSP
Species # 560.0
Band size: 0

Species—Malar streaks relatively indistinct or lacking; terts and wing covs with at least some rufous; rump gray (non-Juvs), contrasting with brown back; wg 63-74; wg-tail usually > 1.5; lower mandible black. The combination of these features should separate dull Juv-HYs from Brewer's and Clay-colored sparrows. [HYs of W. populations have a streaked breast thru fall migration, which further helps with separation.] Juv from Juv Field Sparrow by the relatively heavy and distinct streaking on the breast and (especially) the crown.

Molt—PB: HY partial-incomplete (Jun-Nov), AHY complete (Jul-Nov); PA limited (Mar-Apr). PBs occur on the summer grounds (Jun-Aug) in eastern populations and are suspended or occur on the winter grounds (Aug-Nov) in western populations. The 1st PB often includes the terts.

Skull—Completes in HY/SY from 1 Oct thru Jan.

Age—Rect shape probably not useful for ageing due to pointedness of feathers but relative wear of the flight feathers and contrasts in the wing covs may be of use. Juv (May-Nov) lacks rufous in the crown and has distinct streaking on the breast and flanks; in western populations (see Molt) the presence or absence of this plumage can be used to age AHY/ASYs thru Oct (but beware of eastern vagrants), with some streaking possibly evident on some HY/SYs thru Jan. Look also for a few rusty feathers in the crowns of AHY/ASYs (none in HY/SYs) in Aug-Mar. Otherwise, no plumage criteria known after the 1st PB, although HY/SYs of both sexes average duller than AHY/ASYs (see Sex).

Sex—CP/BP (Mar-Sep). Wg: ♂(n30) 66-74, ♀(n30) 63-72; W > E. No reliable plumage criteria known although ♀ averages duller than ♂, especially in the crown; compare with age and wg.

References—B,R,W,O; Phillips *et al.* (1964); PRBO data.

CLAY-COLORED SPARROW
Spizella pallida

CCSP
Species # 561.0
Band size: 0

Species—Crown with fairly distinct to distinct median stripe; malar streaks well defined; terts and back feathers without rufous; rump brown, not contrasting in base color with lower back; auriculars and breast usually rich buff (when fresh, especially in HY/SYs); wg 56-66, wg-tail usually > 1.5 mm. The combination of these features should readily separate this species from other species of *Spizella* including Brewer's Sparrow (which see).

Molt—PB: HY partial (Jul-Oct), AHY complete (Jul-Aug); PA partial-incomplete (Mar-May). PBs occur primarily on the breeding grounds, with some HYs suspending some contour molt until the winter grounds. The PA may include some flight feathers; this needs verification.

Skull—Completes in HY/SY from 1 Nov thru Jan.

Age—Rect shape probably not useful but relative wear of flight feathers and contrast in wing covs may be of some use, as in Chipping Sparrow. Juv (Jul-Sep) has indistinct but heavy streaking on the breast and flanks; the retention of some streaking on the flanks can be used to age a few HY/SYs thru fall and even (rarely) thru the 1st spring. Otherwise, no reliable plumage criteria known, however, HY/SYs (Aug-Apr) average buffier on the breast than AHY/ASYs, and this can be useful on birds in fresh plumage.

Sex—CP/BP (May-Aug). Wg useful: ♂(n100) 59-66, ♀ (n100) 56-62. No reliable plumage differences are known but the superciliary averages whiter on ♂♂, buffier on ♀♀. Compare this with wg.

References—B,R,W,O; Knapton (1978); PRBO data.

BREWER'S SPARROW
Spizella breweri

BRSP
Species # 562.0
Band size: 0

Species—Crown with very indistinct or no median stripe; malar streaks fairly well defined; terts and back feathers without rufous; rump pale grayish-brown, not contrasting in base color from lower back; auriculars and breast pale grayish-brown; wg 57-66, wg-tail usually < 1.5 mm. The combination of these features should readily separate this species from other species of *Spizella* including Clay-colored Sparrow (which see).

Molt—PB: HY partial (Jul-Aug), AHY complete (Jul-Aug); PA limited-incomplete (Feb-Apr). PBs occur on the summer grounds, although some HYs may retain a few juvenal feathers until the winter grounds are reached, as in other *Spizella* species. The PA may regularly include some flight feathers, especially the terts (this needs more study).

Skull—Completes in HY/SY from 15 Oct thru Jan.

Age—Rect shape probably not useful but flight feather wear and wing covert contrasts may be of some use. Juv (Jun-Aug) has indistinct streaking on the breast and flanks; look for a few streaks in some HY/SYs thru fall/winter. Otherwise, no plumage criteria known.

Sex—♂ = ♀ by plumage. CP/BP (Apr-Aug). Wg: ♂(n30) 58-66, ♀(n30) 56-63.

References—B,O; PRBO data.

FIELD SPARROW
Spizella pusilla

FISP
Species # 563.0
Band size: 0-1

Species—Juv from other species of *Spizella* by no or very indistinct streaking to the crown and breast, and pinker (on the average) bill.

Molt—PB: HY partial-incomplete (Jul-Oct), AHY complete (Jul-Sep); PA absent. PBs occur primarily on the summer grounds. 1st PB may occasionally include some rects.

Skull—Completes in HY/SY from 1 Nov (as early as 15 Oct in extreme southern populations) thru Jan.

Age—Juv (May-Oct) usually has indistinct streaking on the breast and flanks. Look for hints of streaking on occasional HY/SYs thru early spring. Intermediates between the following may not be reliably aged:

HY/SY (Aug-Jul): Rects tapered (fig. 168), usually relatively worn, especially in spring. [Look also for contrasting juvenal and adult rects on some HY/SYs.]

AHY/ASY (Aug-Jul): Rects truncate (fig. 168), relatively unworn.

Sex—CP/BP (Apr-Aug). Wg: ♂(n30) 62-72, ♀(n30) 58-67; W > E. ♂♂ average brighter and darker than ♀♀, and some extremes (both sexes) may be sexable with experience (compare with wg and age). Otherwise, no reliable plumage criteria known.

References—B,R,W,O; Schneider (1981).

BLACK-CHINNED SPARROW
Spizella atrogularis

BCSP
Species # 565.0
Band size: 0

Molt—PB: HY partial (Jul-Aug), AHY complete (Jul-Aug); PA limited (Feb-Apr). PBs occur primarily on the summer grounds. More study is needed on the molts of this species.

Skull—Completes in HY/SY from 1 Nov thru Jan.

Age/Sex—CP/BP (Apr-Aug). Wg: ♂(n30) 60-68, ♀(n30) 57-64; E > W. Rect shape seems unhelpful for ageing despite the retention of the juvenal tail. Juv (Jun-Aug) lacks any black or dark gray in the throat; has more distinct, buffy wing bars; and has faintly streaked underparts (♂ = ♀). Intermediates between the following may occur that are not reliably aged and/or sexed. Alternatively, the combination of subtle plumage characteristics with other criteria may lead to the reliable separation of HY/SY ♂ ♂ and all ♀ ♀ in basic plumage and to ageing in alternate plumage, with experience. More study is needed:

Basic Plumage

AHY/ASY ♂ (Aug-Mar): Chin and (often) throat substantially dark grayish to blackish, contrasting with paler gray breast.

HY/SY ♂ / all ♀ ♀ (Aug-Mar): Chin and throat pale or buffy gray, uniform in color with breast or (on some HY/SY ♂ ♂ and possibly AHY/ASY ♀ ♀) with a few dark gray feathers. [Known AHY/ASYs (by skull) are reliably considered ♀ ♀ and known ♂ ♂ (museum skin or by wg) are HY/SYs. Also, extremely dull birds might be called HY/SY ♀ ♀ with experience and in combination with wg, but plumage distinctions are relative.]

♂ (Feb-Aug)   ♀ (Mar-Aug)

Figure 169. Typical throat patterns of ♂ and ♀ Black-chinned Sparrows in alternate plumage. Look for similar differences in basic plumage.

Alternate Plumage

♂ (Feb-Aug): Crown pure gray; chin and throat patch extensively blackish, contrasting sharply with gray upper breast (fig. 169).

♀ (Mar-Aug): Crown pale gray washed brownish; chin and throat with relatively restricted, dark gray patch, contrasting indistinctly with lighter gray upper breast (fig. 169). [Intermediates are probably SY ♂ ♂ or ASY ♀ ♀. Otherwise, no plumage criteria are known for ageing.]

References—B,O.

VESPER SPARROW
Pooecetes gramineus

VESP
Species # 540.0
Band size: 1B-1

Molt—PB: HY partial-incomplete (Jul-Oct), AHY complete (Jul-Oct); PA absent. PBs occur on the summer grounds. 1st PB may occasionally include the outer p (p9).

Skull—Completes in HY/SY from 15 Nov thru Feb.

Age—Rect shape seems unhelpful for ageing but look for contrastingly fresher outer p on some HY/SYs thru spring. Juv (Jun-Sep) is like adults but is drabber brown, has wider, buffier wing bars, and has little or no chestnut in the les covs. Otherwise, no reliable plumage criteria known although HY/SYs average duller chestnut in the les covs than AHY/ASYs. Extremes are probably reliably aged, with experience.

Sex—♂ = ♀ by plumage. CP/BP (Apr-Sep). Wg: ♂(n30) 74-87, ♀(n30) 72-83; W > E > W Cst.

References—B,R,W,O; Yunick (1984); PRBO data.

LARK SPARROW
Chondestes grammacus

LASP
Species # 552.0
Band size: 1B

Molt—PB: HY partial-complete (Jun-Oct), AHY complete (Jun-Sep); PA limited (Feb-Apr). PBs occur primarily on the summer grounds. Conflicting reports exist concerning the extent of the 1st PB, suggesting that it can be quite variable. PRBO data confirms that HYs often show molting or contrasting new and old flight feathers (especially the inner pp) during migration, indicating at least an incomplete molt in western populations. The 1st PB in this species as a whole deserves a thorough examination.

Skull—Completes in HY/SY from 1 Dec (as early as 1 Nov in California populations) thru Feb; look for windows on some SYs in spring.

Age—Juv (May-Aug) has heavily streaked underparts; look for occasional streaks in HY/SYs thru spring/summer. Intermediates may not be reliably aged by the following; in addition, general plumage probably averages duller in HY/SYs than AHY/ASYs but much overlap seems to occur:

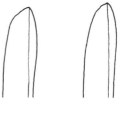

AHY/ASY   most HY/SY
some HY/SY

Figure 170. Juvenal vs. adult rectrix shapes in the Lark Sparrow.

HY/SY (Aug-Jul): Rects tapered (fig. 170), usually relatively worn, especially in spring/ summer. [Look also for contrasting new and old flight feathers during fall migration, possibly indicative of HY/SY.]

AHY (Jan-Sep): Rects truncate (fig. 170), relatively unworn.

Sex—♂ = ♀ by plumage. CP/BP (Apr-Sep). Wg: ♂(n30) 82-94, ♀(n30) 79-88.

References—B,R,O; PRBO data.

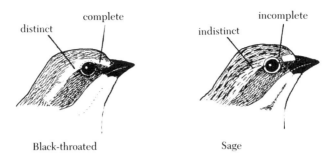

Figure 171. Head patterns in juvenal Black-throated and Sage sparrows.

BLACK-THROATED SPARROW
Amphispiza bilineata

BTSP
Species # 573.0
Band size: 0

Species—Juv-HY from Sage Sparrow by distinct superciliary, extending > 5 mm behind eye (fig. 171) and lack of streaking in the crown.

Molt—PB: HY partial-incomplete (Jun-Nov), AHY complete (Jun-Sep); PA absent. 1st PB often suspended over fall migration; adult PBs occur primarily on the summer grounds. A few flight feathers may molt during the 1st PB in early hatched individuals (more study needed).

Skull—Completes in HY/SY from 15 Nov thru Feb.

Age—The following is reliable on fall birds north of the wintering grounds but becomes increasingly difficult to use through spring and summer:

Juv-HY/SY (Aug-Jul): Throat and chin without black or mixed black and white; upper breast with distinct blackish streaking; some or all scapulars brown with black shaft streaks (plumage criteria good thru Nov only); rects tapered (fig. 172), usually relatively worn, especially in spring/summer.

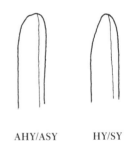

AHY/ASY   HY/SY

Figure 172. Rectrix shape by age in Black-throated and Sage sparrows.

AHY/ASY (Aug-Jul): Throat, chin and upper breast black, without white mottling; scapulars brownish-gray, without shaft streaks (plumage good for AHY thru Sep only); rects truncate (fig. 172), relatively unworn.

Sex—♂ = ♀ by plumage. CP/BP (Apr-Sep). Wg: ♂(n30) 61-70, ♀(n30) 55-67; W > E.

References—B,O.

SAGE SPARROW
Amphispiza belli

SGSP
Species # 574.0
Band size: 1

Species—From Juv Black-throated Sparrow by less distinct supecilliary, extending < 5 mm behind eye (fig. 171) and distinct streaking on the crown.

Molt—PB: HY partial (Jun-Sep), AHY complete (Jun-Sep); PA absent. PBs occur on the summer grounds.

Skull—Completes in HY/SY from 15 Oct thru Jan.

Age—Juv (May-Aug) has a brownish crown with black streaking, and a heavily streaked upperbreast. The following becomes increasingly difficult to use thru spring/summer due to rapid wear of the flight feathers:

HY/SY (Aug-Jul): Rects tapered (fig. 172); usually relatively worn, especially in spring.

AHY/ASY (Aug-Jul): Rects truncate (fig. 172); relatively unworn.

Sex—♂ = ♀ by plumage. CP/BP (Mar-Aug). Wg (interior populations): ♂(n30) 74-82, ♀(n30) 70-78. Wg (coastal/central California populations): ♂(n30) 63-73, ♀(n30) 59-70; SE > NW.

References—B,O.

FIVE-STRIPED SPARROW
Amphispiza quinquestriata

FSSP
Species # 584.2
Band size: 1

Molt—PB: HY partial-incomplete (Aug-Dec), AHY complete (Aug-Nov); PA absent. The 1st PB can include the terts and (rarely) some pp.

Skull—Completes in HY/SY from 1 Oct thru Jan.

Age—Rect shape may be of use for ageing. Juv (Jun-Nov) lacks black in the sides of the throat and has the center of the breast washed yellow. Otherwise, no plumage criteria known.

Sex—♂ = ♀ by plumage. CP/BP (Mar-Sep). Wg: ♂(n28) 63-71, ♀(n9) 60-65.

References—Wolf (1977).

LARK BUNTING
Calamospiza melanocorys

LABU
Species # 605.0
Band size: 1A

Molt—PB: HY incomplete (Jul-Sep), AHY complete (Jul-Sep); PA partial (Jan-Apr). PBs seem to begin on the summer grounds and complete on the winter grounds, perhaps more so in AHYs than HYs. 1st PB usually includes the outer 4 pp and often some rects (possibly more in ♂♂ than ♀♀). The 1st PA may be continuous thru the winter.

Skull—Completes in HY/SY from 15 Nov thru Feb.

Age/Sex—CP/BP (May-Sep). Wg: ♂(n30) 84-92, ♀(n30) 79-87. Juv (Jul-Aug) is like ♀ but is buffier and has bolder spotting on upperparts and stronger streaking on underparts (some juvs sometimes sexed by color and pattern of white in rects; fig. 173). The following should reliably separate the sexes, however, intermediates may not all be aged, especially with the ♀♀:

AHY/ASY ♂ (Aug-Jul): Body plumage mostly grayish-brown and whitish but with a varying amount of black on underparts (Aug-Mar) or entirely glossy black (Mar-Jul); gr covs with white or whitish outer edges; pp covs and flight feathers uniformly blackish; rects truncate (fig. 174). [Use caution and consideration of molt in determining ASY birds in Jul.]

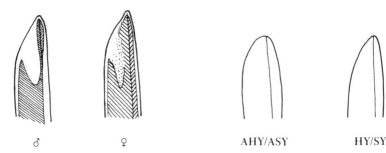

Figure 173. Typical pattern in the juvenal outer rectrices of ♂ vs. ♀ Lark Buntings.

Figure 174. Rectrix shape by age in the Lark Bunting.

HY/SY ♂ (Aug-Jul): Like AHY/ASY ♂ but basic plumage (Aug-Mar) without black on underparts; alternate body plumage (Mar-Jul) often black with some grayish mottling, particularly on upperparts; some gr covs often edged buffy; pp covs, ss, inner pp, and some or all rects brown or brownish, contrasting with blacker outer pp (usually) and sometimes other flight feathers; rects tapered (fig. 174) or mixed tapered and truncate.

AHY/ASY ♀ (Aug-Jul): Body plumage entirely brown and whitish, without black feathers; gr covs with whitish outer edges; pp covs and flight feathers fairly uniformly dark brown; rects truncate (fig.174); white on outer rects distinctly defined (see fig. 173).

HY/SY ♀ (Aug-Jul): Like AHY/ASY ♀ but gr covs with buffy outer edges; pp covs and most flight feathers pale brown, sometimes contrasting with other flight feathers (as in HY/SY ♂); rects tapered (fig. 174) or mixed tapered and truncate; white on outer rects (if juvenal) indistinctly defined (fig. 173).

References—B,R,O; PRBO data.

SAVANNAH SPARROW
Passerculus sandwichensis

SASP
Band size: 1

Savannah Sparrow	Species # 542.0
Ipswich Sparrow (IPSP)	Species # 541.0
Belding's Sparrow (BDSP)	Species # 543.0
Large-billed Sparrow (LBSP)	Species # 544.0

Species—All races from Song Sparrow by shorter tail (41-56).

Molt—PB: HY partial (Jul-Sep), AHY complete (Jul-Sep); PA limited (Feb-Apr). PBs occur on the summer grounds.

Skull—Completes in HY/SY from 15 Nov thru Jan.

Age—Juv (Jun-Aug) resembles adults but has more distinct pale wing bars. Intermediates between the following may not be reliably aged:

HY/SY (Aug-2nd Aug): Rects and outer pp tapered (fig. 175), usually relatively worn, especially in spring/summer.

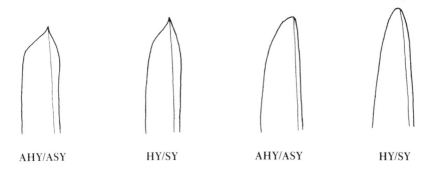

| AHY/ASY | HY/SY | AHY/ASY | HY/SY |

rectrices   primaries

Figure 175. Rectrix and outer primary shapes in the Savannah Sparrow, by age.

AHY/ASY (Aug-Jul): Rects and outer pp truncate (fig. 175), relatively unworn.

Sex—♂ = ♀ by plumage. CP/BP (Apr-Aug). Wg: ♂(n80) 64-80, ♀(n80) 61-77; highly variable, geographically. Wg (Ipswich Sparrow): ♂(n7) 74-83, ♀(n7) 71-79.

References—B,R,W,SK,O; PRBO data.

BAIRD'S SPARROW
Ammodramus bairdii

BDSP
Species # 545.0
Band size: 1

Species—See Table 6 for separation of Juvs from other *Ammodramus* species by measurements.

Molt—PB: HY partial (Jul-Oct), AHY complete (Jul-Sep); PA limited (Feb-Apr). 1st PB can occur on the summer or winter grounds (or both); adult PBs probably occur mostly on the summer grounds.

Skull—Completes in HY/SY from 15 Nov thru Feb.

Age—Rect shape seems unhelpful for ageing despite retention of juvenal tail. Juv (Jul-Sep) is more heavily streaked underneath and has dark back feathers with buffy edging, giving a scaled appearance (vs. a more streaked appearence after the 1st PB). Otherwise, no plumage criteria is known.

Sex—♂ = ♀ by plumage. CP/BP (Jun-Sep). Wg: ♂(n30) 67-75, ♀(n30) 65-72.

References—B,R,O.

GRASSHOPPER SPARROW
Ammodramus savannarum

GRSP
Species # 546.0
Band size: 1

Species—See Table 6 for separation of Juvs from other *Ammodramus* species by measurements. Also from Le Conte's and Sharp-tailed sparrows by p9 usually > p5 by more than 5 mm. Look also for yellow underwing covs vs. white in Le Conte's Sparrow.

TABLE 6.
Measurements of *Ammodramus* sparrows for separation of juveniles.

	Baird's	Grass-hopper	Henslow's	Le Conte's	Sharp-tailed	Seaside
wing	65–75	56–67	47–56	48–56	51–61	54–65
tail	41–58	39–49	46–53	45–56	43–55	46–59
tarsus	20–22	19–21	15–17.5	17–19	19–23	21–24
exp. culmen	9.4–12.7	10.7–12.4	10.2–14.0	8.4–11.2	9.4–13.0	11.9–15.0

Molt—PB: HY complete (Jul-Oct), AHY complete (Jul-Sep); PA limited (Feb-Apr). PBs occur primarily on the summer grounds but may finish on the winter grounds (some HYs).

Skull—Completes in HY/SY from 1 Nov (as early as 1 Oct in Florida and California populations) thru Feb.

Age—Rect shape seems unhelpful for ageing despite retention of the juvenal tail. Juv (May-Aug) has distinct streaking on the upperbreast; look for occasional streaks on some HYs on migration or on the winter grounds thru Oct. Otherwise, no plumage criteria known.

Sex—♂ = ♀ by plumage. CP/BP (Apr-Sep). Wg: ♂(n30) 59-67, ♀(n30) 56-64; W > E.

References—B,R,W,O; PRBO data.

HENSLOW'S SPARROW
Ammodramus henslowii

HESP
Species # 547.0
Band size: 0-1

Species—See Table 6 for separation of Juvs from other *Ammodramus* species by measurements.

Molt—PB: HY complete (Jul-Sep), AHY complete (Jul-Sep); PA limited (Feb-Apr). PBs occur primarily on the summer grounds.

Skull—Completes in HY/SY from 15 Nov thru Feb.

Age—Rect shape seems unhelpful for ageing after the 1st PB. Juv (Jun-Aug) has buffy edging to the scapulars and lacks the malar and distinct breast streaking of older birds. Otherwise no reliable plumage criteria are known.

Sex—♂ = ♀ by plumage. CP/BP (May-Sep). Wg: ♂(n30) 50-56, ♀(n30) 47-54.

References—B,R,W,O.

LE CONTE'S SPARROW
Ammodramus leconteii

LCSP
Species # 548.0
Band size: 1

Species—See Table 6 for separation of Juvs from other *Ammodramus* species by measurements. Also from Juv Grasshopper and Sharp-tailed sparrows by p9 usually > p5 by less than 5 mm. Check also for white underwing covs vs. yellow in Grasshopper Sparrow.

Molt—PB: HY partial (Aug-Oct), AHY complete (Aug-Oct); PA partial-incomplete (Mar-Apr). PBs usually occur on the summer grounds, but can (rarely?) occur on the winter grounds. PA often includes the terts and may include some to all rects. It also may include more flight feathers in SY than ASY birds; this needs more study.

Skull—Completes in HY/SY from 15 Nov thru Jan.

Age—Rect shape seems unhelpful for ageing despite retention of the juvenal tail thru at least the 1st PA. Juv (Jul-Sep) lacks rich orange tones in head and breast and has distinct and fine streaking across upperbreast (look for some HYs retaining the streaking during or for a short time after the fall migration). Otherwise, no reliable plumage criteria known.

Sex—♂ = ♀ by plumage. CP/BP (May-Sep). Wg: ♂(n30) 50-56, ♀(n30) 48-54.

References—B,R,O; Tordoff & Mengel (1951), Dickerman (1962), Murray (1968); PRBO data.

SHARP-TAILED SPARROW
Ammodramus caudacutus

STSP
Species # 549.0
Band size: 1

Species—See Table 6 for separation of Juvs from other *Ammodramus* species by measurements. Also, Juv from Juv Grasshopper and Le Conte's sparrows by p9 usually ≤ p5.

Molt—PB: HY incomplete (Aug-Oct), AHY complete (Aug-Oct); PA partial-incomplete (Mar-Apr). PBs occur on the summer grounds. 1st PB includes the rects and sometimes some ss and pp. PA variable, often includes 3-5 outer pp and the rects. Possible differences in the extent of the PA in SY vs. ASY may occur.

Skull—Completes in HY/SY from 15 Nov thru Feb.

Age—Rect shape not useful after the 1st PB, but look for contrasting new and old pp and ss on some HY/SYs thru Mar. Juv (Jul-Sep) lacks orange in the head, has large black centers to the back feathers, and is distinctly streaked on the underparts; HY/SYs may possibly be separated thru Mar by relatively heavy streaking to the underparts. Otherwise, no plumage criteria known.

Sex—♂ = ♀ by plumage. CP/BP (May-Sep). Wg: ♂(n30) 53-61, ♀(n30) 51-59.

References—B,R,W,O; Tordoff & Mengel (1951), Dickerman (1962), Murray (1968).

SEASIDE SPARROW
Ammodramus maritimus

SESP
Band size: 1B

Seaside Sparrow	Species # 550.0
Dusky Seaside Sparrow (DSSP)	Species # 551.0
Cape Sable Seaside Sparrow (CSSP)	Species # 551.1

Species—See Table 6 for separation of Juvs from other *Ammodramus* species by measurements.

Molt—PB: HY complete (Jul-Sep), AHY complete (Jul-Sep); PA absent-partial (Mar-Apr). PBs occur on the summer grounds.

Skull—Completes in HY/SY from 15 Nov (as early as 15 Oct in southern populations) thru Feb.

Age—Rect shape and wear not useful after the 1st PB. Juv (May-Aug) is generally much buffier and has distinct streaking on the crown, breast, and flanks. Otherwise, no plumage criteria known.

Sex—♂ = ♀ by plumage. CP/BP (Apr-Aug). Wg: ♂(n30) 56-65, ♀(n30) 54-64; N > S.

References—B,W,O; Murray (1968).

FOX SPARROW
Passerella iliaca

FOSP
Species # 585.0
Band size: 1A-1B

Species—From all races of Song Sparrow by yellow or yellowish lower mandible. See also wg by sex.

Molt—PB: HY partial (Jul-Sep), AHY complete (Jul-Sep); PA absent-limited (Mar-Apr). PBs occur on the summer grounds.

Skull—Completes in HY/SY from 1 Dec thru Feb.

Age—Juv (Jun-Aug) is similar to adults but averages duller on the upperparts and has a buffy wash to the underparts. Intermediates between the following may not be reliably aged:

HY/SY (Aug-2nd Aug): Rects tapered (fig. 176), usually relatively worn, especially in spring/summer.

AHY/ASY (Aug-Jul): Rects truncate (fig. 176), relatively unworn.

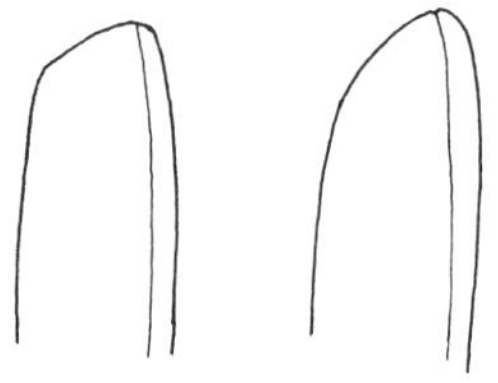

AHY/ASY   HY/SY

Figure 176. Rectrix shape by age in the Fox Sparrow.

Sex—♂ = ♀ by plumage. CP/BP (Apr-Aug). Wg: ♂(n40) 77-92, ♀(n40) 75-88; E > W.

References—B,R,W,O; Stewart (1972a); PRBO data.

SONG SPARROW
Melospiza melodia

SOSP
Species # 581.0
Band size: 1B-1

Species—All races from Savannah Sparrow by longer tail (58-75). From Fox Sparrow by dark lower mandible; see also wg by sex. Juv from Juv Lincoln's and Swamp sparrows by: crown usually mostly brown with relatively indistinct streaks; medium stripe absent or present; throat mostly unstreaked; p9 < p5 by 6-12 mm; and tail ≥ 60.

Molt—PB: HY partial-complete (Jul-Nov), AHY complete (Jul-Oct); PA absent. In migratory (most) races, PBs occur primarily on the breeding grounds, and usually occur in Jul-Aug. 1st PB highly variable and dependant on the race and the brood sequence; usually includes the rects and terts, a variable amount of pp, and often a lesser number of ss.

Skull—Completes in HY/SY from 15 Nov (as early as 15 Oct in certain California populations) thru Feb.

Age—Rect shape seems unhelpful (even on birds that retain the juvenal tail) but check for contrasts in new and old pp in some HY/SYs of certain populations (see Molt). Juv (Apr-Sep) is generally drabber and buffier than adults, with finer streaking below and on face, has less distinct facial and median stripe features and lacks rusty tones to the upperparts. Otherwise, no plumage criteria known for ageing.

Sex—♂ = ♀ by plumage. CP/BP (Feb-Sep). Wg: ♂(n70) 54-83, ♀(n70) 52-79; NW > E > W Coast (highly variable, geographically (see Aldrich 1984); measurements exclude certain insular Alaskan populations, where ♂♂ can reach a wg of 89 mm).

References—B,R,W,SK,O,BBM; Dhondt & Smith (1980), Aldrich (1984), Rimmer (1986); PRBO data.

LINCOLN'S SPARROW
Melospiza lincolnii

LISP
Species # 583.0
Band size: 1

Species—Juv from Juv Song and Swamp sparrows by: crown buffy-brown with distinct black streaking; throat distinctly streaked; roof of mouth gray to grayish-white; p9 ≥ p4 and ≈ p5 (2 mm > to 2 mm <); and tail ≤ 60 mm.

Molt—PB: HY partial (Jul-Aug), AHY complete (Jul-Aug); PA absent-limited (feb-Apr). PBs (and ≈ p5) occur on the summer grounds.

Skull—Completes in HY/SY from 15 Nov thru Feb.

Age—Rect shape and wear seems unhelpful for ageing due to the general pointedness of the feathers. Juv (Jul-Aug) has buffier brown crown and superciliary, and is generally drabber and more coarsely streaked than adults. Otherwise, no plumage criteria known.

Sex—♂ = ♀ by plumage. CP/BP (May-Aug). Wg: ♂(n100) 57-69, ♀(n100) 53-65; W Mts > E & W Coast.

References—B,R,W,O; Rimmer (1986); PRBO data.

SWAMP SPARROW
Melospiza georgiana

SWSP
Species # 584.0
Band size: 1

Species—Juv from Juv Song and Lincoln's sparrows by: crown mostly black or heavily streaked with brown and gray and without a median stripe; throat unstreaked; roof of mouth yellow to yellowish-white; p9 ≤ p4 and < p5 by 3-8 mm; tail 50-65.

Molt—PB: HY partial-incomplete (Jul-Oct), AHY complete (Jul-Oct); PA limited (Feb-Apr). PBs occur on the summer grounds. 1st PB may occasionally include the rects.

Skull—Completes in HY/SY from 15 Nov thru Feb.

Age—Rect shape (see fig. 176) possibly of some use when combined with plumage and sex but beware of renewed rects on occasional HY/SYs. Juv (Jun-Aug) lacks a distinct median stripe and is distinctly streaked below ($\male = \female$). In alternate plumage (Mar-Aug), some SYs might be reliably aged when compared with sex (see below) and other ageing criteria by having a substantially streaked crown with a complete gray median stripe, compared to a full and rufous crown in ASYs. The reliability of this feature should be further studied. The following appears reliable in basic-plumaged birds (compare with sexing criteria on intermediates):

Basic Plumage

HY/SY (Aug-Mar): Nape and superciliary buffy to brownish-gray; crown heavily streaked and with a limited amount or no rufous.

AHY/ASY (Aug-Mar): Nape and superciliary gray or mostly gray; crown lightly streaked and with substantial rufous.

Sex—CP/BP (Apr-Aug). Wg: $\male$(n100) 56-65, $\female$(n100) 52-63. The rufous crown patch may average slightly smaller and more streaked in $\female\female$ than $\male\male$ in alternate plumage (Mar-Aug); this may be of use when compared with age criteria (see above) and wg. Otherwise, $\male = \female$ by plumage.

References—B,R,W,SK,O; Riggins & Riggins (1974), Rimmer (1986); PRBO data.

WHITE-THROATED SPARROW   WTSP
Zonotrichia albcollis   Species # 558.0
                                                             Band size: 1B

Molt—PB: HY partial (Jul-Sep), AHY complete (Jul-Sep); PA limited (Mar-May). PBs occur on the summer grounds.

Skull—Completes in HY/SY from 15 Dec thru Mar; some SYs may show windows thru early summer.

Age/Sex—CP/BP (May-Aug). Wg: $\male$(n100) 68-79, $\female$(n100) 63-73. Rect shape may be useful with extremes (more study needed). Juv (Jun-Aug) has considerable streaking on upperbreast and flanks and a gray-brown iris. Compare the following with wg and plumage (see below):

HY/SY (Jul-Feb): Iris gray-brown to brown.

AHY (Jan-Dec): Iris reddish-brown.

[Plumage variation in relation to age and sex does occur in this species, but polymorphism and substantial overlap in characters complicate the pattern. In all plumages, but especially basic (Aug-Mar), AHY/ASYs and $\male\male$ generally have bolder black and white head patterns, brighter and more yellow on the lores, whiter throats, and grayer and less streaked breasts than HY/SYs and $\female\female$. With experience and comparison with other age/sex criteria, plumage may prove useful for ageing some known-sexed birds and vice versa. But this should not be attempted without a full understanding of the polymorphic variations this species exhibits. For more information, see Lowther (1961), Vardy (1971), Atkinson & Ralph (1980), and Watt (1986).]

References—B,R,W,SK,O,BBM; Lowther (1961), Mellancamp (1969), Vardy (1971), Yunick (1977), Atkinson & Ralph (1980), Prescott (1986), Watt (1986); PRBO data.

GOLDEN-CROWNED SPARROW
Zonotrichia atracapilla

GCSP
Species # 557.0
Band size: 1B-1A

Molt—PB: HY partial (Jul-Nov), AHY complete (Jul-Nov); PA limited-partial (Mar-May). PBs occur primarily on the summer grounds but seem often to be suspended and completed on the winter grounds. [Oct-Nov molt in HYs on the winter grounds includes contours of the upperparts only, and is possibly supplemental to the 1st PB rather than part of it. The "juvenal" plumage (see below) is not found on the winter grounds.]

Skull—Completes in HY/SY from 15 Nov thru Jan.

Age—Rect shape seems unhelpful for ageing despite the retention of the juvenal tail. Juv (Jul-Sep) has distinct streaking on the upperbreast and flanks. No reliable plumage criteria are known for alternate-plumaged (Mar-Aug) birds, although some extremes might be reliably aged by the extent of black in the crown (see fig. 177). In basic plumage the following is reliable but up to 60% will be intermediates and cannot be aged by plumage (fig. 177):

Basic Plumage

HY/SY (Aug-Mar): Crown stripes entirely absent or with a hint of light brown restricted to the area above the lores (fig. 177).

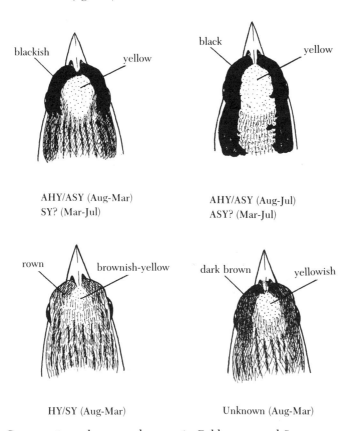

Figure 177. Crown patterns by age and season in Golden-crowned Sparrows.

AHY/ASY (Aug-Mar): Crown stripes with at least some black extending above the lores to at least the eye (fig. 177).

Sex—♂ = ♀ by plumage. CP/BP (May-Aug). Wg: ♂(n30) 75-85, ♀(n30) 72-81.

References—B,O; Stewart (1972a, 1972b); PRBO data.

WHITE-CROWNED SPARROW
Zonotrichia leucophrys

WCSP
Band size: 1B

Eastern White-crowned Sparrow (EWSP)	Species # 554.0
Mountain White-crowned Sparrow (MWSP)	Species # 554.6
Puget Sound White-crowned Sparrow (PWSP)	Species # 554.7
Gambel's White-crowned Sparrow (GWSP)	Species # 555.0
Nuttall's White-crowned Sparrow (NWSP)	Species # 556.0

Subspecies—The Puget Sound, Gambel's, and Nuttall's races can be separated from each other and the other two races as follows (see Mewaldt 1977 for more information). No in hand criteria are known for the separation of the Mountain and Eastern races except, perhaps, by wg with extremes (see Sex):

Eastern/Mountain White-crowned Sparrow—Lores black (AHY/ASY) or dark brown, contrasting with tan malar area (HY/SY; some Mountain HY/SYs may have palish lores, slightly darker than Gambel's); bill dark pinkish; crown stripes relatively pale (HY/SY); wg 66-83 (see Sex).

Gambel's White-crowned Sparrow—Lores white (AHY/ASY) or tan, not contrasting with malar area (HY/SY); breast pale brownish to gray; bend of wing white (sometimes slightly washed yellow); underwing covs silvery-gray; bill orangish to flesh-colored; wg 68-84 (see Sex).

Puget Sound White-crowned Sparrow—Like the Gambel's race but breast darkish brown or brownish-gray; bend of wing yellow; underwing covs washed yellow; bill yellow to orangish-yellow; wg 63-75 (see Sex); wg/lean weight (subtract 0-8 gms for none-much fat present, respectively) > 2.60.

Nuttall's White-crowned Sparrow—Like the Puget Sound race but wg/lean weight ≤ 2.60 (see also differences in the extent of the PA for further clues to separating Feb-Aug birds).

Molt—PB: HY partial (Jul-Oct), AHY complete (Jul-Oct); PA limited-incomplete (Feb-Apr). PBs occur on the summer grounds and are more protracted in Nuttall's than the other races. PAs vary according to race, from mostly limited in Eastern, Mountain, and Nuttall's to incomplete in Puget Sound and Gambel's. The PAs of the latter two races usually include the terts and the central rects. The central rects are also often replaced in the Eastern and Mountain races and occasionally in Nuttall's as well.

Skull—Completes in HY/SY from 15 Nov (as early as 15 Oct in Nuttall's) thru Jan.

Age—Rect shape seems unhelpful for ageing, despite the retention of the juvenal tail. Juv (May-Aug) has distinctly streaked breast and crown.The following is reliable for basic plumage in all races but only for Nuttall's on alternate-plumaged birds. Occasional birds of the other races may show scattered brown and tan feathers in the crown in alternate plumage and if so, they are reliably aged SY:

Basic Plumage

HY/SY (Aug-Apr): Crown tan with brown stripes.

AHY/ASY (Aug-Mar): Crown black and white.

Alternate Plumage (Nuttall's only)

SY (Mar-Aug): Crown with a variable mixture of tan, brown, black, and white, usually with the anterior portion of the crown black and white and the posterior portion mostly tan and brown.

ASY (Mar-Aug): Crown completely black and white (reliable for Nuttall's only; see above).

Sex—♂ = ♀ by plumage. CP/BP (Mar-Aug). Wg: Eastern ♂(n100) 74-83, ♀(n100) 71-80; Mountain ♂(n100) 72-81, ♀(n100) 66-76; Puget Sound and Nuttall's ♂(n100) 67-75, ♀(n100) 63-72; Gambel's ♂(n100) 73-84, ♀(n100) 68-78.

References—B,R,W,SK,O,C(Mewaldt); Michener & Michener (1943), Banks (1964), Mewaldt *et al.* (1968), Morton *et al.* (1969); Morton & Welton (1973); Mewaldt (1973, 1977), Mewaldt & King (1978, 1986); Fugel & Rothstein (1985); PRBO data.

HARRIS' SPARROW
Zonotrichia querula

HASP
Species # 553.0
Band size: 1A

Molt— PB: HY partial (Jul-Sep), AHY complete (Jul-Sep); PA limited-incomplete (Mar-May). PBs occur on the summer grounds. PAs usually include the two central rects.

Skull—Completes in HY/SY from 15 Nov thru Feb.

Age—Rect shape seems unhelpful for ageing despite retention of the juvenal tail. Juv (Jul-Aug) has finely streaked underparts. No reliable plumage criteria known for ageing alternate-plumaged (Apr-Aug) birds, although SYs average more brownish in the crown and face. In basic plumage ageing is reliable for most birds but a few intermediates occur which should not be aged by plumage alone:

Basic Plumage

HY/SY (Aug-Apr): Crown mostly brown with black scalloping to mostly black; lores brown; chin and throat predominantly white.

AHY/ASY (Aug-Apr): Crown entirely black or mostly black with some brown or whitish streaking; lores black or blackish; chin and throat entirely or predominantly black.

Sex—♂ = ♀ by plumage. CP/BP (May-Aug). Wg quite useful: ♂(n55) 84-92, ♀(n50) 77-85.

References—B,R,O; Wolfenden (1955), Rowher *et al.* (1981); PRBO data.

DARK-EYED JUNCO
Junco hyemalis

DEJU
Species # 567.7
Band size: 1

White-winged Junco (WWJU)	Species # 566.0
Slate-colored Junco (SCJU)	Species # 567.0
Oregon Junco (ORJU)	Species # 567.1
Gray-headed Junco (GHJU)	Species # 569.0

Subspecies—White-winged and Gray-headed juncos are readily identified by plumage and longer wg (see Sex). Slate-colored Junco has uniformly colored head and back, and grayish or grayish-brown sides and flanks, while Oregon Junco usually shows a contrast between a black or dark grayish-brown hood and a paler, brown back, and has a pinkish or tan hue to the sides and flanks. Some intermediates or intergrades may occur between Slate-colored and Oregon juncos (especially with younger birds) which are not reliably distinguished. Juveniles may be impossible to separate.

Molt—PB: HY partial (Jul-Oct), AHY complete (Jul-Oct); PA limited (Feb-Apr). PBs occur primarily on the summer grounds.

Skull—Completes in HY/SY from 1 Nov (as early as 1 Oct in some California populations) thru Feb.

Age/Sex—CP/BP (Mar-Sep). Wg: White-winged ♂(n20) 83-90, ♀(n14) 79-86; Slate-colored and Oregon ♂(n100) 74-83, ♀(n100) 68-78; Gray-headed ♂(n20) 78-85, ♀(n20) 75-81. Juv (May-Sep) has distinct streaking above and below (♂ = ♀ except by the amount of white on r4 on the Oregon race, at least; see below). By combining the following with wg, many birds can be reliably aged and sexed. Differences in the shape of the rects can be very subtle, however, and many intermediates will occur (especially in the White-winged and Gray-headed races) which can not be reliably determined. Also, the amount of white in the rects shows age and sex related variation in the Oregon race (fig. 178) and is probably indicative in the other races as well (this should be further investigated):

AHY/ASY ♂ (Aug-Jul): Head, throat, and upper breast relatively dark gray or black (varies with different races), with little or no brownish wash (0-15% brown); terts with pale gray or brownish edging, not contrasting with gr covs; outer 1-5 gr covs without pale tips; rects truncate (fig. 178); r4 with a large patch of white (see fig. 179; Oregon race, at least); iris reddish-brown to dark red.

HY/SY ♂ (Aug-Jul): Head, throat, and upperbreast pale to medium gray or dull blackish, with a moderate brown wash (usually 15-40% brown in Aug-Mar), or as AHY/ASY ♂ (Mar-Aug): terts with brown edging, often contrasting with gray-edged inner gr covs (thru Mar); outer 1-5 gr covs sometimes with pale buffy tips; rects tapered (fig. 178); 4th rect with moderately sized white patch (fig. 179; Oregon race at least); iris grayish-brown to brown (thru Oct-Mar).

AHY/ASY ♀ (Aug-Jul): Head, throat, and upperpart coloration as with HY/SY ♂; terts with pale gray or brownish edging, not contrasting with gr covs; outer 1-5 gr covs without pale tips; rects truncate (fig. 178); r4 with moderately sized white patch (fig. 179; Oregon race, at least); iris reddish-brown to dark red.

HY/SY ♀ (Aug-Jul): Head, throat, and upper breast relatively pale gray or pale blackish, with a moderate to heavy brown wash (usually > 50% brown; Aug-Mar), or mostly dark gray,

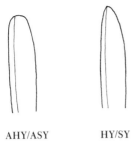

AHY/ASY   HY/SY

Figure 178. Juvenal vs. adult rectrix shapes in juncos.

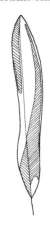

HY/SY ♀   HY/SY ♂

often with a slight brownish wash (Mar-Aug); terts with brown edging, often contrasting with gray-edged inner gr covs (thru Mar); outer 1-5 gr covs sometimes with pale tips; rects tapered (fig. 178); 4th rect with relatively small or no white patch (fig. 179; Oregon race at least); iris grayish-brown to brown (thru Oct-Mar). &179

Figure 179. Typical amounts of white in the fourth rect of HY/SY Oregon Juncos, by sex. Look for more white in AHY/ASY ♂♂, and about the same amount of white in AHY/ASY ♀♀, as is shown for HY/SY ♂. This criterion should also be examined in other races of Dark-eyed Junco.

References—B,R,W,O; Blake (1964), Dow (1966), Grant & Quay (1970), Yunick (1972, 1976b, 1977, 1981b, 1984), Balph (1976), Brackbill (1977), Ryan (1978); R. Yunick data, PRBO data.

YELLOW-EYED JUNCO
Junco phaenotus

YEJU
Species # 570.0
Band size: 1

Molt—PB: HY partial-incomplete (Jul-Sep), AHY complete (Jul-Sep); PA limited (Feb-Apr). 1st PB can include the rects.

Skull—Completes in HY/SY from 15 Oct thru Jan.

Age/Sex—CP/BP (Apr-Aug). Wg ♂(n30) 75-87, ♀(n30) 70-82. Juv (May-Sep) is heavily streaked above and spotted below (♂ = ♀). Most or all of the age and sex plumage criteria useful in Dark-eyed Junco can be applied to this species as well, except for iris color: olive-gray to grayish-yellow in HY/SY (thru Sep-Dec); yellow to orangish-yellow in AHY (Jan-Sep).

References—B; Lamm & Leupke (1981), Bowers & Dunning (1986).

McCOWN'S LONGSPUR
Calcarius mccownii

MCLO
Species # 539.0
Band size: 1

Species—♀ from other longspurs and sparrows by tail pattern (fig. 180) and p7-p6 usually 3-8 mm.

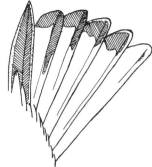

(Aug-Mar)

Figure 181. Pattern of the crown feathers by sex in basic-plumaged McCrown's Longsuprs.

Figure 180. The tail pattern of the McCown's Longspur.

Molt—PB: HY partial (Jul-Sep), AHY complete (Jul-Sep); PA limited (Feb-Apr). PBs occur on the summer grounds.

Skull—Completes in HY/SY from 1 Nov thru Jan.

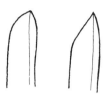

AHY/ASY   HY/SY

Figure 182. Rectrix shape by age in longspurs.

Age—Juv (Jun-Aug) has buffy edging to the back feathers and distinct streaking to the upperbreast ($\male = \female$). In addition to the following, HY/SYs average buffier than AHY/ASYs in both sexes, and in $\male\male$, HY/SYs have relatively less black in the crown and upper breast:

HY/SY (Aug-Jul): Rects tapered (fig. 182), usually relatively worn, especially in spring/summer.

AHY/ASY (Aug-Jul): Rects truncate (fig. 182), relatively unworn.

Sex—CP/BP (May-Aug). Wg useful: $\male$(n30) 86-94, $\female$(n30) 80-88. The following is reliable after the 1st PB:

$\male$: Crown and breast black (Mar-Aug) or mixed brown and black (Aug-Mar); crown feathers as illustrated (fig. 181, Aug-Mar); mid covs relatively dark rufous.

$\female$: Crown and breast brown, with little or no black; crown feathers as illustrated (fig. 181, Aug-Mar); mid covs relatively pale rufous.

References—B,R,O.

LAPLAND LONGSPUR
Calcarius lapponicus

LALO
Species # 536.0
Band size: 1B

Species—From other longspurs and sparrows by the combination of rufous in the gr covs, tail pattern (fig. 183), and p7-p6 usually 5-11 mm.

Molt—PB: HY partial (Jul-Sep), AHY complete (Jul-Sep); PA limited (Mar-May). PBs occur on the summer grounds.

Skull—Completes in HY/SY from 15 Nov thru Jan.

Age—Juv (Jul-Aug) has prominent streaking on upper breast ($\male = \female$). In addition to the following, HY/SYs of both sexes average buffier below and have less rufous in the nape than AHY/ASYs. Also, see sex for basic plumaged birds:

HY/SY (Aug-Jul): Rects tapered (fig. 182), usually relatively worn, especially in spring/summer; central rects without pale edging.

AHY/ASY (Aug-Jul): Rects truncate (fig.182), relatively unworn; central rects often with pale gray edging.

Sex—CP/BP (Jun-Aug). Wg quite useful: $\male$(n40) 90-101, $\female$(n40) 86-94. Intermediates between the following in basic plumage are likely HY/SY $\male\male$ or AHY/ASY $\female\female$; combine with age criteria and wg:

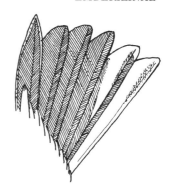

Figure 183. The tail pattern of the Lapland Longspur.

$\male$ $\female$

(Aug-Mar)

Figure 184. Crown feather pattern by sex in Lapland Longspurs.

Basic Plumage

$\male$ (Aug-Mar): Crown feathers as illustrated (fig. 184); nape mostly rufous (feathers tipped buffy when fresh), with no or a few indistinct streaks; upperbreast usually mottled with some black.

$\female$ (Aug-Mar): Crown feathers as illustrated (fig. 184); nape mostly brownish with darker streaking; upperbreast with little or no black.

Alternate Plumage

$\male$ (Mar-Aug): Upperbreast, face, and crown completely black.

$\female$ (Mar-Aug): Upperbreast mostly white with some black streaks; face mostly brownish; crown mixed black and brown.

References—B,R,W,O,Sv; R. Davis (1969b).

SMITH'S LONGSPUR
Calcarius pictus

SMLO
Species # 537.0
Band size: 1-1B

Species—From other longspurs and sparrows by pattern of white in the tail and mid covs (figs. 185 & 186), and p7-p6 usually 0-4 mm.

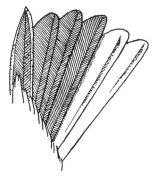

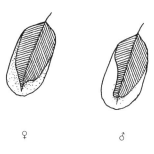

Figure 185. The tail pattern of the Smith's Longspur.

Figure 186. Middle covert pattern by sex in basic-plumaged Smith's Longspurs.

Molt—PB: HY partial (Jul-Sep), AHY complete (Jul-Sep); PA limited (Feb-Apr). PBs occur on the summer grounds.

Skull—Completes in HY/SY from 15 Nov thru Jan.

Age—Juv (Jul-Aug) has distinct streaking on the upperbreast ($\delta = \varphi$). Other than the following, no reliable plumage criteria are known but check the amount of white in the les and mid covs for possible ageing of $\delta\delta$:

HY/SY (Aug-Jul): Rects tapered (fig. 182), usually relatively worn, especially in spring/summer.

AHY/ASY (Aug-Jul): Rects truncate (fig. 182), relatively unworn.

Sex—CP/BP (May-Aug). Wg: δ(n30) 87-97, φ(n30) 84-92. The following is reliable with all birds in alternate plumage (Mar-Aug). Intermediates which occur in basic plumage are likely HY/SY $\delta\delta$ or AHY/ASY $\varphi\varphi$; compare with age criteria and wg:

δ: Crown and face black and white (Mar-Aug); les and mid covs broadly edged white (fig. 186).

φ: Crown and face brownish (reliable in Mar-Aug); les and mid covs narrowly edged white (fig. 186).

References—B,R,O.

CHESTNUT-COLLARED LONGSPUR
Calcarius ornatus

CCLO
Species # 538.0
Band size: 1

Species—From other longspurs and sparrows by the pattern of white in the tail (fig. 187) and p7-p6 usually 0-4 mm.

Molt—PB: HY partial (Jul-Sep), AHY complete (Jul-Sep); PA limited (Feb-Apr). PBs occur on the summer grounds.

Skull—Completes in HY/SY from 1 Nov thru Jan.

Age—Juv (Jul-Aug) has distinct streaking on the upperbreast (♂ = ♀). In addition to the following, HY/SYs (especially ♂♂) average duller than AHY/ASYs. Check also for the amount of white in the les and mid covs of HY/SY and AHY/ASY ♂♂ in both basic and alternate plumage:

HY/SY (Aug-Jul): Rects tapered (fig. 182), usually relatively worn, especially in spring/summer.

AHY/ASY (Aug-Jul): Rects truncate (fig. 182), relatively unworn.

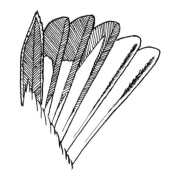

Figure 187. The tail pattern of the Chestnut-collared Longspur.

Sex—CP/BP (Apr-Aug). Wg: ♂(n60) 81-91, ♀(n50) 76-85. The following is reliable after the 1st PB:

♂: Crown and breast black or mixed black and chestnut (Mar-Aug) or black with brown mottling (Aug-Mar); nape chestnut or tinged with chestnut; les covs mostly white.

♀: Crown, breast, nape, and les covs mostly buffy brown.

References—B,R,O.

SNOW BUNTING
Plectrophenax nivalis

SNBU
Species # 534.0
Band size: 1A-1B.

Species—From McKay's Bunting in all plumages by pattern of white on rect 3 (fig. 188).

Molt—PB: HY partial (Jul-Sep), AHY complete (Jul-Sep); PA limited (Feb-Apr). PBs occur on the summer grounds.

Skull—Completes in HY/SY from 15 Nov thru Jan.

Age/Sex—CP/BP (May-Aug). Wg very useful: ♂(n30) 104-117, ♀(n30) 97-105. Juv (Jul-Aug) has head and breast streaked and with a dusky wash; Juv ♂ and ♀ separated by pattern of pp covs (fig. 192) and wg. All birds should be reliably sexed and most birds should be reliably aged when wg is used with the following:

AHY/ASY ♂ (Sep-Aug): Scapulars with blackish, bluntly pointed bases and narrow, buffy tips (fig. 190, Aug-Mar) or entirely black (Mar-Jul); uppertail covs

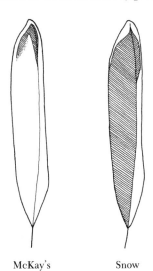

McKay's   Snow

Figure 188. Pattern of the third (from inside) rectrix of McKay's vs. Snow buntings.

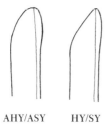

AHY/ASY   HY/SY

Figure 189. Rectrix shape by age in Snow and McKay's buntings.

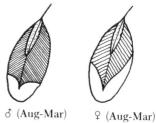

♂ (Aug-Mar)   ♀ (Aug-Mar)

Figure 190. Pattern of the scapulars in ♂ and ♀, basic-plumaged Snow Buntings.

 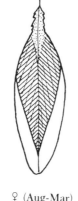

♂ (Aug-Mar)   ♀ (Aug-Mar)

Figure 191. Pattern of the uppertail coverts in ♂ and ♀, basic-plumaged Snow Buntings.

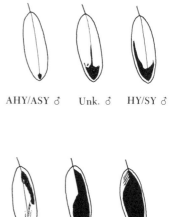

AHY/ASY ♂   Unk. ♂   HY/SY ♂

AHY/ASY ♀   Unk. ♀   HY/SY ♀

Figure 192. Typical patterns of the longest primary coverts in Snow Buntings, by age and sex.

with broad white tip (fig. 191, Aug-Mar); crown white or whitish, without black streaking (Mar-Jul); longest pp covs as illustrated (fig. 192); rects truncate (fig. 189).

HY/SY ♂ (Aug-2nd Aug): Like AHY/ASY ♂ but scapulars tending more towards ♀ (fig. 190, Aug-Mar); longest pp covs as illustrated (fig. 192); rects tapered (fig. 189).

AHY/ASY ♀ (Sep-Aug): Scapulars with dark brownish-gray, sharply pointed bases and broad, buffy-brown tips (fig 190, Aug-Mar) or grayish with black streaking (Mar-Jul); uppertail covs with white edges (fig. 191, Aug-Mar); crown grayish-white with dusky streaking (Mar-Aug); longest pp covs as illustrated (fig. 192); rects truncate (fig. 189).

HY/SY ♀ (Aug-2nd Aug): Like AHY/ASY ♀ but longest pp covs as illustrated (fig.192); rects tapered (fig. 189).

References—B, R, W, Sv.

MCKAY'S BUNTING
Plectrophenax hyperboreus

MCBU
Species # 535.0
Band size: 1B

Species—In all plumages from Snow Bunting by pattern of rect 3 (fig. 188).

Molt—Parallels that of Snow Bunting.

Skull—Completes in HY/SY from 15 Nov thru Jan.

Age/Sex—CP/BP (May-Aug). Wg useful: ♂(n17) 108-122, ♀(n9) 101-113. Juv (Jul-Aug) has dusky wash and streaking to the upperbreast; Juvs sexed by the pattern of the pp covs (fig. 193) and wg. A few intermediates may not be reliably aged but all birds should be reliably sexed (compare with wg) by the following:

AHY/ASY ♂ (Sep-Aug): Back feathers with small black centers or lacking black entirely (fig. 193); alula white, without black tipping (fig. 193); rects truncate (fig. 189).

HY/SY ♂ (Aug-2nd Aug): Like AHY/ASY ♂ but alula tipped black (fig. 193); rects tapered (fig. 189).

AHY/ASY ♀ (Sep-Aug): Back feathers with large, distinct black centers (fig. 193); pp covs mostly white (fig. 193); rects truncate (fig. 189).

HY/SY ♀ (Aug-2nd Aug): Like AHY/ASY ♀ but pp covs mostly blackish (fig. 193); rects tapered (fig. 189).

References—B.

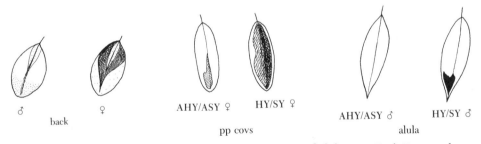

Figure 193. Patterns of the back feathers, primary coverts, and alula in McKay's Bunting, by age and sex.

Blackbirds and Orioles   *Icterinae*

Nineteen species. Subfamily characteristics include generally slender and decurved bills, longish tails, and strong legs. They have 9 primaries, 9 secondaries, and 12 rectrices (occasionally 13 in the meadowlarks). The first prebasic molt is variable, being complete or almost complete in most of the blackbirds and partial to incomplete in most of the orioles. The timing and locality of the prebasic molts in the orioles are also variable. Most species show age and sex related plumage differences and, in some of the blackbirds and the orioles, the shape of the rectricies is a useful ageing criterion. Wing length is also very useful for sexing.

BOBOLINK   BOBO
Dolichonyx oryzivorus   Species # 494.0
                                                Band size: 1A♂-1B♀

Molt—PB: HY partial (Jul-Oct), AHY complete (Jul-Oct); PA complete (Feb-Jun). PBs occur on the summer grounds or may be suspended, completing on the winter grounds. Likewise, PAs may complete on the summer grounds.

Skull—Completes in HY/SY from 1 Nov into Jan.

Age—Juv (Jul-Aug) has indistinct spotting on the throat and upperbreast and lacks streaking on the flanks (♂ = ♀ but see wg and tail). In addition to the following, which is only good in basic plumage, HY/SYs (Aug-Apr) have upperparts and edges to the terts averaging buffier, and underparts averaging richer yellow than AHY/ASYs. Also, some AHY/ASY ♂♂ may have a few black feathers on the throat and upper breast. No plumage criteria known for ageing in alternate plumage although look for duller or slightly more mottled black underparts on HY/SY ♂♂ (Jun-Aug) than on AHY/ASYs:

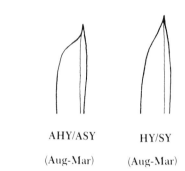

AHY/ASY   HY/SY

(Aug-Mar)   (Aug-Mar)

Figure 194. Rectrix shape by age in the Bobolink.

Basic Plumage

HY/SY (Aug-Apr): Rects tapered (fig. 194).

AHY/ASY (Aug-Apr): Rects relatively truncate (fig. 194).

Sex—CP/BP (May-Aug). Wg useful: ♂(n30) 89-102, ♀(n30) 83-91; tail also useful: ♂(n30) 62-70, ♀(n30) 58-64. The following is reliable in alternate plumage. In basic plumage (Sep-Mar) use wg and tail to sex, and look for a few black feathers on the underparts in occasional AHY/ASY ♂♂:

Alternate Plumage

♂ (Feb-Aug): Crown, underparts and flight feathers entirely or partially black.

♀ (Mar-Aug): Crown and underparts mostly buffy-yellow; flight feathers brown. [Beware of Juv ♂♂ in Jul-Aug.]

References—B,R,W,SK,O; Parkes (1952), Meanley (1967); PRBO data.

RED-WINGED BLACKBIRD
Agelaius phoeniceus

RWBL
Species # 498.0
Band size: 2♂-1A♀

Species—♀♀ and HY/SY ♂♂ from corresponding plumages of Tricolored Blackbird (which see) as follows: Chin and throat (♀♀) often with peach or pinkish wash; central back and/or nape feathers often with chestnut edging; undertail covs usually without pale gray edging; p9 usually ≤ p6 (fig. 195); tail notched (outer—central rect usually > 4 mm); bill relatively short and broad (see table 7, especially ratios of culmen/bill width). See also wg by sex. Some birds may not be reliably identified.

Molt—PB: HY incomplete-complete (Jul-Oct), AHY complete (Jun-Sep); PA: SY limited-partial (Mar-Jun), ASY absent-limited (Mar-May). PBs occur on the summer grounds. The terts and some underwing covs are often (~70% of HYs) retained during the 1st PB.

Skull—Completes in HY/SY from 15 Dec (as early as 15 Oct in certain California populations) thru Feb. Some SYs retain windows and larger areas of non-pneumatisation thru spring and 1st fall. Birds with windows (<5 mm) in Nov-Aug may not be reliably aged by skull; compare with other ageing criteria.

Age/Sex—CP/BP (Mar-Aug). Wg: ♂(n100) 106-126, ♀ (n100) 92-108; wg is very useful for sexing, with little or no overlap between ♂ and ♀ within the geographically varying populations. Generally, ♂ >

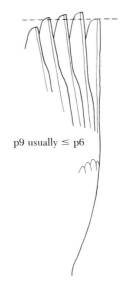

p9 usually ≤ p6

Figure 195. The wing formula of the Red-winged Blackbird.

105 and ♀ < 105 in eastern populations and ♂ > 109 and ♀ < 109 in western populations. Rect shape not useful for ageing after the 1st PB. Juv (May-Sep) is like HY/SY ♀ but is lighter buff colored above and below (♂ = ♀ but check wg). Much variation occurs with plumage of HY/SYs; however, the following, when combined with wg, will lead to reliable determinations of almost all birds:

TABLE 7.
Bill measurements of Red-winged and Tricolored blackbirds. Red-winged #1 represents a random sample. Red-winged #2 is derived from birds with culmen > 17.3 mm (M) or 15.7 mm (F), i.e. a sample of Red-winged Blackbirds with culmen lengths falling within the culmen range of Tricolored Blackbird.

		n	culmen	bill width	width/culmen
Red-winged #1	M	30	13.8–19.0	7.7–10.8	0.491–0.668
	F	30	12.0–16.1	7.5–9.1	0.509–0.722
Red-winged #2	M	30	13.8–17.3	7.7–10.5	0.544–0.668
	F	30	12.0–15.7	7.5–8.9	0.523–0.722
Tricolored	M	30	14.3–17.0	7.2–8.5	0.471–0.555
	F	30	13.5–15.5	6.8–8.0	0.474–0.539

AHY/ASY ♂ (Aug-Jul): Body plumage entirely black (feathers edged brown in fall) without whitish or buffy streaking or mottling; les and mid covs bright red or red and yellow, feathers with little or no blackish; greater underwing covs blackish, with only moderate contrasts between adjacent feathers (fig. 196).

HY/SY ♂ (Aug-Jul): Body plumage varies from almost entirely black (especially in May-Jul) to blackish with heavy white or buff streaking or mottling (especially to upperparts); les and mid covs orangish or orange-red and yellow, many feathers (particularly mid covs) mixed with variable amounts of blackish; some or all gr underwing covs often pale brownish or grayish, contrasting much with adjacent (blacker) feathers (fig. 196).[Some overlap may occur with AHY/ASY ♀; compare with wg.]

AHY/ASY ♀ (Jul-Jun): Body plumage mostly streaked black with buff or whitish; chin often washed with peach or pinkish; les covs variably mixed orange or rusty and (mostly) blackish, forming a small (relative to ♂♂) but distinct patch; underwing covs as AHY/ASY ♂ but paler (fig. 196).

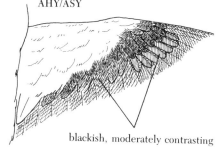

Figure 196. Contrasts in the Underwing coverts, by age, in blackbirds. Some HY/SYs of certain species may show the pattern of AHY/ASY; this needs to be further researched in each of the species.

HY/SY ♀ (Aug-Jun): Body plumage as AHY/ASY ♀ but usually paler buff or whitish overall (blackish streaks thinner); chin usually whitish, without peach or reddish wash; les covs blackish, sometimes with some buffy-orange or orangish, but with little or no rusty; underwing covs as with HY/SY ♂ but paler (fig. 196).

References—DVR,B,R,W,SK,O,C(DeHaven); Packard (1936), Nero (1960), Selander & Giller (1960), Meanley (1967), Payne (1969), Meanley & Bond (1970), DeHaven (1975), Miskimen (1980), Greenwood *et al.* (1983), Linz *et al.* (1983), Linz (1986); PRBO data.

TRICOLORED BLACKBIRD
Agelaius tricolor

TRBL
Species # 500.0
Band size: 2♂-1A♀

Species—♀♀ and HY/SY ♂♂ from corresponding plumages of Red-winged Blackbird (which see) as follows: Chin and throat (♀♀) whitish, rarely with faint pinkish or peach wash; central back and/or nape feathers without chestnut edging; undertail covs usually with distinct pale gray edging; p9 ≥ p6 (fig. 197); tail relatively squared (outer-central rect usually < 4 mm); bill relatively long and narrow (see table 7, especially the ratio of culmen/bill width). See also wg by sex. Some birds may not be reliably identified.

Molt—PB: HY/SY incomplete-complete (usually Jul-Oct but Dec-Feb for offspring of irregular, late fall breeding), AHY complete (Jun-Sep); PA absent?. Terts and some underwing covs are often retained during the 1st PB. The PA may parallel that of Red-winged Blackbird (more study needed).

Skull—Completion in HY/SY is quite variable due to a drawn out nesting season and occasional and irregular late fall breeding. HY/SYs of spring clutches complete as early as 15 Oct in southern populations, and 1 Dec in northern populations, thru Feb. For HY/SYs from late fall breeding, completion occurs from 15 Mar thru Jul. Windows may persist up to a year after hatching. Caution and combination with plumage should be used when ageing by skull, especially in summer and fall.

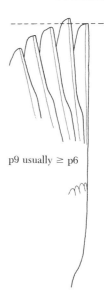

p9 usually ≥ p6

Figure 197. The wing formula of the Tricolored Blackbird.

Age/Sex—CP/BP (Mar-Aug; Sep-Dec for offspring of late fall breeding). Wg: ♂(n30) 115-127, ♀(n30) 101-110. Rect shape not useful for ageing after the 1st PB. Juv (Apr-Aug, Nov-Jan) is like HY/SY ♀ but is generally much lighter gray and buff (♂ = ♀ but check wg). Beware of late fall offspring, which may show irregular plumage timing, when using the following:

AHY/ASY ♂ (Aug-Jul): Body dark glossy black (feathers edged brown in fall) without gray wash or mottling; les and mid covs uniformly red and white or cream, feathers with little or no blackish; greater underwing covs blackish, with only moderate contrasts between adjacent feathers (fig. 196).

HY/SY ♂ (Aug-Jul): Body plumage varies from almost entirely black to blackish-gray or black with grayish mottling, the black not glossy or less glossy than AHY/ASYs; les and mid covs brownish-red or pale orangish and buffy, many feathers (particularly mid covs) mixed with variable amounts of blackish; some or all gr underwing covs often pale brownish or grayish, contrasting much with adjacent (blacker) feathers (fig. 196).

AHY/ASY ♀ (Jul-Jun): Body plumage mostly black with distinct grayish streaks; throat whitish; les covs with reddish-brown forming a small but distinct patch; underwing covs as in AHY/ASY ♂ but paler (fig. 196).

HY/SY ♀ (Aug-Jun): Body plumage as AHY/ASY ♀ but les covs blackish with little or no reddish-brown; underwing covs as with HY/SY ♂ but paler (fig. 196).

References—B,C(DeHaven); Orians (1963), Payne (1969), DeHaven *et al.* (1974), DeHaven (1975).

EASTERN MEADOWLARK
Sturnella magna

EAME
Species # 501.0
Band size: 3-2

Species—From Western Meadowlark (which see) with caution; (this is, perhaps, the most difficult in-hand species identification problem). Crown stripes and upperparts usually average darker than Western Meadowlark; malar region usually whitish, such that yellow of lores and throat are not continuous; rects as in fig. 198 (which show extremes): note especially the amount of white on rect 3 and the width of the shaft streaks on rects 4-6. See also wg by population and sex. [Intermediates may be impossible to reliably identify in the hand, although normally overlapping populations are usually seperable. The palest (southwestern) populations of Eastern Meadowlark, which are closest to Western Meadowlark in upperpart and malar coloration, also show more white on rect 3.]

Molt—PB: HY complete (Aug-Oct), AHY complete (Aug-Oct); PA absent. PBs occur on the summer grounds.

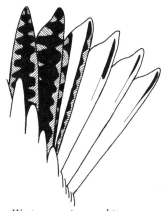

Western maximum white

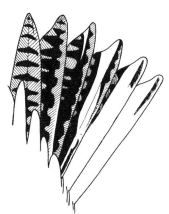

Western minimum white

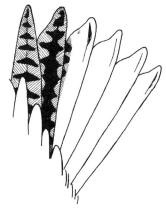

Eastern maximum white

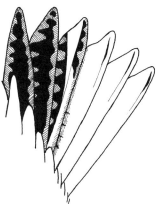

Eastern minimum white

Figure 198. Tail patterns in Eastern vs. Western meadowlarks, to assist in identification.

Skull—Completes in HY/SY from 1 Nov thru Feb. Windows may occur in some SYs thru summer but are difficult to see through skin.

Age—Rect shape not useful after the 1st PB. Juv (May-Sep) has a whitish throat and streaking on the upperbreast (in place of the black "V"). Otherwise, no reliable plumage criteria are known although HY/SYs average paler and buffier than AHY/ASYs.

Sex—♂ = ♀ by plumage. CP/BP (Mar-Sep). Wg best means for sexing but shows geographic variation: NE ♂(n100) 114-131, ♀(n100) 102-117; SE and midwestern ♂(n100) 105-120, ♀(n100) 94-108; SW ♂(n20) 110-123, ♀(n12) 102-112. [Wgs apply to breeding populations only; use caution and consideration of all populations with wintering birds (especially in the Southeast). Also, ranges for intermediate populations may have to be individually determined.]

References—B,R,W,SK,O; Hubbard (1983).

WESTERN MEADOWLARK
Sturnella neglecta

WEME
Species # 501.1
Band size: 3-2

Species—See Eastern Meadowlark. Crown stripes and upperparts usually average paler than Eastern Meadowlark; malar region usually with yellow continuous from lores to throat; rects as in fig. 198: note especially the amount of white on rect 3 and the width of the shaft streaks on rects 4-6. See also wg by population and sex.

Molt—PB: HY complete (Aug-Oct), AHY complete (Aug-Oct); PA absent. PBs occur on the summer grounds.

Skull—Completes in HY/SY from 15 Nov (as early as 1 Nov in California populations) thru Feb. Windows may occur in some SYs thru summer but are difficult to see through skin.

Age—No reliable plumage criteria known after 1st PB; see Eastern Meadowlark.

Sex—♂ = ♀ by plumage. CP/BP (Feb-Sep). Wg best means for sexing: ♂(n100) 117-132, ♀(n100) 104-119.

References—B,R,O; Hubbard (1983); PRBO data.

YELLOW-HEADED BLACKBIRD
Xanthocephalus xanthocephalus

YHBL
Species # 497.0
Band size: 2♂-1A♀

Molt—PB: HY partial (Jul-Aug), AHY complete (Jul-Aug); PA limited-partial (Jan-Apr). PBs occur on the summer grounds. PA probably occurs more extensively in SY ♂ than in other age/sex classes.

Skull—Completes in HY/SY from 15 Nov thru Jan. Some SYs probably retain windows thru spring.

Age/Sex—CP/BP (Apr-Aug). Wg reliable for sexing: ♂(n100) 126-145, ♀(n100) 105-125; wg varies substantially by age as well (see below for ♀♀). Juv (Jun-Aug) has buffy yellow head (extent as in AHY/ASY ♂), dark auriculars and a whitish buffy throat (♂ − ♀ but see wg). In addition to the following, check for underwing covert contrast differences, as in other blackbird species (fig. 196):

AHY/ASY ♂ (Aug-Jul): Body plumage black; head, throat, and upperbreast yellow (feathers tipped blackish in fall); lores black; pp covs and outer gr covs mostly white with black tipping; flight feathers black; rects truncate (fig. 199).

HY/SY ♂ (Aug-2nd Aug): Body plumage blackish-brown (Aug-Mar) or dull black (Mar-Aug); crown and auriculars mostly brown, sometimes with brown mottling (Aug-Mar); superciliary, throat and upper breast dingy yellow mixed with brownish (Aug-Mar); lores brown; pp covs black with white tipping; flight feathers brownish or grayish-black; rects tapered (fig. 199). [Mar-Aug birds may be difficult to age.]

AHY/ASY ♀ (Aug-Jul): Similar to HY/SY ♂ (Aug-Mar) but yellows of head, throat, and upperbreast average duller (but not buffy); lores mixed grayish and olive-brown; pp covs without white tipping; flight feathers blackish; rects truncate (fig. 199); wg 118-125; tail 84-93.

HY/SY ♀ (Aug-2nd Aug): Similar to AHY/ASY ♀ but yellows of head, throat, and upperbreast distinctly buffy and more obscured by brown; flight feathers brownish; rects tapered (fig. 199); wg 105-117; tail 72-85.

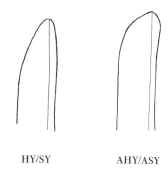

HY/SY   AHY/ASY

Figure 199. Rectrix shape by age in the grackles and Yellow-headed Blackbird.

References—B,R,O; Crawford & Hohman (1978); PRBO data.

RUSTY BLACKBIRD
Euphagus carolinus

RUBL
Species # 509.0
Band size: 2

Species—HY/SY in fall from Brewer's Blackbird by the presence of rusty edging to the terts, and a shorter tail: 83-92.

Molt—PB: HY incomplete-complete (Jul-Sep), AHY complete (Jul-Sep); PA absent. PBs occur on the summer grounds. Most if not all HYs retain some underwing covs during the 1st PB. Look also for retention of terts in some HYs as with other blackbirds; otherwise, all flight feathers are replaced..

Skull—Completes in HY/SY from 15 Nov thru Jan. Look for windows on some SYs thru spring.

Age/Sex—CP/BP (Apr-Aug). Wg reliable for sexing most birds: ♂(n100) 111-123, ♀(n100) 101-113. Rect shape not useful for ageing after the 1st PB. Juv (Jun-Aug) has distinct, buffy wing bars (♂ = ♀ but see wg). Some intermediates between the following (particularly those resembling AHY/ASY) may not be reliably aged:

AHY/ASY ♂ (Aug-Jul): Body plumage glossy black (edged moderately with rusty in fall-winter); rump black; flight feathers uniformly black; greater underwing covs blackish, showing only moderate contrasts between adjacent feathers (fig. 196).

HY/SY ♂ (Aug-Jul): Body plumage dull to glossy black (edged substantially with rusty in fall-winter, some often remaining thru spring); rump black; flight feathers black (terts may occasionally be contrastingly paler); some or all gr underwing covs often pale brownish or grayish, contrasting much with adjacent (blacker) feathers (fig. 196).

AHY/ASY ♀ (Aug-Jul): Body plumage gray or grayish-brown (edged with some rusty in fall-winter); rump gray; flight feathers uniformly dark brownish; underwing covs as in AHY ♂ but paler (fig. 196).

HY/SY ♀ (Aug-Jul): Like AHY/ASY ♀ but body plumage with relatively more rusty edging (fall and spring); terts occasionally contrastingly faded; underwing covs as in HY/SY ♂ but paler (fig. 196). [Experience is probably required to reliably age ♀♀.]

References—B,R,W,SK,O; Meanley (1967).

BREWER'S BLACKBIRD
Euphagus cyanocephalus

BRBL
Species # 510.0
Band size: 2

Species—Some HY/SYs resemble Rusty Blackbird but can be distiguished by the lack of rusty or tawny on the terts and longer tail (92-104).

Molt—PB: HY incomplete-complete (Jul-Sep), AHY complete (Jul-Aug); PA absent. PBs occur on the summer grounds. Most if not all HYs retain underwing covs, and some may retain the terts during the 1st PB. Otherwise, all flight feathers are replaced.

Skull—Completes in HY/SY from 15 Nov (as early as 15 Oct in California populations) thru Feb. Look for windows thru spring.

Age/Sex—CP/BP (Mar-Aug). Wg reliable for sexing most birds: ♂(n100) 125-137, ♀(n100) 113-125. Rect shape not useful after the 1st PB. Juv (Jun-Aug) resembles ♀♀ but flight feathers brownish, without gloss (♂ = ♀ but see wg). Some birds (especially those resembling AHY/ASY in spring) may not be reliably aged by the following:

AHY/ASY ♂ (Aug-Jul): Plumage dark glossy black (feathers occasionally tipped brownish in fall); flight feathers uniformly glossy black; greater underwing covs blackish, showing only moderate contrasts between adjacent feathers (fig. 196); iris yellowish.

HY/SY ♂ (Aug-Jul): Plumage dull to dark glossy black (feathers tipped brownish in fall); flight feathers black (terts sometimes contrastingly browner); some or all gr underwing covs pale brownish or grayish, contrasting much with adjacent (blacker) feathers (fig. 196); iris yellowish.

AHY/ASY ♀ (Aug-Jul): Plumage dark grayish-brown; flight feathers uniformly dark brown; underwing covs as in AHY/ASY ♂ (fig. 196) but paler; iris brown.

HY/SY ♀ (Aug-Jul): Plumage dull to dark grayish-brown; flight feathers brown (terts sometimes contrastingly paler brown); underwing covs as in HY/SY ♂ but paler (fig. 196); iris brown. [Experience may be required to reliably age ♀♀ by plumage.]

References—B,R,W,SK,O; Selander & Giller (1960); Meanley (1967); PRBO data.

GREAT-TAILED GRACKLE
Quiscalus mexicanus

GTGR
Species # 512.0
Band size: 4♂-3♀

Species—Iris pale to bright yellow (dark brown in Juvs thru mid-summer); Juvs with indistinct but obvious streaking on the underparts; ♀♀ with distinct superciliary, contrasting with darker crown; wg ≤ tail. A combination of the above with wg and tail by sex and age (see below) should reliably separate this species from Boat-tailed and Common grackles.

Molt—PB: HY incomplete-complete (Jun-Oct), AHY complete (Jul-Oct); PA absent-limited (Mar-Apr). 1st PB is usually incomplete, some underwing covs and terts usually retained, occasionally other flight feathers. PA may be confined to SY ♂♂ only.

Skull—Completes in SY from 1 Feb thru Aug. May be difficult to see through skin.

Age/Sex—CP/BP (Mar-Aug). Wg reliable: ♂(n100) 165-200; ♀(n100) 135-164. Juv (May-Aug) is like ♀♀ but has indistinct streaking to the underparts and a dark iris (generally, ♂ = ♀ in Juvs, but ♂♂ average darker, and this combined with wg and tail should make sexing reliable). Sexing is reliable after the 1st PB, and almost all ♂♂ and most ♀♀ are reliably aged during and after the 1st PB, as follows:

AHY/ASY ♂ (Aug-Jul): Plumage glossy purplish or black; flight feathers uniformly black; greater underwing covs blackish, showing only moderate contrasts between adjacent feathers (fig. 196); wg 173-200; tail relatively broad, 178-232; rects truncate (fig. 199); iris yellow.

HY/SY ♂ (Aug-2nd Aug): Plumage black, usually with little gloss; some underwing covs (fig. 196), terts, and (occasionally) other flight feathers brownish and faded, contrasting with blacker, fresher adjacent feathers; wg 165-188; tail relatively narrow, 165-200; rects tapered (fig. 199) or truncate; iris brownish to brownish-yellow (thru Oct-Mar). [Some HY/SY ♂♂ may approach AHY/ASY in measurements and plumage (especially in Apr-Jul).]

AHY/ASY ♀ (Aug-Jul): Upperparts dark brown; throat and upperbreast tan; flight feathers uniformly dark brown; underwing covs as with AHY/ASY ♂ but paler (fig. 196); tail 135-170; rects truncate (fig. 199); iris yellow.

HY/SY ♀ (Aug-2nd Aug): Upperparts brown washed buffy or cinnamon; throat and upperbreast buffy or brownish; some underwing covs (fig. 196), terts and (occasionally) other flight feathers pale brown, contrasting with darker adjacent feathers; tail 122-145; rects tapered (fig. 199) or truncate; iris brownish to brownish-yellow (thru Oct-Mar).

References—DVR,B,O; Selander (1958).

BOAT-TAILED GRACKLE
Quiscalus major

BTGR
Species # 513.0
Band size: 4♂-3♀

Species—Iris yellow (Atlantic coast populations) to brown or brownish-yellow (Gulf coast populations.); Juvs with little or no indistinct streaking on the underparts; ♀♀ with superciliary indistinct, contrasting gradually with darker crown; wg usually > tail. A combination of the above with wg and tail by sex and age (see below) should reliably separate this from the other grackles.

Molt—PB: HY incomplete-complete (Jul-Oct), AHY complete (Jul-Oct); PA absent-limited (Mar-Apr). See Great-tailed Grackle.

Skull—Completes in SY from 1 Jan thru June. May be difficult to see through skin.

Age/Sex—CP/BP (Feb-Aug). Wg: ♂ 155-197, ♀ 129-148; Gulf > Atlantic. The criteria of Great-tailed Grackle is reliable for sexing and ageing most birds, except that Juv resembles ♀ but is paler and has a more distinct superciliary. Eye color useful, as with Great-tailed Grackle, for ageing Atlantic coast forms. Useful measurements are as follows:

AHY/ASY ♂ (Aug-Jul): Wg 167-197; tail 161-193.

HY/SY ♂ (Aug-2nd Aug): Wg 155-178; tail 152-165.

AHY/ASY ♀ (Aug-Jul): tail 121-139.

HY/SY ♀ (Aug-2nd Aug): tail 111-126.

References—B,W,O; Selander (1958), Meanley (1967).

COMMON GRACKLE
Quiscalus quiscula

COGR
Species # 511.0
Band size: 3

Species—From Boat-tailed and Great-tailed grackles by measurements (see below).

Molt—PB: HY incomplete-complete (Jul-Oct), AHY complete (Jul-Oct); PA absent. PBs occur primarily on the summer grounds. Some underwing covs and terts are usually retained during the 1st PB. Watch for a limited PA in SY ♂ ♂, as in the other grackles.

Skull—Completes in HY/SY from 15 Dec thru Apr. May be difficult to see through skin.

Age/Sex—CP/BP (Mar-Aug). Wg: ♂ 129-149, ♀ 118-134; tail: ♂ 120-140, ♀ 102-125 (N > Gulf coast and Florida for both wg and tail; local populations show no overlap between the sexes). Rect shape not useful after the 1st PB. Juv (Jun-Sep) has dull brown body plumage and flight feathers (♂ = ♀ but check wg and tail). The following is relative, and much overlap occurs, especially with HY/SYs that have a complete 1st PB. By combining with wg, many birds should be reliably determined:

AHY/ASY ♂ (Aug-Jul): Plumage dark glossy; flight feathers uniformly glossy black; greater underwing covs blackish, with only moderate contrasts between adjacent feathers (fig. 196).

HY/SY ♂ (Aug-2nd Aug): Plumage dull glossy (head may become brighter in spring); one or more terts often dull brownish-black, contrasting in color with black ss; some or all gr underwing covs often pale brownish or grayish, contrasting much with adjacent (blacker) feathers (fig. 196). [Some birds may show underwing covs like AHY/ASY.]

AHY/ASY ♀ (Aug-Jul): Like HY/SY ♂ but flight feathers uniformly blackish; underwing covs as in AHY/ASY ♂ (fig. 196). [Compare with wg for separation from HY/SY ♂.]

HY/SY ♀ (Aug-2nd Aug): Plumage blackish with little gloss; terts and underwing covs as in HY/SY ♂ ♂ (fig. 196).

References—B,R,W,SK,O; Selander & Giller (1960); Meanley (1967).

BRONZED COWBIRD
Molothrus aenus

BRCO
Species # 496.0
Band   size:
2♂-1A♀

Species—From Brown-headed Cowbird by larger size: wg 97-123 (compare with sex; see below); tail 64-84; culmen > 12.5 mm (fig. 200).

Molt—PB: HY incomplete-complete (Jul-Oct), AHY complete (Jul-Oct); PA absent-limited (Feb-Mar). PBs occur primarily on the summer grounds. Some underwing covs are sometimes retained in most HYs during the 1st PB, as in other Icterids. Otherwise, all flight feathers are molted. A limited PA usually occurs in SY ♂ ♂ only.

Skull—Completes in HY/SY from 15 Nov thru Feb. Check for windows in some spring SYs.

Age/Sex—CP (Mar-Jul); BP does not occur in this species. Wg reliable for sexing: ♂(n100) 112-123, ♀(n100) 97-110. Rect shape is not useful after the 1st PB. Juv (May-Aug) is uniformly brownish to brownish-gray (♂ = ♀ but see wg):

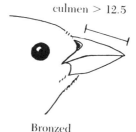

culmen > 12.5

Bronzed

culmen < 12.5

Brown-headed

Figure 200. Relative head and bill dimensions of Brown-headed vs. Bronzed cowbirds.

AHY/ASY ♂ (Aug-Jul): Body plumage and
   flight feathers uniformly glossy; greater underwing covs blackish, showing only moderate contrasts between adjacent feathers (fig. 196).

HY/SY ♂ (Aug-Jul): Body plumage mixed dull glossy and black (head uniformly glossy in spring, Texas populations); or mixed black and gray (SW populations; more black in Mar-Aug); flight feathers and upperwing covs black with slight gloss; some or all gr underwing covs often pale brownish or grayish, contrasting much with adjacent (blacker) feathers (fig. 196). [Some may have underwing covs as with AHY/ASY.]

AHY/ASY ♀ (Aug-Jul): Plumage uniformly black with little gloss (Texas populations) or uniformly slate gray (SW populations); underwing covs as with AHY/ASY ♂ (fig. 196). [Combine with wg for accurate sexing, hence ageing of Texas populations. ♀ ♀ of SW populations, and intermediates between this and HY/SY ♀ (which have molted all underwing covs) are not reliably aged.]

HY/SY ♀ (Aug-Jul), Texas populations only: Body plumage uniformly dull black, with little or no gloss; terts sometimes pale brownish or brownish-gray, contrasting with darker ss; underwing covs as with HY/SY ♂ (fig. 196).

References—DVR,B,O.

BROWN-HEADED COWBIRD
Molothrus ater

BHCO
Species # 495.0
Band size: 1A♂-
1B♀

Species—From Bronzed Cowbird by smaller size: Wg 87-117 (compare with sex; see below); tail 59-80; culmen < 12.5 mm (fig. 200).

Molt—PB: HY incomplete-complete (Jul-Oct); AHY complete (Jul-Oct); PA absent. PBs occur primarily on the summer grounds. 1st PB is rarely complete, with a varying number of underwing covs, and one or more terts usually retained; often scattered body feathers are retained as well.

Skull—Completes in HY/SY from 1 Dec thru Mar. Check for windows in some SYs thru summer.

Age—Rect shape not useful for ageing after the 1st PB. Juv (May-Aug) is similar to ♀♀ but body feathers and wing covs edged buff, creating two buffy wing bars (see wg for sexing; also, ♂♂ have darker underwing covs than ♀♀, which is useful with experience; otherwise, Juv ♂ = ♀ by plumage). The following is reliable with ♂♂. Contrasts in the underwing and terts may be used to age some HY/SY ♀♀ thru Feb, with experience:

AHY/ASY ♂ (Aug-Jul): Body plumage (except head) and flight feathers entirely glossy black; greater underwing covs blackish, showing only moderate contrasts between adjacent feathers (fig. 196).

HY/SY ♂ (Aug-2nd Aug): Body plumage (except head) dull to glossy black sometimes with a few pale gray feathers; one or more terts often brownish and abraded, contrasting with blacker ss; some or all gr underwing covs often pale brownish to grayish, contrasting much with adjacent (blacker) feathers (fig. 196). [A few HYs have complete 1st PBs and are not distinguishable from AHY/ASYs; compare with skull.]

Sex—CP (Mar-Aug), BP does not develop in this species. Wg reliable for sexing almost all birds: ♂(n100), 101-115 ♀(n100) 90-101 (excludes certain small S. Arizona and Texas populations where ♂(n20) 95-104, ♀(n20) 85-95). The following is reliable during or after the 1st PB:

♂: Body plumage entirely or partially black.

♀: Body plumage entirely gray. [Careful with Juvs; see Age.]

References—B,R,W,O,BBM; Baird (1958), Selander & Giller (1960), Meanley (1967), Hill (1976); PRBO data.

ORCHARD ORIOLE
Icterus spurius

OROR
Species # 506.0
Band size: 1B

Species—♀♀ and HY/SY ♂♂ from Hooded and Scott's orioles by: back unstreaked; bill broader based and shorter (fig. 201); tail relatively square (outer—central rect usually 8-15 mm); and by smaller measurements: wg 69-84 (compare with sex, see below); tail 63-75; exposed culmen 14.0-17.3.

Molt—PB: HY partial (Sep-Nov), AHY complete (Aug-Oct); PA absent-limited (Mar-Apr). PBs occur primarily on the winter grounds. PA molts may occur more extensively in SY ♂♂ than in other age/sex classes.

Skull—Completes in HY/SY from 1 Nov thru Feb.

Age/Sex—CP/BP (Apr-Sep). Wg useful: ♂(n30) 74-84, ♀(n30) 69-78. Juv (Jun-Oct) is like ♀♀ but has buffy wing bars and fresher feathers at that time of year (♂ = ♀ but see HY/SY ♀, below). Most birds should be reliably aged and sexed when the following is combined with wg:

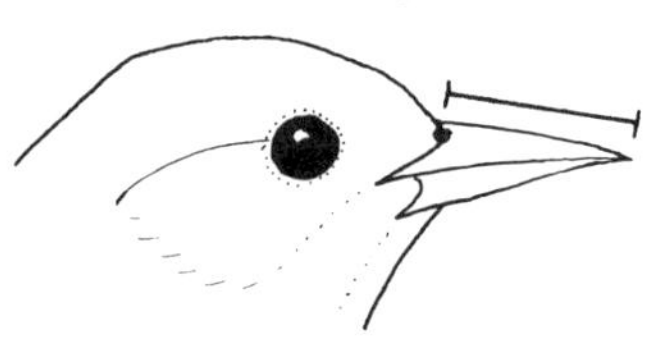

exp. culm. 14.0-17.3

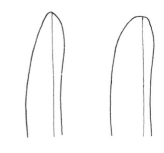

Figure 201. Head and bill dimensions in the Orchard Oriole.

HY/SY   AHY/ASY

Figure 202. Rectrix shape by age in orioles. Look for differences in amount of wear, as well.

AHY/ASY ♂ (Oct-Sep): Body plumage mixed black and chestnut; flight feathers black; rects truncate (fig. 202).

HY/SY ♂ (Sep-2nd Oct): Head, rump and belly mostly greenish-yellow; back mottled black; chin and throat yellow with a few black feathers (Oct-Mar; occasionally none) or mostly black (Mar-Sep); a few body feathers often chestnut; pp covs, pp and ss mostly pale brownish (look for occasional black replacements), contrasting with darker gr covs; rects brownish-green, tapered (fig. 202), quite abraded in spring. [SY separated from HY in Aug-Sep by extremely worn vs. fresh flight feathers. See HY/SY ♀.]

AHY/ASY ♀ (Aug-Jul): Body plumage entirely greenish-yellow; wing covs, pp and ss uniformly darkish brown; throat without black; rects greenish, truncate (fig. 202), relatively unworn.

HY/SY ♀ (Aug-Jul) Like AHY/ASY ♀ but pp covs, pp and ss pale brown, contrasting with darker brown gr covs; rects brownish-green, tapered (fig. 202); usually quite abraded in spring. [Probably not reliably separated from Juv-HY ♂ in Aug-Oct except by wg; most HY/SYs reliably sexed by wg: ♂ ≥ 73, ♀ ≤ 73. Also, some black feathering may occur on throats of occasional Juv-HY ♂♂.]

References—DVR,B,W,SK,O; PRBO data.

HOODED ORIOLE
Icterus cucullatus

HOOR
Species # 505.0
Band size: 1A-1B

Species—♀♀ and HY/SY ♂♂ from Orchard and Scott's orioles by: back unstreaked; bill longer and with relatively narrower base (fig. 203); tail relatively rounded (outer—central rect usually 15-22 mm); and by measurements: wg 77-93 (compare with sex, see below); tail 80-100; exposed culmen 18.5-22.5.

Molt—PB: HY partial (Jul-Sep), AHY complete (Aug-Oct); PA absent-limited (Feb-Apr). The 1st PB occurs primarily on the summer grounds, adult PBs occur mostly on the winter grounds (apparently the case in California populations (at least with SYs); this should be further researched elsewhere). The PA may occur more extensively in SY ♂♂ than in other age/sex classes.

exp. culm. 18.5-22.5

Figure 203. Head and bill dimensions in the Hooded Oriole.

Skull—Completes in HY/SY from 1 Nov thru Mar.

Age/Sex—CP/BP (Mar-Sep). Wg: ♂(n40) 80-93, ♀(n30) 77-85 (W > Texas); tail: ♂(n40) 82-100, ♀(n30) 80-90 (Texas > W). Juv (May-Aug) is like ♀ in plumage coloration but has buffier wing bars and fresher feathers at this time of year (♂ = ♀):

AHY/ASY ♂ (Sep-Aug): Body plumage (except throat and back) mostly orange; flight feathers black; rects truncate (fig. 202).

HY/SY ♂ (Jul-2nd Oct): Body plumage mostly green or greenish-yellow; lores, throat, and upper breast black; pp covs, pp and ss pale brownish, contrasting with darker brown gr covs; rects brownish-yellow, tapered (fig. 202), usually quite abraded in spring/summer. [In Jul-Oct, SYs are easily separated from HYs by extensive wearing, especially on the pp and rects.]

AHY/ASY ♀ (Sep-Aug): Plumage mostly greenish-yellow; throat without black; wing covs, pp and ss uniformly darkish brown; rects yellowish, truncate (fig. 202), relatively unworn.

HY/SY ♂ (Aug-2nd Aug): Like AHY/ASY ♀ but pp covs, pp and ss pale brownish, contrasting with darker gr covs; rects brownish-yellow; tapered (fig. 202), usually quite abraded in spring/summer.

References—B,O; PRBO data.

ALTAMIRA ORIOLE
Icterus gularis

ALOR
Species # 503.1
Band size: 3

Species—From other orioles by thick bill (fig. 204) and larger size: wg 103-119, tail 95-111.

Molt—PB: HY partial (Aug-Oct), AHY complete (Aug-Sep); PA absent-limited (Feb-Apr). PAs may occur more in SY ♂♂ than other age/sex classes.

exp. culm. 23.6-26.7

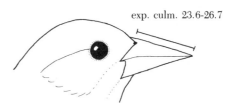

Skull—Completes in HY/SY from 1 Dec thru Mar.

Age—Juv (Jun-Sep) resembles HY/SY but lacks black on the throat:

Figure 204. Head and bill dimensions in the Altimira Oriole.

HY/SY (Sep-2nd Oct): Body plumage generally greenish-yellow or orangish yellow; back dusky yellow; throat mixed yellow and black; flight feathers pale grayish-brown; rects brownish edged yellow, tapered (fig. 202).

AHY/ASY (Sep-Aug): Head, rump and belly orange; back, throat, and flight feathers black; rects truncate (fig. 202).

Sex—CP/BP (Apr-Sep). Wg: ♂(n23) 108-119, ♀(n21) 103-111. No reliable plumage criteria yet known for sexing although ♂♂ average more black on the throat than ♀♀ (especially with HY/SYs); extremes are probably reliably sexed, with experience and consideration of age.

References—DVR,B,O.

AUDUBON'S ORIOLE
Icterus graduacauda

AUOR
Species # 503.0
Band size: 2

Species—From Scott's Oriole by greenish-yellow upper back (without streaks), entirely black (AHY/ASY) and longer and more tapered tail: (100-108, outer—central rect > 20 mm); and thicker and shorter culmen (fig. 205).

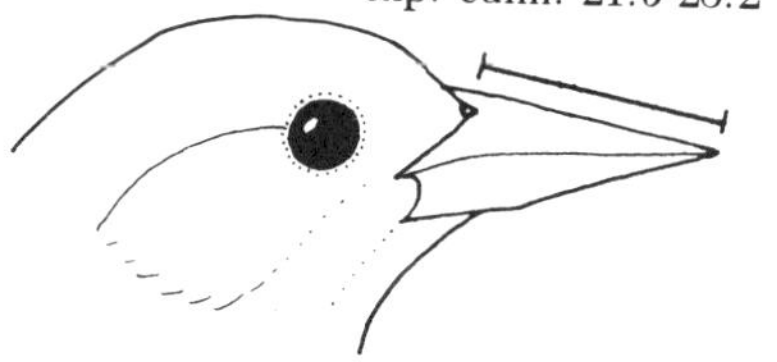

Molt—PB: HY partial (Jul-Sep), AHY complete (Jul-Sep); PA absent.

Skull—Completes in HY/SY from 1 Dec thru Feb.

Age—Juv (May-Aug) lacks black on the head:

exp. culm. 21.9-28.2

Figure 205. Head and bill dimensions in the Audubon's Oriole.

HY/SY (Aug-2nd Sep): Flight feathers brownish, rects edged with greenish when fresh; rects tapered (fig. 202). [SY is separated from HY in Aug-Sep by very worn flight feathers.]

AHY/ASY (Sep-Aug): Flight feathers black (faded blackish in summer); rects truncate (fig. 202).

Sex—CP/BP (Mar-Aug). Wg useful: ♂(n19) 94-103, ♀(n16) 89-98. Otherwise, no reliable criteria are known for sexing although ♂♂ average brighter than ♀♀, within both age groups.

References—B,O.

NORTHERN ORIOLE
Icterus galbula

NOOR
Band size: 1A

Baltimore Oriole (BAOR)
Bullocks Oriole (BUOR)

Species # 507.0
Species # 508.0

Species—♀♀ and HY/SY ♂♂ usually with at least some orange on the throat; bill broad-based, relatively short and straight (fig. 206); wg 85-105; tail 66-85; exposed culmen 16.0-20.1. The combination of plumage with measurements should readily separate this from other oriole species.

Subspecies—♀♀ and HY/SY ♂♂ (Aug-Mar) separated as follows; see also the age/sex accounts (below) for other plumage and wg differences, and beware of intergrades:

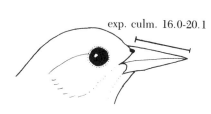

Bullock's   Baltimore

Figure 206. Head and bill dimensions in the Northern Oriole.

Figure 207. Scapular patterns in Baltimore vs. Bullock's orioles.

Baltimore—Upperparts relatively dark brownish-orange; scapulars with large blackish centers (fig. 207); throat and underparts (including flanks and belly) yellowish-orange.

Bullocks—Upperparts relatively pale, grayish-brown; scapulars with small dusky centers (fig. 207) throat pale orange-yellow; flanks and belly white.

Molt—PB: HY partial (Jun-Sep), AHY complete (Jun-Sep); PA absent-partial (Feb-Apr). PBs occur primarily on the summer grounds and (in some SYs) during the early stages of fall migration. The PA occurs more extensively in SYs than ASYs (it may not occur at all in ASYs).

Skull—Completes in HY from 15 Nov (as early as 15 Oct in California populations of Bullock's) thru Feb. Look for windows in spring SYs.

Age/Sex—CP/BP (Apr-Aug). Wg useful: Baltimore ♂(n40) 91-103, ♀(n28) 85-94; Bullock's ♂(n40) 94-105, ♀(n35) 86-101 (Inland > California populations). Juv (both subspecies) are relatively pale grayish, with buffy wing bars (♂ = ♀). Except for sexing first basic-plumaged Baltimores, most birds of both subspecies should be reliably aged and sexed when wg is combined with the following:

AHY/ASY ♂ (Aug-Jul): Plumage bright black and orange (black tipped with orange in fall); flight feathers black or (rects) black and bright orange; rects truncate (fig. 202).

HY/SY ♂ (Aug-2nd Sep): Crown, upper back, and throat usually mixed grayish-green or orangish and black, varying from mostly greenish with a few black feathers (Aug-Mar; some Baltimores may lack black) to mostly blackish with varying amounts of orange (Mar-Aug, more so in Baltimore); les covs usually with some orange (Mar-Aug); pp covs, pp and ss brownish or pale brownish-gray, contrasting with darker brown gr covs; rects brownish-yellow, tapered (fig. 202), usually quite abraded in spring/summer. [Baltimores may lack black in Aug-Mar and are then not reliably separated from HY/SY ♀♀ except by wg.]

AHY/ASY ♀ (Aug-Jul): Crown and upperback mostly brownish-orange with some black mixed in (Baltimore) or pale grayish-brown, usually with some dark brownish mixed in (Bullock's); throat usually with some black; les covs brown or grayish-brown with white tipping; wing covs and pp and ss uniformly darkish brown; rects yellowish, truncate (fig. 202), relatively unworn.

HY/SY ♀ (Aug-Jul): Crown and back dark brown (Baltimore) or pale grayish-brown (Bullock's), without black; underparts pale orange or yellowish and whitish, without black;

pp covs, pp, and ss pale brown contrasting with darker brown gr covs; rects brown-ish-yallow, tapered (fig. 202), usually quite abraded in spring/summer. [Baltimores in Aug-Mar are probably not reliably sexed by plumage; see HY/SY ♂.]

References—DVR,B,R,W,SK,O; Hubbard (1974), Fisk (1975), Sealy (1979); PRBO data.

SCOTT'S ORIOLE
Icterus parisorum

SCOR
Species # 504.0
Band size: 1A

Species—♀♀ and HY/SY ♂♂ from Orchard and Hooded orioles by: back mostly streaked; bill straight and narrow (fig. 208); tail relatively square to somewhat rounded (outer—central rect 6-17 mm); and by measurements: wg 93-107 (compare with sex, see below); tail 79-92; exposed culmen 20.0-25.0. From Audubon's Oriole by the above and by outer rects black with yellow bases in AHY/ASY ♂.

Molt—PB: HY partial (Jul-Aug), AHY complete (Jul-Aug); PA partial (Feb-Apr). PBs occur on the summer grounds. The PA probably is more extensive in SY ♂♂ than other age/sex classes.

Skull—Completes in HY/SY from 15 Nov thru Feb.

exp. culm. 20.0-25.0

Figure 208. Head and bill dimensions in the Scott's Oriole.

Age/Sex—CP/BP (Apr-Aug). Wg: ♂(n20) 95-107, ♀(n20) 93-103. Juv is like HY/SY ♀ but is washed brownish and has broader, yellowish wing bars (♂ = ♀). The body plumage varies substantially within the following but most should be reliably aged and sexed when combined with skull and wg:

AHY/ASY ♂ (Aug-Jul): Head, upper back, and throat black (edged thinly with yellowish in fall); les covs yellow; flight feathers black or black and yellow; rects truncate (fig. 202).

HY/SY ♂ (Aug-2nd Aug): Head and throat mostly blackish with yellow mottling; upper back blackish with yellow streaking; les covs variable, black with whitish or yellowish edging to mostly yellow; pp covs, pp, and ss pale brownish, contrasting with darker brown gr covs; rects brownish-green, tapered (fig. 202), usually quite abraded in spring/summer. [Percent of black in head and throat increases in Mar-Apr.]

AHY/ASY ♀ (Aug-Jul): Head and throat mostly olive green with some black mottling; upper back olive streaked with black; les covs grayish with white edging; wing covs, pp and ss uniformly darkish brown; rects dusky-greenish, truncate (fig. 202), relatively unworn. [Plumage overlap occurs with HY/SY ♂ in Aug-Mar; separate with wg and rects.]

HY/SY ♀ (Aug-Jul): Head and throat greenish-olive, with little or no black (may acquire some after the 1st PA); upper back olive streaked with black; pp covs, pp, and ss pale brownish, contrasting with darker brown gr covs; rects brownish-green, tapered (fig. 202), usually quite abraded in spring/summer.

References—B,O.

FINCHES   *FRINGILLIDAE*

Fourteen species. Family characteristics include relatively large, conical bills, short tails, and short legs. They have 10 primaries (10th spurious), 9 secondaries, and 12 rectrices. The first prebasic molt is most often partial and the shape of the rectrices is generally a good ageing criterion. Most age/sex classes can be distinguished by plumage.

ROSY FINCH   ROFI
Leucosticte arctoa   Band size: 1B

    Gray-crowned Rosy-Finch (GCFI)   Species # 524.0
    Black Rosy-Finch (BLFI)   Species # 525.0
    Brown-capped Rosy-Finch (BCFI)   Species # 526.0

Molt—PB: HY partial (Jul-Sep), AHY complete (Jul-Sep). PA absent. PBs occur on the summer grounds.

Skull—Completes in HY/SY from 1 Nov thru Feb.

Age—Juv (Jun-Aug) is uniformly brown or grayish-brown with buffy wing bars ($\male = \female$). The following plumage criteria may be difficult to use with $\female\female$ of Black and Gray-crowned rosy-finches (use rect shape with these) but should be reliable with all $\male\male$, and $\female$ Brown-capped:

    HY/SY (Aug-Jul): Pp, ss and pp covs (fig. 209) uniformly browish-black or (when fresh) with narrow, whitish-pink or buffy edges; rects tapered (fig. 210).

    AHY/ASY (Aug-Jul): Pp, ss and pp covs (fig. 209) black with distinct pink edges; rects truncate (fig. 210). [Caution is necessary in spring/summer, when flight feathers become worn.]

Sex—CP/BP (May-Sep). Wg useful: $\male$(n30) 102-114, $\female$(n30) 94-106 (excludes certain Alaska populations, which can be much larger). The following is reliable with Black and Brown-capped rosy-finches but is less so with the Gray-crowned form, where overlap occurs (combine with age and wg to sex Gray-crowned):

    $\male$—Forecrown black; hindcrown with some to much grayish-silver; uppertail covs, wing covs, flight feathers, and underparts with extensive pink coloration.

wide pink edging   narrow buffy-pink edging

AHY/ASY   HY/SY   HY/SY   AHY/ASY

Figure 209. Pattern of the primary coverts by sex in the Rosy Finch. This criteria is more useful in the Brown-capped than the other two races.

Figure 210. Rectrix shape of the Rosy Finch, by age.

♀—Forecrown brownish, feathers with grayish edging; hindcrown with relatively little or no grayish-silver (Black and Brown-capped); uppertail covs, wing covs, flight feathers, and underparts with little or no pink.

References—B; French (1959).

PINE GROSBEAK
Pinicola enucleator

PIGR
Species # 515.0
Band size: 1A

Molt—PB: HY partial (Jul-Oct), AHY complete (Jul-Sep); PA absent. PBs occur on the summer grounds.

Skull—Completes in HY/SY from 1 Nov thru Feb.

Age/Sex—CP/BP (May-Sep). Wg: ♂(n30) 108-127, ♀(n30) 105-120; NW > S (excludes Queen Charolette Is. populations, which are much smaller). Juv (Jun-Aug) has body plumage mostly brown with buffy wing bars (♂ = ♀):

AHY/ASY ♂ (Sep-Aug): Body plumage primarily pink or reddish; rects truncate (fig. 211).

AHY/ASY ♀ (Sep-Aug): Lower back and underparts mostly gray; crown, nape, and uppertail covs with varying amounts of olive, yellowish or russet; rects truncate (fig. 211).

HY/SY (Aug-2nd Sep): Like AHY/ASY ♀ but rects tapered (fig. 211). [HY/SY ♀♀ average duller (especially on the crown and rump) than ♂♂, and some ♂♂ have a few pink or reddish feathers in the body plumage and are reliably distinguished (look for this especially in spring, the result of a limited PA?). Also, brown birds with a CP and birds molting from brown to red in Aug-Oct are SY ♂♂. Most birds should probably not be reliably sexed, however, except in combination with wg and experience.]

References—B,R,W,Sv; Adkisson (1977).

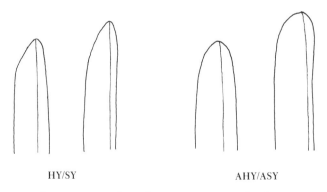

HY/SY   AHY/ASY

Figure 211. Inner and outer rectrix shape by age in Pine Grosbeaks.

PURPLE FINCH
Carpodacus purpureus

PUFI
Species # 517.0
Band size: 1

Species—Eye line and malar usually distinct and undertail covs often (but not always) without heavy streaks (HY/SY ♂♂ & ♀♀); back with purple or reddish (AHY/ASY ♂♂); wg 74-87 (compare with sex; see below); wing tip (longest p—longest s) 16-25 mm; culmen 8.2-10.1, distinctly but not substantially curved (fig.212); tail notched, central—outer rect usually > 4 mm; often attempts to bite; usually silent when released. The combination of the above should separate this from Cassin's and House finches (which see). Be careful with Juvs (especially in western populations), which can resemble House Finch quite closely in bill and plumage features.

Molt—PB: HY partial (Aug-Oct), AHY complete (Jul-Oct); PA limited (Apr). PBs occur mostly on the summer grounds but can complete during fall migration.

Skull—Completes in HY/SY from 15 Nov thru Feb. Some SYs (2-3%, mostly ♂♂) show windows thru summer.

Age/Sex—CP/BP (May-Sep); brown plumaged birds with neither a CP nor a BP in Jun-Aug are reliably sexed ♂. Wg: ♂(n100) 76-87, ♀(n100) 74-84. Juv (Jun-Sep) is washed brown and has streaking on throat and undertail covs (which are also loosely textured). Along with the following, use careful consideration of both outgoing and incoming plumage in molting, Aug-Oct birds:

AHY/ASY ♂ (Oct-Sep): Upperparts, head, and breast with substantial purple or reddish; rects truncate (fig. 213).

AHY/ASY ♀ (Aug-Jul): Upperparts, head, and breast brown and whitish, with little or no reddish (some birds show a slight pink or yellowish wash); rects truncate (fig. 213). [Rect shape can be difficult; some of these may not be reliably aged (thus sexed) by plumage alone.]

HY/SY (Aug-2nd Oct): Like AHY/ASY ♀♀ but rects tapered (fig. 213). [Some HY/SYs may be reliably sexed ♂ by: the presence of a distinctive pinkish or yellowish tinge to the plumage (known HY/SYs only); a CP (reliable for SY ♂

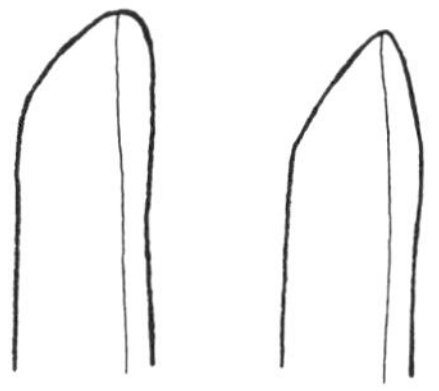

AHY/ASY   HY/SY

Figure 213. Rectrix shape by age in the *Carpodacus* finches.

culmen 9.6-11.8   culmen 8.2-10.1   culmen 6.9-9.0

Cassin's   Purple   House

Figure 212. Bill shape and dimensions in the *Carpodacus* finches.

on brown plumaged birds); or, in Aug-Oct SYs, a brown plumaged bird molting in red feathers. HY/SY ♀♀ are not reliably called, however, except in combination with BP or wg.]

References—B,R,O,W,BBM; Duvall (1945), Blake (1954b, 1955), Kennard (1962), Ryan (1969), Yunick (1979a, 1983a); R. Yunick data, PRBO data.

CASSIN'S FINCH
Carpodacus cassinii

CAFI
Species # 518.0
Band size: 1B-1

Species—Similar to Purple Finch but plumage generally paler; undertail covs with heavy streaks; wg 86-97 (compare with sex; see below); wing tip 25-37 mm; culmen 9.6-11.8, virtually straight (fig. 212). These criteria should easily separate Cassin's from Purple and House finches.

Molt—PB: HY partial (Jul-Sep), AHY complete (Jul-Sep); PA limited (Mar-May). PBs occur on the summer grounds.

Skull—Completes in HY from 15 Nov thru Feb. Some SYs probably show windows thru spring.

Age/Sex—CP/BP (Apr-Sep); brown plumaged birds with niether a CP or a BP in Jun-Jul are possibly reliably considered ♂♂ (this needs further study). Wg: ♂ (n100) 89-97, ♀(n100) 86-92. See Purple Finch for plumage criteria (the only difference being that rect shape (fig. 213) may be easier with Cassin's; 10% intermediates reported).

References—B,O,C(Samson),BBM; Duvall (1945), Samson (1974, 1976), Balph (1977); PRBO data.

HOUSE FINCH
Carpodacus mexicanus

HOFI
Species # 519.0
Band size: 1

Species—Eye line and malar indistinct or lacking and undertail covs streaked (HY/SY ♂♂ & ♀♀); back without reddish or yellow (AHY/ASY ♂♂); wg 70-83 (compare with sex; see below); wing tip 16-23 mm; culmen 6.9-9.0, substantially curved (fig. 212); tail square, central—outer rect usually < 3 mm; seldom attempts to bite; usually calls when released. The combination of the above should separate this from Purple and Cassin's finches (which see).

Molt—PB: HY partial-complete (Jul-Oct), AHY complete (Jun-Oct); PA absent. PBs occur on the summer grounds. The 1st PB may include none, some, or all flight feathers, with the ss and inner pp most often retained during incomplete molts. Southern populations show a higher percentage of complete 1st PBs than northern populations.

Skull—Completes in HY/SY from 1 Oct thru Jan.

Age/Sex—CP/BP (Apr-Oct). Wg: ♂(n30) 74-83, ♀(n30) 70-80. Rect shape (fig. 212) seems unhelpful, even in birds that retain the juvenal tail during the 1st PB. Juv (Apr-Oct) is washed brownish and has heavy streaking and loosely textured undertail covs (♂ = ♀). The following is reliable for sexing during and after the 1st PB and for ageing most ♂♂:

AHY/ASY ♂ (Sep-Aug): Crown, breast, and rump with distinct red or gold; mid and les covs and alula edged pink; rump patch bright red (or yellow) and relatively extensive (width 17-28 mm; length 21-40 mm).

HY/SY ♂ (Sep-Aug): Like AHY/ASY ♂ but mid and les covs and alula without pink edging; rump patch often washed brownish (but can be bright), relatively less extensive (width 10-24 mm; length 12-38 mm).

♀ ♀ : Crown, breast, and rump brown, sometimes with slight reddish or gold tinging. [♀ ♀ are not reliably aged by plumage, except, perhaps by contrasting flight feathers in some HY/SYs (look especially for the outer 4-7 pp being contrastingly fresher.]

References—B,O,BBM,C(R.Tweit); Michener & Michener (1940), Gill & Lanyon (1965), McEntee (1970a), Klimkiewicz (1980), Stangel (1985), Yunick (1987); PRBO data.

RED CROSSBILL
Loxia curvirostra

RECR
Species # 521.0
Band size: 1B

Species—Juvs and some ♀ ♀ of certain populations may show pale buffy or whitish wing bars, but these are ≤ 2.5 mm in width and not sharply defined (see White-winged Crossbill).

Molt—PB: HY partial-incomplete (Jun-Dec), AHY complete (May-Nov); PA: SY ♂ partial (Feb-May), ASY ♂ limited (Mar-Apr). PBs usually occur in the vicinity of the summer grounds. The 1st PB can include the central rects. The PAs, especially in ♀ ♀, need further investigation. Exceptions to the above may occur with some frequency, due to year-round breeding in this species.

Skull—May complete in HY/SY at all times of the year but most often from Dec-Feb. AHYs are reliably aged by skull only through Jun; use plumage instead.

Age/Sex—CP/BP (Apr-Oct, sometimes Nov-Mar). Wg: ♂(n50) 82-103, ♀(n50) 79-98; Arizona > N, generally shows substantial geographic variation. Juv (Jan-Dec) is entirely brownish with heavy streaking (♂ = ♀ but see wg). Ageing codes in this species are complicated by occasional winter breeding:

AHY/ASY ♂ (Aug-Jul): Plumage entirely red or red-orange (usually) or mixed red and yellowish; flight feathers and wing covs uniformly blackish-brown with red edging; wing bars absent; rects truncate (fig. 214). [Some ASY ♂ ♂ (Apr-Jul) will lack red edging to the flight feathers; age these by rect shape only.]

HY/SY ♂ (May-2nd Oct): Plumage mixed dull red or yellow and brownish (thru Apr); flight feathers and pp covs pale brown, often with greenish or pale edging, contrasting with darker brown gr and mid covs (possibly more so in 2nd Apr-Sep); wing bars, if present, buffy (thru Apr); rects tapered (fig. 214). [The central rects may also be contrastingly truncate, darker, and edged red. Use consideration of molt and flight feather criteria for ageing SY in Aug-Oct.]

AHY/ASY ♀ (Aug-Jul): Plumage brown or greenish, usually with substantial yellow (a few may show somw reddish but not as bright as in ♂ ♂); flight feathers and wing covs uniformly dark brown; wing bars absent; rects truncate (fig. 214).

HY/SY ♀ (May-2nd Sep): Plumage brown or greenish, usually without substantial yellow; flight feathers and pp covs pale brown, contrasting with darker gr covs (Apr-Sep, if contrasting at all); wing bars buffy (Jun-Mar); rects tapered (fig. 214).

References—B,R,W,O,Sv; Tordoff (1952), Jollie (1953), Kemper (1959), Phillips (1977), Yunick (1984), Dickerman (1986); PRBO data.

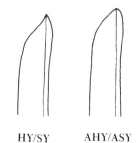

HY/SY   AHY/ASY

Figure 214. Rectrix shape by age in the Crossbills.

WHITE-WINGED CROSSBILL
Loxia leucoptera

WWCR
Species # 522.0
Band size: 1B

Species—White wing bars distinctly defined, ≥ 2.5 mm in width (see Red Crossbill).

Molt—PB: HY partial-incomplete (Jun-Nov), AHY complete (Jun-Nov); PA absent-limited (Mar-Apr). The molts and erratic breeding of this species probably parallel those of the Red Crossbill (which see).

Skull—see Red Crossbill.

Age/Sex—CP/BP (Jan-Oct). Wg: ♂(n30) 83-91, ♀(n30) 80-89. Otherwise, ageing and sexing criteria are the same as in Red Crossbill.

References—B,R,W,Sv.

COMMON REDPOLL
Carduelis flammea

CORE
Species # 528.0
Band size: 0

Species—From Hoary Redpoll (which see) with caution; some intermediates or hybrids may not be safely separable. Nape, back, rump, and flanks brownish-white with moderate to heavy streaking; undertail covs with large blackish centers and upper mandible strongly curved (fig. 215). The undertail cov difference is usually the most reliable; combine all criteria for accurate separation of most birds.

Molt—PB: HY partial (Aug-Sep), AHY complete (Aug-Sep); PA absent. PBs occur on the summer grounds.

Skull—Completes in HY/SY from 1 Nov thru Jan.

Age/Sex—CP/BP (May-Sep). Wg: ♂(n100) 70-81, ♀(n100) 67-78; N > S. Juv (Jul-Aug) lacks red cap and black throat patch (♂ = ♀). Intermediates between the following will occur, which are not reliably aged and/or sexed:

AHY/ASY ♂ (Sep-Aug): Breast and flanks heavily washed pink; rects truncate (fig. 216); relatively unworn.

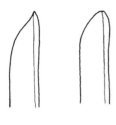

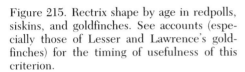

HY/SY   AHY/ASY

Figure 215. Rectrix shape by age in redpolls, siskins, and goldfinches. See accounts (especially those of Lesser and Lawrence's goldfinches) for the timing of usefulness of this criterion.

Figure 216. Bill shape and uppertail covert pattern for identifying Common Redpoll.

HY/SY ♂ (Aug-2nd Aug): Breast and flanks lightly washed pink; rects tapered (fig. 216), relatively abraded, especially in spring/summer.

AHY/ASY ♀ (Sep-Aug): Breast and flanks usually tinged lightly (but sometimes without) pink; rects truncate (fig. 216), relatively unworn.

HY/SY ♀: Breast and flanks entirely without pink; rects tapered (fig. 216), relatively abraded, especially in spring/summer.

References—B,R,W,C(Collins and West),Sv; Houston (1963), Brooks (1973), Yunick (1979); R. Yunick data.

HOARY REDPOLL
Carduelis hornemanni

HORE
Species # 527.0
Band size: 0

Species—Nape and back white with light to moderate streaking; rump and flanks white to whitish with sparse to no brown streaks; longest undertail cov with narrow or (usually) no blackish center (fig. 217); upper mandible relatively straight (fig. 217). See Common Redpoll.

Molt—PB: HY partial (Jul-Sep), AHY complete (Jul-Sep); PA absent. PBs occur on the summer grounds.

Skull—Completes in HY/SY from 1 Nov thru Jan.

Age—Juv (Jul-Aug) lacks red cap and black throat patch (♂ = ♀). Intermediates between the following will occur, which are not reliably aged (see also Sex):

Figure 217. Bill shape and uppertail covert pattern for identifying Hoary Redpoll.

HY/SY (Aug-Jul): Rects tapered (fig. 216).

AHY/ASY (Aug-Jul): Rects truncate (fig. 216).

Sex—CP/BP (May-Sep). Wg: ♂(n30) 71-87, ♀(n30) 67-84; E > W. The following is reliable only with some (probably AHY/ASY only) ♂. Compare with Common Redpoll criteria for possible determinations of other classes on some birds, when age and wg are combined:

♂: Breast and rump moderately washed with pink.

♂/♀: Breast and rump without pink.

References—B,R,Sv.

PINE SISKIN
Carduelis pinus

PISI
Species # 533.0
Band size: 0

Molt—PB: HY partial (Jul-Dec), AHY complete (Jun-Oct); PA absent. The PBs occur primarily in the vicinity of the summer grounds but may complete on migration or the winter grounds in some HYs.

Skull—Completes in HY/SY from 15 Nov thru early March.

Age—Juv (Apr-Sep) has a buffy or yellowish wash to the upperparts and breast (some birds possibly sexed by amount of yellow in flight feathers; see Sex). Otherwise, the following is the only reliable plumage-related criterion known:

HY/SY (Aug-2nd Aug): Rects tapered (fig. 216), usually relatively abraded, especially in spring.

AHY/ASY (Sep-Aug): Rects truncate (fig. 216), relatively unworn.

Sex—CP/BP (Mar-Sep). Wg: ♂(n100) 69-79, ♀(n100) 66-76. The amount and brightness of yellow in the flight feathers is related to sex and may be useful for separating up to 35% of birds when combined with age and wg (see McEntee 1970b; Yunick 1970b, 1976a). The specifics for reliable sexing within age groups have yet to be determined, however.

References—B,R,W,SK,O,BBM; Lowther and Walker (1967), McEntee (1970b), Yunick (1970b, 1976a, 1976c, 1977c), Leberman (1984); PRBO data, R. Yunick data.

LESSER GOLDFINCH
Carduelis psaltria

LEGO
Species # 530.0
Band size: 0

Species—Distinctly yellow undertail covs will separate this from the other two goldfinch species.

Molt—PB: HY incomplete (Aug-Nov), AHY complete (Aug-Nov); PA incomplete (Mar-Apr). PBs occur during migration or on the winter grounds. The 1st PB is variable but usually includes the tail. The PA can include some or all rects. Molt in this species deserves further study.

Skull—Completes in HY/SY from 15 Nov thru Mar. Unpneumatized areas can be difficult to see due to subtle contrasts with pneumatized sections.

Age/Sex—CP/BP (Mar-Oct). Wg: ♂(n40) 60-69, ♀(n40) 58-66; E (black-backed) > W (green-backed). Rect shape (fig. 216) useful for only a small percentage of HY/SYs after the 1st PB

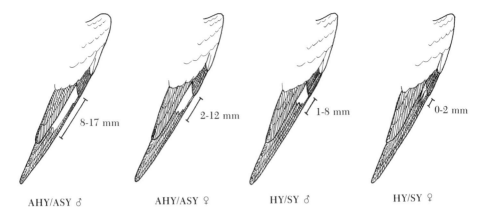

AHY/ASY ♂   AHY/ASY ♀   HY/SY ♂   HY/SY ♀

Figure 218. Amounts of white at the base of the primaries in the Lesser Goldfinch, by age and sex. This may be reliable in basic plumage only.

(Sep-Nov), and is probably only good thru Apr with these. Juv (May-Aug) is like HY/SY ♀ but is drabber and has buffy wing bars (Juvs can be sexed by the amount of white in the flight feathers; see below). The following should be reliable for sexing and for ageing most birds; beware of the possibility that some HY/SYs may have a complete 1st PB and/or PA:

AHY/ASY ♂ (Oct-Sep): Forehead and crown completely black (may show slight greenish edging in late fall); wing covs uniformly black; underparts bright yellow; inner pp with white extending 8-17 mm from tips of pp covs (fig. 218); white patch in outer rects relatively distinct and large.

HY/SY ♂ (Sep-2nd Sep): Forehead and crown usually mixed green and black (especially in Sep-Mar); underparts dull yellow (thru Mar); pp covs brown, contrasting in color with blacker gr covs (gr covs may not molt in until Oct on some HYs); inner pp with white extending 2-12 mm from tips of pp covs (fig. 218); white patch in outer rects indistinct to fairly distinct and small to moderate in size (thru Mar only?).

AHY/ASY ♀ (Sep-Aug): Forehead and crown usually without black; wing covs uniformly blackish; inner pp with white extending 1-8 mm beyond tips of pp covs (fig. 218); white patch in outer rects lacking to fairly distinct and moderately large. [♀ ♀ may be difficult to age; look for a few black feathers in the crown of some AHY/ASYs and for flight feather contrasts in some HY/SYs.]

HY/SY ♀ (Sep-Aug): Forehead and crown without black; pp covs and other flight feathers brown, contrasting in coloration with blacker gr covs (from Oct on some birds); inner pp with white extending 0-2 mm beyond tips of pp covs (fig. 218); white patch in outer rects lacking (often) to indistinct and small.

References—B,O,C(Sheppard),BBM; PRBO data.

LAWRENCE'S GOLDFINCH
Carduelis lawrencei

LAGO
Species # 531.0
Band size: 0

Molt—PB: HY incomplete-complete (Aug-Oct); AHY complete (Jul-Sep); PA incomplete (Mar-Apr). PBs occur mostly on the summer grounds. The 1st PB includes a variable number of flight feathers, usually all rects. The PA appears to include the rects but not the pp or ss. More study is needed on the molt of this species.

Skull—Completes in HY/SY from 15 Sep thru Feb. The pneumatization pattern may be difficult to see, as with Lesser Goldfinch.

Age—Rect shape (fig. 216) useful for ageing prior to the 1st PB and for a few HY/SYs thru Apr. Juv (May-Aug) has generally dull yellowish-brown plumage with indistinct streaks to the upperparts (see Sex). Otherwise, nothing reliable is known for ageing in this species but the amount of yellow in the pp, the amount of white in the rects, the general plumage brightness, and wing cov contrasts (all as in Lesser Goldfinch) should be examined for age/sex related differences.

Sex—CP/BP (Mar-Sep). Wg: ♂(n30) 64-71, ♀(n30) 61-68. The following is reliable during and after the 1st PB (some Juvs may be sexable by the amount of white in the rects as in Lesser Goldfinch):

♂: Throat, lores, and crown partially or entirely black.

♀: Throat, lores, and crown without black.

References—B,O.

AMERICAN GOLDFINCH
Carduelis tristis

AMGO
Species # 529.0
Band size: 0

Species—From Lesser Goldfinch by white or whitish undertail covs.

Molt—PB: HY partial (Sep-Dec), AHY complete (Aug-Dec); PA partial (Feb-Jul). PBs commence on the summer grounds and finish on the winter grounds; vice versa for PAs. Continuous, limited molting occurs through the winter.

Skull—Completes in HY/SY from 15 Dec thru Mar. The pattern of pneumatization in this species is atypical (see Yunick 1979b).

Age/Sex—CP/BP (Jun-Oct). Wg: ♂(n50) 68-78, ♀(n50) 65-74. Juv (Jul-Oct) is brownish-yellow, often with streaks in the upperparts, and has buffy brown wing bars (see below for sexing Juvs). The following is reliable for sexing in all plumages (including Juv) and for ageing ♂♂. A few ♀♀ may be difficult to age. Look also for the presence (HY/SY ♂) or absence (AHY/ASY ♂) of white spots in the outer webs of pp 4-8, which is not reliable for ageing but may be an indicator:

AHY/ASY ♂ (Oct-Sep): Plumage black and yellow (Mar-Oct only); les covs bright yellow; wing bars white; flight feathers glossy black; rects truncate (fig. 216).

HY/SY ♂ (Oct-Sep): Plumage black and yellow (Mar-Oct only); les covs olive to yellowish-olive; wing bars buffy-white (thru Apr); flight feathers dull black; rects tapered (fig. 216).

AHY/ASY ♀ (Oct-Sep): Plumage without yellow and black (reliable for ♀ in Mar-Aug only); flight feathers dark brown; rects truncate (fig. 216).

HY/SY ♀ (Oct-Sep): Like AHY/ASY ♀ but flight feathers slightly paler; rects tapered (fig. 216).

References—B,R,W,SK,O,C(D. Foster),BBM; Parks & Parks (1968), Olyphant (1972), Fisk (1973b), Middleton (1974, 1977), Prescott (1983), Yunick (1979b, 1983); R. Yunick data, PRBO data.

EVENING GROSBEAK
Coccothraustes vespertinus

EVGR
Species # 514.0
Band size: 1A

Molt—PB: HY partial-incomplete (Aug-Nov), AHY complete (Aug-Nov); PA limited (Mar-May). PBs occur primarily on the summer grounds. The 1st PB may occasionally include the terts.

Skull—Completes in HY/SY from 15 Nov thru Feb.

Age/Sex—CP/BP (May-Sep). Wg: ♂(n30) 108-117, ♀(n30) 103-114. Juv (Jun-Oct) has dingy grayish or brownish plumage and yellow inner gr covs (Juvs sexed by pattern of flight feathers; see below.). The following should reliably sex all and age most birds:

AHY/ASY ♂ (Sep-Aug): Forehead yellow; crown black; flight feathers and pp covs uniformly black; terts white; rects relatively truncate (fig. 219); outer rects without whitish spots.

HY/SY ♂ (Aug-2nd Aug): Like AHY/ASY ♂ but flight feathers and pp covs brownish-black, contrasting with blacker gr covs; terts edged gray (beware of some that may have renewed terts at the 1st PB); rects tapered (fig. 219); outer rects with indistinct whitish spots to the inner webs (some HY/SY ♂ ♂ may have very indistinct or no whitish spots).

AHY/ASY ♀ (Sep-Aug): Forehead and crown grayish; pp 3-6 with white bases; rects with conspicuous white patches; terts mixed black and and grayish or white; flight feathers and wing covs uniformly dark brown; rects truncate (fig. 219).

HY/SY ♀ (Aug-2nd Aug): Like AHY/ASY ♀ but flight feathers and pp covs pale brown, contrasting with darker brown gr covs; rects tapered (fig. 219).

References—B, R, W, SK, O, BBM; Yunick (1977a); R. Yunick data.

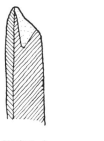 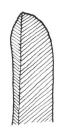

HY/SY ♂   AHY/ASY ♂

Figure 219. Rectrix shape and pattern by age in ♂ ♂ Evening Grosbeaks. The shape (but not the pattern) is applicable to ♀ ♀, as well.

OLD WORLD SPARROWS

PASSERIDAE

Two species. Family characteristics include stout, conical bills; robust postures; and short tails. They have 10 primaries (10th spurious), 9 secondaries, and 12 rectrices. The first PBs are complete, resulting in little if any plumage differences between the ages. The sexes are different in one species, alike in the other.

HOUSE SPARROW
Passer domesticus

HOSP
Species # 688.2
Band size: 1B

Molt—PB: HY complete (Jun-Dec), AHY complete (Aug-Nov); PA absent.

Skull—Completes in HY/SY from 15 Sep thru Feb. Northern populations may be reliably called AHY by skull as late as 15 Nov. Some SYs retain windows thru the first breeding season (thru Jul).

Age—Rect shape not useful after the 1st PB. Juv (May-Oct) is like ♀ but is buffier and has looser plumage (see Sex). Some ♂♂ may be aged by the porportion of brown (more in HY/SYs) and gray (more in AHY/ASYs) in the cheeks. Extremes are reliably aged (with experience) when compared with fullness of the throat patch and crown plumage. Otherwise, no plumage criteria known for ageing.

Sex—CP/BP (Mar-Sep). Wg: ♂(n30) 72-83, ♀(n30) 70-81. The following is reliable during and after the 1st PB. Many Juvs can also be reliably sexed by throat color, being white in ♀♀ and dusky gray in ♂♂ (look also for a more prominent postocular spot on Juv ♂♂ than ♀♀):

♂: Throat and lores partially or entirely black; crown gray and chestnut.

♀: Throat and lores whitish-brown; crown brown.

References—B,R,W,O,Sv; Nero (1951), R. Johnston (1967), Selander & Johnston (1967), Niles (1973), Blackmore (1973), Casto (1974); PRBO data.

EURASIAN TREE SPARROW
Passer montanus

ETSP
Species # 688.3
Band size: 1B

Molt—PB: HY complete (Aug-Nov); AHY complete (Aug-Oct); PA absent.

Skull—Completes in HY/SY from 1 Oct thru Jan. Look for windows in some SYs thru spring/summer.

Age—Rect shape not useful for ageing after the 1st PB. Juv (May-Sep) resembles adult in pattern but is faded overall. Otherwise, no reliable criteria known.

Sex—♂ = ♀ by plumage. CP/BP (Mar-Sep). A sample of wgs by sex for the N.A. population is needed.

References—B,Sv.

Literature Cited

Adkisson, C.S. 1977. Morphological variation in North American Pine Grosbeaks. *Wilson Bull* 89(3): 380-395.

Aldrich, J.W. 1968. Population characteristics and nomenclature of the Hermit Thrush. *Proc. U.S. Nat. Mus.* 124(3637): 1-33.

‗‗‗‗‗ 1984. Ecogeographic variation in size and proportions of Song Sparrows (*Melospiza melodia*). *Ornith. Monographs* 35: 1-134.

American Ornithologist's Union. 1957. Check-list of North American birds. Fifth edition. Amer. Ornith. Union, Baltimore. 691 pp.

‗‗‗‗‗ 1983. Check-list of North American birds. Sixth edition. Amer. Ornith. Union, Lawrence, Kansas. 877 pp.

Anderson, B.W. and R.J. Daugherty. 1974. Characteristics and reproductive biology of grosbeaks (*Pheuticus*) in the hybrid zone in South Dakota. *Wils. Bull.* 86(1): 1-11.

Atkinson, C.T. and C.J. Ralph. 1980. Acquisition of plumage polymorphism in White-throated Sparrows. *Auk* 97(2): 245-252.

Austin, G.T. and A.M. Rea. 1971. Key to age and sex determination of Verdins. *Western Bird Bander* 46(3): 41.

Bailey, R.E. 1952. The incubation patch of passerine birds. *Condor* 54(3): 121-136.

Baird, J. 1958. The postjuvenal molt of the male Brown-headed Cowbird. *Bird-Banding* 29(4): 224-228.

‗‗‗‗‗ 1964. Aging birds by skull ossification. *EBBA News* 27(4): 162- 163.

‗‗‗‗‗ 1967. Arrested molt in Tennessee Warblers. *Bird-Banding* 38(3): 236-237.

Balph, M.H. 1975. Wing length, hood coloration, and sex ratio in Dark- eyed Juncos wintering in northern Utah. *Bird-Banding* 46(2): 126- 130.

‗‗‗‗‗ 1977. On the use of rectrix shape and wing length to determine age and sex in the Cassin's Finch. *N. Am. Bird Bander* 2(4): 157- 158.

Bancroft, G.T. and G.E. Woolfenden. 1982. The molt of the Scrub Jays and Blue Jays in Florida. *Ornith. Monog.* 29: 1-51.

Bangs, O. 1925. The history and characters of *Vermivora crissalis* (Salvin and Goodman). *Auk* 42(2): 251-253.

Banks, R.C. 1964. The White-crowned Sparrow, *Zonotrichia leucophrys*. *Univ Calif. Pubs. Zool.* 70: 1-123.

‗‗‗‗‗ 1970. Molt and taxonomy of Red-Breasted Nuthatches. *Wilson Bull.* 82(2): 201-205.

‗‗‗‗‗ 1978. Prealternate molt in Nuthatches. *Auk* 95(1): 179-181.

Bateman, G.C. and R.P. Balda. 1973. Growth, development and food habits of young Piñon Jays. *Auk* 90(1): 39-61.

Baumgartner, A.M. 1986. Sex reversal in banded cardinal. *North Am. Bird Bander* 11(1): 11.

Bent, A.C. 1942. Life histories of North American flycatchers, larks, swallows, and their allies. *U.S. Nat. Mus. Bull.* # 179. Wash. D.C.

‗‗‗‗‗ 1946. Life histories of North American jays, crows, titmice and their allies. *U.S. Nat. Mus. Bull.* # 191. Wash. D.C.

‗‗‗‗‗ 1948. Life histories of North American nuthatches, wrens, thrashers and their allies. *U.S. Nat. Mus. Bull.* # 195. Wash. D.C.

‗‗‗‗‗ 1949. Life histories of North American thrushes, kinglets and their allies. *U.S. Nat. Mus. Bull.* # 196. Wash. D.C.

‗‗‗‗‗ 1950. Life histories of North American wagtails, shrikes, vireos and their allies. *U.S. Nat. Mus. Bull.* # 197. Wash. D.C.

‗‗‗‗‗ 1953. Life histories of North American wood warblers. *U.S. Nat. Mus. Bull.* # 203. Wash. D.C.

_____ 1958. Life histories of North American blackbirds, orioles, tanagers and their allies. *U.S. Nat. Mus. Bull.* # 211. Wash. D.C.

_____ *et al.*, comps. 1968. Life histories of North American cardinals, buntings, towhees, finches, sparrows and their allies, ed. O.L. Austin. *U.S. Nat. Mus. Bull.* # 237, parts 1-3. Wash. D.C.

Binford, L.C. 1971. Identification of Northern and Louisiana Waterthrushes. *California Birds* 2(1): 1-10.

Blackmore, F.H. 1973. Seasonal variation and energetics of molt in captive outdoor House Sparrows (Abstract). *Ornith. Monogr.* 14: 94.

Blake, C.H. 1954a. Leg color of Blackpoll and Bay-breasted Warblers. *Bird-Banding* 25(1): 16.

_____ 1954b. Notes on the wing length of Eastern Purple Finch (*Carpodacus p. purpureus*). *Bird-Banding* 25(3): 97-101.

_____ 1955. Notes on the Eastern Purple Finch. *Bird-Banding* 26(3): 89-116.

_____ 1964. Color and wing length in the Slate-colored Junco. *Bird- Banding* 35(2): 125-126.

_____ 1965a. Comments on difficult decisions. *EBBA News* 28(4): 179.

_____ 1965b. Replaced primaries in first nuptual plumage of *Passerina cyanea*. *Bird-Banding* 36(4): 270.

_____ 1965c. Sexing by wing length. *EBBA News* 28(5): 227-228.

_____ 1969. Notes on the Indigo Bunting. *Bird-Banding* 40(2): 133-139.

Bohlen, H.D. and V.M. Kleen. 1976. A method for aging Orange-crowned Warblers in fall. *Bird-Banding* 47(4): 365.

Bowers, R.K. Jr. and J.B. Dunning Jr. 1986. Weights and measurements # 1—Arizona sparrows. *North Am. Bird Bander* 11(2): 59-60.

Brackbill, H. Protracted prebasic head molt in the Dark-eyed Junco. *Bird-Banding* 48(4): 370.

Briggs, D. 1975. Baby Blue Jay with barred alula. *EBBA News* 34(5): 238.

Brooks, W.S. 1973. A tentative key for sex determination of Common Redpolls (*Acanthis flammea flammea*) in the northern United States during winter. *Bird-Banding* 44(1): 13-21.

Canadian Wildlife Service. 1984. North American bird banding. Vol. I. Can. Wildl. Serv., Ottawa.

_____ and U.S. Fish and Widlife Service. 1977. North American bird banding techniques. Vol. II. Can. Wildl. Serv., Ottawa (parts revised, 1981).

Cannell, P.F., J.D. Cherry, and K.C. Parkes. 1983. Variation and migration overlap in flight feather molt of the Rose-breasted Grosbeak. *Wilson Bull.* 95(4) 621-627.

Carpenter, T.W. 1979. An observation of an AHY Gray Catbird with a gray iris. *N. Am. Bird Bander* 4(4): 157.

Casto, S.D. 1974. Molt schedule of House Sparrows in northwestern Texas. *Wilson Bull.* 86(2): 176-177.

Cherry, J.D. 1985. Early autumn movements and prebasic molt of Swainson's Thrushes. *Wilson Bull.* 97(3): 368-370.

_____ and P.F. Cannell. 1984. Rate and timing of prebasic molt of adult Boreal Chickadees. *Journ. Field Ornith.* 55(4): 487-489.

Cohen, R.R. 1984. Criteria for distinguishing breeding male Tree Swallows from brightly colored females prior to capture. *N. Am. Bird Bander* 9(3): 2-3.

Crawford, R.D. and W.L. Hohman. 1978. A method for aging female Yellow-headed Blackbirds. *Bird-Banding* 49(3): 201-207.

Dater, E. 1970. Dorsal wing coverts of Blue Jay (*Cyanocitta cristata*). Guide to age. *EBBA News* 33(3): 125-129.

Davis, D.E. 1960. Comments on the migration of Starlings in the eastern United States. *Bird-Banding* 31(4): 216-219.

Davis, J. 1951. The Brown Towhees. *Univ. Calif. Pubs. Zool.* 52: 1-120.

_____ 1954. Seasonal changes in bill length of certain passerine birds. *Condor* 56(3): 142-149.

_____ 1957. Determination of age in the Spotted Towhee. *Condor* 59(3): 195-202.

Davis, R.S. 1969a. Northern Prairie Horned Larks. *IBB News* 41(4): 145.

_____ 1969b. Lapland Longspur data. *IBB News* 41(5): 185.

Davis, T.H. 1971. A key to fall *Piranga* tanagers—females and immatures. *EBBA News* 34(4): 237-238.

DeHaven, R.W. 1975. Plumages of the Tricolored Blackbird. *Western Birds* 50(4): 59-60.

_____, F.T. Crase and M.R. Miller. 1974. Aging Tricolored Blackbirds by cranial ossification. *Bird-Banding* 45(2): 156-159.

Dennis, J.V. 1958. Some aspects of the breeding ecology of the Yellow- breasted Chat (*Icteria virens*). *Bird-Banding* 29(3): 169-183.

_____ 1967. Fall departure of the Yellow-breasted Chat (*Icteria virens*) in eastern North America. *Bird-Banding* 38(2): 130-135.

DeSante, D.F., N.K. Johnson, R. LeValley and R.P. Henderson. 1985. Occurrence and identification of the Yellow-bellied Flycatcher on Southeast Farallon Island, California. *West. Birds* 16(4): 153-160.

Dhondt, A.A. and J.N.M. Smith. 1980. Postnuptual molt of the Song Sparrow on Mandarte Island in relation to breeding. *Can. Journ. Zool.* 58: 513-520.

Dickerman, R.W. 1962. Identification of the juvenal plumage of the Sharp-tailed Sparrow (*Ammospiza caudacuta nelsoni*). Bird-Banding 33(4): 202-204.

_____ 1986. A review of the Red Crossbill in New York state. Part 2. Identification of specimens from New York. *Kingbird* 36: 127-134.

Dickey, D.R. and A.J. Van Rossem. 1938. The birds of El Salvador. *Zool. Series* 23: 1-609, Field Museum of Natural History, Chicago.

Dixon, K.L. 1962. Notes on the molt schedule of the Plain Titmouse. *Condor* 64(2):134-139.

Dow, D.D. 1966. Sex determination of Slate-colored Junco by means of plumage characteristics. *Ontario Bird Banding* 2:1-14.

Dunning, J.B. Jr. 1984. Body weights of 686 species of North American birds. *West. Bird Banding Assoc. Monograph* 1: 1-38.

Duvall, A.J. 1945. Variation in *Carpodachus purpureus* and *Carpodacus cassinii*. *Condor* 47(5): 202-204.

Dwight, J. Jr. 1900. The sequence of plumages and moults of the passerine birds of New York. *Ann. Acad. Sci.* 13: 73-360.

Eaton, S.W. 1957a. Variation in *Seiurus novaboracensis*. *Auk* 74(2): 229-239.

_____ 1957b. A life history study of *Seiurus noveboracensis* (with notes on *Seiurus aurocapillus* and the species of *Seiurus* compared). *Sci. Studies St. Bonaventure Univ.* 19: 7-36.

_____ 1958. A life history study of the Louisiana Waterthrush. *Wilson Bull.* 70(3): 211-236.

Eisenmann, E. 1969. Wing formula as a means of distinguishing Summer Tanager, *Piranga rubra*, from Hepatic Tanager, *P. flava*. *Bird- Banding* 40(2): 144-145.

Emlen, J.T. Jr. 1936. Age determination in the American Crow. *Condor* 38(2): 99-102.

Erpino, M.J. 1968. Age determination in the Black-billed Magpie. *Condor* 70(1): 91-92.

Ervin, S. 1975. Iris coloration in young Bushtits. *Condor* 77(1): 90- 91.

Ewert, D.N. and W.E. Lanyon. 1970. The first prebasic molt of the Common Yellowthroat (Parulidae). *Auk* 87(2): 362-363.

Fairfield, D.M. and P.A. Shirkoff. 1978. Aging North American kinglets: a new technique. *Blue Bill* (suppl.) 25:19-21.

Felt, A.C. 1967. Ageing Mountain Chickadees. *Western Bird Bander* 42(1): 3.

Fisk, E.J. 1970. A note on wintering Myrtle Warblers. *EBBA News* 33(4): 174.

_____ 1972. Bander's shoptalk. *EBBA News* 35(1): 58-62.

_____ 1973a. Further notes on the iris color of Mockingbird eyes. *Bird-Banding* 44(2): 124.

_____ 1973b. Do not age American Goldfinch by the Olyphant system. *EBBA News* 36(3): 179.

_____ 1973c. Further speculations on Myrtle Warblers in winter plumage. *EBBA News* 36(suppl.): 38-41.

_____ 1971. Wintering populations of Painted Buntings in southern Florida. *Bird-Banding* 45(4): 353-359.

_____ 1975. On Northern Oriole plumages: questions for banders to answer. *EBBA News* 38(3): 146-147.

Foster, M.S. 1967a. Pterylography and age determination in the Orange- crowned Warbler. *Condor* 69(1): 1-12.

_____ 1967b. Molt cycles of the Orange-crowned Warbler. *Condor* 69(2): 169-200.

Foy, R.W. 1974a. Aging and sexing American Redstarts in fall. *EBBA News* 37(1): 43-44.

_____ 1974b. Aging and sexing American Redstarts in the fall: a note of caution. *EBBA News* 37(3-4): 128.

Freer, V. and B. Belanger. 1981. A technique for distinguishing the age classes of adult Bank Swallows. *Journ. Field. Ornith.* 52(4): 341-343.

French, N.R. 1959. Life history of the Black Rosy Finch. *Auk* 76(2): 159-180.

Fugle, G.N. and S.I. Rothstein. 1985. Age and sex related variation in size and crown plumage brightness in wintering White-crowned Sparrows. *Journ. Field Ornith.* 56(4): 356-368.

Gebhardt, S. 1971. Eye color in Blue Jays. *IBB News* 43(2-3): 52-53.

George, W.G. 1973. Molt of juvenile White-eyed Vireos. *Wilson Bull.* 85(3): 327-330.

Gill, D.E. and W.E. Lanyon. 1965. Establishment, growth, and behavior of an extralimital population of House Finches in Huntington, New York. *Bird-Banding* 36(1) 1-14.

Gochfield, M. 1977. Plumage variation in Black-capped Chickadees: is there sexual dimorphism? *Bird-Banding* 48(1): 62-66.

Goodpasture, K.A. 1963. Age, sex and wing length of tower casualties: fall migration, 1962. *Bird-Banding* 34(4): 191-199.

_____ 1972. A rarely reported sex-plumage association in a Rose-breasted Grosbeak. *Bird-Banding* 43(2): 136.

Grant, G.S. and T.L. Quay. 1970. Sex and age criteria in the Slate- colored Junco. *Bird-Banding* 41(4): 274-278.

Gray, D.R. III. 1973. Report on aging and sexing criteria for American Redstart. *EBBA News* 36(3): 143-146.

Greenwood, H., P.J. Weatherhead and R.D. Titman. 1983. A new age- and sex-specific molt scheme for the Red-winged Blackbird. *Condor* 85(1): 104-105.

Hall, G.A. 1979. Hybridization between Mourning and MacGillivray's Warblers. *Bird-Banding* 50(2): 101-107.

Hamel, P.B., J.L. Beacham and A.E. Ross. 1983. A laboratory study of cranial pneumatization in Indigo Buntings. *Journ. Field Ornith.* 54(1): 58-66.

_____ and M.K. Klimkiewicz. 1981. Standard abbreviations for common names of birds—revisited. *N. Am. Bird Bander* 6(2): 46.

Hawthorn, I. 1972. Some differences between juvenile, first year and adult wrens. *The Ringers Bulletin* 3(9): 9-11. [Reprinted in *EBBA News* 35(1): 35-38.]

Hedenstrøm, A. and J. Petterson. 1986. Differences in fat deposits and wing pointedness between male and female Willow Warblers caught in spring migration at Ottenby, SE Sweden. *Ornis Scandinavica* 17(2): 182-185.

Heydweiller, A.M. 1936. Sex, age and individual variation of winter Tree Sparrows. *Bird-Banding* 7(2): 61-68.

Hill, R.A. 1976. Sex ratio and sex determination of immature Brown- headed Cowbirds. *Bird-Banding* 47(2) 112-114.

Houston, C.S. 1963. Redpoll identification—a problem. *Bird-Banding* 34(2): 94-95.

Howard, D.V. 1968. Criteria for aging and sexing Bay-breasted Warblers in the fall. *Bird-Banding* 39(2): 132.

Hubbard, J.P. 1969. The relationships and evolution of the *Dendroica coronata* complex. *Auk* 86(3): 393-432.

_____ 1970. Mensural separation of Black-capped and Carolina chickadees. *EBBA News* 33(5): 211-213.

_____ 1974. Identification of wintering Orioles in the northeast. *Delmarva Ornithologist* 7(2): 10-12. [Reprinted in *EBBA News* 37(2): 70-73.]

_____ 1983. The tail pattern of meadowlarks in New Mexico. *New Mex. Ornith. Soc. Bull.* 11: 61-66.

Humphrey, P.S. and K.C. Parkes. 1959. An approach to the study of molts and plumages. *Auk* 76(1): 1-31.

_____ and _____ 1963. Comments on the study of plumage succession. *Auk* 80(4): 496-503.

Hussell, D.J.T. 1980. The timing of fall migration and molt in Least Flycatchers. *Journ. Field Ornith.* 51(1): 65-71.

_____ 1982a. The timing of fall migration in Yellow-bellied Flycatchers. *Journ Field Ornith.* 53(1): 1-6.

_____ 1982b. Migrations of the Yellow-bellied Flycatcher in southern Ontario. *Journ. Field Ornith.* 53(3): 223-224.

_____ 1983. Age and plumage color in female Tree Swallows. *Journ Field Ornith.* 54(3): 312-318.

Johnson, N.K. 1963a. Biosystematics of sibling species of flycatchers in the *Empidonax hammondii-oberholseri-wrightii* complex. *Univ. Calif. Pubs. Zool.* 66(2): 79-238.

_____ 1963b. Comparative molt cycles in the Tyrannid genus *Empidonax*. *Proc XIIIth Int. Ornith. Cong.* 1963: 870-873.

_____ 1974. Molt and age determination in Western and Yellowish flycatchers. *Auk* 91(1): 111-131.

_____ 1980. Character variation and evolution of sibling species in the *Empidonax difficilis-flavescens* complex (Aves: Tyrannidae). *Univ. Calif. Pubs. Zool.* 112: 1-151.

Johnston, D.W. 1967. The identification of autumnal Indigo Buntings. *Bird-Banding* 38(3): 211-214.

Johnston, R.F. 1967. Sexual dimorphism in juvenile House Sparrows. *Auk* 84(2): 275-277.

Jollie, M. 1953. Plumages, molt and racial status of Red Crossbills in northern Idaho. *Condor* 55(4): 193-197.

Kale, H.W. 1966. Plumages and molts in the Long-billed Marsh Wren. *Auk* 83(1): 140-141.

Katholi, C. 1966. Titmouse postjuvenal molt. *EBBA News* 29(5): 200.

Kemper, T. 1959. Notes on the breeding cycle of the Red Crossbill (*Loxia curvirostra*) in Montana. *Auk* 76(2): 181-189.

Kennard, J.H. 1962. Further notes on the occurrence of pink coloration in Purple Finches. *Bird-Banding* 33(2): 90-92.

Kessel, B. 1951. Criteria for sexing and aging European Starlings (*Sturnus vulgaris*). *Bird-Banding* 22(1): 16-23.

Klimkiewicz, M.K. 1980. Notes from the BBL. *N. Am. Bird Bander* 5(3): 96.

_____ and C.S. Robbins. 1978. Standard abbreviations for common names of birds. *N. Am. Bird Bander* 3(1): 16-25.

Knapton, R.W. 1978. Sex and age determination in the Clay-colored Sparrow. *Bird-Banding* 49(2): 152-156.

Kowalski, M.P. 1983. Identifying Mourning and MacGillivrays warblers: geographic variation in the MacGillivray's Warbler as a source of error. *N. Am. Bird Bander* 8(2): 56-57.

_____ 1986. Weights and measurements of Prothonotary Warblers from southern Indiana, with a method of aging males. *N. Am. Bird Bander* 11(4): 129-131.

Lamb, W.A., A.H. Kelley and S.M. Cohen. 1978. Age determination of Blue Jays. *Bird-Banding* 49(3): 215-217.

Lamm, D.W. and J.C. Luepke. 1982. Iris changes in hatching year Yellow-eyed Juncos. *N. Am Bird Bander* 7(3): 93.

Lanyon, W.E. 1961. Specific limits and distribution of Ash-throated and Nutting flycatchers. *Condor* 63(6): 421-449.

Lanyon, W.E. and J. Bull. 1967. Identification of Connecticut, Mourning, and MacGillivrays warblers. *Bird-Banding* 38(3): 187-194.

Leberman, R.C. 1967. The influence of fat on bird weight. *EBBA News* 30(4): 181-184.

_____ 1970. Pattern and timing of skull pneumatization in the Ruby- crowned Kinglet. *Bird-Banding* 41(2): 121-124.

_____ 1973. A study of Tufted Titmouse weights. *EBBA News* 36(1): 34- 38.

_____ 1984. Rose underwings in female Rose-breasted Grosbeaks. *Journ Field Ornith.* 55(4): 486-487.

Ligon, J.D. and J.L. White. 1974. Molt and its timing in the Piñon Jay, *Gymnorhinus cyanocephalus. Condor* 76(1) 274-287.

Linsdale, J.N. 1937. The natural history of Magpies. *Pacific Coast Avifauna* # 25: 1-234.

Linz, G.M. 1986. Temporal, sex, and population characteristics of the first prebasic molt of Red-winged Blackbirds. *Journ Field Ornith.* 57(2): 91-98.

_____, S.B. Bolen and J.F. Cassel. 1983. Postnuptual and postjuvenal molts of Red-winged Blackbirds in Cass County, North Dakota. *Auk* 100(1): 206-209.

Lloyd, J.A. 1965. Seasonal development of the incubation patch in the Starling. *Condor* 67(1): 67-72.

Lloyd-Evans, T.L. 1983. Incomplete molt of juvenile White-eyed Vireos. *Journ Field Ornith.* 54(1): 50-57.

Lowther, J.K. 1961. Polymorphism in the White-throated Sparrow, *Zonotrichia albicollis* (Gmelin). *Can. Journ. Zool* 39: 281-292.

_____. and R.E. Walker. 1967. Sex ratios and wing chord lengths of Pine Siskins (*Spinus pinus*) in Algonquin Park, Ontario. *Can. Field-Naturalist* 81(3): 220-222.

Lunk, W.A. 1952. Notes on the variation in the Carolina Chickadee. *Wilson Bull.* 64(1): 7-24.

Mayfield, H. 1960. The Kirtland's Warbler. Cranbrook Institute of Science, Bloomfield Hills, Michigan. *xv* + 242 pp.

McEntee, E. 1970a. Age determination of House Finches by plumage change. *EBBA News* 33(2): 70-76.

_____ 1970b. Pine Siskins—some observations on color, size and sex. *EBBA News* 33(2): 100-101.

McNicholl, M.K. 1977. Measurements of Wilson's Warblers in Alberta. *N. Am. Bird Bander* 2(3): 108-109.

Meanley, B. 1967. Aging and sexing blackbirds, Bobolinks and starlings. Special report to Patuxent Wildlife Research Center; work unit F-24.1.

_____ and G.M. Bond. Molts and plumages of the Red-winged Blackbird with particular reference to fall migration. *Bird-Banding* 41(1): 22-27.

Meigs, J.B., D.C. Smith and J. Van Buskirk. 1983. Age determination of Black-capped Chickadees. *Journ. Field Ornith.* 54(3): 283-286.

Mellancamp, W.R. 1969. Skull ossification in the White-throated Sparrow. *EBBA News* 32(3):109-111.

Mengel, R.M. 1952. Certain molts and plumages of Acadian and Yellow- bellied Flycatchers. *Auk* 69(3): 273-283.

Mewaldt, L.R. 1952. The incubation patch of the Clark's Nutcracker. *Condor* 54(6): 361.

_____ 1958. Ptrylography and natural and experimentally induced molt in Clark's Nutcracker. *Condor* 60(3): 165-187.

_____ 1973. Wing-length and age in White-crowned Sparrows. *Western Bird Bander* 48(4): 54-56.

_____ 1977. White-crowned Sparrow. Banding worksheet for Western birds. Suppl. to *N. Am. Bird Bander* 2(4).

_____, S.S. Kibby and M.L. Norton. 1968. Comparative biology of Pacific White-crowned Sparrows. *Condor* 70(1): 14-30.

_____ and J.R. King. 1978. Latitudinal variation in prenuptial molt in wintering Gambel's White-crowned Sparrows. *N. Am. Bird Bander* 3(4): 138-144.

_____ and _____ 1986. Estimation of sex ratio from wing-length in birds when sexes differ in size but not coloration. *Journ. Field. Ornith.* 57(2): 155-167.

Michener, H. and J.R. Michener. 1940. The molt of House Finches of the Pasadena region, California. *Condor* 42(2): 140-153.

_____ and _____ 1943. The spring molt of the Gambel Sparrow. *Condor* 45(3): 113-116.

Michener, J.R. 1953. Molt and variations in plumage pattern of Mockingbirds at Pasadena, California. *Condor* 55(2): 75-89.

_____ and H. Michener. Notes on banding records and plumages of the Black-headed Grosbeak. *Condor* 53(2): 93-96.

Middleton, A.L.A. 1974. Age determination in the American Goldfinch. *Bird-Banding* 45(4): 293-296.

_____ 1977. The molt of the American Goldfinch. *Condor* 79(4): 440- 444.

Miller, A.H. 1928. The molts of the Loggerhead Shrike *Lanius ludovicianus* linnaeus. *Univ. Calif. Pubs. Zool.* 30: 393-417.

_____ 1931. Systematic revision and natural history of American shrikes (*Lanius*). *Univ. Calif. Pubs. Zool.* 38: 11-242.

_____ 1933. Postjuvenal molt and appearance of sexual characters of plumage in *Phainopepla nitens*. *Univ. Calif. Pubs. Zool.* 38: 425- 444.

_____ 1946. A method for determining the age of live passerine birds. *Bird-Banding* 17(1): 33-35.

Miskimen, M. 1980. Red-winged Blackbirds: I. Age-related epaulet color changes in captive females. *Ohio Journ. Sci.* 80(5): 232-235.

Moore, R.T. Notes on Middle American *Empidonaces*. *Auk* 57(3): 349-389.

Morton, M.L., J.R. King and D.S. Farner. 1969. Postnuptual and postjuvenal molt in White-crowned Sparrows in central Alaska. *Condor* 71(4): 376-385.

_____ and D.E. Welton. 1973. Postnuptual molt and its relation to reproductive cycle and body weight in Mountain White-crowned Sparrows (*Zonotrichia leucoprys oriantha*). *Condor* 75(2): 184-189.

Mosher, J.I. and S. Lane. 1972. A method of determining the sex of captured Black-capped Chickadees. *Bird-Banding* 43(2): 139-140.

Murray, B.G. Jr. 1968. The relationships of sparrows in the genera *Ammodramus, Passerherbulus* and *Ammospiza* with a description of a hybrid Le Conte's x Sharp-tailed sparrow. *Auk* 85(4): 586-593.

Nero, R.W. 1951. Pattern and rate of cranial "ossification" in the House Sparrow. *Wilson Bull.* 63(1): 84-88.

_____ 1960. Additional notes on the plumage of the Redwinged Blackbird. *Auk* 77(3): 298-305.

Nichols, J.T. 1953a. Eye-color in the Red-eyed Towhee. *Bird-Banding* 24(1): 16-17.

_____ 1953b. Eye-color in the Brown Thrasher. *Bird-Banding* 24(1): 17.

_____ 1955. A criterion for young-of-the-year in the Blue Jay. *Bird- Banding* 26(1): 27.

Niles, D.M. 1972a. Determining age and sex of Purple Martins. *Bird- Banding* 43(2): 137-138.

_____ 1972b. Molt cycles of Purple Martins (*Progne subis*). *Condor* 74(1): 61-71.

_____ 1973. Geographic and seasonal variation in the occurrence of incompletely pneumatized skulls in the House Sparrow. *Condor* 75(3): 354-356.

Nisbet, I.C.T., W.H. Drury Jr. and J.Baird. 1963. Weight loss during migration. Part I: deposition and consumption of fat by the Blackpoll Warbler *Dendroica striata*. *Bird-Banding* 34(3): 107-159.

_____, J. Baird, D.V. Howard and K.S. Anderson. 1970. Statistical comparison on wing lengths measured by four observers. *Bird-Banding* 41(4): 307-308.

Nolan, V. Jr. 1978. The ecology and behavior of the Prairie Warbler *Dendroica discolor*. *A.O.U. Monograph #* 26. *xxii* + 595 pp.

———— and R.E. Mumford. 1965. An analysis of Prairie Warblers killed in Florida during nocturnal migration. *Condor* 67(4): 322-338.

Norris, R.A. 1952. Postjuvenal molt of tail feathers in the Pine Warbler. *Oriole* 17: 29-31.

———— 1958a. Comparative biosystematics and life history of the nuthatches *Sitta pygmaea* and *Sitta pusilla*. *Univ. Calif. Pubs. Zool.* 56(2): 119-300.

———— 1958b. Notes on a captive Wood Thrush and its prenuptual molt. *Bird-Banding* 29(4): 245.

———— 1961. A modification of the Miller method of aging live passerine birds. *Bird-Banding* 32(1): 55-57.

Oberholser, H.C. 1974. The bird life of Texas. Vol. 2, pp 531-1069. University of Texas Press, Austin.

Olyphant, J.C. 1972. A method for aging American Goldfinches. *Bird-Banding* 43(3): 173-181.

Orians, G.H. 1963. Notes on fall-hatched Tricolored Blackbirds. *Auk* 80(4): 552-553.

Packard, F.M. 1936. Notes on plumages of the Eastern Red-wing. *Bird- Banding* 7(2): 77-80.

Palmer, R.S. 1972. Patterns of molting. Pp 65-102 *in* Farner, D.S. and J.R. King, eds., Avian biology. Vol. II. Academic press, New York.

Parkes, K.C. 1951. The genetics of the Golden-winged X Blue-winged warbler complex. *Wilson Bull.* 63(1): 5-15.

———— 1952. Post-juvenal molt in the Bobolink. *Wilson Bull.* 64(3): 161-162.

———— 1953. The incubation patch in males of the suborder Tyranni. *Condor* 55(4): 218-219.

———— 1967. Prealternate molt in the Summer Tanager. *Wilson Bull.* 79(4): 456-458.

———— 1979. Plumage variation in female Black-throated Blue Warblers. *Continental Birdlife* 1(6): 133-135.

———— 1985. Sexing Blue-gray Gnatcatchers (*Polioptila caerulea*). *Ontario Birds* 3: 104-106.

Parks, G.H. 1962. A convenient method of sexing and aging the Starling. *Bird-Banding* 33(3): 148-151.

———— (Mr. and Mrs.). 1968. About the sexing and aging of wintertime American Goldfinches. *EBBA News* 31(3): 115-119.

Patterson, R.M. 1981. Latitudinal variation in length of Barn Swallow tails in North America. *N. Am. Bird Bander* 6(4): 151-154.

Payne, R.B. 1969. Breeding seasons and reproductive physiology of Tricolored Blackbirds and Redwinged Blackbirds. *Univ. Calif. Pubs. Zool.* 90: 1-137.

———— 1972. Mechanisms and control of molt. Pp 103-105 *in* Farner, D.S. and J.R. King, eds. Avian biology. Vol II. Acedemic Press, New York.

Phillips, A.R. 1951. The molts of the Rufous-winged Sparrow. *Wilson Bull.* 63(4): 323-326.

———— 1974. The first prebasic molt of the Yellow-breasted Chat. *Wilson Bull.* 86(1): 12-15.

———— 1977. Sex and age determination of Red Crossbills (*Loxia curvirostra*). *Bird-Banding* 48(2): 110-117.

————, M.A. Howe and W.E. Lanyon. 1966. Identification of the flcatchers of eastern North America, with special emphasis on the genus *Empidonax*. *Bird-Banding* 37(3): 153-171.

———— and W.E. Lanyon. 1970. Additional notes on the flycatchers of eastern North America. *Bird-Banding* 41(3): 190-197.

———— J. Marshall and G. Monson. 1964. The birds of Arizona. Univ. Arizona Press, Tucson. 220 pp.

————, S. Speich and W. Harrison. 1973. Black-capped Gnatcatcher, a new breeding bird for the United States; with a key to the North American species of *Polioptila*. *Auk* 90(2): 257-262.

Pinkowski, B.C. 1974. Criteria for sexing Eastern Bluebirds in juvenile plumage. *IBB News* 46(3): 88-91.

_____ 1976. Photoperiodic effects on the postjuvenal molt of the Eastern Bluebird. *Ohio Journ. Sci.* 76(6): 268-273.

Pitelka, F.A. 1945. Pterylography, molt and age determination of American jays of the genus *Aphelcoma. Condor* 47(6): 229-260.

_____ 1946. Age in relation to migration in the Blue Jay. *Auk* 63(1): 82-84

_____ 1958. Timing of molt in Steller Jays of the Queen Charlotte Islands, British Columbia. *Condor* 60(1): 38-49.

_____ 1961. A curtailed postjuvenal molt in the Steller Jay. *Auk* 78(4) 634-636.

Pitts, D.T. 1985. Identification of second-year and after-second-year Eastern Bluebirds. *Journ Field Ornith.* 56(4): 422-424.

Prescott, K.W. 1972. An adult Mockingbird with a pale white iris. *Bird-Banding* 43(3): 219-220.

_____ 1980a. Weight, fat class and wing measurements of Ruby-crowned Kinglets during migration. *Inland Bird Banding* 52: 1-7.

_____ 1980b. Weight, fat class, and wing measurements of Golden- crowned Kinglets during migration. *Inland Bird Banding* 52: 41-48.

_____ 1981. Weight, fat class, and wing measurements of Yellow-rumped Warblers during migration. *Inland Bird Banding* 53: 39-48.

_____ 1982. Weight, fat class and wing measurement of Gray Catbirds during migration. *N. Am. Bird Bander* 7(4): 146-149.

_____ 1983. Weight, fat, and wing measurement variations of adult American Goldfinches in New Jersey. *N. Am. Bird Bander* 8(4): 149- 152.

_____ 1986. Weight, fat, and wing measurement variations during migration and overwintering of White-throated Sparrows in New Jersey. *N. Am. Bird Bander* 11(2): 46-51.

Pustmueller, C.J. 1975. New method for sexing Steller's Jays. *Bird- Banding* 46(4): 342-343.

Quay, W.B. 1987. Physical characteristics and arrival times of Indigo Buntings in eastern Missouri. *N. Am. Bird Banding* 12(1): 2-7.

Radke, E.L., A.M. Craig and R.G. McCaskie. 1968. Bushtit (*Psaltriparus minimus*). *Western Bird Bander* 43(1): 5.

Raitt, R.J. 1967. Relationships between black-eared and plain-eared forms of Bushtits. *Auk* 84(4): 503-528.

Rappole, J.H. 1983. Analysis of plumage variation in the Canada Warbler. *Journ. Field Ornith.* 54(2): 152-159.

_____, E.C. Rappole and C. P. Barkan. 1979. Basic plumage in the male Blue-gray Gnatcatcher. *Bird-Banding* 50(1): 71.

Raveling, D.G. 1965. Geographic variation and measurements of Tennessee Warblers killed at a TV tower. *Bird-Banding* 36(2): 89- 101.

_____ and D.W. Warner. 1965. Plumages, molts and morphometry of Tennessee Warblers. *Bird-Banding* 36(3): 169-179.

_____ and _____ 1978. Geographic variation of Yellow Warblers killed at a TV tower. *Auk* 95(1): 73-79.

Raynor, G.S. 1979. Weight and size variation in the Gray Catbird. *Bird-Banding* 50(2): 124-144.

Rea, A.M. 1967. Age determination of Corvidae. Part 1: Common Crow. *Western Bird Bander* 42(4): 44-47.

_____ 1969. Species, age and sex determination in the genus *Tyrannus. Western Bird Bander* 44(3): 32-35.

_____ 1970. Status of the Summer Tanager on the Pacific Slope. *Condor* 72(2): 230-232.

_____ 1972. Notes on the Summer Tanager. *Western Bird Bander* 47(4): 52-53.

_____ and D. Kanteena. 1968. Age determination of Corvidae. Part 2. Common and White-necked ravens. *Western Bird Bander* 43(1): 6-9.

Reese, J.G. 1975. Fall remix and rectrix molt in the Cardinal. *Bird-Banding* 46(4): 305-310.

Reese, K.P. and J.A. Kadlec. 1982. Determining the sex of Black-billed Magpies by external measurements. *Journ Field Ornith.* 53(4): 417- 418.

Ricklefs, R.E. 1972. Latitudinal variation in breeding productivity of the Rough-winged Swallow. *Auk* 89(4): 826-836.

Riggins, J. and H. Riggins. 1974. Aging Swamp Sparrows by plumage. *IBB News* 46(1): 5-9.

Rimmer, C.C. 1986. Identification of juvenile Lincoln's and Swamp sparrows. *Journ Field Ornith.* 57(2): 114-125.

Rising, J.D. and F.W. Schueler. 1980. Identification and status of wood pewees (*Contopus*) from the Great Plains: what are sibling species? *Condor* 82(3): 301-308.

Robbins, C.S. 1959. Mimeographed notes. U.S. Fish and Wildlife Service, Washington, D.C.

———— 1964. A guide to the aging and sexing of wood warblers (Parulidae) in fall. *EBBA News* 27(3): 199-215.

———— 1972. Mimeographed notes. *IBB News* 44(2): 72-76.

———— 1975. Atlantic Flyway review—region V. *EBBA News* 38(1): 31- 35.

Robbins, M.B., M.J. Braun and E.A. Tobey. 1986. Morphological and vocal variation accross a contact zone between the chickadees *Parus atricapillus* and *P. carolinensis*. *Auk* 103(4): 655-666.

Roberts, T.S. 1955. A manual for the identification of the birds of Minnesota and neighboring states. Univ. Minnesota Press, Minneapolis.

Rowher, S.A. 1986. A previously unknown plumage of first-year Indigo Buntings and theories of delayed plumage maturation. *Auk* 103(2): 281-292.

————, P.W. Ewald and F.C. Rowher. 1981. Variation in size, appearance and dominance within and amoung the sex and age classes of Harris' Sparrows. *Journ. Field Ornith.* 52(4): 291-303.

————, S.D. Fretwell and D.M. Niles. 1980. Delayed maturation in passerine plumages and the deceptive acquisition of resources. *Am. Nat.* 115: 400-437.

————, W.P. Klein Jr. and S. Heard. 1983. Delayed plumage maturation and the presumed prealternate molt in American Redstarts. *Wilson Bull.* 95(2): 199-208.

Ryan, L.S. 1969. Sexing Purple Finches. *IBB News* 41(4): 123-125.

———— 1978. Dark-eyed Junco wing chord lengths. *IBB News* 50(2): 43- 45.

Saiza, A. 1968. Age determination of Corvidae. Part III. Juveniles. *Western Bird Bander* 43(2): 20-23.

Samson, F.B. 1974. On determining sex and age in the Cassin's Finch. *Western Bird Bander* 49(3): 4-7.

———— 1976. Pterylosis and molt in Cassin's Finch. *Condor* 78(4): 505- 511.

Schneider, K.J. 1981. Age determination by skull pneumatization in the Field Sparrow. *Journ Field Ornith.* 52(1): 57-59.

Schwab, R.G. and R.E. Marsh. 1967. Reliability of external sex characteristics of the Starling in California. *Bird-Banding* 38(2): 143-147.

Scott, D.M. 1967. Postjuvenal molt and determination of age of the Cardinal. *Bird-Banding* 38(1): 37-51.

Sealy, S.G. 1979. Prebasic molt of the Northern Oriole. *Can Journ. Zool.* 57: 1473-1478.

———— 1985. Analysis of a sample of Tennessee Warblers window killed during spring migration in Manitoba. *N. Am. Bird Bander* 10(4): 121- 124.

Selander, R.K. 1958. Age determination and molt in the Boat-tailed Grackle. *Condor* 62(1): 355-375.

———— 1964. Speciation in Wrens of the genus *Campylorhinchus*. *Univ. Calif. Pubs. Zool.* 74: 1-305.

———— and D.R. Giller. 1960. First-year plumages of the Brown-headed Cowbird and Red-winged Blackbird. *Condor* 62(3): 202-214.

———— and R.F. Johnston. 1967. Evolution in the House Sparrow. I. Intra-population variation in North America. *Condor* 69(3): 217- 258.

Sheppard, J.M. and M.K. Klimkiewicz. 1976. An update to Wood's Bird Bander's Guide. *N. Am. Bird Bander* 1(1): 25-27.

Short, L.L. 1963. Hybridization in the wood-warblers *Vermivora pinus* and *V. chrysoptera*. *Proc. XIII Int. Ornith. Congr.* (1962): 147-160.

_____ and C.S. Robbins. 1967. An intergeneric hybrid wood warbler (*Seiurus* X *Dendroica*). *Auk* 84(4): 534-543.

Shortt, T.M. On the juvenal plumages of North American pipits. *Auk* 68(3): 265.

Simon, S.W. 1960. Occurrence and measurements of Black-capped Chickadees at Monkton, Md. *EBBA News* 23(1): 11-12.

Smith, C.E. 1966. Preliminary notes on a six-year study of Rose-breasted Grosbeak plumages. *Bird-Banding* 37(1): 49-51.

Smith, W.P. 1979. Timing of skull ossification in Kinglets. *N. Am. Bird Bander* 4(3): 103-105.

Smithe, F.B. 1975 & 1981. Naturalist's color guide. 3 parts. American Museum of Natural History, New York.

Stangel, P.W. 1985. Incomplete first prebasic molt of Massachusetts House Finches. *Journ Field Ornith.* 56(1): 1-8.

Stein, R.C. 1963. Isolating mechanisms between populations of Traill's Flycatchers. *Proc. Am. Phil. Soc.* 107(1): 21-50.

Stewart, R.E. 1952. Molting of Northern Yellow-throat in southern Michigan. *Auk* 69(1): 50-59.

Stewart, R.M. 1971. Application of an analysis of wing length in Swainson's Thrushes. *Western Bird Bander* 46(4): 52-53.

_____ 1972a. The reliability of aging some fall migrants by skull pneumatization. *Bird-Banding* 43(1): 9-14.

_____ 1972b. Age and crown types in the Golden-crowned Sparrow. *Western Bird Bander* 47(2): 32-33.

_____ 1972c. Determining sex in western races of adult Wilson's Warbler: a reexamination. *Western Bird Bander* 47(3): 45-48.

Stiles, F.G. and R.G. Campos. 1983. Identification and occurrence of Blackpoll Warblers in southern Middle America. *Condor* 85(2): 254- 255.

Storer, R.W. 1951. Variation in the Painted Bunting (*Passerina ciris*) with special reference to wintering populations. *Occ. Papers Mus. Zool. Univ. Mich.* # 532: 1-11.

Stutchbury, B.J. and R.J. Robertson. 1987. Two methods of sexing adult Tree Swallows before they begin breeding. *Journ. Field Ornith.* 58(2): 236-242.

Svensson, L. 1970. Identification guide to European Passerines. L. Svensson, Stockholm.

_____ 1975 Identification guide to European Passerines. 2nd ed. L. Svensson, Stockholm.

_____ 1984. Identification guide to European Passerines. 3rd ed. L. Svensson, Stockholm.

Tanner, J.T. 1952. Black-capped and Carolina Chickadees in the southern Appalachian Mountains. *Auk* 69(3): 407-424.

Taylor, W.K. 1970. Molts of the Verdin, *Auriparus flaviceps*. *Condor* 72(4): 493-496.

_____ 1972. Analysis of Ovenbirds killed in central Florida. *Bird- Banding* 43(1): 15-19.

_____ 1973. Aging of Ovenbirds by rusty-tipped tertials and skull ossification. *EBBA News* 36(1): 71-72.

_____ 1976. Variations in the black mask of the Common Yellowthroat. *Bird-Banding* 47(1): 72-73.

Thompson, C.F. 1973. Postjuvenal molt in the White-eyed Vireo. *Bird-Banding* 44(1): 63-65.

Tipton, S.R. and I.H. Tipton. 1978. Some notes on Painted Buntings. *N. Am. Bird Bander* 3(1): 26.

Tordoff, H.B. 1952. Notes on plumages, molts, and age variation of the Red Crossbill. *Condor* 54(4): 200-203.

_____ and R.M. Mengel. 1951. The occurrence and possible significance of a spring molt in Le Conte's Sparrow. *Auk* 68(4): 519-522.

Traylor, M.A. 1968. Winter molt in the Acadian Flycatcher, *Empidonax virens*. *Auk* 85(4): 691.

_____ 1979. Two sibling species of *Tyrannus* (Tyrannidae). *Auk* 96(2): 221-233.

van Rossem, A.J. 1935. A note on the color of the eye of the bush-tit. *Condor* 37(5): 254.

Vardy, L.E. 1971. Color variation in the crown of the White-throated Sparrow (*Zonotrichia albicollis*). *Condor* 73(4): 401-414.

Verbeek, N.A.M. 1973a. The exploitation system of the Yellow-billed Magpie. *Univ. Calif. Pubs. Zool.* 99: 1-58.

_____ 1973b. Pterylosis and timing of molt in the Water Pipit. *Condor* 75(3) 287-292.

Walters, P.M. 1983. Notes on the first banding of the Cave Swallow (*Hirundo fulva*) in Arizona. *N. Am. Bird Bander* 8(3): 103.

_____ and D.W. Lamm. 1980. A Hooded Warbler (*Wilsonia citrina*) in South-east Arizona. *N. Am. Bird Bander* 5(1): 15.

_____ and _____ 1986. Notes on the ageing and sexing of the Curve- billed Thrasher (*Toxostoma curvirostrae*). *N. Am. Bird Bander* 11(1): 2-3.

Watt, D.J. 1986. Plumage brightness index for White-throated Sparrows. *Journ. Field Ornith.* 57(2): 105-113.

Webster, J.D. 1958. Systematic notes on the Olive Warbler. *Auk* 75(4): 469-472.

_____ 1959. A revision of the Botteri's Sparrow. *Condor* 61(2): 136-146.

_____ 1961. A revision of the Grace's Warbler. *Auk* 78(4): 554-566.

_____ 1962. Systematic and ecological notes on the Olive Warbler. *Wilson Bull.* 74(4): 417-425.

West, D.A. 1962. Hybridization in grosbeaks (*Pheucticus*) of the Great Plains. *Auk* 79(3): 399-424.

Whitney, B. 1983. Bay-breasted, Blackpoll and Pine warblers in fall plumage. *Birding* 15(6): 219-222.

Wiseman, A.J. 1968a. Ageing by skull ossification. *IBB News.* 40(2): 47-52.

_____ 1968b. Ageing Cardinals by juvenal secondaries and secondary coverts. *IBB News* 40(5): 172-173.

_____ 1969. The geographically erratic chickadees. *IBB News* 41(5): 164-168.

_____ 1977. Interrelation of variables in postjuvenal molt of Cardinals. *Bird-Banding* 48(3): 206-223.

Wolf, L.L. 1977. Species relationships in the avian genus *Aimophila*. *Ornith. Monographs* 23: 1-220.

Wolfson, A. 1952. The cloacal protuberance—a means for determining breeding condition in live male passerines. *Bird-Banding* 23(4): 159-165.

Wood, D.L. and D.S. Wood. 1972. Numerical color specification for bird identification: iris color and age in fall migrants. *Bird-Banding* 43(3): 182-190.

Wood, M.S. 1969. A bird-bander's guide to the determination of age and sex of selected species. College of Agriculture, The Pennsylvania State Univ., University Park, Pennsylvania. 181 pp.

_____ 1970. Corrections by the author for "A bird-bander's guide to the determination of age and sex of selected species." *West. Bird Bander* 45:43. [Also *EBBA News* 33(3): 107-108.]

Woodward, J. 1975. [On the use of roof-of-mouth color for ageing Tufted Titmice.] *EBBA News* 38(1): 19.

Woolfenden, G.E. 1955. Spring molt of the Harris Sparrow. *Wilson Bull.* 67(3): 212-213.

Yunick, R.P. 1970a. On Bank Swallow banding. *EBBA News* 33(2): 85-96.

_____ 1970b. The Pine Siskin wing stripe and its relation to age and sex. *EBBA News* 33(6): 267-274.

_____ 1970c. An examination of certain aging criteria for the Cedar Waxwing (*Bombycilla cedrorum*). *Bird-Banding* 41(4): 291-299.

_____ 1972. Variations in the tail spotting of the Slate-colored Junco. *Bird-Banding* 43(1): 38-46.

_____ 1973. An age technique for female Evening Grosbeaks. *EBBA News* 36(1): 69-70.

_____ 1976a. Further examination of the wing stripe of the Pine Siskin. *N. Am. Bird Bander* 1(2): 63-66.

_____ 1976b. Incomplete prebasic molt in a Dark-eyed Junco. *Bird-Banding* 47(3): 276-277.

_____ 1976c. Delayed molt in the Pine Siskin. *Bird-Banding* 47(4): 306-309.

_____ 1977a Evening Grosbeak age-sex determining criteria. *N. Am. Bird Bander* 2(1): 12-13.

_____ 1977b. Eye color changes in the Dark-eyed Junco and White- throated Sparrow. *N. Am. Bird Bander* 2(4): 155-156.

_____ 1977c. Timing of completion of skull pneumatization in the Pine Siskin. *Bird-Banding* 48(1): 67-71.

_____ 1979a. Timing of completion of skull pneumatization of the Purple Finch and the Common Redpoll. *N. Am. Bird Bander* 4(2): 49- 51.

_____ 1979b. Variation in skull pneumatisation patterns of certain passerines. *N. Am. Bird Bander* 4(4): 145-147.

_____ 1980. Timing of completion of skull pneumatization of the Black-capped Chickadee and the Red-breasted Nuthatch. *N. Am. Bird Bander* 5(2): 43-46.

_____ 1981a. Further observations on skull pneumatization. *N. Am. Bird Bander* 6(2): 40-43.

_____ 1981b. Age determination of winter and spring Dark-eyed Juncos. *N. Am. Bird Bander*. 6(3): 97-100.

_____ 1983a. Age and sex determination of Purple Finches during the breeding season. *N. Am. Bird Bander* 8(2): 48-51.

_____ 1983b. Age determination of female American Goldfinches. *N. Am. Bird Bander* 8(4): 152.

_____ 1984. Toward more effective age determination of banded birds. *N. Am. Bird Bander* 9(1): 2-4.

_____ 1986. Carpal compression as a variable in taking wing chord measurements. *N. Am. Bird Bander* 11(3): 78-83.

_____ 1987. Age determination of male House Finches. *N. Am. Bird Bander* 12(1): 8-11.

Index

Notes

SOME ABBREVIATIONS AND INTERPRETATIONS

MONTHS (see also p. 23)

All months are abbreviated to the first 3 letters. Parentheses surrounding the months indicate that the plumage or condition described may be encountered between and/or within the months listed, but is usually not found or can't be reliably used outside of them.

FEATHERS (see also p. 2)

p (pp) — primary (primaries).
pN — (ex. p10) the Nth (10th or outermost) primary.
s (ss) — secondary (secondaries).
terts — tertials.
covs — coverts.
pp covs — (greater) primary coverts.
gr covs — greater (secondary) coverts.
mid covs — middle (secondary) coverts.
les covs — lesser (secondary) coverts.
rect(s) — rectrix (rectrices).
flight feathers — collective for pp, ss, and rects.

MEASUREMENTS (see also p. 3)

wg — length of wing chord (unflattened) in mm.
wg (flat) — length of flattened wing in mm.
p6-p10 (example) — distance from the tip of p6 to the tip of p10 in mm.
tail — tail length in mm.
culmen — culmen (anterior end of nares to bill tip) in mm.
exp culmen — exposed culmen (bill from edge of feathers on ridge, to tip) in mm.
wt — weight in grams.

MOLT (see also p. 12)

PB — Prebasic (postjuvenal and/or postnuptial) molt.
1st PB — First prebasic (postjuvenal) molt.
Adult PB — Adult prebasic (postnuptial) molt.
PA — Prealternate (prenuptial) molt.
1st PA — Prealternate molt in first-year birds.
Adult PA — Prealternate molt in adults (at least 1½ years old).
Absent — No molt or feather replacement occurs (many PAs).
Limited — Some, but not all, body feathers and no flight feathers are replaced (some PAs).
Partial — Most or all body feathers but no flight feathers are replaced (many 1st PBs, some PAs).
Incomplete — Usually all body feathers and some, but not all, flight feathers are replaced (some 1st PBs, a few PAs).
Complete — All body and flight feathers are replaced (all adult PBs, some 1st PBs, a few PAs).

AGE/SEX (see also p. 26)

CP/BP — Cloacal protuberance and brood patch are reliable indicators of sex within the months given.
Juv — Juvenile. A bird in juvenal plumage, before the first prebasic molt.
HY — A bird in first basic plumage and in its first calendar year (i.e. from the first prebasic molt until December 31st of the year it fledged).
SY — A bird in its second calendar year (i.e. January 1st of the year following fledging through December 31st of the same year).
AHY — A bird in *at least* its second calendar year (at least an SY).
TY — A bird in its third calendar year.
ASY — An adult in at least its third calendar year (i.e. a bird in at least the year following its first breeding season and 2nd prebasic molt).